Cognition, Emotion, and Aesthetics in Contemporary Serial Television

This book posits an interconnection between the ways in which contemporary television serials cue cognitive operations, solicit emotional responses, and elicit aesthetic appreciation.

The chapters explore a number of questions, including: How do the particularities of form and style in contemporary serial television engage us cognitively, emotionally, and aesthetically? How do they foster cognitive and emotional effects such as feeling suspense, anticipation, surprise, satisfaction, and disappointment? Why and how do we value some serials while disliking others? What is it about the particularities of serial television form and style, in conjunction with our common cognitive, emotional, and aesthetic capacities, that accounts for serial television's cognitive, socio-political, and aesthetic value and its current ubiquity in popular culture?

This book will appeal to postgraduates and scholars working in television studies as well as film studies, cognitive media theory, media psychology, and the philosophy of art.

Ted Nannicelli is Senior Lecturer in Film and Television Studies at The University of Queensland. He is editor of *Projections: The Journal for Movies and Mind*, co-editor of *Cognitive Media Theory* (2014), and author of *Appreciating the Art of Television: A Philosophical Perspective*.

Héctor J. Pérez is Associate Professor of Audiovisual Narrative at the Universitat Politècnica de València. He has published widely in scientific journals such as *Projections*, *Culture & Psychology*, *Aisthesis*, and *L'Atalante*. He is editor of *SERIES, International Journal of TV Serial Narratives*.

Routledge Advances in Television Studies

11 Reading Contemporary Serial Television Universes
A Narrative Ecosystem Framework
Edited by Paola Brembilla and Ilaria A. De Pascalis

12 Children, Youth, and American Television
Edited by Adrian Schober and Debbie Olson

13 American Television and the Sensate Body
Affect and Meaning
Marsha F. Cassidy

14 Creating Reality in Factual Television
The Frankenbite and Other Fakes
Manfred W. Becker

15 A European Television Fiction Renaissance
Premium Production Models and Transnational Circulation
Edited by Luca Barra and Massimo Scaglioni

16 Difficult Women on Television Drama
The Gender Politics of Complex Women in Serial Narratives
Isabel C. Pinedo

17 Global Trafficking Networks on Film and Television
Hollywood's Cartel Wars
César Albarrán-Torres

18 Cognition, Emotion, and Aesthetics in Contemporary Serial Television
Edited by Ted Nannicelli and Héctor J. Pérez

Cognition, Emotion, and Aesthetics in Contemporary Serial Television

Edited by
Ted Nannicelli and Héctor J. Pérez

Routledge
Taylor & Francis Group
LONDON AND NEW YORK

First published 2022
by Routledge
2 Park Square, Milton Park, Abingdon, Oxon OX14 4RN

and by Routledge
605 Third Avenue, New York, NY 10158

Routledge is an imprint of the Taylor & Francis Group, an informa business

British Library Cataloguing-in-Publication Data
A catalogue record for this book is available from the British Library

Library of Congress Cataloging-in-Publication Data
A catalog record has been requested for this book

ISBN: 978-1-032-03715-8 (hbk)
ISBN: 978-1-032-03716-5 (pbk)
ISBN: 978-1-003-18864-3 (ebk)

DOI: 10.4324/9781003188643

Typeset in Bembo
by Deanta Global Publishing Services, Chennai, India

Contents

Contributors

Sarah Cardwell is Honorary Fellow in the School of Arts, University of Kent. She specializes in television aesthetics and adaptation studies, and is the author of *Adaptation Revisited* (2002) and *Andrew Davies* (2005) as well as numerous articles and papers on television and film aesthetics, literary adaptation, and contemporary British literature. Cardwell is founding co-editor of "The Television Series" (book series, Manchester University Press) and is on the advisory boards for the journal *Critical Studies in Television* and "Adaptation and Visual Culture" (book series, Palgrave Macmillan).

Kathrin Fahlenbrach (Dr. phil.) is Professor of Film and Media Studies at the Department for Media and Communication at the University of Hamburg (Germany). Her main research focus is on cognitive film and media theory, embodiment and moving images, and cognitive metaphors in audiovisual media; furthermore, she works on visual performances and the role of visual media in protest movements. She is the author of several publications on audiovisual metaphors in moving images. In her book on audiovisual metaphors (2010), she offers a theoretical framework on embodied and emotion metaphors in audiovisual mass media, including film and television. She edited the volume *Embodied Metaphors in Film, Television, and Video Games: Cognitive Approaches* (2016) London/New York: Routledge. She is a board member of the Society for the Cognitive Study of the Moving Image.

Alberto N. García is an Associate Professor of Film and Television Studies at the School of Communication, Universidad de Navarra (Spain). During 2018, he was a Visiting Professor at the University of Queensland (Australia). He has also been Visiting Scholar at George Washington University (Washington, DC) and Visiting Professor at the University of Stirling (United Kingdom). He has published his work in journals such as *Continuum*, *Quarterly Review of Film and Video*, and *Horror Studies*. He has edited the books *Landscapes of the Self: The Cinema of Ross McElwee* (2007) and *Emotions in Contemporary TV Series* (Palgrave, 2016).

Oliver Kroener is an independent media scholar from Berlin, Germany. His main research interests are television genre, seriality, and viewer engagement.

His work on Quality TV has been published in *SERIES, International Journal of TV Serial Narratives*, and his work on television wrestling has been published in *Convergent Wrestling: Participatory Culture, Transmedia Storytelling, and Intertextuality in the Squared Circle* (Routledge, 2019).

Birger Langkjær is an Associate Professor in the Department of Communication at the University of Copenhagen. His main research is within film sound, cognitive film theory, and realism in Danish cinema. He has published articles on film sound and music, empirical studies of TV audiences and on film editing, metaphors in film, action heroes and affordances, and realism as a narrative mode in Danish cinema. He has published monographs on sound effects and music in movies (*Filmlyd og filmmusik*, 1996, and *Den lyttende tilskuer*, 2000) and on realism in Danish cinema (*Realismen i dansk film*, 2012). From 2013 to 2016, he was head of the research network "Film, experimental designs and quantitative analysis."

Elliott Logan is Lecturer in Media and Communication at The University of Queensland. He is the author of *Breaking Bad and Dignity* (Palgrave Macmillan, 2016) and is Associate Editor of the television studies journal *SERIES*.

Joseph P. Magliano (PhD) is a Professor of Educational Psychology in the Department of Learning Sciences at Georgia State University. He studies the basic cognitive processes that support the ability to comprehend narratives conveyed across different media, such as text, comics, and film. He and his collaborators explore how perceptual, attentional, and comprehension processes are coordinated. He also studies what it means to be ready to read for college and what can be done to help those who are not ready for college.

Ted Nannicelli teaches at The University of Queensland. He is editor of *Projections: The Journal for Movies and Mind*, co-editor of *Cognitive Media Theory* (2014), and author of *Appreciating the Art of Television: A Philosophical Perspective*.

María J. Ortiz is Associate Professor in the Department of Communication and Social Psychology in the University of Alicante (Spain) and director of the "Media, Discourse, and Audio-visual Expression" research group. She teaches different subjects related to filmmaking and narrative. She has been a researcher on the R&D/Innovation project financed by the Ministry of Economy and Competitiveness, entitled "Strategies of Theoretical Innovation in the Analysis of Serial Audiovisual Narrative" led by Héctor J. Pérez (Universitat Politècnica de València).

Héctor J. Pérez is associate professor of audiovisual narrative at the Universitat Politècnica de València (Escola Politècnica Superior de Gandia). A main line of his research is the cognitive aesthetics of television series. He is the author of five books on different aesthetic topics, co-editor of three anthologies, and has published widely in scientific journals such as *Projections*, *Psychology and Culture*, *Aisthesis*, and *L'Atalante*. He is one of the founding editors of *SERIES, International Journal of TV Serial Narratives* and Principal Researcher, with Jesús Jiménez Varea, of the Spanish National research project: Interactions between cognitive value and aesthetic properties in contemporary serials (RTI2018-096596-B-I00). He is a member and Fellow of the Society for Cognitive Studies of the Moving Image.

Carl Plantinga is Arthur H. DeKruyter Chair of Communication at Calvin University. He is primarily a film and media theorist. His two latest books are *Alternative Realities* (2020), which examines the relationship between the imagination and realism in film, and *Screen Stories: Emotion and the Ethics of Engagement* (2018), a treatise on emotion and ethics in spectatorship. He is former president of the Society for Cognitive Studies of the Moving Image.

Rainer Reisenzein is Professor of General Psychology at the University of Greifswald, Germany. His research is focused on emotion and motivation, and it is marked by an interdisciplinary orientation. He is the author of numerous articles on emotion-related topics, including emotional experience, facial expressions, emotion measurement, emotion theory, and the history of emotion research. He is on the editorial board of *Cognition and Emotion* and *Experimental Psychology* and is an associate editor of *Emotion Review*.

Jeffrey E. Saerys-Foy is an Associate Professor of Psychology at Quinnipiac University in Connecticut. He earned his PhD in Experimental Psychology at Stony Brook University under the mentorship of Richard Gerrig. His research focuses on how people comprehend fictional stories.

Murray Smith is Professor of Film and Director of the Aesthetics Research Centre at the University of Kent. He was President of the Society for Cognitive Studies of the Moving Image from 2014 to 2017 and a Laurance S. Rockefeller Fellow at Princeton University's Center for Human Values for 2017–2018. He has published widely on film, art, and aesthetics. In addition to the recent *Film, Art, and the Third Culture: A Naturalized Aesthetics of Film* (Oxford, 2017), his publications include *Engaging Characters: Fiction, Emotion, and the Cinema* (Clarendon; revised ed. forthcoming 2021); *Trainspotting* (BFI; revised ed. 2021); *Film Theory and Philosophy* (co-edited with Richard Allen) (Clarendon); *Contemporary Hollywood Cinema* (co-edited with Steve Neale) (Routledge); and *Thinking through Cinema* (co-edited with Tom Wartenberg) (Blackwell).

Aaron Taylor is Associate Professor of Drama and a Board of Governors' Research Chair (Tier 2) at the University of Lethbridge. He is the editor of *Theorizing Film Acting* (Routledge, 2012), co-editor of *Screening Characters*

(Routledge, 2019), and Associate Editor of *Projections: The Journal for Movies and Mind*. His essays on performance and on comics and cinema have been published in numerous journals and anthologies.

Malcolm Turvey is Sol Gittleman Professor in the Department of History of Art and Architecture and Director of the Film and Media Studies Program at Tufts University. He is also an editor of the journal *October*. He is the author of *Doubting Vision: Film and the Revelationist Tradition* (Oxford University Press, 2008) and *The Filming of Modern Life: European Avant-Garde Film of the 1920s* (MIT Press, 2011) and the co-editor of *Wittgenstein, Theory, and the Arts* (Routledge, 2001). His *Play Time: Jacques Tati and Comedic Modernism* was published by Columbia University Press in 2019.

Margrethe Bruun Vaage is a Senior Lecturer in Film and Media at the University of Kent. She explores the spectator's engagement with fictional films and television series, more specifically the imagination, the emotions, and the moral psychology of fiction. Her latest book is entitled *The Antihero in American Television* (Routledge). She has published widely in journals such as the *British Journal of Aesthetics, Midwest Studies in Philosophy, Screen* and *Poetics Today* as well as in *The Routledge Encyclopedia of Film Theory* and anthologies such as *Cognitive Media Theory* and *The Oxford Handbook of Cognitive Literary Studies*.

Iris Vidmar Jovanović is an assistant professor and a chair in aesthetics in the Department of Philosophy, University of Rijeka. She works primarily in the philosophy of narrative art, but her interests include Kant's aesthetics, cognitive approaches to aesthetics, and issues in metaphilosophy. She is one of the organizers of the Philosophy of Art conference in Dubrovnik, a secretary of the Croatian Society for Analytic Philosophy, and a member of the Executive Committee of the European Society for Aesthetics.

Acknowledgments

This book has been supported by a research project funded by the Spanish Government: *Interactions between cognitive value and aesthetic properties in contemporary serials* (RTI2018-096596-B-I00).

1 Introduction

Cognition, emotion, and aesthetics in contemporary serial television

Ted Nannicelli and Héctor J. Pérez

On May 19, 2019, nearly 20 million people around the world stopped what they were doing, temporarily ignoring deadlines, stresses, or whatever else might have been preoccupying them, and, despite differences in age, gender, race, class, political affiliation, nationality, and religion, were temporarily united by a common interest: How would *Game of Thrones* end? It is easy to forget, in our contemporary moment of narrowcasting and individualized media "curation," the extent to which television is nevertheless capable of eliciting widely shared cognitive, emotional, and aesthetic responses from a broad spectrum of viewers. This book's overarching goal is to explore how this happens.

Our book's title, *Contemporary Serial Television: Cognition, Emotion, and Aesthetics*, posits an interconnection between the ways in which contemporary television serials cue cognitive operations, solicit emotional responses, and elicit aesthetic appreciation. By "cognitive operations," we mean activities such as remembering and ordering some narrative events and anticipating or inferring the occurrence of others. By emotional responses, we have in mind both general, fiction-directed moods such as dread or anxiety, and more narrowly focused emotions such as suspense or fear, sometimes with a more specifically directed object – such as anger at a character. And by aesthetic appreciation, in this context, we roughly mean experiences that, in virtue of the close attention to an object's formal elements and their interrelations, are special or valuable in their own right, including, for example, the apprehension of beauty, balance, unity, elegance, and the like, as well as the more general feelings of wonder, awe, fascination, and admiration that are engendered by such apprehension. Aesthetic appreciation thus contains a cognitive element as well as a sensory or perceptual aspect and an affective dimension.

These foci – cognition, emotion, and aesthetic appreciation – are not typical of most contemporary scholarship on television. Why not? The long answer is complicated; the short answer is simply that television studies developed in such a way that its key theoretical concerns lie elsewhere. To see this, one need only look at some of the recent textbooks that survey the field. For example, Jonathan Bignell writes that his *An Introduction to Television Studies* "is concerned with the most commonly studied theoretical issues in television

DOI: 10.4324/9781003188643-1

courses," which include "analytical study of television programmes as texts," "the television industry as an institution and its production practices and organization," "television in contemporary culture and the sociological study of audiences," and "television history and developments in broadcasting policy" (2013, 2). And in a chapter titled "Introduction to Television Studies" in *Television: Visual Storytelling and Screen Culture*, Jeremy Butler claims that "the most significant … strains of television studies" are

> approaches that focus mostly on TV programs "themselves," without theorizing extensively about the TV viewer or the TV industry (authorship, stylistics, genre study, and semiotics) … and approaches that examine how TV's meanings, its discourses, are received by viewers and produced by TV-industry workers (ideological analysis, political economy, feminism, queer theory, and race and ethnic studies).
>
> (2018, 311)

Notably absent from these lists is a consideration of television programs as *artworks*. By using the term "artwork," we do not mean to bestow any special honor or value on television. Rather, we are talking about "art" in a descriptive, classificatory sense that picks out a cluster of artifacts, performances, and the practices of creating them. Artworks, like other artifacts, are designed with particular aims and purposes. The aims and purposes of narrative artworks, including narrative television programs, typically include the enjoyable or otherwise rewarding cognitive and emotional engagement of the readers or viewers. Furthermore, what we might call popular artworks, or "mass artworks," to use Noël Carroll's more precise term, are designed to be "accessible virtually on contact, without specialized background training and/or effort by vast numbers of people" (1998, 196). While mainstream television studies tends to emphasize "polysemy" and the diversity of viewing perspectives, it seems to us that one of the most interesting features of contemporary serial television is its ability to elicit intended effects – ranging from misdirection and surprise to the feeling of sympathy to aesthetic pleasure – from mass audiences.

We think that the nature of the phenomenon under investigation ought to determine the research methods to be employed. Accordingly, this volume assembles contributors from a variety of fields and disciplines whose approaches are suitable for the task of exploring contemporary serial television's ability to foster congruent cognitive, emotional, and aesthetic experiences of screen stories. By "congruent," we do not mean "universal" but "widely shared" or "common." The fact that contemporary serial television is able to elicit such widely shared responses among *mass* audiences is important because it allows us to think about our research problem in a slightly different way: It means that contemporary serial television is able to appeal to something(s) that is/are shared by large numbers of viewers who might otherwise be extremely heterogeneous. In Carroll's words, mass artworks like serialized television "aim at engaging what is common among huge populations" (1998, 196).

The research approaches adopted in this book – media psychology, cognitive media theory, and television aesthetics – take this observation as a starting point. As Carroll wrote in an early and influential argument for a cognitive approach to theorizing the power of movies to engage mass audiences,

> only by focusing on cognitive capacities, especially ones as deeply embedded as pictorial recognition, practical reason, and the drive to get answers to our questions, will we be in the best position to find the features of movies that account for their phenomenally *widespread* effectiveness; since cognitive capacities … seem the most plausible candidate for what mass-movie audiences have in common. That is, the question of the power of movies involves explaining how peoples of different cultures, societies, nations, races, creeds, educational backgrounds, age groups, and sexes can find movies easily accessible and gripping.
>
> (1996, 92)

For all three approaches featured in the present volume – media psychology, cognitive media theory, and television aesthetics – the foundational assumption from which we need to begin to explain widely shared cognitive, emotional, and aesthetic responses to serial television is that despite whatever differences exist between individual viewers and collective audiences, those responses depend upon our evolved cognitive capacities.

In the pages that follow, we try to illuminate further relevant connections between these three research approaches. Some of these links are historical, so we spend a bit of time developing a historical narrative that aims to bring forth commonalities in the intellectual histories of these research traditions. Other connections are conceptual, involving shared research questions, aims, and methodological assumptions. Our overall ambition in this book is to foster closer collaboration between researchers across these three traditions working on similar questions and problems; our overall goal in the rest of the Introduction is to demonstrate that these three research traditions already have more in common than might be apparent at first sight and with regard to the study of television, are pursuing similar questions pitched at varying, potentially complementary levels of specificity.

Media psychology

The first of these approaches represented here – media psychology – might be thought of as a road not taken by television studies. According to Karen Dill-Shackleford's definition in the introduction to *The Oxford Companion to Media Psychology*, "media psychology is the scientific study of human behavior, thoughts, and feelings experienced in the context of media use and creation" (2013, 6). Although the formal establishment of the field might be traced to the American Psychological Association's 1987 establishment of a dedicated division (46) to the topic, media psychology is widely regarded as an "emerging field" (Dill 2013, 4; Rutledge 2013, 44): a journal and a textbook bearing the title *Media Psychology* first appeared in 1999 and 2003, respectively (Giles 2003). As we shall soon see, recent work in this interdisciplinary field has increasingly intersected with research being conducted under the banner of cognitive film theory or cognitive media theory. But before we get to this, let us provide some historical and intellectual context to explain this exchange and media psychology's relative lack of exchange with television studies.

Media psychology's roots lie in the disciplines of mass communications and psychology, especially social psychology. The reason we claim that media psychology might be thought of as a road not taken for television studies is that mass communications was also central to the development of the scholarly study of television before other research traditions like literary studies, sociology, and cultural studies gained more prominence as television studies came into its own as a field (Allen 1992, 13–16; Butler 2018, 371–377; Gray and Lotz 2019, 14–15; Spigel 2009, 150). Mass communications' own development as a field is ineluctably tied to World War II, both because of the influx of German and Austrian emigres like Paul Lazarsfeld and Kurt Lewin, whose work would come to shape the discipline, and because of the ways in which the American government's interest in propaganda and communication fostered a number of well-resourced research projects in these areas.

It is important to understand that mass communications emerged in concert with contemporary American social psychology, which had a particularly *cognitive* inflection in the time immediately preceding and throughout World War II in the United States thanks, also, to the European intellectual migration. As Robert M. Farr writes in his historical study *The Roots of Modern Social Psychology*, "social psychologists in America were cognitive theorists at a time when it was not fashionable to be so, i.e., in the heyday of behaviourism" (1996, 7). Moreover, he explains, "This was mainly due to the influence of the Gestalt psychologists" (Farr 1996, 7). By the time John B. Watson's classic *Behaviorism* was published in a revised version in 1930 (the original having been published in 1925), the behaviorist paradigm was ensconced in the psychology departments of the major U.S. universities (Mandler and Mandler 1969, 376).

It was in this intellectual context that the founders of Gestalt psychology arrived in the United States from their institutional home at the Berlin School of Experimental Psychology – Kurt Koffka in 1927, Max Wertheimer in 1933, and Wolfgang Kohler in 1935. Less central to the establishment of the Gestalt movement, but also working in the Berlin School before emigrating to the United States, were Hans Wallach and Kurt Lewin. Wallach was employed by Kohler – who had taught him in Berlin – at Swarthmore College, where he taught a number of students who went on to be major figures in the establishment of cognitive psychology and perceptual psychology, including Ulric Neisser, Irvin Rock, and Julian Hochberg. Hochberg's research on the perception of motion images eventually came to influence the development of cognitive film theory, as did the work of Rudolf Arnheim, who studied under Kohler and Wertheimer before emigrating.

At this rich confluence of Gestalt psychology, or the psychology of perception more broadly, social psychology, and cognitive psychology, Regina M. Tuma finds a plausible candidate for an early and important work of media psychology which has a connection to motion pictures that is somewhat ironic given the failure of the promising interdisciplinary methodology to take hold in film and television studies until decades later. The research in question is Hadley Cantril's *The Invasion from Mars: A Study in the Psychology of Panic*, published in 1940, which investigates Orson Welles's infamous radio adaptation of H. G. Wells's *War of the Worlds*. Aspects of Cantril's study have been criticized by contemporary media historians, but the important methodological point isn't about Cantril's data collection or experiment design, which admittedly may have been flawed (Pooley and Socolow 2013). Rather, it is his general approach, which attempts to account for the perceiver's perception and cognition of the artwork itself *and* the contextual or environmental factors that shape and influence those processes. According to Tuma,

> in paying attention to the listening situation, Cantril is introducing a very different model of media. Instead of the traditional transmission model that flows from medium to individual, Cantril is opening up the possibility of "otherness" as a mediating variable in relation to media.
>
> (Tuma 2013, 70–71)

Unfortunately, Cantril's work had little influence on the direction of mass communications as a field. In no small part, this was because at The Rockefeller Seminars, which Cantril attended while working on *The Invasion from Mars* in 1939, Harold Lasswell was also developing the "five-question" model that eventually took hold for the next phase of communications research: "*Who* says *what* to *whom* in *what channel* and with *what effects*?" In the words of media historian Daniel Czitrom, Lasswell's model "became the dominant paradigm defining the scope and problems of American communications research. The behavioral science of communication became restricted to a rather narrow model that explained communication as essentially a process of persuasion" (1982, 132). As a result of the influence of Lasswell's work, along with that of Lazarsfeld and Lewin, the early institutionalization of mass communications at places like Stanford University, the University of Illinois, and the University of Wisconsin "shaped the field in directions that were empirical, quantitative, and effects oriented" (Rogers 1994, 492).

Although research in mass communications (and later, media psychology) has evolved significantly since its academic institutionalization in the 1950s and 1960s, this is the rough picture of an approach to the study of media that the founders of television studies ultimately rejected, sometimes tacitly and sometimes explicitly. In part for this reason, it is probably fair to say that historically, mainstream television studies has focused on the reception context (broadly construed) of television at the expense of attention to individual perceivers. But it is also true that part of what this tradition rejected was the emphasis of mass communications – and more broadly, social psychology – on empirical and quantitative methods, as well as its "individualization of the social and the desocialization of the individual" (Graumann 1986), which was arguably continued into the development of cognitive psychology.

This history we've described has no doubt shaped contemporary media psychology, but it is important to acknowledge that the field has also evolved in ways that seek to acknowledge and redress some of the theoretical and methodological tendencies to which mainstream television studies has often objected.[1] Indeed, as one of media psychology's contemporary advocates writes, a

> reductionist tradition is evident in much of the research on the effects of mass media that employed experimental quantitative methods in an attempt to isolate and quantify the actual and potential impact of media exposure on individual and group behavior and norms. The inherent problem with this type of specificity is that it creates an artificial user environment and strips away the subjective experience and relational context that is a fundamental feature of media use.
>
> (Rutledge 2013, 50)

Certainly, much cutting-edge research in media psychology has made and continues to make methodological and theoretical progress on these points. Recent applications of research on motivated cognition (Lang 2006), complexity theory (Sherry 2015), dynamic systems theory (Lang 2014; Han and Lang 2019), neuropsychology (Weber, Sherry, and Mathiak 2009; Weber et al. 2015), and psychophysiology (Lang, Potter, and Bolls 2009; Potter and Bolls 2012), and the social contexts of media use (Cohen 2017; Tal-Or 2019), have, in different ways, attempted to re-situate perceivers in their environmental contexts.

Cognitive film and media theory

Because cognitive film theory's roots lie partly in the same experimental psychology that gave rise to mass communications and later, media psychology, there are some noteworthy parallels evident in the sorts of objections made against early cognitive film theory and in its trajectory as a research program. In the same way that mainstream television studies objected to mass communications' emphasis on the individual over the social and cultural in reception contexts, so too did mainstream film studies make this complaint about cognitive film theory – in particular, as it was initially championed by David Bordwell (1985; 1989a; 1989b). The sort of objections we have in mind focused primarily on Bordwell's *Narration in the Fiction Film* – the first book in the discipline to advocate a cognitive approach to film viewing. As Bordwell himself later described it, the book argued "that the regularities of narration revealed by film analysis indicated that films were designed to elicit particular activities from spectators … In effect [it] was proposing perceptual and inferential mechanisms underlying the 'natural understanding' of cinematic expression" (2009, 360).

Critics at the time worried that Bordwell's emphasis on a hypothetical spectator, defined by a standard perceptual-cognitive stock, abstracted film viewing from its socio-historically determined environment. As Robert Stam brusquely put it, "Cognitivists say that all viewers have the same perceptual apparatus. That's like saying we all defecate. So what?" (quoted in Quart 2000, 41). (Stam does not elaborate on how our shared defecation capacities might subtend or partly explain our ability to understand and enjoy movies.) Bill Nichols offered a more explicit statement of the point: "Given his linear, one-dimensional model, Bordwell must neglect the subjective and socially constrained processes of interpretation" (1992, 72). Picking up steam, Nichols concludes that Bordwell's cognitivism is an approach that

> neglects differences that make a difference, that achieves coherence by excluding history and subjectivity, that treats narrative as data or information for genderless, classless, stateless "processors" … As such it is of value wherever narrative is processed by "hypothetical" entities or "organisms" – better called, perhaps, cyborgs.
>
> (1992, 75)

We think such criticisms of Bordwell's cognitivism are ill-founded for a number of reasons that other scholars have described elsewhere. However, it is true that early work in cognitive film theory, like Bordwell's, did tend to focus on individualistic cognition – assuming, not implausibly, that the individual embodied brain is the seat of *much* cognition and that the basic functions and capacities are nearly universally possessed across societies, cultures, and historical epochs, given the evolution of our cognitive architecture over several million years.

More important than the parallelism in the objections lodged against mass communications research and cognitive film theory is the infrequently noted parallelism in intellectual roots. As mentioned earlier, the Gestaltist forerunners of the mass communications and media psychology research traditions – Koffka, Wertheimer, Kohler, Wallach, Lewin – also taught and influenced the psychologists who would go on to pioneer the New Look movement and later, cognitive psychology. It is precisely these New Look/early cognitivist researchers – Bruner, Hochberg, Neisser, Rock – whom Bordwell cites as he develops his Constructivist account of the viewer's perceptual-cognitive activity in *Narration in the Fiction Film* (1985, 342–343; also see Bordwell 2009, 359–360). Ten to fifteen years later, the major publications of the 1990s and early 2000s that marked the emergence of cognitive film theory as an emerging research program (Carroll 1990; M. Smith 1995; Bordwell and Carroll 1996; Tan 1996; Grodal 1997; Plantinga and Smith 1999) reflected the fact that cognitive psychology had since shifted its emphasis from "cold" cognition based on reason to "hot" cognitive operations driven or influenced by emotion.

Thus, in the 1990s, there was a slightly peculiar situation in which, for reasons of intellectual lineage and disciplinary organization, the publication of books of cognitive film theory such as *The Philosophy of Horror* (Carroll 1990), *Emotion and the Structure of Narrative Film* (Tan 1996), and *Moving Pictures: A New Theory of Film Genres, Feelings, and Cognition* (Grodal 1997) paralleled the publication of books in media psychology like *Responding to the Screen: Reception and Reaction Processes* (Bryant and Zillman 1991), *Suspense: Conceptualizations, Theoretical Analyses, and Empirical Explorations* (Vorderer, Wulff, and Friedrichsen 1996), and *Horror Films: Current Research on Audience Preferences and Reactions* (Weaver and Tamborini 1996).

While there were, at this point in the development of media psychology and cognitive film theory, some productive exchanges and collaborations, for the most part work in the two fields proceeded separately. Since then, as cognitive science and its various branches, like cognitive psychology, have shifted their emphasis to the way cognition is, as the phrase goes, "embodied, embedded, extended, and enacted," so too has cognitive film theory – or what we might now term cognitive *media* theory, some areas of which are increasingly indistinct from contemporary media psychology.

"Cognitive media theory" is not an easy concept to define. It is best considered as a tradition of research that brings together the likes of film, television, and media theorists, narratologists, philosophers of art, psychologists, and neuroscientists in an interdisciplinary effort to answer questions about the ways our perceptual, cognitive, emotive, and imaginative capacities subtend our experience of various kinds of media. The editors of the recent book *Cognitive Media Theory* characterized this research tradition in terms of four features:

> (1) a dedication to the highest standards of reasoning and evidence in film and media studies and other fields (including, but not limited to, empirical data from the natural sciences); (2) a commitment to stringent inter-theoretical criticism and debate; (3) a general focus on the mental activity of viewers as the central (but not the only) object of inquiry; and (4) an acceptance of a naturalistic perspective, broadly construed.
>
> (Nannicelli and Taberham 2014, 5)

As indicated earlier, cognitive media theory began as cognitive film theory in the 1980s, when David Bordwell, Noël Carroll, and other film scholars turned to cognitive science (itself an interdisciplinary field, constituted by anthropology, artificial intelligence, linguistics, philosophy, psychology, and neuroscience) to develop an alternative approach to the study of film at a time when film studies was dominated by "Grand Theory," or what Bordwell called SLAB theory for its combination of Saussurean semiotics, Lacanian psychoanalysis, Althussarian Marxism, and Barthesian structuralism. In those early days, there were not yet many alternatives to Grand Theory, but the first meeting of the group that was eventually to become the Society for Cognitive Studies of the Moving Image (SCSMI) in 1997 marked a turning point. SCSMI now holds an annual conference, which alternates between European and American universities and attracts an increasingly diverse and interdisciplinary group of scholars.

The productive aspect of these and other meetings – and indeed, a main feature of the research program itself – lies in the fact that in addition to stimulating mutual curiosity and dialogue, they have been opening spaces of productive exchange between the sciences and the humanities. Dialogue about the limitations of a perspective on a given problem may well lead to the development of different methodologies for approaching it, influencing the construction of theories or the clarification of concepts. For example, in his proposal for a "third culture" bridging the humanities and the sciences, film theorist and aesthetician Murray Smith (2017) advocates a methodological triangulation between phenomenological, psychological, and neurophysiological levels. Other proposals in the same spirit of "consilience" – to use E.O. Wilson's term – have been developed from the other side of the "divide," notably with the concept of *psychocinematics*, a term coined by cognitive neuroscientist Arthur P. Shimamura (2013).

As we suggested earlier, cognitive theory has, over the years, also expanded its scope of inquiry beyond film to include a variety of other media – most importantly for our present purposes, television. As noted by early pioneers of cognitivist and aesthetic studies of television like Greg M. Smith, television and film share enough narrative and stylistic similarities for the application of broadly cognitivist ideas from film studies to illuminate our understanding of television. But television also differs in important ways. Influenced by Bordwell's complementary cognitivist and poetic approaches to film narrative, Smith turned his attention to television in the 1990s, identifying specific elements of serial TV that have continued to merit close attention years later.[2] For example, Smith's (1995) work on *Seinfeld* reveals a sharp and insightful understanding of the subtleties of the multi-plot architecture of this narratively innovative sitcom. Next, Smith (2006) examined the British comedy-drama *Cold Feet*, again demonstrating the relevance and utility of research on film narrative in the context of television. Then, drawing upon the same Russian formalist concepts that Bordwell had introduced to film studies, Smith (2007) offered a sustained analysis of the poetics and aesthetics of the serialized comedy-drama series *Ally McBeal*. Here, Smith's analysis identified and analyzed narrative processes unique to serials, in which the "emphasis is on what plot events tell us about the interconnected world of the serial, how actions inflect our understanding of the dramatic community, and how the closed system of the serial sets up comparisons among characters" (2007, 73).

Smith's observation about seriality's effect upon the portrayal of and engagement with television characters points to another important area in which cognitive film theory has been brought to bear upon the study of television: character engagement. Given cognitive film theorists' research on the relationship between emotion, moral judgment, and sympathy for characters, it is no surprise that Tony Soprano of *The Sopranos* piqued their interest. The theoretical question that intrigued them can be stated as an apparent paradox: how is it possible for us to feel sympathy for Tony when we would feel antipathy towards his real-life equivalent (Carroll 2004)? The apparent paradox drew cognitive film theorists not only to *The Sopranos* (e.g., Smith 2011) but to television more generally, thanks in part to the emergence of other television characters who were just as popular and just as morally ambiguous (like Dexter Morgan and Walter White). At the same time, cognitivists' study of television began to lead to the refinement of arguments and concepts (e.g., empathy and sympathy) in the earlier literature (Vaage 2014; 2016).

Particularly noteworthy in this respect is the recent work of Margrethe Bruun Vaage, who has argued, for example, that viewers can be morally "blinded by familiarity" with characters in serial television programs (2014). Similarly to how we tend to be biased in favor of our real-life friends and family members, our "familiarity" with television characters over long periods of time might partly explain our strong pro-attitudes towards morally ambiguous characters. At the same time, it has led to a sustained discussion about the nature of moral judgments and an exploration of the reasons for the popularity of antiheroes and other characters who constantly transgress moral norms, particularly their extraordinary prominence in contemporary television. Vaage's research is a good example of the ways in which the particularities of television have prompted refinements of cognitivist concepts and arguments in the literature on film.[3]

It may be true, as Greg Smith suggests, that "[a]pplying cognitive research schemata (assumptions about what the 'text' is, for instance) to television or games may not be as simple as exchanging one object of study for another" (2014, 286). But on the other hand, the studies reviewed here reveal significant lines of continuity between earlier cognitivist research on film and emerging cognitivist work on television, particularly serial television. Smith's own work is an important example of this, and furthermore, it points to an important point of connection between cognitivism and television studies that may be overlooked if one misconstrues cognitive theory as simply the scientific study of film and media. The point of connection is aesthetics.

Aesthetics

Thus far, we have been emphasizing the affinities between media psychology and cognitive media theory – particularly in terms of their intellectual histories, their research foci, and their foundational, theoretical assumptions. And we have framed these affinities as something of a departure from mainstream film and television studies. However, it is now time to trace some connections between media psychology, cognitive media theory, and a relatively more orthodox research program in film and television studies – namely, film and television aesthetics. "Aesthetics" is something of a term of art, meaning rather different things in different contexts. Here, used to describe a research program, it carries with it connotations related not only to its etymological root *aisthesis* – Greek for "perception by sense" or "sensuous perception" – but also to the related Greek concept of *poeisis*, meaning, in general terms, "making," and most commonly associated with Aristotle's *Poetics*.

Sometimes forgotten in discussions foregrounding the cognitivism of Bordwell's *Narration in the Fiction Film* is the fact that, as he himself points out, the book also falls "within a recognizable tradition of film aesthetics, addressing familiar problems of how structure and style functioned in cinematic storytelling" (2009, 360). More specifically, *Narration in the Fiction Film* inaugurates Bordwell's career-spanning research program on what he calls, following the Russian formalists, "the poetics of the cinema" (see Taylor 1982). As Bordwell describes,

> The poetics of any artistic medium studies the finished work as the result of a process of construction – a process that includes a craft component (such as rules of thumb), the more general principles according to which the work is composed, and its functions, effects, and uses.
>
> (2008, 12)

Here, it is important to understand the connection between Bordwell's poetics of cinema and his cognitivism. Interestingly, the former project has gained much more traction within mainstream film studies (Keill 2001; Buckland 2006; Keating 2010; Bettinson 2015; Bettinson and Udden 2016) and television studies (Newman 2006; Butler 2010; Mittell 2015). Indeed, one can embrace poetics without cognitivism, but the two are in fact complementary. For Bordwell, poetics, like cognitivism, belongs to "the overarching tradition of rational and empirical inquiry to which science and kindred disciplines belong" (2008, 16). Both poetics and cognitivism are concerned with the effects that films are designed to elicit. Poetics emphasizes the design; cognitivism emphasizes the elicitation of effects. The two research programs share a guiding research question, and their line of inquiry is continuous; the difference is in the points of focus and emphasis. "The elicitation of effects" is a helpful term insofar as it, too, makes an explicit connection to media psychology, noting that traditionally, it has placed an even greater focus on "effects" than cognitive theory and has concretely operationalized that term in ways that allow researchers to analyze audiences rather than films themselves.[4]

However, the domain of aesthetics is, of course, also concerned with effects. This is true whether we conceive of aesthetics as a descriptive endeavor – along the lines of *aisthesis*, pertaining to sensuous perception – or as a normative matter, according to which aesthetics somehow involves apprehending a certain kind of value that issues from sensuous perception. For example, on the minimalist conception of aesthetic experience advocated by Noël Carroll (2010), aesthetic experience of art is roughly a matter of the apprehension of an artwork's content, broadly construed, in ways that engage the perceiver's perceptual, cognitive, emotive, and imaginative capacities. A more robust, value-laden conception of aesthetic experience characterizes it in terms of the pleasure a perceiver takes in appreciating the sensuous form of an object or artwork. The cruder versions of this sort of account, often operationalized by scholars in the natural sciences and social sciences, sometimes boil down to a kind of aesthetic hedonism, according to which aesthetic experience is any pleasurable perceptual experience (Zeki 1999; Calvo-Merino et al. 2008.) More sophisticated versions of this sort of account of aesthetic experience typically emphasize the necessity of attending to the artwork or object in a particular sort of way and sometimes expand the understanding of "pleasure" to encompass other sorts of "rewarding" experience (Levinson 2016; Matthan 2017; Gorodeisky 2021a; Gorodeisky 2021b).

On this topic, we see an overlap of the concerns of media psychology and television aesthetics that might appear surprising at first blush. The rawer versions of aesthetic hedonism have a parallel in hedonistic theories of media reception, according to which one's media entertainment preferences are a function of the enjoyment or pleasure afforded by those media. According to a more recent and sophisticated statement of this view, "at the core of the [media] entertainment experience there is a 'pleasant' experiential state that we term enjoyment, which includes physiological, cognitive, and affective components" (Vorderer, Klimmt, and Ritterfeld 2004, 393). However, pioneering work in media psychology is now also grappling with the sorts of issues that fall under the banner of what philosophers of art call "the paradox of negative emotion." Noting that audiences also seek out forms of media entertainment that are not "pleasurable" in the sense operationalized by natural and social scientists, entertainment psychologists Mary Beth Oliver and Anne Bartsch (2010; 2011) have sought to carve out space for nonhedonic gratifications by borrowing a term more commonly found in the aesthetics literature: appreciation. In particular, Oliver and Bartsch describe their focus as being "aspects of entertainment experience that are intrinsically rewarding for media users without necessarily being associated with enjoyment proper" (2010, 56). Two such aspects emphasized by Oliver and Bartsch are the apprehension of artistic achievement and a more emotionally and cognitively complex, contemplative response. Although Oliver and Bartsch do not make the connection explicit, it should be evident, in light of our discussion here, that their interest is in the media-psychological basis of what philosophers of art would call aesthetic appreciation.

Here, we see a potential bridge between cognitive theory, media psychology, and the emergent research program of television aesthetics, which as the name suggests, focuses on the aesthetic appreciation of television. Although the formation of television aesthetics as a research program has only occurred within the last two decades or so, it is important to acknowledge that there is a longer history of studying television as an aesthetic object or, if one prefers, as an object that affords aesthetic appreciation. In fact, despite the well-known history of television's status as a "bad object" within the academy, arguably one of the founding documents of television studies was Horace Newcomb's *Television: The Most Popular Art* (1974). It bears remembering that Newcomb's starting premise – in 1974, no less, before the institutionalization of television studies as a field – was that television afforded a particular kind of aesthetic attention. Stanley Cavell also assumed this premise in his 1982 essay "The Fact of Television," a phrase he used, in part, to refer to "the acceptance of television as a mature medium of art" (77). In both of these publications, however, as well as in Herbert Zettl's 1978 essay "The Rare Case of Television Aesthetics," some initial defensive maneuvers were still required – no doubt in part because of snobbery, but also because as noted by Cavell and Zettl, in particular, nearly all of the academic discourse around television at the time comprised "effects research" undertaken in mass communications.

Not coincidentally, the initial exceptions to this trend emerged from across the Atlantic, where the study of media and communications had a different intellectual trajectory. The most important development here was the cultural studies tradition developed at the Centre for Contemporary Cultural Studies at the University of Birmingham, which also emphasized the close "reading" of television but for the purposes of analyzing the dissemination of ideology rather than aesthetic appreciation. As we know, it was this latter concern with ideology and the research traditions dedicated to its study that took hold in the nascent field of television studies and came to shape its research priorities. Nevertheless, it would be too simplistic to say that an interest in television as an aesthetic object then disappeared from the field. On the contrary, one sees its continuation throughout the 1990s and 2000s in the work of scholars such as John T. Caldwell (1995), Charlotte Brunsdon (1997), Robin Nelson (1997), Robert J. Thompson (1997), John Caughie (2000), Jason Jacobs (2000, 2003) Glen Creeber (2005), and Janet McCabe and Kim Akass (2007); importantly, though, this sort of research tends to be described as exploring questions about television's particular forms or about "quality" television rather than *aesthetics*.[5]

It was not until the mid-2000s that scholars began to address the cluster of issues regularly and explicitly under the banner of the specific term "television aesthetics" (Geraghty 2003; Jacobs 2006; Cardwell 2006). In her pioneering work, Sarah Cardwell characterizes television aesthetics as a research program in television studies that "draws upon a generalized understanding of the key foci of philosophical aesthetics: the criticism and evaluation of art, and the raising and tackling of questions that arise from our engagement with works of art" (2006, 73). In line with Cardwell's description, we may think of television aesthetics as comprising a more applied line of inquiry, which focuses on analyzing and evaluating the form and style of individual television programs or episodes, as well as a more theoretical line of inquiry that explores, for example, the normativity or warrant of our evaluative judgments of such programs or episodes. Cardwell (2013) and Nannicelli (2017) have described the activities comprising the applied line of inquiry as the *appreciation* of television. As Cardwell argues, "appreciation is more than just the contemplation of a work or, as [John] Corner rather dismissively puts it, the study of 'how pleasing things are done.'" Rather, Cardwell explains, it is the activity of understanding and evaluating the "purpose" realized by the work (2013, 36). Nannicelli, in turn, draws upon philosopher James Grant's conception of appreciation, according to which "[a]ppreciating an artwork involves having appropriate perceptual, cognitive, cogitative, affective, or conative responses to the right aspects of the work for the right reasons" (quoted in Nannicelli 2017, 9). We might phrase this notion less formally and more roughly in film theorist Andrew Klevan's terms as "taking proper account" of a work by correctly perceiving its qualities, understanding it, and perhaps, valuing it on these bases (2018, 39). The key to this sort of account of appreciation is that it is a *normative* concept and can be undertaken more or less successfully.

The normative conception of appreciation is, at the bottom, what separates television aesthetics from the rest of television studies. Moreover, the fact that one of the two major lines of inquiry comprising television aesthetics is normative through and through has resulted in some talking at cross purposes with scholars working on evaluation from outside television aesthetics. For example, scholars working outside of television aesthetics have taken Jason Mittell, in his recent discussions of evaluation, to be talking about aesthetic judgment (e.g., Griffin 2017) in a way that is "brave" for arguing for the need "to allow evaluation into our scholarly arsenal" (Kozloff 2016, 161). But for those working within television aesthetics, Mittell's discussion of evaluation merely attempts to explain away what is so contested about evaluation in the first place – namely, its normativity (Nannicelli 2016; 2017). Because Mittell thinks that evaluative claims do not aspire to truth (2015, 207–208), his conception of evaluation is similar to that of those working in television aesthetics in name only. In fact, television studies' perennial debates about evaluative judgment have likely occluded the fact that the truly contentious premise of television aesthetics, embedded in the concept of appreciation, is, in Grant's terms, that there are more or less appropriate perceptual, cognitive, cogitative, affective, or conative responses one can have to a television program *before* one even broaches the issue of evaluation.

Cognition, emotion, and aesthetics: The challenge of reconciling naturalism and normativity

We have spent the bulk of this Introduction tracing and emphasizing connections between the intellectual histories and conceptual concerns of the three research traditions represented in this volume. We'd like to conclude with a more concrete discussion that addresses one of the challenges that attend the bridging of these fields of research. The problem can be stated like this: Media psychology and cognitive media theory, it seems, traffic in explanations of responses to television (perceptual, cognitive, emotional) that viewers, as a matter of empirical fact, actually have. On the contrary, television aesthetics (and aesthetics in general) advances and defends claims about responses that are appropriate to appreciation – responses that viewers *should* have. The challenge is to reconcile these two apparently incongruous approaches to studying viewer responses to television. Aren't their aims and purposes fundamentally different? This is a complex and difficult question that neither the Introduction nor the overall volume will be able to answer in a sustained way. Our aim here is to offer some preliminary ideas about how it might be approached.

Let's consider a case that is perhaps atypical in the scale and intensity with which it elicited congruent emotion responses, but which will, for that reason, be well known and clear to many readers: the "death" of Jon Snow in the season finale of the fifth season of *Game of Thrones*. As Héctor J. Pérez and Rainer Reisenzein (2019) have documented, there is compelling evidence to suggest that shock – negatively valenced surprise – was a widely shared reaction to the apparent murder of Snow. The first thing to say about this example is that it is a paradigmatic case of diverse audiences experiencing congruent cognitive and emotional responses to a television episode. As we acknowledge, the case is also atypical in the scale and depth of emotion elicited. However, it should be noted that variations on this sort of case are easily found within *Game of Thrones* (e.g., the beheading of Ned Stark and the "Red Wedding") and in other television programs. In fact, as another analysis on plot twists by Pérez (2020) suggests, the very concept of a plot twist depends upon the fact that television programs can reliably elicit surprise from viewers. As we indicated at the start of the chapter, there is room in this account for individual and socio-cultural variation; the claim is not that Snow's death (or any other television moment) is universally surprising. Nevertheless, given the plausibility that certain emotional responses, like surprise, *are* pancultural, it is reasonable to suppose that surprise responses to events on television, as with events in real life, will be widely shared.

A second point that is demonstrated by Pérez and Reisenzein's study concerns the integration of cognition and emotion in common audience responses like surprise. On any plausible account of surprise, including the one endorsed by Pérez and Reisenzein, surprise necessarily involves a kind of discrepancy between one's beliefs or expectations and newly acquired perceptions or beliefs. Drawing upon earlier research of Reisenzein and his colleagues, Pérez and Reisenzein explain that the felt experience of surprise results from "a discrepancy or conflict between [one's] activated schemas and the newly acquired information [whereby] ongoing information processing is automatically interrupted [and] processing resources are reallocated to the unexpected event (i.e., attention is shifted to the event)" (2019). Pérez and Reisenzein point out that in the context of *Game of Thrones*, the narrative's establishment of particular beliefs and expectations among viewers was essential to elicit surprise at Snow's death.

Moreover, surprise is either an emotion itself or at the very least, a cognitive state that is closely linked to the generation of emotion. Whether or not one regards surprise as an emotion itself tends to depend on the conception of emotion one endorses, but let us sidestep conceptual debates about the nature of emotions for now. For some psychologists, like Paul Silvia, surprise is part of a larger category of *knowledge emotions*. Silvia endorses an appraisal theory of emotion, by which emotions necessarily have a cognitive component; in the case of surprise, there is "one core appraisal – appraising something as novel and unexpected – although appraisals can shift the subjective feeling of surprise or shift the emotion from surprise to another emotion" (2009, 49). Moreover, knowledge emotions like surprise involve cognition in an additional way – namely, "their appraisals are metacognitive: the emotions stem from people's appraisals of what they know, what they expect to happen, and what they think they can learn and understand" (Silvia 2009, 49). On this view, surprise is an emotion in virtue of the fact that it involves this sort of appraisal as well as a typical expressive component, a subjective or feeling component, a behavioral component, and a physiological component (Silvia 2009, 48).[6]

With this conception of surprise as a knowledge emotion in mind, we can see the rationale for Pérez and Reisenzein's poetic analysis of Snow's death scene. In order to explain how the scene elicited a very intensely experienced sensation of surprise, they needed to reverse-engineer its construction, looking back to see how the narration cued the formation of particular hypotheses and expectations about narrative events and how the stylistic features of the death scene emphasized its sudden, unexpected, and negatively valenced nature. Here, we see the integration of the cognitive, the emotional, and the poetic in action.

What about the aesthetic? One might wonder how there could be a normative dimension to the way a scene is designed to elicit an emotional response such as surprise. Perhaps the first step in responding to this challenge is to note that non-experts usually talk and act as *if* there were a normative, aesthetic element to the design of such scenes. Pérez and Reisenzein documented viewers' web-based "aesthetic reflections" on Snow's death scene, and similar critical debates occurred about the aesthetic merit of the plot twist at the end of *Westworld*'s first season, which Foy and Magliano discuss in this volume. Foy and Magliano focus on the psychological mechanisms that underpin our narrative comprehension of television serials in general. Yet, like Pérez and Reisenzein, they also track some of the design features of *Westworld* that provide enough narrative information to establish expectations to support a twist (which is narratively coherent) and withhold enough narrative information for the twist to elicit surprise. In the case of *Westworld*, however, it is plausible that the revelation that the Man in Black is William's future-self elicited less intense surprise from viewers. For example, according to *Washington Post* critic Alyssa Rosenberg, "that much-telegraphed reveal was the least interesting thing about the season finale of 'Westworld'" (2016). Likewise, critic Genevieve Valentine asserts that *Westworld* "telegraphs … many of its twists" (2016).

The critical discussion around *Westworld* suggests, at least, that viewers whose approach to the show is *appreciative* sometimes render aesthetic judgments on the basis of how successful a program has been in its aim of eliciting a particular emotion. For Rosenberg, *Westworld*'s reveal is not aesthetically meritorious in part because it is *not* surprising – it is not unexpected and does not cue what Reisenzein et al. would call a "schema revision process" (2012). Valentine agrees that the twist is not surprising but suggests that it is nevertheless aesthetically successful in part because it is not designed to elicit surprise but to cue a meta-level reflection on the nature of storytelling. The point is that it is common to aesthetically evaluate a television program in terms of how well its design successfully realizes the aim of eliciting a particular emotion. For this reason, we might call emotions such as surprise elicited in aesthetic contexts "aesthetic emotions"; they are "emotions aroused by specifically aesthetic properties of a work of art" (Juslin 2013, 238) and in turn, they contribute to our aesthetic evaluation of the work (Fingerhut and Prinz 2020; also see Menninghaus et al. 2019). Furthermore, because the question of whether the design of a television program successfully realizes the aim of eliciting a particular emotion is an objective matter, a given evaluative judgment of a television program is objective inasmuch as it is made on the basis of how elegantly, clumsily, coherently, or unexpectedly the program elicits an intended emotional response (Carroll 2008; Nannicelli 2016; 2017). And this fact explains the apparent normative force of fans' and critics' overall aesthetic evaluations of television shows with reference to "evidence" such as a particular show being funny, being predictable, being suspenseful, and the like.

Conclusion

There is much more to be said on this topic and others pertaining to the relationship between cognition, emotion, and aesthetics in contemporary serial television, as the following chapters attest. We have tried to organize the chapters in a way that makes their connections clear but that also suggests linkages between each of the broad sections of the book. The first section, "The Nature of Television Contemporary Televisual Seriality," comprises essays that attempt to stake out the distinctive features of contemporary serial television. This section is thus designed to identify, describe, and delimit the boundaries of our object of inquiry. As suggested earlier, the guiding research question of our volume asks how contemporary serial television is designed to elicit particular cognitive, emotional, and aesthetic effects from audiences. In the first section, the emphasis is on establishing what constitutes *contemporary serial television*. The second section, "Audiences," comprises three chapters from researchers in media psychology whose particular area of analysis is, as the title suggests, the audiences of contemporary serial television. In the second section of the book, the emphasis is on *audiences*. In the third section, "Poetics," the emphasis is, in turn, on how television is *designed* to elicit effects from those audiences. Finally, the fourth section, "Value: Aesthetic and Beyond," focuses on the difficult question of how the various "effects" that contemporary serial television elicits from audiences – cognitive, emotional, and aesthetic – bear upon how we value it. Aesthetic value is obviously a key issue here, but ethical value also looms large given the close connections to cognition, emotion, and moral judgment that have intrigued scholars across a number of disciplines. In all four sections, the contributions necessarily juggle discussions and analyses of the cognitive, emotional, and aesthetic responses we experience while watching contemporary serial television.

Notes

1 However, this is not at all to say that all earlier work in media psychology assumed a methodologically naïve media effects framework. For example, research from the 1980s and 1990s on viewer responses to horror films studied viewers in co-viewing situations – in particular, in co-viewing situations with a member of the opposite sex – with the understanding that the reception environment informed the psychological and behavioral responses of viewers (Zillmann et al. 1986; Zillmann and Weaver 1996).
2 In relation, see Thompson (2003).
3 For other recent cognitivist work that expands its purview to include television, see Riis and Taylor (2019).
4 Oftentimes, this distinction is phrased in a way that suggests media psychology is "empirical" or "more empirical" than cognitive film theory or film theory in general. Insofar as cognitive theory is also defined by a tradition of conceptual analysis, there is a partial truth in this claim. Yet, we must not forget Bordwell's point: the analysis of form and style in film (and television) is *also* a form of empirical inquiry.
5 There are exceptions, of which Jacobs (2000; 2003) is one. Also see Thorburn (1987) and Metallinos (1996).
6 Also see Reisenzein et al. (2012) and Reisenzein et al. (2019).

References

Allen, Robert C. 1992. "Introduction to the Second Edition: More Talk about TV." In *Channels of Discourse, Reassembled*, edited by Robert C. Allen, 1–30. Chapel Hill, NC: University of North Carolina Press.

Bettinson, Gary. 2015. *The Sensuous Cinema of Wong Kar-wai: Film Poetics and the Aesthetic of Disturbance*. Hong Kong: Hong Kong University Press.

Bettinson, Gary, and James Udden, eds. 2016. *The Poetics of Chinese Cinema*. Basingstoke: Palgrave Macmillan.

Bignell, Jonathan. 2013. *An Introduction to Television Studies*, 3rd ed. New York: Routledge.

Bordwell, David. 1985. *Narration in the Fiction Film*. Madison, WI: University of Wisconsin Press.

Bordwell, David. 1989a. "A Case for Cognitivism." *Iris* 9: 11–41.

Bordwell, David. 1989b. *Making Meaning: Inference and Rhetoric in the Interpretation of Cinema*. Cambridge, MA: Harvard University Press.

Bordwell, David. 2008. *Poetics of Cinema*. New York: Routledge.

Bordwell, David. 2009. "Cognitive Theory." In *The Routledge Companion to Philosophy and Film*, edited by Paisley Livingston and Carl Plantinga, 356–367. New York: Routledge.

Bordwell, David, and Noël Carroll, eds. 1996. *Post-Theory: Reconstructing Film Studies*. Madison, WI: University of Wisconsin Press.

Brunsdon, Charlotte. 1997. *Screen Tastes: Soap Opera to Satellite Dishes*. London: Routledge.

Bryant, Jennings, and Dolf Zillmann, eds. 1991. *Responding to the Screen: Reception and Reaction Processes*. Mahweh, NJ: Lawrence Erlbaum.

Buckland, Warren. 2006. *Directed by Steven Spielberg: Poetics of the Contemporary Hollywood Blockbuster*. London: Continuum.

Butler, Jeremy G. 2010. *Television Style*. New York: Routledge.

Butler, Jeremy G. 2018. *Television: Visual Storytelling and Screen Culture*. New York: Routledge.

Caldwell, John Thornton. 1995. *Televisuality: Style, Crisis, and Authority in American Television*. New Brunswick, NJ: Rutgers University Press.

Calvo-Merino, Beatriz, Corrine Jola, Daniel E. Glaser, and Patrick Haggard. 2008. "Towards a Sensorimotor Aesthetics of Performing Art." *Consciousness and Cognition* 17, no. 3: 911–922.

Cantril, Hadley. (1940) 2009. *The Invasion from Mars: A Study in the Psychology of Panic*. New Brunswick, NJ: Transaction Publishers.

Cardwell, Sarah. 2006. "Television Aesthetics." *Critical Studies in Television* 1, no. 1: 72–80.

Cardwell, Sarah. 2013. "Television Aesthetics: Stylistic Analysis and Beyond." In *Television Aesthetics and Style*, edited by Jason Jacobs and Steven Peacock, 23–44. London: Bloomsbury.

Carroll, Noël. 1990. *The Philosophy of Horror, or Paradoxes of the Heart*. New York: Routledge.

Carroll, Noël. 1996. "The Power of Movies." In his *Theorizing the Moving Image*, 78–93. Cambridge: Cambridge University Press.

Carroll, Noël. 1998. *A Philosophy of Mass Art*. Oxford: Clarendon Press.

Carroll, Noël. 2004. "Sympathy for the Devil." In *The Sopranos and Philosophy: I Kill, Therefore I Am*, edited by Richard Greene and Peter Vernezze, 121–136. Peru, IL: Open Court.

Carroll, Noël. 2008. *The Philosophy of Motion Pictures*. Malden, MA: Blackwell.

Carroll, Noël. 2010. "Aesthetic Experience: A Question of Content." In his *Art in Three Dimensions*, 77–108. Oxford: Oxford University Press.

Cavell, Stanley. 1982. "The Fact of Television." *Daedalus* 111, no. 4: 75–96.

Caughie, John. 2000. *Television Drama: Realism, Modernism, and British Culture*. Oxford: Oxford University Press.

Cohen, Elizabeth L. 2017. "Social Context of Media Use." In *The International Encyclopedia of Media Effects*, edited by Patrick Rössler, Cynthia A. Hoffner, and Liesbet van Zoonen, 1–12. Boston, MA: Wiley-Blackwell.

Creeber, Glen. 2005. *Serial Television: Big Drama on the Small Screen*. London: BFI.

Czitrom, Daniel J. 1982. *Media and the American Mind: From Morse to McLuhan*. Chapel Hill, NC: University of North Carolina Press.

Dill, Karen E. 2013. "Introduction." In *The Oxford Handbook of Media Psychology*, edited by Karen E. Dill, 3–9. Oxford: Oxford University Press.

Farr, Robert M. 1996. *The Roots of Modern Social Psychology*. Oxford: Blackwell.

Fingerhut, Joerg, and Jesse Prinz. 2020. "Aesthetic Emotions Reconsidered." *The Monist* 103: 223–239.

Geraghty, Christine. 2003. "Aesthetics and Quality in Popular Television Drama. *International Journal of Cultural Studies* 6, no. 1: 25–45.

Giles, David. 2003. *Media Psychology*. Mahweh, NJ: Lawrence Erlbaum Associates.

Gorodeisky, Keren. 2021a. "The Authority of Pleasure." *Noûs* 55: 199–220. doi:10.1111/nous.12310

Gorodeisky, Keren. 2021b. "On Liking Aesthetic Value." *Philosophy and Phenomenological Research* 102, no. 2: 261–280. doi:10.1111/phpr.12641

Graumann, Carl F. 1986. "The Individualization of the Social and the Desocialization of the Individual: Floyd H. Allport's Contribution to Social Psychology." In *Changing Conceptions of Crowd Mind and Behavior*, edited by Carl F. Graumann and Serge Moscovivi, 97–116. Berlin: Springer-Verlag.

Gray, Jonathan, and Amanda D. Lotz. 2019. *Television Studies*, 2nd ed. Cambridge: Polity.

Griffin, Hollis. 2017. "Evaluating Television: Affect as a Critical Optic." *Cinema Journal* 57, no. 1: 71–93.

Grodal, Torben. 1997. *Moving Pictures: A New Theory of Film Genres, Feelings, and Cognition*. Oxford: Clarendon Press.

Han, Jingjing, and Annie Lang. 2020. "It's a Journey: From Media Effects to Dynamic Systems." *Media Psychology* 23, no. 3: 415–435. doi:10.1080/15213269.2019.1604236.

Jacobs, Jason. 2000. *The Intimate Screen: Early British Television Drama*. Oxford: Oxford University Press.

Jacobs, Jason. 2003. *Body Trauma TV: The New Hospital Dramas*. London: BFI.

Jacobs, Jason. 2006. "Television Aesthetics: An Infantile Disorder." *Journal of British Cinema and Television* 3, no. 1: 19–33.

Jacobs, Jason, and Steven Peacock, eds. 2013. *Television Aesthetics and Style*. London: Bloomsbury.

Juslin, Patrik N. 2013. "From Everyday Emotions to Aesthetic Emotions: Towards a Unified Theory of Musical Emotions." *Physics of Life Reviews* 10, no. 3: 235–266.

Keating, Patrick. 2010. *Hollywood Lighting: From the Silent Era to Film Noir*. New York: Columbia University Press.

Keil, Charlie. 2001. *Early American Cinema in Transition: Story, Style, and Filmmaking, 1907–1913*. Madison, WI: University of Wisconsin Press.

Klevan, Andrew. 2018. *Aesthetic Evaluation and Film*. Manchester: Manchester University Press.

Kozloff, Sarah. 2016. "Complex TV: The Poetics of Contemporary Television Storytelling (Review)." *Cinema Journal* 55, no. 3: 159–164.

Lang, Annie. 2006. "Motivated Cognition (LC4MP): The Influence of Appetitive and Aversive Activation on the Processing of Video Games." In *Digital Media: Transformation in Human Communication*, edited by Paul Messaris and Lee Humphreys, 237–256. New York: Peter Lang.

Lang, Annie. 2014. "Dynamic Human-Centered Communication Systems Theory. *The Information Society* 30, no. 1: 60–70.

Lang, Annie, Robert F. Potter, and Paul Bolls. 2009. "Where Psychophysiology Meets the Media:Taking the Effects Out of Mass Media Research." In *Media Effects: Advances in Theory and Research*, edited by Jennings Bryant and Mary Beth Oliver, 3rd ed., 185–206. New York: Routledge.

Levinson, Jerrold. 2016. "Toward an Adequate Conception of Aesthetic Experience." In his *Aesthetic Pursuits: Essays in the Philosophy of Art*, 28–46. Oxford: Oxford University Press.

Mandler, Jean Matter, and George Mandler. 1969. "The Diaspora of Experimental Psychology: The Gestaltists and Others." In *The Intellectual Migration: Europe and America, 1930–1960*, edited by Donald Fleming and Bernard Bailyn, 371–419. Cambridge, MA: Harvard University Press.

Matthen, Mohan. 2017. "The Pleasure of Art." *Australasian Philosophical Review* 1, no. 1: 6–28.

McCabe, Janet, and Kimm Akass, eds. 2007. *Quality TV: Contemporary American Television and Beyond*. London: I.B. Tauris.

Menninghaus, Winfried, Valentin Wagner, Eugen Wassiliwizky, Ines Schindler, Julian Hanich, Thomas Jacobsen, and Stefan Koelsch. 2019. "What Are Aesthetic Emotions?" *Psychological Review* 126, no. 2: 171–195.

Metallinos, Nikos. 1996. *Television Aesthetics: Perceptual, Cognitive, and Compositional Bases*. Mahweh, NJ: Lawrence Erlbaum Associates.

Mittell, Jason. 2015. *Complex TV: The Poetics of Contemporary Television Storytelling*. New York: New York University Press.

Nannicelli, Ted. 2016. "In Defence of the Objectivity of Evaluative Television Criticism." *Screen* 57, no. 2: 124–143.

Nannicelli, Ted. 2017. *Appreciating the Art of Television: A Philosophical Perspective*. New York: Routledge.

Nannicelli, Ted, and Paul Taberham, eds. 2014. *Cognitive Media Theory*. New York: Routledge.

Nelson, Robin. 1997. *TV Drama in Transition: Forms, Values, and Cultural Change*. Basingstoke: Macmillan.

Newcomb, Horace. 1974. *TV: The Most Popular Art*. Garden City, NY: Anchor Press.

Newman, Michael Z. 2006. "From Beats to Arcs: Toward a Poetics of Television Narrative." *The Velvet Light Trap* 58: 16–28.

Nichols, Bill. 1992. "Form Wars: The Political Unconscious of Formalist Theory." In *Classical Hollywood Narrative: The Paradigm Wars*, edited by Jane Gains, 49–78. Durham, NC: Duke University Press.

Oliver, Mary Beth, and Anne Bartsch. 2010. "Appreciation as Audience Response: Exploring Entertainment Gratifications Beyond Hedonism." *Human Communication Research* 36: 53–81.

Oliver, Mary Beth, and Anne Bartsch. 2011. "Appreciation of Entertainment: The Importance of Meaningfulness via Virtue and Wisdom." *Journal of Media Psychology* 23: 29–33.

Pérez, Héctor J. 2020. "The Plot Twist in TV Serial Narratives." *Projections: The Journal for Movies and Mind* 14, no. 1: 58–74.

Pérez, Héctor J., and Rainer Reisenzein. 2019. "On Jon Snow's Death: Plot Twist and Global Fandom in *Game of Thrones*." *Culture and Psychology*. doi:10.1177/1354067X19845062.

Plantinga, Carl, and Greg M. Smith, eds. 1999. *Passionate Views: Film, Cognition, and Emotion*. Baltimore: The Johns Hopkins University Press.

Pooley, Jefferson, and Michael J. Socolow. 2013. "The Myth of the *War of the Worlds* Panic." *Slate*, October 28, 2013. https://slate.com/culture/2013/10/orson-welles-war-of-the-worlds-panic-myth-the-infamous-radio-broadcast-did-not-cause-a-nationwide-hysteria.html

Potter, Robert F., and Paul Bolls. 2012. *Psychophysiological Measurement and Meaning: Cognitive and Emotional Processing of Media*. New York: Routledge.

Quart, Alissa. 2000. "The Insider: David Bordwell Blows the Whistle on Film Studies." *Lingua Franca* 10, no. 2: 34–43.

Reisenzein, Rainer, Gernot Horstmann, and Achim Schützwohl. 2019. "The Cognitive-Evolutionary Model of Surprise: A Review of the Evidence." *Topics in Cognitive Science* 11: 50–74.

Reisenzein, Rainer, Wulf-Uwe Meyer, and Michael Niepel. 2012. "Surprise." In *Encyclopedia of Human Behavior*, edited by V.S. Ramachandran, 564–570. London: Elsevier.

Riis, Johannes, and Aaron Taylor. 2019. *Screening Characters: Theories of Character in Film, Television, and Interactive Media*. New York: Routledge.

Rogers, Everett M. 1994. *A History of Communication Study*. New York: The Free Press.

Rosenberg, Alyssa. 2016. "'Westworld' Season 1, Episode 10 Review: 'The Bicameral Mind.'" *The Washington Post*, December 5, 2016. https://www.washingtonpost.com/news/act-four/wp/2016/12/04/westworld-season-1-episode-10-review-the-bicameral-mind/.

Rutledge, Pamela Brown. 2013. "Arguing for Media Psychology as a Distinct Field." In *The Oxford Handbook of Media Psychology*, edited by Karen E. Dill, 43–61. Oxford: Oxford University Press.

Sherry, John L. 2015. "The Complexity Paradigm for Studying Human Communication: A Summary and Integration of Two Fields." *Review of Communication Research* 3, no. 1: 22–54. doi:10.12840/issn.2255-4165.2015.03.01.007

Shimamura, Arthur P., ed. 2013. *Psychocinematics: Exploring Cognition the Movies*. Oxford: Oxford University Press.

Silvia, Paul J. 2009. "Looking Past Pleasure: Anger, Confusion, Disgust, Pride, Surprise, and Other Unusual Aesthetic Emotions." *Psychology of Aesthetics, Creativity, and the Arts* 3, no. 1: 48–51.

Smith, Greg M. 1995. "Plotting a TV Show about Nothing: Patterns of Narration in *Seinfeld*." *Creative Screenwriting* 2, no. 1: 82–90.

Smith, Greg M. 2006. "A Case of *Cold Feet*: Serial Narration and the Character Arc." *Journal of British Cinema and Television* 3, no. 1: 82–94.

Smith, Greg M. 2007. *Beautiful TV: The Art and Argument of Ally McBeal*. Austin, TX: University of Texas Press.

Smith, Greg M. 2014. "Coming Out of the Corner: The Challenges of a Broader Media Cognitivism." In *Cognitive Media Theory*, edited by Ted Nannicelli and Paul Taberham, 285–302. New York: Routledge.

Smith, Murray. 1995. *Engaging Characters: Fiction, Emotion, and Cinema*. Oxford: Clarendon Press.

Smith, Murray. 2011. "Just What Is It that Makes Tony Soprano such an Appealing, Attractive Murderer?" In *Ethics at the Cinema*, edited by Ward E. Jones and Samantha Vice, 66–90. Oxford: Oxford University Press.

Smith, Murray. 2017. *Film, Art, and the Third Culture: A Naturalized Aesthetics of Film*. Oxford: Oxford University Press.

Spigel, Lynn. 2009. "My TV Studies… Now Playing on a YouTube Site Near You." *Television and New Media* 10, no. 1 (January 2009): 149–153.

Tal-Or, Nurit. 2019. "The Effects of Co-viewers on the Viewing Experience." *Communication Theory*. Online first: doi:10.1093/ccc/qtz012

Tan, Ed S. 1996. *Emotion and the Structure of Narrative Film: Film as an Emotion Machine*. Mahweh, NJ: Lawrence Erlbaum.

Taylor, Richard, ed. 1982. *The Poetics of Cinema*. Oxford: Russian Poetics in Translation.

Thompson, Kristen. 2003. *Storytelling in Film and Television*. Cambridge, MA: Harvard University Press.

Thompson, Robert J. 1997. *Television's Second Golden Age: From Hill·Street Blues to ER*. Syracuse: Syracuse University Press.

Thorburn, David. 1987. "Television as an Aesthetic Medium." *Critical Studies in Mass Communication* 4, no. 2: 161–173.

Tuma, Regina M. 2013. "Media Psychology and Its History." In *The Oxford Handbook of Media Psychology*, edited by Karen E. Dill, 62–74. Oxford: Oxford University Press.

Vaage, Margrethe Bruun. 2014. "Blinded by Familiarity: Partiality, Morality, and Engagement with Television Series." In *Cognitive Media Theory*, edited by Ted Nannicelli and Paul Taberham, 268–284. New York: Routledge.

Vaage, Margrethe Bruun. 2016. *The Antihero in American Television*. New York: Routledge.

Valentine, Genevieve. 2016. "Westworld's Twists Are Easy to Predict Because They're Not the Point of the Show." *Vox*, December 2, 2016. https://www.vox.com/culture/2016/12/2/13807370/westworld-twists-mystery-myth.

Vorderer, Peter, Christoph Klimmt, and Ute Ritterfeld. 2004. "Enjoyment: At the Heart of Media Entertainment." *Communication Theory* 14, no. 4: 388–408.

Vorderer, Peter, Hans J. Wulff, and Mike Friedrichsen, eds. 1996. *Suspense: Conceptualizations, Theoretical Analyses, and Empirical Explorations*. Mahweh, NJ: Lawrence Erlbaum.

Weaver, James III, and Ron Tamborini. 1996. *Horror Films: Current Research on Audience Preferences and Reactions*. Mahweh, NJ: Lawrence Erlbaum.

Weber, René, Klaus Mathiak, and John Sherry. 2009. "The Neurological Perspective in Mass Communications Research." In *Biological Dimensions of Communication: Perspectives, Methods, and Research*, edited by Michael J. Beatty, James C. McCroskey, and Kory Floyd, 43–73. Creskill, NJ: Hampton Press.

Weber, René, Allison Eden, Richard Huskey, J. Michael Mangus, and Emily Falk. 2015. "Bridging Media Psychology and Cognitive Neuroscience: Challenges and Opportunities." *Journal of Media Psychology* 27: 146–156.

Zeki, Semir. 1999. *Inner Vision: An Exploration of Art and the Brain*. Oxford: Oxford University Press.

Zettl, Herbert. 1978. "The Rare Case of Television Aesthetics." *Journal of the University Film Association* 30, no. 2: 3–8.

Zillmann, Dolf, James B. Weaver, Norbert Mundorf, and Charles F. Aust. 1986. "Effects of an Opposite-Gender Companion's Affect to Horror on Distress, Delight, and Attraction. *Journal of Personality and Social Psychology* 51, no. 3: 586–594.

Zillmann, Dolf, and James B. Weaver, III. 1996. "Gender-Socialization Theory of Reactions to Horror." In *Horror Films: Current Research on Audience Preferences and Reactions*, edited by James B. Weaver, III and Ron Tamborini, 81–102. Mahweh, NJ: Lawrence Erlbaum.

Part I

The nature of contemporary televisual seriality

2 Television's temporality

Seriality and temporal prolongation

Alberto N. García and Ted Nannicelli

Introduction: Television and the passage of time

This chapter aims to provide a critical survey of thought about a key aspect of television's temporal dimension – namely, its extended duration. We begin by hazarding some assumptions that we hope are uncontentious. We then pose some questions that have yet to be satisfactorily addressed in the recent media studies literature on seriality, as we try to demonstrate with a subsequent critique of extant conceptions of "seriality" in the field – some too narrow and some too broad. The productive part of the chapter outlines quite different understandings of "seriality" in philosophical aesthetics. We argue that these subtler conceptions of "seriality" come closer to accounting for television's particularity and that they bear significant affinities with a recent account one of us has advanced. Nevertheless, we argue that the ambiguity of the term "seriality" threatens to mislead, particularly since some of the phenomena for which we want to account are not intuitively described as involving seriality – at least in the standard sense of that term. For this reason, we maintain that our label – temporal prolongation – is preferable, and we try to support this claim by working through some specific examples at the end of the chapter.

Having set out an overview of the chapter, let us now lay out our starting assumptions. It is commonly accepted that an important part of the interest we have in contemporary television as an art form has to do with artistic effects it achieves in virtue of its handling of time.[1] Consider a couple of different examples. 1) The current popularity of television reboots like *Twin Peaks: The Return*, *The X-Files*, and *Roseanne* partly depends upon an interest in how these programs handle the time elapsed during their "hiatuses." There are too many dimensions to this to summarize them adequately here, but we can think about this in relation to, say, the changed political context of reception for *Roseanne*, *The X-Files*' stalled resolution of the alien mythology it developed intermittently over nine seasons, and the cliff-hangers regarding Cooper's fate at the end of the second season of *Twin Peaks*. Part of our interest in such programs *as* artworks is in their relative success or failure in handling these challenges raised by the long passage of time. 2) Whether we call them "prestige," "Quality," "high-end," "complex," or so forth, it is clear that in recent years some serial

DOI: 10.4324/9781003188643-2

television dramas such as *The Sopranos*, *The Wire*, and *Game of Thrones* have garnered praise for their innovative, multi-threaded narrative structures. The praise and, indeed, the programs' artistic achievements depend in part upon the creators' successful orchestration of plotlines, characters, and narrative details. There are, of course, many other examples to which we could point; we highlight these three sorts of cases because they are likely the most recognizable.[2]

Our chapter is driven by what we take to be two central research questions about this particular feature of television's temporal character: What, if anything, about television's capacity for extended duration is specific to *television*? And what, if any, distinctive artistic effects are realizable in the television medium in virtue of its particular capacity for extended duration?[3] As a field, media studies (within which we include television studies for our present purposes) has, of course, already had much to say about television's extended temporal duration. We can only gesture towards that literature here. In our opinion, one of the most valuable insights of the literature is that the recent wave of serial television drama is very similar, in narrative structure, to older cultural forms – most proximately, television soap operas, but of course, radio soap operas before them (Newcomb 1974; Feuer 1984; Allen 1985; Hayward 1997; Newman and Levine 2012). And the narrative structure of *radio soap operas* was, in turn, related to the narrative structure of *other* radio serials as well as the film serials. And on and on back to the Victorians (Hagedorn 1995; Hayward 1997). Noting the uptake of seriality across (popular) media, several scholars pursuing research under the headings of "transmedia" or "seriality" studies claim that seriality is a transcultural, transhistorical phenomenon of which television seriality is a particular instance (Allen and van den Berg 2014; Kelleter 2017). If this is right, then the questions we want to ask about the artistic capacities television has in virtue of its extended temporal duration can be answered by appealing to "seriality" as conceived in the transmedia/seriality studies literature.

The "simple" and "expanded" conceptions of seriality

There are two standard conceptions of seriality in the literature, either of which may be thought to offer a full account of television's particular temporal character and the artistic capacities it has thanks to that temporal character. The first holds that serials are narratives told in successive installments (e.g., Williams 1974; Kozloff 1992; Hagedorn 1995; Carroll 1996; Hayward 1997; Mittell 2015). Call this "the simple conception" of seriality. According to the second view, seriality is a much broader phenomenon. In Frank Kelleter's words, "what looks like a simple matter of narrative technique on closer inspection turns out to be a core problem of modernity itself: the problem of renewing something by duplicating it" (2017, 29). For Kelleter, this is the core problem of capitalism. Call this "the expanded conception" of seriality. We will begin by showing that neither the simple nor the expanded conception of seriality sufficiently addresses what we take to need explaining about television's particular temporality and the artistic capacities it affords. The simple conception, we will argue, is too narrow insofar as it does not account for non-narrative forms. The expanded conception is too broad because it cannot distinguish salient differences between television and other media (in a non-medium essentialist sense to be explained presently). If we look beyond television and media studies to philosophical aesthetics, there are conceptions of seriality that split the difference between overly narrow and overly broad, and they offer insight into television's particular temporal affordances (Mag Uidhir 2013; Cavell 1982). Nevertheless, here, too, "serial" is used in a somewhat idiosyncratic fashion. In part, because we think that the term "seriality" itself threatens to confuse rather than clarify matters, we prefer the term "temporal prolongation." In what follows, we will track the senses in which temporal prolongation involves seriality and those in which it does not. We then offer some analysis of various ways in which television's temporal prolongation affords the medium distinctive artistic capacities.

On our view, the simple conception of seriality describes a widely prevalent and significant way in which television's capacity for extended duration is realized – namely, in terms of the processional mode of storytelling common to soap operas as well as contemporary "prestige" or "complex" dramas whose narratives unfold over successive episodes and seasons. As an example of this conception of seriality, consider Carroll's account: "The serial form, in whatever medium, relies on the same principle: the narrative generates certain questions that the audience expects will be answered either in the present installment or a subsequent one" (1996, 120). Carroll's characterization of seriality is advanced in the context of a discussion of soap opera, which of course bears seriality as one of its hallmark features. But seriality, conceived in this way, is a feature of *much* contemporary narrative television. It is something of a critical commonplace now to note that with a few notable exceptions (for example, *The Simpsons*), most contemporary narrative television takes a particular hybrid form that combines elements of series and serials (Kozloff 1992; Mittell 2015).

Lest proponents of the expanded understanding of seriality object that the narrow conception is purely formalistic, let us quickly add that all of the extant characterizations of seriality we would regard as falling under the simple conception refer to extratextual considerations. In Carroll's account in the preceding paragraph, seriality is a formal feature that *cues* audience expectations in particular ways. This idea recurs in Christy Mag Uidhir's formalized definition of serial art. According to Mag Uidhir:

W is a *serial artwork* if and only if:

1. *W* is itself an artwork.
2. *W* is wholly (nontrivially) composed of some (nontrivial) sequence $\{w_1, w_2, \ldots w_n\}$.
3. Properly attending to (engaging with) *W* qua artwork – that is, access to any and all of the constitutive art-relevant features for that *W* – requires

> properly attending to each element in that sequence (in the order/arrangement prescribed by that *W*) (2013, 262).

The similarity with Carroll's characterization of seriality is Mag Uidhir's emphasis on the audience's engagement with the work: "Serial artworks prescribe reception of, attention to, or engagement with elements in sequence" (2013, 262). There are more nuances to Mag Uidhir's definition, which we shall discuss presently. But first, consider one more characterization of seriality that, on our view, falls under the simple conception. According to literary scholar Jennifer Hayward:

> [Serial literature] is not constituted, then, by purely formal and thematic considerations. Rather, these considerations are inseparable from the unique reading practices and interpretive tactics developed by audiences, practices that include collaborative, active reading; interpretation; prediction; occasional rewriting or the creation of new subplots; attempts to influence textual production; and, increasingly often, a degree of success in those attempts.
>
> (1997, 4)

We hope the similarities between Hayward's characterization of seriality and those of Carroll and Mag Uidhir are evident, and that this passage also makes clear that the simple conception circulates across disciplines.

As we indicated earlier, we think the simple conception of seriality is satisfactory as far as it goes. The only point we wish to make about it is that it is only one, particular manifestation of television's capacity for extended duration. Seriality, on the simple conception, is a specific realization of a broader phenomenon – and it is that broader phenomenon that we are trying to describe. Mag Uidhir's definition offers a helpful way of distinguishing between seriality on the simple conception and the broader phenomenon that we want to call temporal prolongation. One point that Mag Uidhir makes, which has not received sufficient recognition, is that the simple conception of seriality has a normative component built into it. That is, there is a proper way to attend to a serial artwork – namely, by attending to *all* elements or installments of the work *in* the sequence prescribed by the work. We think this is right, and, furthermore, it allows us to see how many of the other realizations of television's capacity for extended duration fall *outside* the simple conception of seriality. For in many cases, it seems implausible that proper attention to a given television series or program depends upon attending to all of its installments in just the sequence prescribed by the work. We will discuss some examples later, but for now, you might consider formats like talk shows, game shows, sporting events, and certain reality television series.

Let us make one final point as a segue to a discussion of the expanded conception of seriality. Mag Uidhir's article also has affinities with some of the work being conducted under the banner of seriality studies, since it recognizes seriality as a widespread, transmedia phenomenon. Assuming this is right, it is not clear that being marked by serials (in the simple sense) would be sufficient to differentiate television's temporal character from that of other media that traffic in serials. But given our insistence that the simple conception of seriality is too narrow for our purposes anyway, we won't worry about this further problem here.

If the simple conception of seriality is too narrow to account for television's capacity for extended duration *in general*, then what of the expanded notion of seriality? This is a more idiosyncratic view of seriality, and we are not sure how common it is. Nevertheless, we've chosen to address it briefly here because the view appears in a recent book project – *The Media of Serial Narrative* – that seeks to make a decisive intervention in our understanding of seriality. In his introductory essay to that book, Frank Kelleter acknowledges that what we are calling the expanded conception of seriality may "seem like a risky 'broadening' of the concept of seriality, almost encompassing the notion of popular culture itself" (2017, 14). Nevertheless, he claims:

> once we shift our attention to networked cultural practices, seriality will become visible in ostensibly nonserialized textual structures as well, precisely because these structures can now be investigated as (inter)actions that have been consolidated in domain-specific forms. My point, therefore, is to encourage an understanding of seriality as a practice *of* popular culture, not a narrative formalism within it. This is not an issue of "broad" versus "narrow" concepts but of scholastic versus systemic-praxeological models of description. Or, in other words: one and the same text can be regarded as simultaneously serial and nonserial, depending on the perspective from which it is seen – or, more properly, depending on the historical situation in which its textual activities are mobilized in one way or another.
>
> (2017, 15)

We find Kelleter's discussion of seriality hard to understand.[4] None of the characterizations of the simple conception of seriality we discussed earlier are purely formalistic or divorced from reception practices in the way he suggests. Furthermore, from the acknowledgment that extratextual factors like reception practices partly constitute the notion of seriality, it hardly follows that one needs to accept Kelleter's theoretical assumptions (i.e., systems theory; praxeology) or subsequent claims such as "one and the same text can be regarded as simultaneously serial and nonserial."

On our view, the constitutive features of serials are determined by their makers, since serials are artifacts – human creations over which their makers have a particular kind of authority. For example, *Great Expectations* is, on this view, a serialized work, even though most contemporary readers regard it as a one-off, self-contained novel. The facts that it sits on a bookshelf in a single volume and might be read in its entirety in just one sitting do not change the fact that it is a work of serial fiction insofar as this is how Charles

Dickens created it. As the work's creator, Dickens determined certain facts about what the work is like and about what sorts of engagement are necessary for a proper experience of the work. To return to Mag Uidhir's definition, Dickens *prescribed* that the installments of *Great Expectations* be read in a particular sequence.

In contrast, Kelleter overestimates the feedback loop between the producers and consumers of serials. He claims that "serial aesthetics does not unfold in a clear-cut, chronological succession of finished composition and responsive actualization ... Repeated temporal overlap between ongoing publication and ongoing reception allows serial audiences to become involved in a narrative's progress" (2017, 13). Maybe, but the actual creators of serials determine the extent of this audience "involvement." The creators' involvement is of a very different nature than that of the audiences because of the ontological and epistemic privilege they have over their creations. So, we don't see the motivation to think that a single work might be variously serial or nonserial depending on one's perspective or about how audiences approach the work *after* its creation.

More importantly, insofar as Kelleter's claim actually involves the simple conception of seriality, his expanded use of the term alongside his continued use of the term in its simple sense threatens to muddy the conceptual waters. Even if one accepted Kelleter's claims regarding seriality as a "practice of popular culture," we'd still want a term to distinguish *this* concept from seriality in the simple sense. But as we have indicated, we are not in fact persuaded that it is cogent to think of seriality in this expanded sense. Kelleter's characterization of seriality explains too much and not enough: If the concept he seeks is meant to describe general patterns of replication and variation in popular culture, then we see neither why the term for this concept should be "seriality" nor how such a concept could illuminate any differential features of television's extended duration. At the same time, throughout his discussion, Kelleter continues to use the term "narrative" in conjunction with seriality in his expanded sense, which is odd, because the expanded sense of the term would apparently need to include non-narrative forms by his definition of it.

Towards a definition of temporal prolongation

As one would suppose, our particular interest in television's expanded duration includes both narrative and non-narrative forms, and for this reason, as well as the others we've presented, neither the simple conception of seriality nor the expanded conception of seriality accounts for what we want to describe. At this point, we want to return to Mag Uidhir's paper, because he supplements his basic definition of seriality with several related concepts, one of which offers a congenial starting point for developing our own account. Mag Uidhir proposes using the term *loosely serial artworks* to describe "artworks for which there is no nontrivial ordering of elements in the sequence composing them" (2013, 264). Formally, according to Mag Uidhir:

W is a *loosely serial artwork* if and only if:

1. *W* is an artwork.
2. *W* is composed (in a nontrivial way) or a (trivial) sequence or a (nontrivial yet nonordered) set $\{p_1, p_2, \ldots p_n\}$.
3. There is some art-relevant feature φ but no $p_m \in \{p_1, p_2, \ldots p_n\}$ that has φ.
4. Properly attending to (engaging with) *W* qua artwork requires properly attending to each element in that sequence or member of that set (in the *nonordered* manner prescribed by *W*) (2013, 264).

In rough terms, the basic idea is that there are some artworks, comprising multiple distinct works, of which the proper appreciation requires one to attend to each constitutive part but not in a particular order. This idea offers a way to account for two sorts of art that have parallels in television, in particular – namely, series (both fiction and non-fiction) and non-narrative works.[5] In the following, we will suggest a number of ways in which television's extended duration might bear upon our appreciation of both.

Mag Uidhir's discussion of "loosely serial artworks" is helpful because it is sufficiently capacious to cover series in the standard, television-specific sense of that term as well as other sorts of television that might be more commonly thought of as "formats." Consider, for example, Kozloff's characterization of series as "those shows whose characters and setting are recycled but [whose] story concludes in each individual episode" (1992, 90–91). Much like Raymond Williams's (1974) description of series before hers, Kozloff's use of the term denotes narrative fictions. That's fine as far as it goes, but again, one of our hypotheses is that television's extended duration has implications for our engagement with non-narrative, non-fiction programs that share the same sort of processional, temporally extended character as series. We are thinking in particular of things like newscasts and sportscasts as well as certain reality television shows. This, however, suggests the need for a still broader concept than Mag Uidhir's "loosely serial artworks," because on his account, the proper appreciation of the work as a whole (e.g., the series or format) "requires properly attending to each element" of it. And that, we think, is too strong a requirement on our appreciation of the sorts of television formats we've mentioned.

There is, finally, one extant conception of seriality that we think is broad enough to account for *all* of the different kinds of television whose proper appreciation is shaped by its particular temporality yet narrow enough to say something informative about those particularities. The sense of seriality to which we refer is that described by Stanley Cavell in his surprisingly unheralded article "The Fact of Television" (1982). Cavell offers an expansive discussion, which we will not try to summarize here. Rather, we want to focus upon his understanding of serialization as it relates to our aesthetic interest in television. We can start by picking up a connection with Mag Uidhir's paper – namely, Cavell's analogy to painting in series. Raising an objection to the idea that serialization – in a sense to be clarified momentarily – might mark a "principle of composition" of "the popular arts," Cavell argues that, like the paintings of Mark Rothko, Morris Louis, Kenneth Noland, Jules Olitski, and Frank Stella, black-figure and red-figure vase paintings and 19th-century American quilts all "exist essentially as items of a series" (1982, 83). Therefore, Cavell argues, "the concept of existence in a series, of being composed according to a serial-episode principle, does not distinguish popular from high arts" (1982, 83) – assuming, for the sake of argument, that one accepts the popular/high distinction.

So, how exactly does Cavell conceive of serialization? As we foreshadowed earlier, it is in close connection with the ideas of formulas and formats. Cavell begins by suggesting, "What is memorable, treasurable, criticisable, is not primarily the individual work, but the program, the format" (1982, 77). Note here that Cavell's idea about the aesthetic character of television is already somewhat different from ours. Whereas Cavell claims that "the primary object of aesthetic interest in television is not the individual piece, but the format" (1982, 79), our less ambitious claim is that insofar as television's "rule of format" (1982, 78) is a kind of manifestation of its temporal capacities, this is an artistically relevant feature that bears upon our appreciation of television as art.

"Format" here has a kind of double meaning for Cavell: it connotes a television format in the ordinary sense (e.g., *Big Brother*, *60 Minutes*) as well as "an artistic *kind*" (1982, 79). In this latter sense of the term, Cavell claims, formats may be generated according to a "serial-episode principle" or a "genre-member principle" (1982, 79). Television, on his view, "works aesthetically according to a serial-episode principle" (1982, 79). In both cases, however, "each instance [each episode or member] is a perfect exemplification of the format, as each solution of an equation, or each step in a mathematical series, is a perfect instance of the formula that 'generates' it [...] and whether an instance 'belongs' to the formula is as settled by the formula as is the identity of the instance" (1982, 82). Again, the affinities to Mag Uidhir's discussion of serial art in terms of sequences and sets are clear in Cavell's analogy to set theory in mathematics. Roughly speaking, however, what Cavell has in mind are formats like sitcoms and police procedurals, wherein the episodes need not share a specific plot but probably must share certain characters, settings, and perhaps even certain plot elements, such as a crime that needs to be solved. We hasten to remind readers that Cavell is using terms like "seriality" and "serialization" in a sense that is broader than the simple conception, such that these sorts of television programs, which we would normally call "series" in *contrast* to "serials" like soap operas and complex television drama, nonetheless operate according to the serial-episode principle. In Cavell's words, he has the

> intuition that the repetitions and recurrences of soap operas bear a significant relation with those of series, in which the narrative comes to a

> classical ending each time, *and indeed that these repetitions and recurrences are modes of a requirement that the medium of television exacts in all its formats.*
> (1982, 81, emphasis added)

As we have explained, we share the first part of Cavell's "intuition": We think that there is something important about the temporal character of series as well as serials – hence our exploration of broader conceptions of seriality than that offered by the simple conception. Furthermore, we think that Cavell is also on to something important in referring to still more formats beyond the serial and the (narrative fiction) series, and as we have indicated, we will discuss a few of these, such as the newscast, presently. On the other hand, we are less persuaded by the claim that these sorts of issues around temporality, processionality, repetition, and recurrence pertain to *all* of television's formats. We suspect there are specific one-off programs, such as live music specials or made-for-television movies, that are *not* satisfactorily analyzed in such terms precisely because they neither evince repetition nor indeed, make any use of the medium's specific capacity for extended duration.

Cavell's characterization of serialization in television is illuminating and extremely close to accounting for the temporal capacities of TV that we think bear upon the appreciation of television artworks *qua* artworks in the medium of television. Notwithstanding the qualms noted earlier, we subscribe to much of it and will seek to build upon it in what follows. Nevertheless, to both register certain differences in the scope and foci of our claims and perhaps more importantly, to eschew the ambiguity of "serial" and its cognate terms as well as the attendant conceptual confusions such ambiguity often raises, we will advance a different term – to wit, *temporal prolongation.*

We do not deploy the neologism lightly. Instead, we believe that a precise, distinct term is genuinely needed to describe television's particular temporal character and the artistic possibilities it affords. We use the term in the same sense as one of us has previously used it – namely, to describe a differential feature of television that is constituted by a variety of practices for creating television works with diffuse and expansive temporal boundaries. Beyond merely needing a term that distinguished this idea from seriality (in any of its varied senses), the choice of the term "temporal prolongation" is influenced by its use in music theory, where it "carries with it connotations of a temporally unfolding, yet organically unified structure" (Nannicelli 2017, 65). The motivating thought behind the introduction of the term is that it captures a use or artistic realization of television's capacity for extended duration typical of serials like *As the World Turns* and *Game of Thrones*, series like *The Simpsons* and *Law and Order*, newsmagazines like *60 Minutes*, sports programs like *Sports Center* and *Monday Night Football*, game shows like *Jeopardy!*, and reality television programs of both the serial (*The Bachelor*) and the nonserial (*Kitchen Nightmares*) varieties.

In all the examples mentioned here and the detailed cases we describe later, the temporally prolonged nature of the work bears upon what the program achieves artistically and how it engages its viewers. Or, to put it another way, the proper appreciation of all of these programs requires understanding their temporally prolonged character. It is hard to move beyond reasonably general statements at this level of analysis because temporal prolongation has a different significance for different kinds of programs. In some cases, our appreciation of a show requires us to attend to the episodes in chronological order, thanks to the serialization (in the simple sense) that temporal prolongation affords. In other cases, like sitcoms or sports programs, we do not need to watch episodes or installments in a particular sequence, let alone watch *all* of the episodes or parts in a set. Yet, a proper appreciation of such programs *does* seem to depend upon a recognition of how the format shapes its discrete instances as well as some level of familiarity with prior instances.[6] If we wanted to put this more formally, we might, following Mag Uidhir, phrase it this way: Properly attending to (engaging with) a television artwork requires appropriately attending to how the format of which it is an instance affords particular artistic possibilities. And adequately attending to how a given television format affords specific artistic possibilities is, in turn, a matter of appropriately attending to what options are open to *it* in virtue of television's capacity for temporal prolongation.

We conceive of temporal prolongation as a differential feature of the television medium because we see it manifested in a wide variety of television contexts and with different artistic effects. Therefore, in what follows, we try to outline some broad categories across which the artistic effects of temporal prolongation vary in interesting and illuminating ways. We describe the specific artistic effects or more simply, the artistic relevance of temporal prolongation in these distinct contexts as we go. This survey of the different sorts of television in which temporal prolongation gives rise to artistic effects is not meant to be exhaustive, nor is it meant to show that temporal prolongation is an essential feature of the television medium. Rather, our argument here is an abductive one: The presence and artistic relevance of temporal prolongation in these diverse television contexts at least lends strong *prima facie* plausibility to our claim that the phenomenon is a differential feature of the medium.

Case study I: Non-fiction, non-narrative television

The first case we are going to explore is that of formats, such as newscasts or sports programming, that prominently feature the TV presenter. It seems obvious that part of the appeal that some TV programs cultivate is related to the figure of the presenter because of his/her personality as well as his/her physical appearance. Furthermore, in some cases, the passing of time and the recurrence of watching such presenters fosters a kind of familiarity – perhaps even an emotional bond or a sort of friendship with them. As Frances Bonner puts it,

> We see television personalities so often and their persona is so consistent and coherent that we feel we know them, and in knowing them our entry

> into the programme they are associated with is made easier and more predictable and our likelihood of remaining for whatever it is that makes them appeal to us – their signature distinctiveness – enhanced.
>
> (2003, 66)

This sense of knowing the individuals on television has a long history of study in media studies and communications, where it was initially described as "para-social interaction" (Horton and Whol 1956).

Is there any essential difference between the "familiarity" that the viewer establishes with Sheldon Cooper (*The Big Bang Theory*), Michele Beadle (ESPN), Tucker Carlson (Fox News), or Gordon Ramsay (several cooking shows and contests), to cite characters from such disparate genres? In psychology, the jury is still out (see Giles 2002). But in the context of normative questions around artistic appreciation, the answer seems to be no. There is some evidence to suggest that repeated exposure to the same soap opera character, news anchor, sports commentator, or reality TV presenter can, under the right conditions, foster an emotional bond, which is predicated on two interwoven elements related to the notions of both time and relationship: repetition and memory (see the literature review in Klimmt et al. 2011). Yet, the point we wish to make is slightly different: As a feature that affords the realization of particular artistic effects, temporal prolongation is common to both fiction and factual television formats. Therefore, the proper appreciation of the artistic effects of these formats requires the same sort of attention to the handling of a television personality in both cases. In both cases, what is required is attention to the repeated, ongoing textual presence of those personalities, notwithstanding their ontological status.[7] Stanley Cavell foresaw this feature in 1982 when he pointed out, as an example, how Johnny Carson could "instruct his audiences' responses with a glance in our direction [...] – a power the comedian shares with the lion tamer" (88).

Notwithstanding this claim about the similar ways temporal prolongation requires attending to both factual and fictional formats, we maintain that temporal prolongation may bear upon our engagement with formats that feature TV presenters in more specific ways. To reiterate, we are not pursuing an empirical question, recently debated by Blanchet and Vaage (2012) and Turvey (2019), about how viewers *actually* respond in such contexts – e.g., whether they are more likely to develop pro-attitudes towards the TV personalities or not. Instead, we are asking a normative question about our appreciation of television as art: What do these formats' use of temporal prolongation make necessary for a proper appreciation of their artistic effects and achievements? Repetition appears to be the most noticeable element of the viewer's engagement with TV presenters. In every new instance of a program, there are always some elements that remain consistent, be it the set, the tone, the schedule, the talking-head format, and so on. In the case of newscasts, for example, every night is different and fresh because the very definition of news demands, well, to have new information to report. But at the same time, there are also several features that remain stable, familiar, or even identical to the previous installment (the set, the presenter, the opening music, the structure).

Properly attending to the use of repetition afforded by temporal prolongation requires us to exercise our memories – sometimes consciously, at other times unconsciously – to assess that something is being repeated. Otherwise, the spectator would miss artistically salient effects involving such repetition, variation, and patterning and the aesthetic pleasures they afford. Therefore, the memory of previous viewings facilitates detailed semantic iterations: ways of decoding this or that gesture, political inclinations before specific issues, and even, running catchphrases or signing-off idioms. This last item is worth unpacking because those particular phrases delivered by the presenters become a kind of signature that rely on temporal prolongation for their effects. Be it Michael Buffer declaiming his resounding and emphatic "Let's get ready to rumbleeee!" before any boxing match, or the legendary Edward R. Murrow's serene bidding farewell ("Good night and good luck"), these catchphrases work as markers of familiarity, a trait that depends on temporal prolongation.

Of course, the same applies to the nonverbal cues we have sketched in the prior paragraph, echoing the Cavellian comment on how Johnny Carson instructed his audience's response with a simple glance. The news presenter Tucker Carlson, for example, has made his audience used to fixed body gestures and subtle exclamations that are full of meaning. Carlson interviews are a mixture of obnoxiousness and irony, filtered through his conservative lens. Understandably, this ideological leaning creates assumed expectations of how the talk is going to result. But moreover, the split screen encourages the spectator to quickly identify the presenter's code of meaning by watching him react to the responses of his interviewees: his disbelieving smile, his pugnacious replies, or his ironic "uh" to suggest doubt. All these gestures from Carlson cue the spectator to anticipate imminent verbal escalation whereby sarcasm, constant interruptions, and heated debate will follow. In this case, the spectator able to read the signs thanks to exposure to temporal prolongation can anticipate a climactic moment in the show or a memorable interview.

The same applies to Bill Maher, to take an example from the other end of the political spectrum. The viewer enters into his show aware of his liberal mindset, expecting cruel and witty jokes at the expense of Republicans. But again, there are also visual expectations acquired through temporal prolongation. Maher's weekly monologue, for example, adds to generic comedy strategies his characteristic way of containing his own laughter after a "serious" joke, or his specific way of interacting with the live public. An example can illustrate this last point on how a casual viewer would not get the same artistic pleasure as a committed viewer from the way Maher relates to his very progressive in-studio audience. In a program from April 2012, Maher made a harsh joke involving the trial of George Zimmerman (shooter of African American teenager Trayvon Martin) and the Irish-British pop music boy band One Direction. The audience, usually very cheerful and supportive of Maher puns, kept oddly silent. And the host responded, giving the finger ostensibly with each hand while cursing:

> Oh, fuck you!! I mean, seriously. People, the show has started. We're on HBO; we're in California! You can get the stick out of your ass. It's just a joke! We're not really going to shoot the kids from One Direction.

To get the most out of this example, the spectator must be aware of Maher's tendency to political incorrectness, his proclaimed liberal values, and of course, the customary ideological collusion with his lived audience; otherwise, one could not enjoy – let alone make sense of – Maher's sudden outburst.

Case study II: Non-fiction episodic television: *Kitchen Nightmares*

Yet in the realm of non-fiction, temporality is also an essential feature to understand the allure of reality TV in such disparate formats such as *Got Talent*, *Survivor*, *Pawn Stars*, *The Deadliest Catch*, *Duck Dynasty*, or *Master Chef*. Firstly, the resemblances between these formats and seriality seem evident: most of them are episodic and offer a narrative progression, where the spectator needs to take into account previous events from the narrative. The most explicit examples in this regard are the contest formats, such as *Survivor* or *Big Brother*, where narrative progression is obviously the core mechanism of the program. It is impossible to restore the order when every week there are characters/players expelled from the program.

But as we are arguing in this chapter, the notion of seriality does not address all the distinctive features of television's temporality. Let's make our case by choosing a famous nonserial (that is, not a docu-soap) reality TV program: *Kitchen Nightmares*. The Gordon Ramsay franchise is the *CSI* procedural equivalent in the field of culinary reality TV. Every episode recycles its character types and setting types, but the story concludes in each installment. Every week there is a new decaying restaurant to fix, problematic owners to deal with, and full menus to redesign. How does our notion of temporal prolongation explain the effects achieved by *Kitchen Nightmares*' use of temporality? First, there are the concomitant traits explained in the previous section: Ramsay, as presenter of the show, has gotten his audience used to his culinary dissatisfaction at every restaurant he visits for the first time, his epic outbursts, and even his verbal and physical tics (the swearing, the hand slap, the "Ugh? Yes?"). Those are familiar mannerisms for the audience, who have forged dramatic and narrative bonds through repeated exposure to the protagonist of the show.

Nevertheless, beyond the Ramsay persona, there is a structural pattern in *Kitchen Nightmares* whereby temporal prolongation plays a crucial role in the most basic sense – narrative accumulation. As explained before, temporal prolongation links to repetition and memory. Indubitably, a first-time casual viewer of *Kitchen Nightmares* can follow and enjoy the episode, because it is a self-contained narrative. But a committed viewer can get a different, richer kind of aesthetic experience due to temporal prolongation. While the narrative structure remains pretty consistent along the episodes,[8] mirroring the template of any four-act dramatic TV series episode, the main novelty of every episode has to do with location. Every new restaurant brings a new place with its idiosyncrasies and its problematic people. Therefore, besides the ongoing relationship with the star of the show (Ramsay himself), the viewer can find pleasure in the variety of both the thematic and dramatic possibilities every new episode opens. Instead of the attraction of the monster-of-the-week or the killing-of-the-week typical of episodic/procedural TV series such as *CSI* or *Supernatural* (which we tackle later), the viewer faces every new episode expecting a fresh culinary choice (be it bakeries, pizzas, bistros, sushi, and so on), a new group of antagonists (the disastrous owner, the arrogant chef, the careless waiter …), and variations on the usual problems (relational, creative, financial, hygienic, familial, personal …). By triangulating these three expectations, the show finds refreshing stories that the viewers accommodate into the narrative and dramatic patterns with which they are already familiar. As happens with the so-called "special episodes" in some TV series (we will explain them later), *Kitchen Nightmares* eventually plays with surprise by breaking some of its core expectations. For example, there were six times when Ramsay *did* like the food he tasted in the restaurants, and most starkly, the "Amy's Baking Company" episode (6.16.) has been the only one when Ramsay walked away, accepting he was not able to help the business. Other variations worth mentioning – strictly related to seriality, in this case – are those episodes when Ramsay comes back to check how a previous re-launching is currently going.

To a lesser extent, temporal prolongation also serves to make sense of the hiatus between seasons. Be it the comparison between the new *Big Brother* pool of contestants and those from the past year, or the new exotic location for *Survivor* or the new juries in the recent edition of *The Voice* or *Master Chef*, the aesthetic experience of entertainment programs is enhanced by the cognitive effort the spectator has to make to reconcile – that is, to fully make sense – of the disparities among memory, repetition, and variation. Reality TV is a very self-conscious genre, populated by "reunions," "all-stars," "comebacks," and several contestants crossing over from one branch of the franchise to another (Nick Viall from *The Bachelorette*, *Bachelor in Paradise*, and *The Bachelor* can serve as a paradigm). This last trait implies that beyond the temporal prolongation we are trying to explain, the programs usually add some layers of explicit seriality into the temporality mix, as shown, for example, in the several *Survivor* editions including contestants from past seasons (*Survivor: All-Stars*, 2004, and *Survivor: Micronesia – Fans vs. Favorites*, 2008, are among the most popular cases in this sense).

Case study III: Fictional episodic TV

Another "format" we want to flesh out is episodic television, be it the drama series (usually referred to as "procedurals") or the traditional sitcom. As we have stated before, the narrative and dramatic structure of the TV series is similar to the reality TV example we have scrutinized, the Doylesque narrative. The self-contained series narrative offers a balance that is broken at the beginning of each episode, so that the *peripeteia* of the protagonists involves restoring the lost order: solving a riddle, finding a culprit, curing a patient, winning a court case, or learning a lesson. Each of the cases solved by the hero of Baker Street offers the same type of closure as an episode of *Law & Order* or *CSI Las Vegas*. As a result, in series with stand-alone stories, each episode is relatively independent – characters, settings, and relationships carry over across episodes, but the plots stand on their own, such that there is little need for consistent viewing or knowledge of diegetic history to comprehend the narrative [itself]. (cf. Mittell 2007, 163) This does not imply that episodic series make a clean sweep of what happened in previous chapters and lack memory. The important thing is not a character's memory – which, although it may be very slight, obviously has to exist to ensure the internal coherence of the text – but the memory of the spectators, who "need no memory of the previous episodes to understand and appreciate the present one [because] [e]pisodes may be seen in any order and may be skipped without compromising future comprehension and engagement" (Newman 2006, 23).

Nonetheless, episodic television offers certain characteristics that cannot be explained through the concept of seriality but through the notion of temporal prolongation. We are going to explore three peculiarities, which can be found both in comedy and in drama.

1. Running gags

The "TV Tropes" website offers a succinct but widespread definition of a running gag: "A joke whose humor derives from repetition, ideally becoming funnier each time it is repeated." The notion of a running gag can apply to a single episode (or a single movie), but television, due to its extended duration, offers a specific way of dealing with running gags. The most usual method is that of peppering the narrative occasionally with such recurring jokes. *Friends*, for example, made its audience familiar with the "swearing" signal – which allows the characters to "give the finger without actually having to give the finger" – and offered several variations on the "Smelly Cat" Phoebe performance during its ten-season run. In such cases, the scene can work for a casual viewer, unaware of the callback, but the aesthetic achievement is more intense and satisfactory, due to temporal prolongation, for those viewers who are usually followers of the show. The enjoyment of the gag derives partially from its prolonged existence, but also from the ways temporal prolongation can trigger and modify it. This statement is also backed up by studies on the psychology of humor. As Martin and Ford argue, citing Wyer and Collins, "people perceive jokes that have high elaboration potential as funny even after many repetitions because they prompt new humor-relevant elaborations with each repetition" (Martin and Ford 2018, 83).

More precisely, the usual followers are those who get the most from another possibility offered by the intersection between running gags and temporal prolongation. Sometimes, the running joke can become something the audience expects every episode, to see its originality or to laugh at how the writers shoehorn it into the narrative. This is illustrated, for example, by Kramer entering Jerry's apartment without knocking in *Seinfeld* or by Kenny's surreal death in every episode of *South Park*. But also, the running gags can work in a more "serial" way, even in an episodic series. *How I Met Your Mother* can serve to illustrate this point. In the episode "The Slap Bet" (2.9.), Marshall wins a bet with Barney. The loser has an option: "Either 10 slaps right now in a row or 5 slaps that can be doled out at any point from here to eternity." As Barney opts for the latter, this becomes a sort of narrative and comic Sword of Damocles that hangs over the sitcom until the end of its run (the last slap being given in the third episode from last). As Nannicelli summarizes,

> after the initial payoff of a running gag, the gag may be interwoven with others to realize an additional, amplified pay-off down the line. There is a particular cognitive pleasure in perceiving how such gags are interwoven, in catching moments where the set up seems to be established, in anticipating how the pay-off will be implemented, and, once the pay-off has been realized, in reflecting back on the structural choices made to set it up. (2017, 81)

2. Monster-of-the-week

Even in genres or formats where the structure is repetitive, temporal prolongation can explain some of the aesthetic achievements of certain TV shows. One of the usual narrative tropes in self-contained TV series is the monster-of-the-week. As explained before by Kozloff, Newman, and Mittell, this is the kind of narrative thread that can get closure within a single episode. But here, we would like to call attention to how the recurring exposure to several installments (sequential order is not necessary for the validity of our argument) can create in the viewers a distinctive aesthetic effect.

We have already mentioned Carroll's erotetic conception of seriality, where the narrative generates questions that the audience expects to have answered. Without denying his claim, we run a lateral view on the self-contained TV series. Our account of temporal prolongation adds another layer of aesthetic enjoyment: our familiarity with a particular template (a narrative structure, a web of emotional relations between the characters) alleviates our cognitive effort while allowing us to devote more interpretive resources to each new monster, crime, disease, or legal case. That is, the specifics of every new narrative setup dialogues with previous ones the spectator has watched and accordingly, judges its ingenuity, oddness, plausibility, and so on. The audience wants not only to resolve the narrative crisis proper to this kind of narrative but also to marvel at the originality of the new situation posed by the showrunners. At first sight, Jason Mittell seems to have proposed a similar concept ("serialized routine"), arguing that "one of the most exciting pleasures of contemporary fictional television is when a series breaks from its intrinsic norms to offer a new take on its conventional storytelling mode" (Mittell 2015, 28). Nonetheless, our concept does not need a break from the norm. On the contrary, we claim that the series, per se, due to its temporal prolongation, encourages us to focus on the narrative and aesthetic differences provided by every new episode.

Let's try to shed light through a sound and juicy example. Despite offering a relevant series arc (the uncovering of Hannibal Lecter), during its first two seasons, *Hannibal* followed a procedural structure: every week, FBI profiler Will Graham had to help resolve a new and juicy murder. Beyond the weekly mystery, part of the appeal of the narrative had to do with the sinister visual inventiveness of the crimes depicted. Temporal prolongation not only made the spectator anxious to discover the next *tableau vivant* that *Hannibal* had to offer but also configured a museum of horrors, where gory images became stuck in the memory of the audience.

3. Special episodes

The last distinctive use of temporal prolongation we want to underline is the "special episode," not to be confused with the "Very Special Episode" that populated TV series during the 1980s trying to raise social awareness of certain issues. By "special episode," we are addressing the episodes where a TV show changes its usual aesthetic and narrative features. By its own definition, the possibilities are endless, but it is not unlikely that these episodes usually concentrate on singular periods of the year (the Christmas Special, the Halloween Special, the April Fool's Special) or that they can adopt specific narrative or aesthetic structures (Bottle Episode, Clip Episode, pastiche, narratological games).

In every case, the notion of temporal prolongation is essential for the special episode to fire on all cylinders, because the very essence of a "special episode" is to break the continuity of the formula, to surprise the spectator, to bend the template. That is, a "special episode" works against the backdrop of the perceived stability that the audience bestows on the narrative. Among the countless examples, let us take one of the most critically acclaimed "special episodes" ever to explain our idea. TV critics and scholars praise *Buffy* as one of the most relevant shows in expanding its template through bold aesthetic and narrative innovations. "Once More, With Feeling" (6.7.) offered a whole musical episode that shocked the audience by its formal audacity. Again, the notion of temporal prolongation is essential to capture the artistic achievements of the episode accurately, because the audience are continually accommodating the extemporary musical genre codes to the narrative they are used to. TV series are always playing with stability and novelty; the "special episode" turns the narrative up a notch, because stability is rocked, and through the surprise factor, the viewer gets a sort of pleasurable cognitive dissonance from trying to familiarize themselves with the new rules of the game.

Conclusion

The capacity for an extended duration is one of the defining traits of television as a medium. Within the fields of philosophical aesthetics and media studies, academics have frequently explored this issue under the label of "seriality" in both the simple and expanded theoretical conceptions we have summarized in the first part of this chapter. Nonetheless, we have offered a more precise term to account for all the temporal capacities of television: "temporal prolongation." Our label encompasses television's medium-specific handling of temporality and the effects it creates. It serves to make sense of the artistic achievements that temporality accomplishes in disparate formats and genres – both fiction and non-fiction – such as soap operas, packed-with-continuing-storylines serial dramas, episodic procedurals, sitcoms, daily newscasts, sports broadcasting, weekly gameshows, reality TV, and even documentaries.

Casting light on our theory, we also have examined several cases in depth in the second part of our chapter. For reasons of space, we have deliberately chosen examples from American television because it is the most popular around the world. But we are confident that our theory can work – no matter what the geography or the type of TV program – to accurately distill the artistic possibilities of television's temporality. To support our claims, we have surveyed the case of some of the most common genres: newscasts, reality television, and TV fiction shows. However, we are aware that some of the main counter-arguments to our idea can be found in two different elements (a format and a practice) that have been gaining traction in the television ecosystem during the last decade: the anthology series and binge-watching. We hope to flesh out their specific temporality in future works. Paraphrasing the end of a famous (conceived initially as a serial) Dostoyevski novel, that might be the subject of a new article, but our present one is ended.

Notes

1 By "artistic effects," we simply mean what the artwork does as an artwork – for example, whether it engenders laughter, suspense, and so forth. For a broader discussion, see Nannicelli (2017).

2 The other temporal feature of television about which much has been written is liveness; we do not have the space to address that topic here.

3 A defense of the sense in which we are advancing medium-specific claims is beyond the purview of this chapter. For an extended discussion of medium-specificity and a defense of a moderate form of it, see Nannicelli (2017).

4 We find the "scholastic"/"systems-praxeological" distinction particularly abstruse in the absence of further explanation.

5 As Mag Uidhir notes, there is a potential confusion here, because in the art world, series like Walter de Maria's *Statement Series* (2011) [his example] or Andy Warhol's Jackie Kennedy series [ours] are often referred to as "serial art." According to *The Oxford Dictionary of Art*, the term "serial art" "has been applied to works of art that are conceived in series or as part of a larger group; often the individual work is regarded as incomplete in itself, needing to be seen within the context of the whole" (Chilvers 2011).

6 On the normative aspect of the appreciation of the art of television, see Nannicelli (2017).
7 This idea can be reinforced, for example, by attending to the recent success achieved by true crime, not only in television (the TV series *The Jinx* or *Making a Murderer*) but also by the significant trend of true crime podcasting after the *Serial* phenomenon. See the recent Punnett (2018).
8 See a more detailed outline of the plot structure of *Kitchen Nightmares* in Thompson and Haigh (2017, 3).

References

Allen, Rob, and Thijs van den Berg. 2014. "Introduction." In *Serialization in Popular Culture*, edited by Rob Allen and Thijs van den Berg, 1–7. New York: Routledge.

Allen, Robert C. 1985. *Speaking of Soap Operas*. Chapel Hill, NC: University of North Carolina Press.

Blanchet, Robert, and Margrethe Bruun Vaage. 2012. "Don, Peggy, and Other Fictional Friends? Engaging with Characters in Television Series." *Projections: The Journal for Movies and Mind* 6, no. 2: 18–41.

Bonner, Frances. 2003. *Ordinary Television*. London: Sage.

Carroll, Noël. 1996. *Theorizing the Moving Image*. Cambridge: Cambridge University Press.

Carroll, Noël. 2002. *Engaging the Moving Image*. New Haven, CT: Yale University Press.

Cavell, Stanley. 1982. "The Fact of Television." *Daedalus* 111, no. 4: 75–96.

Chilvers, Ian. 2011. *The Oxford Dictionary of Art*, 3rd ed. Oxford: Oxford University Press. http://www.oxfordreference.com/view/10.1093/acref/9780198604761.001.0001/acref-9780198604761

Feuer, Jane. 1984. "Melodrama, Serial Form and Television Today." *Screen* 25: 4–16.

Giles, David C. 2002. "Parasocial Interaction: A Review of the Literature and a Model for Future Research." *Media Psychology* 4, no. 3: 279–305.

Hagedorn, Roger. 1995. "Doubtless to Be Continued: A Brief History of Serial Narrative." In *To Be Continued… Soap Operas Around the World*, edited by Robert C. Allen, 27–48. London: Routledge.

Hayward, Jennifer. 1997. *Consuming Pleasures: Active Audiences and Serial Fictions from Dickens to Soap Opera*. Lexington, KY: The University Press of Kentucky.

Horton, Donald, and R. Richard Wohl. 1956. "Mass Communication and Para-Social Interaction: Observations on Intimacy at a Distance." *Psychiatry* 19, no. 3: 215–229.

Kelleter, Frank. 2017. "Five Ways of Looking at Popular Seriality." In *Media of Serial Narrative*, edited by Frank Kelleter, 7–34. Columbus, OH: The Ohio State University Press.

Klimmt, Christoph, Tilo Hartmann, and Holger Schramm. 2011. "Parasocial Interaction and Relationships." In *Psychology of Entertainment*, edited by Jennings Bryant and Peter Vorderer, 291–314. New York: Routledge.

Kozloff, Sarah. 1992. "Narrative Theory and Television." In *Channels of Discourse, Reassembled*, edited by Robert C. Allen, 67–100. London: Routledge.

Mag Uidhir, Christy. 2013. "How to Frame Serial Art." *The Journal of Aesthetics and Art Criticism* 71, no. 3: 261–265.

Martin, Rod A., and Thomas Ford. 2018. *The Psychology of Humor: An Integrative Approach*. Cambridge and Oxford: Academic Press.

Mittell, Jason. 2007. "Film and television narrative." In *The Cambridge Companion to Narrative*, edited by David Herman, 156–171. Cambridge: Cambridge University Press.

Mittell, Jason. 2015. *Complex TV: The Poetics of Contemporary Television Storytelling*. New York: New York University Press.

Nannicelli, Ted. 2017. *Appreciating the Art of Television: A Philosophical Perspective*. New York: Routledge.

Newcomb, Horace. 1974. *TV: The Most Popular Art*. Garden City, NY: Anchor Books.

Newman, Michael Z. 2006. "From Beats to Arcs: Toward a Poetics of Television Narrative." *The Velvet Light Trap* 58: 16–28.

Newman, Michael Z., and Elana Levine. 2012. *Legitimating Television: Media Convergence and Cultural Status*. New York: Routledge.

Punnett, Ian Case. 2018. *Toward a Theory of True Crime Narratives: A Textual Analysis*. New York: Routledge.

Thompson, Kirrilly, and Laura Haigh. 2017. "Representations of Food Waste in Reality Food Television: An Exploratory Analysis of Ramsay's *Kitchen Nightmares*." *Sustainability* 9, no. 7: 1–10.

Turvey, Malcolm. 2019. "'Familiarity Breeds Contempt': Why Fascination, Rather than Repeat Exposure, Better Explains the Appeal of Antiheroes on Television." In *Screening Characters: Theories of Character in Film, Television, and Interactive Media*, edited by Johannes Riis and Aaron Taylor, 231–247. New York: Routledge.

Williams, Raymond. 1974. *Television: Technology and Cultural Form*. London: Fontana.

3 Multi-plot structure in television serials

Héctor J. Pérez and María J. Ortiz

Introduction

The multi-plot structure has existed in all kinds of formulations, in both written literature and audiovisual narratives. In cinema, the traditional single-plot form consisted of one main plot and two related subplots (Thompson 2003). Although according to Bordwell (2006), films that depart from this canonical formula have existed since the earliest days of cinematic history, in the last two decades, their number has increased considerably. Films like *Pulp Fiction* (Tarantino 1994), *Secrets and Lies* (Leigh 1996), *Eternal Sunshine of the Spotless Mind* (Gondry 2004), and *Inception* (Nolan 2010) are often cited as examples of "complex narratives" (Simons 2014).

However, there is one field where multi-plot narratives have been especially widespread, and more systematically employed than in cinema: TV serials. It could also be argued that this practice originated in the field of the soap opera. Thompson (2003) suggests that this structure was imported to prime-time television with *Dallas* (Jacobs 1978–1991) and *Dynasty* (R. Saphiro and E. Saphiro 1981–1989), which in turn, served as the inspiration for professional dramas like *The West Wing* (Sorkin 1999–2006) or *L.A. Law* (Bochco and Fisher 1986–1994). *Hill Street Blues* (Bochco and Kozoli 1981–1987) was the American series that pioneered the idea of wrapping up at least one plotline in each episode while continuing with others over the course of a season, an approach that has since become common practice in contemporary seriality.

Considering the consolidation of the multi-plot structure in soap operas and its extension to other serial genres, we might assume that the temporal prolongation specific to the television medium pointed out by Ted Nannicelli (2017) particularly favors this type of narration. Although it is not the aim of this chapter to establish further differences between cinema and television, our research shows that certain differences may exist between the two media in relation to the purposes behind the use of a multi-plot structure. While in cinema, its use is aimed more often at producing cognitively challenging complex narratives for the spectator, in TV serials, it appears to be geared towards stimulating and maintaining spectator interest over time by focusing on longer individual and social interactions. However, this distinction should not be viewed as absolute.

DOI: 10.4324/9781003188643-3

On the one hand, the category of the multi-protagonist narrative is a significant defining feature of many multi-plot films, and many of the traits of multi-protagonist films identified by María del Mar Azcona (2010) can be found in serials too: (1) a broad spectrum of characters involved in different storylines, (2) stories that may be narrated either in parallel or consecutively, (3) a tendency to focus more on characters than on actions, and (4) the establishment of unexpected and unlikely connections between characters. On the other hand, there is a growing group of serials that should obviously be defined as complex narratives given their systematic use of plot twists and playing with time frames, such as *Lost* (Abrams et al. 2004–2010), *Mr. Robot* (Esmail 2015–present), *Westworld* (Nolan 2016–present), *Dark* (Odar and Friese 2017–present), or *The Haunting of Hill House* (Flanagan 2018).

It could be argued that the theory of the multi-protagonist narrative defended by Azcona is an ideal paradigm for understanding the multi-plot phenomenon in seriality, given that in most cases, a diversity of plots corresponds to a diversity of protagonists. So, can we assert that the use of different storylines in a series is closer to the notion of the multi-protagonist narrative defined in film studies than to the concept of complex narratives, despite the fact that the latter, introduced by Jason Mittell (2015), is firmly established as the most commonly used term to refer to the narrative qualities of contemporary seriality?

In the interest of defining the concept of the multi-plot narrative with the greatest conceptual precision, the first thing we must take into consideration is the fact that the concept of complex narratives is used differently in film and television studies. Film studies, following the boom in "complexity studies," has taken a clear interest in "complex narratives," used as an umbrella term, which, according to Jan Simons (2014), would include other concepts such as "forking path narratives," "mind-game films," "modular narratives," "hyperlink cinema," "fractal films," "network narratives," "tandem narratives," "ensemble narratives," and "multi-protagonist films." In the field of TV studies, although Mittell (2015) uses complexity as a term to designate the narrative qualities of contemporary television series, it is in a general sense applied to a wide range of works best exemplified by serials like *The Wire* (Simon 2002–2008) and *Breaking Bad* (Gilligan 2008–2013), which are not narratives that could be defined as posing particular cognitive challenges. The difference in the use of the term is found in that while in film studies, complexity is associated with cognitive challenges, in television studies, it is considered, rather, a formal quality, a structural feature that entails greater narrative and/or aesthetic sophistication.

Our approach to the multi-plot phenomenon is global in nature, because we argue that it is a key quality that can be found in all kinds of series, independent of genre, and in their multiple hybrid forms. Multi-plot structures are, of course, considered complex, and in fact, this study is partly based on a plot-mapping technique that has often revealed a very rich and complex structure. However, we argue that the multi-plot structure is not necessarily associated with a difficult cognitive experience, since we consider that in most cases, the multi-plot structure facilitates the spectator's cognitive access to the narrative. It is true that it can serve to create extreme cognitive experiences, puzzles with a much greater number of pieces that are distributed in plots with very ambiguous and constantly changing relationships or that entail a greater effort than in cinema because they require memory to connect elements that are chronologically much further apart than they could be in a film, as happens in the series *Westworld*, for example. But this happens only in certain cases and is not something common to all of them. The multi-plot structure can be considered complex in a structural sense in series such as *Downton Abbey* (Fellowes 2010–2015), *Vår tid är un* (*The Restaurant*, Hamrell et al. 2017–2018), or *Orange Is the New Black* (Kohan 2013–2019), where the numerous storylines facilitate the representation of realities that are rich in cognitive value: the inner life of the residents of a fictional English estate, the workers in a Swedish restaurant, or the inmates of an American prison. But rather than hindering it, structural complexity actually facilitates cognitive access to these realities by offering the diversity of narrative lines necessary to more fully represent social realities and their different interactions in order to help us better understand the relationships between them. The opposite can also happen, in that a series with a smaller number of plots and therefore, greater structural simplicity may nevertheless pose cognitive challenges by giving us access to realities or experiences whose meaning is not easy to grasp, as happens with *Rectify* (McKinnon 2013–2016).

We are therefore going to explore an aspect that is crucial in series and as such, has attracted considerable academic interest. Mittell (2015) offers valuable reflections on the use of multi-plot structures and their narrative consequences, as have a significant number of other scholars of contemporary television narrative. There are reflections of interest on multi-plot narratives covering all genres and types of serials, from the sitcom (G. Smith 1995) to the drama (Logan 2013), and from perspectives that include narratology (Newman 2006; Skoptsov 2015), reception studies, where the diversity of plots may receive comparatively different appraisals depending on the national context (Crofts 1995), production studies, where storylines are proposed as production strategies to adapt the narrative to the producer's scheduling practices (A. Smith 2018), and fandom studies, where the similarities between celebrity culture and the social canvasses of soap operas are explored with some thought-provoking results (De Kosnik 2011).

The objective of our study is to approach the phenomenon from a different perspective than all of these, exploring it in global terms. Firstly, our approach will be sensitive to the cognitive value that we have already associated with the use of the multi-plot strategy. Of course, the multi-plot structure works well in the terrain of seriality because of the greater scope of time offered by a serial, but we believe that this aspect has significance in cognitive terms as well. One hypothesis to explain why a series can be successful while experimenting with narrative form, from a cognitive point of view, is that its temporal prolongation makes it possible to represent a wider range of temporal processes, with the obviously distinguishing feature of being able to include processes of a longer duration, which other narrative forms, such as cinema, have to represent in another way (although this too can be done with excellent results). In his discussion of the qualities of the soap opera, Robert Allen points out what may be the best direction for our analysis:

> By contrast, the serial spreads its narrative energy among a number of plots and a community of characters, and, what is even more important, sets these plots and characters in complex, dynamic, and unpredictable relationship with each other. Because serials cut between scenes enacting separate plot lines, the viewer is prompted to ask not only "Where is each of these plot lines going?" but also "What might be the relationship between different plot lines?"
>
> (2001,17–18)

Allen refers to expectations about relationships between different plots. The temporal factor is crucial here, as in seriality, it is possible to represent processes that go beyond a simple causal relationship to show several forces interweaving/intersecting and influencing the final result. It is this element, the playing with a more complex and therefore more unpredictable causal network, that enhances the cognitive appeal of the series. Having said this, any analysis of the cognitive dimension must include the aesthetic factor. Fiction can teach us things using all kinds of aesthetic resources, making use of them to enhance its cognitive efficiency.

Our analysis will be structured around the concepts of beats, episodes, and arcs proposed by Michael Z. Newman (2006) in relation to contemporary seriality. We have chosen these concepts because they can be related to what we consider some of the main cognitive dimensions of the multi-plot structure. Thus, in the section dedicated to a micro-structural level of the beats, we will deal with the main way in which a multi-plot organization unleashes effects on the spectator's perception. In the section dedicated to the episodic and inter-episodic dimension, we will address cognitive processes such as the generation of hypotheses and expectations at the beginning of a series and the continuity and evolution that the spectator's cognitive activities can acquire, stimulated by the interaction of numerous plots both in the central phase of the narration and in its closing moments. By looking at the evolution of the arcs, we will see that they are not isolated elements of continuity but components in a deep interaction that actually constitutes one of the main ways of helping the spectator to formulate and develop schemes, ideas, and hypotheses with the aim of enhancing the spectator's interest and emotions in relation to the narrative.

Multi-plot narrative in serial micro-structures or beats

Beats are the "television's most basic storytelling unit," according to Newman (2006, 17). Each beat lasts about two minutes, pushing the plot forward, reminding us of certain details, and telling us something new that we want to know while at the same time increasing our desire to know more. The division of contemporary serials into beats facilitates our understanding of current standards of plot alternation. In this section, we compare the beats of two very different shows. Following Elliot Panek (2014), we use diagrams as a tool for understanding complex narratives and as a diagnostic aid in the analytical process. Time is depicted along the x-axis and the plots along the y-axis to illustrate how the beats of different plots alternate in time.

The distribution of beats in *Game of Thrones* (Benioff and Weiss 2011–2019) reveals a different treatment between the first episode and the others. The first is the only episode where there are up to nine consecutive beats following a single plotline (Figure 3.1). Four locations are presented (The Wall, Winterfell, King's Landing, and across the narrow sea), and six changes of plot and setting occur. In terms of duration, there is a main plotline that takes place in Winterfell and takes up most of the episode's running time, with shorter periods of time spent in the other locations. Each set of beats ranges from 4 to 13 minutes. Basically, the alternation is between two plots in two locations (Winterfell/Stark vs. across the narrow sea/Targaryen siblings), so this episode could be considered the easiest one in terms of cognitive effort. According to Newman, the typical prime-time serial episode has 20-40 beats, the average being about 25, and the main plot tends to have 6 or more beats, while the rest of the plots have fewer. Our analysis reveals that the number of beats in *Game of Thrones* is within the average, and Winterfell/Stark could be considered the main plotline because it has the largest number of beats.

However, from episode 3 onwards, we find another type of structure that will be the predominant one throughout the season (Figure 3.2). The plot alternation is faster, and the groups of beats are shorter.

In episodes 4 and 5, two differentiated sections can be identified (Figure 3.3). In the first 15–20 minutes, most of the plots featured in the episode are introduced. Then, some plots are picked up again, and near the end of the episode, one or two more are added. In our diagram, this presentation of plots takes the form of a staircase, because the storylines change constantly over 25 minutes, and afterwards some of them continue. Although the number of beats remains close to the average (about 25), there are no significant differences in the number of beats between plots. For example, episode 3 has eight plots, four of which include two beats, while the others have between five and eight beats. However, only once are there four consecutive beats from the same plot; the usual distribution is one or two beats. Similarly, episode 5 has 11 plots, but they are presented in an alternating pattern of 1 or 2 beats each, and the longer one contains 5 beats. In our view, these diagrams show the kind of thread structure defined by Evan Smith, which is characterized by "snapshots of assorted characters, relationships and events" (1999, 95).

The diagram of the series *Mad Men* (Weiner 2007–2015) is visually quite different. The storylines are based on the relationships between the characters, so it is sometimes difficult to decide where one plot ends and another plot

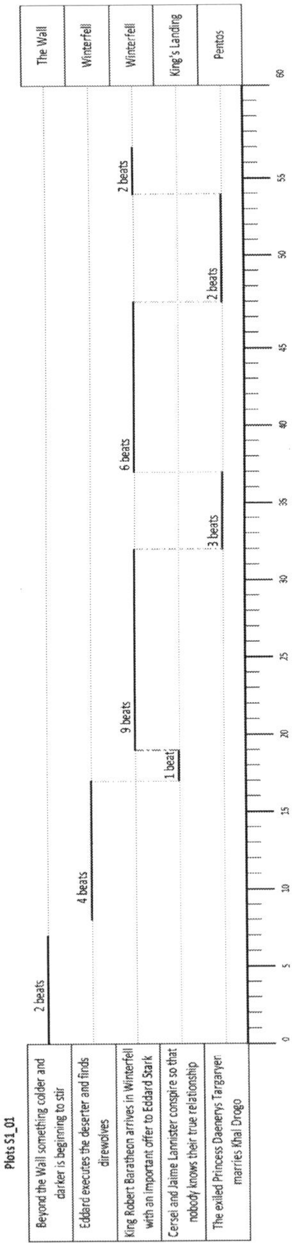

Figure 3.1 Plots and beats in *Game of Thrones*, episode 1.

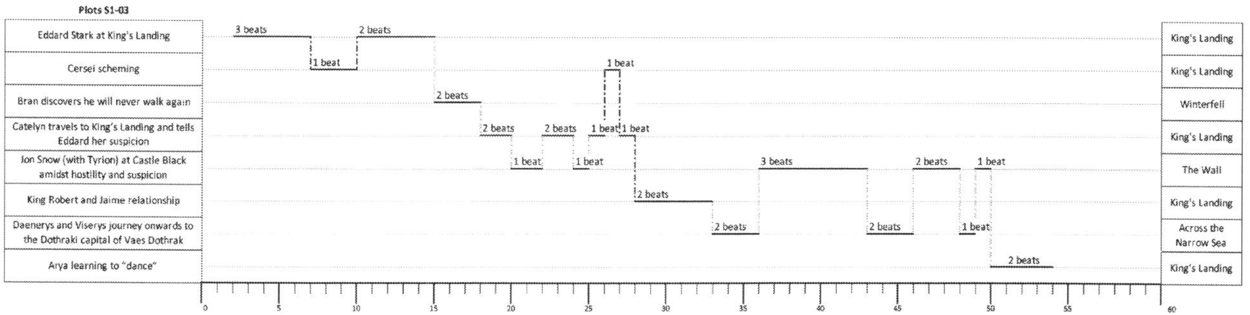

Figure 3.2 Plots and beats in *Game of Thrones*, episode 3 (in gray when both plot and location change, in black when there is a change of plot but not of location).

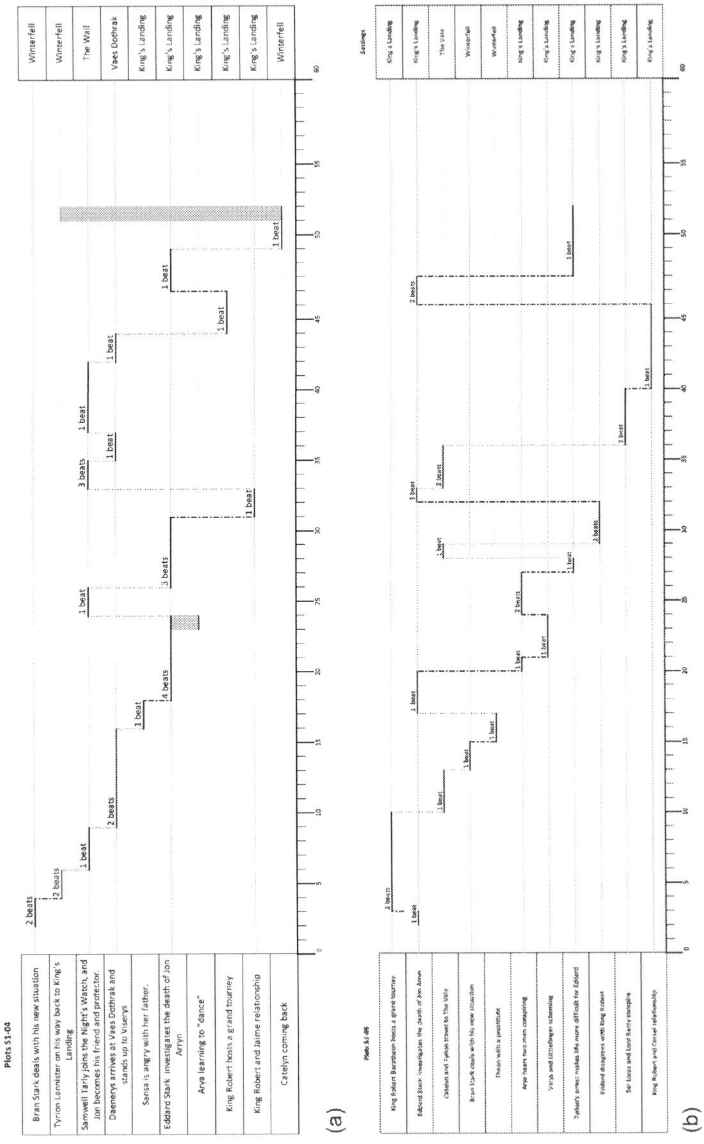

Figure 3.3 Examples of staircase structure in *Game of Thrones*. (a) Episode 4, (b) episode 5. In gray when both plot and location change, in black when there is a change of plot but not of location.

begins. Michael J. Porter et al. (2002) argue that many television narratives focus more on character than plot, which is why characters, and not plotlines, are the focus of the study. When beats include multiple main characters, we have shaded them in gray.

Figure 3.4 shows that the total number of beats per episode for the character of Don (Jon Hamm) is higher than for the other characters throughout the episodes. Moreover, the plots alternate between character pairs. For example, in episode 1, the pairs are Don and Salvatore (Bryan Batt), Don and Peter (Vincent Kartheiser), Don and Roger (John M. Slattery), and Don and Peggy (Elisabeth Moss), while in episode 2 they are Don, Roger, and Betty (January Jones) and Peggy and Joan (Christina Hendricks). The number of beats per episode is higher than in *Game of Thrones*, between 35 and 45, but the number of plots/characters is lower. Nevertheless, it is rare to find more than six consecutive beats for the same plot; the usual distribution is from one to three beats. Thus, once again, we find a thread structure with multiple stories and minimal exposition.

One conclusion that could be drawn from the comparison between these two cases is that the multi-plot structure can take a wide variety of forms due to the range of possible combinations. A beat analysis of other multi-plot series would reveal other possible plot groupings and alternations. However, we can infer that this interplay between continuity and interruption should have an effect on the viewer's attention, although the shifts are not jarring or disconcerting.

Some psychological theories propose that segmentation is a key component of perception. According to Jeffrey Zacks et al. (2010), the structure of the most popular films reflects this type of cognitive process, which depends on the perception of significant changes to a situation. James E. Cutting and Catalina Iricinschi (2015) argue that viewers segment the movie stream into events and encode them into a mental model. Changes in narrative attributes, called indices, would force viewers to update this model. Since narrative shifts usually demand greater cognitive resources, certain techniques are used in order to adjust the viewer's need to update. An example of this is the establishing shot and the re-establishing shot. In a structure like the one we have seen in *Game of Thrones*, there are not only changes in events but also changes of plot. Changing from one plotline to a different one is of special interest because it raises two questions. On the one hand, how can this interplay between continuity and interruption take place without causing confusion? On the other hand, is the link between plots where multi-plot narratives display a characteristic style, as Azcona (2010) suggests, in relation to multi-protagonist films?

In *Game of Thrones*, we find ten narrative shifts per episode on average, making it essential to use signals that will help spectators shift their attention. The most common techniques are establishing shots, mentions, character exits, and point-of-view shots. One distinctive feature of the establishing shots in this series is that from the first episode, each setting is identified with a color. In this way, in the spectator's mind, each character can be associated not only

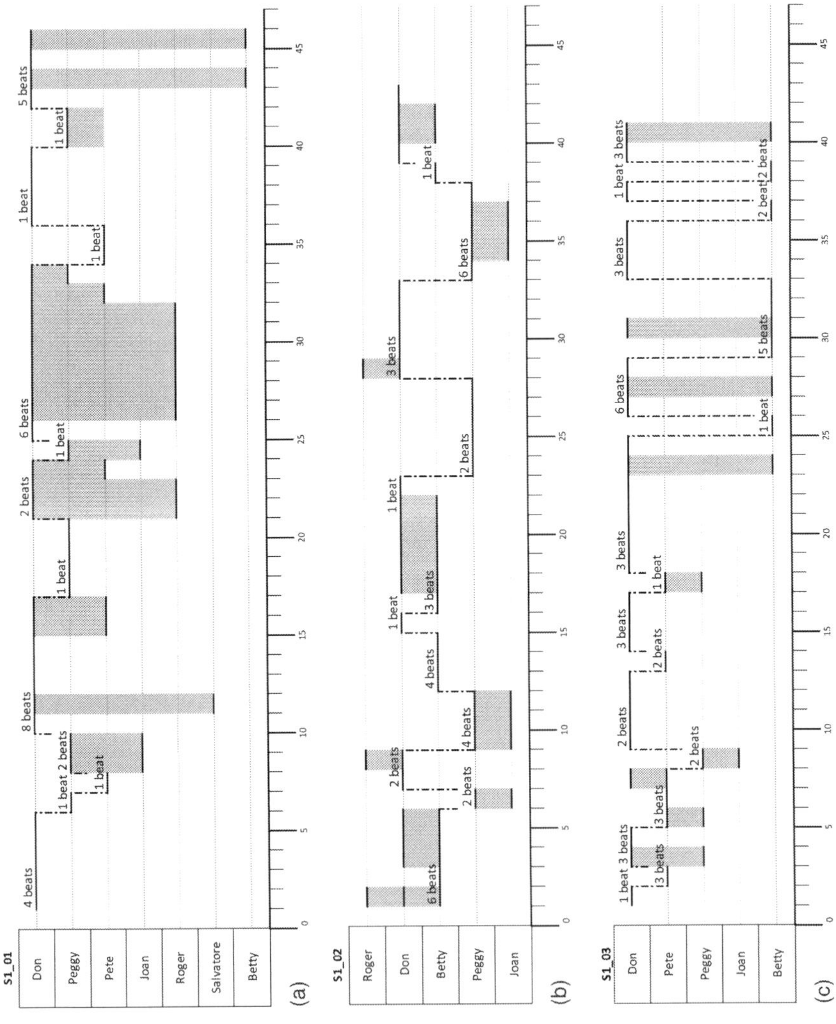

Figure 3.4 Plots and beats in *Mad Men*. (a) Episode 1, (b) episode 2, and (c) episode 3 (shaded in gray when two plots coincide).

with a geographical space but also with a particular color. The color of each plot is maintained regardless of the shot distance, the time of day, or whether it is an indoor or an outdoor shot. According to Tim J. Smith (2012), color is a bottom-up visual factor that grabs our attention. In this case, it signals that the narrative is shifting from one plot to another, so spectators need to update their narrative schemata.

On the other hand, cognitive experiments show that some relevant interruptions are not disruptive but can serve as reinforcement (Gould et al. 2013). Timing is also fundamental, because interruptions are considered less jarring when they take place at the end rather than in the middle of a subtask (Iqbal and Bailey 2005). Bearing these points in mind, our analysis of *Game of Thrones* might reveal that the interruption of plots is usually relevant because someone is mentioned before the beat change. In others, the timing allows the plot shift to be perceived as natural because the character is leaving the scene or gazing at something outside the frame, so that the viewer can conclude that the subtask or event is finished. In short, we would argue that the constant interruptions are mitigated by their relevance, by their timing, and because the different techniques employed direct the spectator's attention. These elements are not just tricks designed to enhance the spectator's experience; they can be developed into systematic strategies that may be used to give a series an aesthetic identity, like the use of colors in *Game of Thrones* or the systematic marking of beat/plot transitions with diegetic and nondiegetic music and sound in *Stranger Things* (R. Duffer and M. Duffer 2016–present).

Multi-plot narrative from episodes to inter-episodic arcs

In this section, we consider the value of the multi-plot narrative with respect to the episodic narrative structure and also to inter-episodic arcs. It is important to consider the current predominance in the most successful series of inter-episodic plots, clearly much more common now than episodic seriality, which enjoyed predominance some decades ago.

Our hypothesis to explain this circumstance is that a plurality of arcs developing in time throughout episodes and over entire seasons in a pattern that leads to interactions between plots allows the multi-plot structure to realize its full potential. The mere coexistence of parallel plots prompts spectators to think about the possible relationships between them. When these relationships become explicit, this may often serve to renew viewers' interest or elicit cognitively enriching experiences such as surprise. We could thus assume that a specific pattern of interacting narrative arcs provides a more cognitively active (and probably more pleasurable) experience for the spectator.

Conversely, the development of a multi-plot structure in an episodic environment in general does not offer the same wealth of possibilities of combining plots, nor can the interactions between those plots achieve a similar aesthetic dimension. The most obvious effect produced by a multi-plot structure for the episodic form is the definition of an episodic ending, when the episodic plot concludes. Such effects often occur because what happens in one or more of the subplots influences the ending, thus preparing the viewer. There are, we would argue, some highly innovative and effective achievements in this regard. For example, the first season of *Gomorra* (*Gomorrah*, Saviano 2014–present) presents the rivalry between two mafia clans in Naples and the ongoing battles and betrayals within each clan. The life of the Sevastano clan stands out: Pietro Sevastano (Fortunato Cerlino), the head of the clan, Imma (Maria Pia Calzone), his wife, Genna (Salvatore Sposito), his son, and Ciro (Marco D'Amore), his best friend, all have specific plots. But the uniqueness of the first episode is that it starts and ends with an apparently secondary subplot. Near the beginning of the episode, a scene shows Imma Sevastano deciding to get a new sofa and offering the old one as a present to Ciro. In a later scene, Ciro takes the sofa away in his car with the help of his friend Genna. The episode's closing scene begins with the news on the television of the vendetta that seems to bring the battle with the Sevastanos' rival clan to an end, while the camera moves over to the newly bought luxury sofa. Salvatore and his wife Imma start talking about the sofa, a conversation that ends with Salvatore saying that it is uncomfortable. The sofa is then taken away and ends up serving as a game prop for a child who is effectively training to become a lookout for the neighborhood's drug dealers. The subplot ending offers a visual juxtaposition of a piece of luxury furniture with a desolate landscape and human degradation, and with children beginning their integration into the drug world. The screenwriters may have designed this subplot strategy as a means of enriching the meaningfulness of an opening episode. It not only offers us a hint as to the future evolution of the story but also raises expectations about its critical interpretation.

However, in addition to the value of the multi-plot narrative with respect to episode endings, its use in relationship to arcs is also of great interest. In many series, simply ending an episode results in a cliffhanger that increases the viewer's interest in an inter-episodic arc. This approach can be found at crossover moments of a series that constitute the beginning of the inter-episodic arc and that can give rise to a rather sophisticated narrative strategy.

How much information is necessary to begin an inter-episodic arc? In relation to classical cinema, Jason Gendler proposes a cognitive criterion for an apparently formal question as the dimensions of a recognizable narrative moment:

> a classical narrative beginning concludes when the narration has introduced enough information for viewers to form a probable and exclusive global hypothesis about the direction of the rest of the narrative.
>
> (2012, 75)

Gendler draws the idea of the hypothesis from David Bordwell (2006), who considers hypothesis-forming one of the spectator's main cognitive activities. From this perspective, narration is conceived as a process in which the spectator is presented with numerous questions that are answered with a hypothesis, in a similar way to the idea of erotetic narration proposed by Noël Carroll (2007).

In the pilot episode of *Game of Thrones*, viewers are introduced immediately to the wide array of plotlines in the series: beyond Winterfell, the White Walkers seem to be on the move after thousands of years; in the South, the Targaryens form an alliance and want to reclaim the throne; Jon Arryn, the Hand of the King (John Standing), has died, and Robert Baratheon (Mark Addy) travels north to get Ned Stark to replace him and unite their families. Ned (Sean Bean) and Catelyn (Michelle Fairley) receive news that the Lannisters were behind Jon Arryn's murder and that Robert wants to keep Ned close to protect them. This array of plots depicts an unstable world that is being threatened from many directions. Almost every storyline conveys a moment of transition, and there are signs of potential conflict between them. Based on this, viewers may posit an initial general hypothesis: that the world depicted will evolve from a situation of instability to one of conflict. In the final scene, Jaime Lannister (Nikolaj Coster-Waldau) throws the youngest son of the rival clan, Bran Stark (Isaac Hempstead-Wright), out of a window after the latter catches him committing incest with his sister. This event connecting two main plots might serve to support the aforementioned hypothesis, because the assault on Bran clearly suggests that the changes that lead to Ed Stark's appointment as Hand of the King to Robert Baratheon, who is married to Cersei Lannister (Lena Headey), will lead to a conflict between the Stark and Lannister families.

Gendler (2012) argues that the global hypothesis needs to be made more probable but also more exclusive. The closure described in the previous paragraph clearly fulfills that second condition, since the end of the episode actually contributes information on previous elements that modifies the perception of one particular direction as being more likely than another: we recast and refine our global hypothesis with the introduction of more information, or causally necessary conditions, and as certain directions for a narrative appear increasingly likely.

The *Game of Thrones* pilot episode shows how the multi-plot structure cognitively determines the narrative form, fulfilling the requirements of probability and exclusivity. The beginning of a season extends throughout the first episode and concludes with its end, often resulting in a cliffhanger. Season beginnings where the first episode presents similarities to the beginnings of classical Hollywood movies in terms of the definition of a hypothesis could be identified in serials like *Six Feet Under* (Ball 2001–2005), *Lost* (Abrams et al. 2004–2010), *Bron/Broen* (*The Bridge*, Georgsson et al. 2011–2018), and *La casa de papel* (*Money Heist*, Pina 2017–present), among others. All of these serials share the feature of introducing multiple storylines that hint at something and a closure that connects some of the plots introduced to allow us to confirm and refine our initial hypothesis.

The following paragraphs explore the relationships developed between narrative arcs as a serial progresses. To this end, we will leave the discussion of serial beginnings and turn our attention to the analysis of an intermediate point especially relevant for the development of a series. An example of such a point is the final scene in Season 3 episode 4 of *The Americans* (Weisberg 2013–2018), in which we see Philip (Matthew Rhys) hugging a teenage girl, Kimberly (Julia Garner), and smoking pot in a parking lot at night to the tune of Yazoo's 1980s hit "Only You." In the final shot, which lasts only a few seconds, while the girl smiles innocently as if she were in love, Philip's expression is serious. Although this image might elicit all kinds of reactions in spectators, I would argue that the sad tone of the music and the sight of Matthew Rhys's gloomy expression would most probably compel them to question the significance of this moment in Philip's life. But to do this, they would need to place elements from three previously developed plots in relation with each other. Accessing prior knowledge of the narrative is thus the key to interpreting the scene (Kintsch 1988; Myers and O'Brien 2005). One of the plots in question is the espionage plot of which this scene is a part, as Philip has won Kimberly's heart in order to spy on her father, an American CIA agent. Another is the family plot related to the coming-of-age of his daughter Paige (Holly Taylor), who is now a teenager and beginning her quest for an identity of her own. There is also a third plot arising from the second, related to Philip's relationship with his KGB supervisor, Gabriel (Frank Langella), which is characterized by a conflict over Paige's future, as while the KGB believes it is time for Paige to begin her training, Philip doesn't want his fourteen-year-old daughter to be turned into a secret agent. Based on their knowledge of these three plots, viewers might develop a hypothesis along the following lines: Philip's sad expression reflects his recognition of the contradiction of deceiving and sleeping with a girl his daughter's age and involving her in a KGB plot while he himself wants to keep his own daughter out of the world of espionage.

A moment like this acquires strategic importance, as it enables viewers to establish a new network of associations between arcs in order to understand the narrative. In psychological terms, and following some of the concepts proposed by Jeffrey Foy and Joseph Magliano in their contribution to this book, we could argue that the scene consolidates Philip's status as a high-level node, a hierarchically structured network of pieces of information that will gain more importance by consolidating and enriching the set of connections that will emerge in the subsequent course of the narrative. For example, in the next episode, almost every scene in which Philip appears, and therefore every plot he participates in, seems to be asking viewers to read his mind in the same way: when he buys a dress for his daughter; in his discussion with Elizabeth (Keri Rusell); and in his conversations with his supposed friend, FBI agent Stan Beeman (Noah Emmerich). Indeed, the inner conflict between his private feelings (developed as a subplot to the main family storyline) and his professional career as spy (the core of another main plot) becomes explicit and more acute as this episode progresses. Philip's feelings about working with a young girl like Kimberly will be made explicit after these scenes in a conversation with his KGB supervisor, Gabriel, who concludes their discussion by saying to him: "You have a conscience, Philip. There's nothing wrong with that. But conscience can be dangerous." Finally, episode 5 ends with a conversation between Philip and Elizabeth in which he confesses his "problems" of conscience. This turns his professional dilemma into an important element in the plot related to the couple's relationship as well.

As the different plots converge, they form some interesting patterns. At the beginning of episode 6, when Paige is being baptized, the scene includes several close-ups where Philip's expression can be read in light of his inner conflict in relation to the baptism. Later, in the storyline of his false relationship with Kimberly, just when it seems that Philip will consummate the charade, there is a surprising twist: when Kimmy undresses, Philip covers her and tells her that he has become religious, practically repeating the words he had heard his daughter speak earlier, thus reinforcing the connection between the two plots established in the scene in episode 4. A unique feature of *The Americans* is that the spectator always knows that the Jennings are pretending in most situations, and the dialogues create a sustained suspense around their ability to handle very delicate situations that can even lead Philip and Elizabeth to lie to each other. This happens in one of the typical scenes of intimacy between the couple: Elizabeth becomes pensive when Philip tells her that he does not want to sleep with Kimmy, although he may do so if the operation requires it when she is older. But the conflict sharpens when Gabriel tells Philip that his spying on Kimmy's father is essential to KGB operations and orders him to see her weekly. In addition, Gabriel reveals that he has a son born out of his relationship with another spy.

Philip's inner moral conflict becomes a main factor of narrative continuity, as it will be developed in the different plots where it resonates. There are clear efforts to involve as many plots as possible at certain key points: for example, when Gabriel explains to Elizabeth that he suspects that Philip is losing confidence in him because of his relationship with Paige and presses her to maintain a harder line than Philip. However, in the last scene of the episode, when Philip and Kimmy meet, he expands on his lie about his newly found faith, explaining that his conversion is related to his discovery that he is the father of a child. He asks her to pray with him, and after they finish, she tells him she is sure he will be a good father. Of course, it is true that Philip lies and suffers in his efforts to protect his moral bond with his real daughter (Paige), but viewers will interpret Kimmy's words as an unwitting description of a paradoxical life and will probably by this point engage in a meta-discursive reflection on the mastery of the screenwriters in the development of this subplot.

The way that Philip's crisis serves to connect the different arcs of the show develops into an organic feature of the narrative over the course of the serial, as it will eventually lead him to leave the KGB in the fifth season, while Elizabeth will become even more firmly committed to her work in espionage. In this way, Philip's crisis will prompt viewers to sustain a hypothesis that his private/family life and strong moral sense may end up undermining his/the Jennings' future as spies. The hypothesis itself raises new expectations about the direction the main plots will take as the rest of the season unfolds, for example regarding Paige's exploration of her own identity as a central theme of the second half of the series, and also Philip and Elizabeth's romantic relationship.

In this way, beginning with a subtle reading of a scene where a mental event is suggested, the multiple storylines of the show will converge to reinforce the event's capacity to push forward the dramatic core of the series related to the conflict between personal and professional life. This will trigger the viewer's coherent cognitive activity, enhancing a systematic use of empathetic access throughout the serial and the development of expectations that determine the main hypothesis related to the outcome of the show, which will only be possible for spectators who actively make inferences about the content of different plotlines and their interactions.

Another important consideration for this study is how the interaction between long arcs serves to shape the conclusion to a season. In many cases, the end of a season has a two-part structure: the resolution of the main plots in a climactic moment, and an epilogue that serves to provide a sense of completion and where unresolved secondary plots that have not been addressed in the climax are also sometimes closed. A diversity of plots can be an effective resource, although the plurality and dissimilarity of narrative lines can also make this decisive stage of the narrative especially challenging to get right. The ending is the moment when we most clearly perceive the aesthetic implications of the multi-plot narrative, since it is the moment that can especially trigger the reflective impulse needed for aesthetic evaluation. The last part of this chapter looks briefly at both examples of both cases: firstly, a climactic moment; and secondly, an epilogue.

In the second season of *Fargo* (Hawley 2015), the multi-plot structure has the appearance of an organic system organized around a main event: a bloody war between two mafias. When one of the members of one mafia is the victim of a hit-and-run that actually has nothing at all to do with the conflict, his death triggers the outbreak of the war. There is also a plot involving a police investigation that begins in response to a triple murder, although at a certain point the only aim the police officers have is to try to stop a spiral of violence. In the final episodes, there are secondary plots about characters that acquire a greater intensity, especially the plot featuring the person responsible for the hit-and-run: Peggy Blumquist (Kirsten Dunst), along with her husband, Ed the butcher (Jesse Plemons). These plots produce a subtle shift of narrative focus from the conflict between the two mafias to certain consequences of that conflict. At the end of episode 7, Milligan (Bokeem Woodbine), the boss of the Kansas City Mafia, receives a call from Ed, who makes a deal with him to deliver the boss of the Gerhardt Crime Syndicate, Dodd Gerhardt (Jeffrey Donovan), who has been kidnapped by Peggy and her husband following a bizarre turn of events. Thus, episode 8 will be dedicated to showing how the butcher and his wife treat the kidnapped mob boss in a situation that is interesting because it turns the focalization of the narrative towards the transformation of two apparently ordinary individuals (Ed and Peggy). Moreover, in another unexpected turn, a mafia mercenary working for the Gerhardts appears: the Native American Hanzee Dent (Zahn McClarnon), who is searching for Ed and Peggy, supposedly to free his boss. At this point comes the twist that will lead to the crucial climactic situation that constitutes the culmination of the season: instead of rescuing Dodd, Hanzee kills him. A mercenary in a secondary role thus becomes the protagonist in episodes 9 and 10 alongside the butcher and his wife. In this way, we can see how a set of subplots that might otherwise have remained secondary acquire importance as the moment of narrative resolution approaches.

In one of their numerous reflections on climaxes, David Bordwell and Kristin Thompson (2009) suggest that a narrative "will typically resolve its causal issues by bringing the development to a high point, or climax. In the climax, the action is presented as having a narrow range of possible outcomes" (2009, 83). It is clear that the climactic scene of the whole second season of *Fargo*, at the point where all possibilities are reduced to just a few, is the motel scene in episode 9. Here, for the first time, all the main plotlines converge, and all the participants in the story appear together in the same place: the police, the two mafia gangs, and Ed and Peggy. The scene depicts an ambush by the police to bring an end to the war between the two gangs at the very moment when they were supposed to be meeting to make a pact. But the final result is the annihilation of all the members of the Gerhardt family. This outcome is not the result of the feud between gangs but the work of Hanzee, who kills the family that gave him a home and a job. What was until then a secondary character carries out a drastic reduction of possibilities for the continuity of the narrative, and his story now becomes the main plot. Viewers may consider this narrative resolution to be questionable, even gratuitous. The surprise of this turn undoubtedly leads to these kinds of doubts about the narrative; on the other hand, given that the season is approaching its conclusion, this structuring of the narrative could itself conceivably be considered a strategy to convey the meaning of the story. What does this mean for the logic of the story up to this moment, when the only event consistent with Hanzee's actions is his earlier murder of Dodd Gerhardt? Instead of sidestepping this question, for the first time in the series, the narrative introduces a voice-over, together with certain visual resources, to present a metanarrative perspective that underscores the mysterious nature of Hanzee's actions. In this way, the mystery that surrounds a secondary character ends up creating a new plotline.

Thus, at the end of the second season of *Fargo*, viewers are inevitably led to consider that the story is not really about a confrontation between mafias but about how a random accident can direct human fate. It is as if the story were asking us: What might we have become if this had happened to us? The shift of focus prior to the climax onto Ed and Peggy, insofar as they are two ordinary characters with whom most spectators can empathically engage, points in this direction. The last episode offers new perspectives on how this situation pushes Peggy over the edge into madness while confirming how a simple man like Ed can end up becoming a criminal without even seeming to be aware of the fact. And the same could be said of Hanzee's story. In both cases, fiction reveals where human nature could take us when chance comes into play. Might Hanzee have remained unswervingly loyal to his bosses if Peggy had not run over the Gerhardts' little brother?

A fairly common formula for concluding the epilogue to a series is the juxtaposition of parallel images from different plots by means of a montage sequence. In most cases, this seems to express a temporal coordination between the different storylines. Montage sequences offer a parallel view of the scenes that conclude the different plots developed over the course of the season. These sequences often constitute a synthetic way of expressing the most common procedure for a narration distributed in multiple storylines: temporal parallels between plots. This formula also encourages cognitive activity aimed at considering the totality of the narration, so that the spectator's reflection on the meaning behind any ending is oriented decidedly towards the whole, which tends to add to the cognitive and aesthetic value of the series. For example, the final sequence of *The Deuce* (Simon 2017–2019) runs through all the plots, showing us Larry (Gbenga Akinnagbe), Alston (Lawrence Gilliard Jr.), Bobby (Chris Bauer), Frankie (James Franco), and Lori (Emily Meade) in scenes that even contribute narrative content offering some sense of closure in relation to their stories, such as Barbara's (Kayla Foster) arrival at the prison, the publication of Sandra's (Matalie Paul) article and her frustration when she sees it, or Eileen (Maggie Gyllenhaal) finally directing a porno film scene with Darlene (Dominique Fishback). The whole sequence is formally encapsulated by the music that begins when Vincent (James Franco) puts on "Careless Love" by Ray Charles and concludes with the image of another jukebox in the parlor where Bernice (Andrea-Rachel Parker) is working overtime. The result is an ellipsis, which calls attention to the formal framework but at the same time has a narrative value, because it concludes several plots and especially, because it places all the stories on an equal level. Yet, its most powerful effect seems to be that of calling on the spectator in the final moment to engage in a direct act of reflection that may range from a rational analysis to an association tinged more with emotion and lyricism. Such cognitive activity serves as the basis for understanding, feeling, and aesthetically evaluating the narrative. Thus, if spectators take the larger narrative design as the basis for an aesthetic judgment, assuming that the subtle strategy of plot interactions is a successful way of conveying the dramatic content of the series, they will be able to engage in a very coherent act of evaluation.

Conclusion

In this chapter, we have identified a range of specific relationships between cognitive effects and formal solutions that are characteristic of contemporary serials. First of all, alternating plots through constant scene changes may take a wide range of different forms that effectively define the formal structure of the narrative. This can be particularly important from a perceptual perspective, because the transitions employed to soften the impact of such narrative shifts can even turn into systematic norms that represent overarching serial aesthetic features of the narration.

In addition, we have offered an overview of the episodic narrative structure and inter-episodic arcs. We have addressed cognitive conditions such as the knowledge not only of the overarching main plot but also of the main interacting plots that are central to defining the formal structure of different kinds of beginnings. Our analysis of the middle has shown how this key moment may stimulate the spectator's perception of the interaction between narrative threads over the course of different episodes to elicit effects ranging from powerful emotions, like surprise, to sustained cognitive attitudes, like a particular empathetic attachment to a particular character. Finally, we have outlined some plot interactions of great significance for climax and closure strategies, insofar as they elicit reflection in order to produce a global sense of the narration as a whole. As we have shown, the formal possibilities are many, and the plasticity and adaptability of the multi-plot structure to the cognitive experience that screenwriters want to elicit from spectators results in a diversity of forms. That is perhaps one of the secrets of the success of serial television in recent years.

References

Abrams, J.J. Damon Lindelof, Jeffrey Lieber, and Carlton Cuse. 2004–2010. *Lost*. USA: CBS Television Studios, Touchstone Television, Bad Robot, and Grass Skirt Productions.

Allen, Robert C., ed. 2001. *To Be Continued... Soap Operas around the World*. New York: Routledge.

Azcona, María del Mar. 2010. *The Multi-Protagonist Film*. London: John Wiley & Sons.

Ball, Allan. 2001–2005. *Six Feet Under*. USA: HBO, The Greenblatt Janollari Studio, Actual Size Films, and Actual Size Productions.

Benioff, David, and D.B. Weiss. 2011–2019. *Game of Thrones*. USA: HBO.

Bochco, Steven Michael, and Kozoll. 1981–1987. *Hill Street Blues*. USA: MTM Enterprises, NBC.

Bordwell, David, and Kristin Thompson. 2009. *Film Art: An Introduction*. New York: McGraw-Hill.

Bordwell, David. 2006. *The Way Hollywood Tells It: Story and Style in Modern Movies*. Berkeley, CA: University of California Press.

Carroll, Noël. 2007. "Narrative Closure." *Philosophical Studies* 135, no. 1: 1–15.

Crofts, Stephen. 1995. "Global Neighbours." In *To Be Continued...: Soap Operas Around the World*, edited by Robert C. Allen, 98–120. London: Routledge.

Cutting, James, and Catalina Iricinschi. 2015. "Re-Presentations of Space in Hollywood Movies: An Event-Indexing Analysis." *Cognitive Science* 39, no. 2: 434–456.

De Kosnik, Abigail. 2011. "Soaps for Tomorrow: Media Fans Making Online Drama from Celebrity Gossip." In *The Survival of Soap Opera: Transformations of a New Media Era*, edited by Sam Ford De Kosnik and C. Lee Harrington, 233–249. University of Mississippi Press.

Duffer, Matt, and Ross Duffer. 2016–present. *Stranger Things*. USA: Netflix, and 21 Laps Entertainment.

Esmail. Sam. 2015–2019. *Mr. Robot*. USA: Universal Cable Productions, and Anonymous Content.

Fellowes, Julian. 2010–2015. *Downton Abbey*. UK: Carnival Film & Television.

Flanagan, Mike. 2018. *The Haunting of Hill House*. USA: Amblin Television, and Paramount Television.

Gendler, Jason. 2012. "Where Does the Beginning End? Cognition, Form, and Classical Narrative Beginnings." *Projections: The Journal for Movies and Mind* 6, no. 2: 64–83.

Gilligan, Vince. 2008–2013. *Breaking Bad*. USA: Gran Via Productions, High Bridge Productions, and Sony Pictures Television.

Gondry, Michel. 2004. *Eternal Sunshine of the Spotless Mind*. USA: Focus Features.

Gould, Sandy J.J., Duncan P. Brumby, and Anna L. Cox. 2013. "What Does It Mean for an Interruption to be Relevant? An Investigation of Relevance as a Memory Effect." *Proceedings of the Human Factors and Ergonomics Society Annual Meeting* 57, no. 1: 149–153.

Hamrell, Harald, Anna Zackrisson, Andrea Östlund, and Molly Hartleb. 2017–2018. Vår tid är nu (The Restaurant). Sweden: SVT, Film I Väst, Jarowskij AB, Viaplay.

Hawley, Noah. 2015. Fargo. USA: 26 Keys Productions, FX Productions, Littlefield Company.

Iqbal, Shamsi, and Bryan Bailey. 2005. "Investigating the Effectiveness of Mental Workload as Predictor of Opportune Moments for Interruption." *CHI'05 Extended Abstracts on Human Factors in Computing Systems*, 1489–1492.

Jacobs, David. *Dallas*. 1978–1991. USA: Lorimar Television.

Kintsch, Walter. 1988. "The Role of Knowledge in Discourse Comprehension: A Construction-integration Model." *Psychological Review* 95, no. 2: 163–182.

Kohan, Jenji. 2013–2019. *Orange Is The New Black*. USA: Netflix, Lionsgate Television.

Leigh, Mike. 1996. *Secrets and Lies*. UK: Thin Man Films, Film4 Productions, Ciby 2000.

Logan, Elliott. 2013. "Flashforwards in Breaking Bad: Openness, Closure and Possibility." In *Television Aesthetics and Style*, edited by Jason Jacobs and Steven Peacock, 219–226. New York: Bloomsbury.

McKinnon, Ray. 2013–2016. *Rectify*. USA: SundanceTV, Gran Via Productions, Zip Works.

Mittell, Jason. 2015. *Complex TV: The Poetics of Contemporary Television Storytelling*. New York: NYU Press.

Nannicelli, Ted. 2017. *Appreciating the Art of Television: A Philosophical Perspective*. New York: Taylor and Francis.

Newman, Michael Z. 2006. "From Beats to Arcs: Toward a Poetics of Television Narrative." *The Velvet Light Trap* 58, no. 1: 16–28.

Nolan, Christopher. 2010. *Inception*. USA & UK: Warner Bros., Legendary Pictures, Syncopy Production.

Nolan, Jonathan. 2016–present. *Westworld*. USA: Jerry Weintraub Productions, Warner Bros. Television, and Bad Robot.

Odar; Baran bo and Jantje Friese. 2017–2020. *Dark*. Germany. Wiedemann & Berg Television.

Panek, Elliot. 2014. "Show, Don't Tell: Considering the Utility of Diagrams as a Tool for Understanding Complex Narratives." In *Hollywood Puzzle Films*, edited by Warren Buckland, 72–88. New York: Routledge.

Pina, Alex. 2017–present. *La casa de papel (Money Heist)*. Spain: Vancouver Media, Atresmedia Televisión.

Porter, Michael J., Deborah L. Larson, Allison Harthcock, and Kelly Berg Nellis. 2002. "Re(de)fining Narrative Events Examining Television Narrative Structure." *Journal of Popular Film and Television* 30, no. 1: 23–30.

Rosenfeldt, Hans. 2011–2018. *Bron/Broen (The Bridge)*. Sweden: Filmlance International AB, Nimbus Film Productions, SVT, ZDF, Radio (DR), Norsk Rikskringkasting, ZDF Enterprises, Film I Väst.

Saphiro, Richard, and Esther Saphiro. 1981–1989. *Dynasty*. USA: Aaron Spelling.

Saviano, Roberto. 2014–present. *Gomorra*. Italy: Cattleya, Sky Cinema, Fandango Produzione.

Simon, David. 2002–2008. *The Wire*. USA: HBO.

Simon, David. 2017–2019. *The Deuce*. USA: HBO, and Blown Deadline Productions.

Simons, Jan. 2014. "Complex Narratives." In *Hollywood Puzzle Films*, edited by Warren Buckland, 17–34. London/New York: Routledge.

Skoptsov, Mikhail L. 2015. "Prophetic Visions, Quality Serials: *Twin Peaks*' New Mode of Storytelling." *Series - International Journal of TV Serial Narratives* 1, no. 1: 39–50.

Smith, Anthony. 2018. *Storytelling Industries: Narrative Production in the 21st Century*. London: Palgrave Macmillan.

Smith, Evan. 1999. "Thread Structure: Rewriting the Hollywood Formula." *Journal of Film and Video* 51, no. 3–4: 88–96.

Smith, Greg M. 1995. "Plotting a Show about Nothing: Patterns of Narration in Seinfeld." *Creative Screenwriting* 2, no. 1: 82–90.

Smith, Tim J. 2012. "The Attentional Theory of Cinematic Continuity." *Projections: The Journal for Movies and Mind* 6, no. 1: 1–27.

Tarantino, Quentin. 1994. *Pulp Fiction*. USA: Miramax, Band Apart, Jersey Films.

Thompson, Kristin. 2003. *Storytelling in Film and Television*. Cambridge, MA: Harvard University Press.

Weiner, Mathew. 2007–2015. *Mad Men*. USA: Lionsgate Television.

Weisberg, Joseph. 2013–2018. *The Americans*. USA: Amblin Television, DreamWorks Television.

Zacks, Jeffrey M., Nicole K. Speer, Khena M. Swallow, and Corey J. Maley. 2010. "The Brain's Cutting-room Floor: Segmentation of Narrative Cinema." *Frontiers in Human Neuroscience* 4: 1–15.

4 "Oh my God, they didn't kill Kenny"

Seriality and viewer engagement in contemporary animated television

Oliver Kroener

At the end of the mid-season finale of *South Park*'s (Comedy Central, 1997–) 15th season, Stan's parents Randy and Sharon have an argument about Randy's newest obsession to become a professional musician. While their confrontation starts out like any other argument the two characters have had over the course of the animated show's 15-season run, it eventually becomes a meta-textual statement on *South Park's* narrative format. Sharon argues that the real problem is not that Randy suddenly wants to be a musician but that he has a new obsession each week. Referring to past episodes of the show, Sharon states: "You do this all the time! First, you're obsessed with baseball fights! Then you need to play Warcraft! Then you've gotta be a celebrity chef!" The conversation turns meta-textual when Sharon asks: "How much longer can we keep doing this? It's like the same shit just happens over and over, and then in a week it just all resets until it happens again." She continues her monologue while slowly walking towards the camera. Now directly addressing the audience, Sharon proclaims: "Every week it's kind of the same story in a different way but it just keeps getting more and more ridiculous." Shortly after, the episode ends with a montage that teases that the events of "You're Getting Old" are going to have major narrative consequences for future episodes of *South Park*: Stan is struggling with depression, Randy and Sharon get a divorce and move into separate apartments, and Cartman and Kyle, whose relationship has always been antagonistic, are shown enjoying each other's company.

When "You're Getting Old" first aired, some television critics saw it as an indicator that *South Park* was about to abandon its episodic format. Meanwhile, others interpreted it as the creators of the show signaling to the audience that the show would end soon. Ultimately, both of these readings proved to be inaccurate. Although the beginning of the next episode plays with the idea that the events of "You're Getting Old" have had a lasting effect on the characters and their relationships, this impression is completely ridiculed by the end of the episode when *South Park*'s familiar status quo is re-established in a quick succession of events.

One might interpret the way in which these two episodes tease the introduction of serial storytelling as Trey Parker and Matt Stone (the creators of *South Park*) playing an elaborate prank on the audience. Yet, such a reading

DOI: 10.4324/9781003188643-4

neglects the degree to which "You're Getting Old" exploits the desire for narrative consequences and character growth that many long-time viewers of *South Park* might have felt at this point in the show's run. In the context of this chapter, this example is noteworthy for how it teases the potential of seriality to deepen the viewer's emotional engagement with the characters.

This chapter focuses on viewer engagement with animated television characters. However, I should note that my investigation of animated television characters is based on a broader assumption, namely, that how we relate to television characters is dependent on the narrative context they exist in. For example, this means that how we relate to animated television characters is not predominantly determined by one narrative element, such as the structure of the narration (i.e., episodic or serial) or the fact that the characters are animated. Rather, as I argue throughout this chapter, the viewer's relationship with the characters from *South Park* and *The Legend of Korra* (Nickelodeon, 2012–2014) is shaped by the distinct ways in which these programs combine different narrative components (i.e., visual style, narrative structure, and performances). While this might seem like a somewhat obvious argument, in the past, cognition-based studies on viewer engagement with television characters (i.e., Mittell 2015) have often examined this subject in relation to other types of storytelling such as those found in film or literature. In contrast, I argue that when studying viewer engagement with television characters, we need to pay more attention to the narrative setup of individual programs.

Throughout this chapter, I take an interdisciplinary approach to the study of animated characters that, although it originates from cognitive media theory, draws from a number of disciplines, particularly animation and television studies. I begin this chapter with a brief overview of the differences between engaging with animated and with live-action characters. This is followed by a discussion of Donald Crafton's (2013) theory of animated performances. In this section, I discuss how figurative animated performances, which primarily emphasize gestures and movement, and embodied animated performances, which suggest that animated characters possess a complexity beyond what is shown on screen, lead to different engagement patterns. In the second half of this chapter, I specifically analyze viewer engagement with animated characters from *The Legend of Korra* and *South Park*. Firstly, I use *The Legend of Korra* to investigate the influence of embodied animated performances and serial storytelling on viewer engagement. Secondly, I examine how *South Park* complicates character engagement by frequently oscillating between episodic and serial storytelling.

Most existing studies on viewer engagement with animated characters originate from animation studies (Bukatman 2012; Cholodenko 2007; Wells 1998). As a result, they often share a similar focus. For example, many studies on viewer engagement that are based in animation theory are concerned with the uncanny valley effect or examine the relationship between animators and animated characters. At the same time, aside from a few exceptions (Harrison and Stable 2003; Mittell 2004), viewer engagement with animated television characters has rarely been analyzed within television studies or cognitive media theory. Instead, many recent cognition-based studies on the viewer/character relationship in contemporary television tend to focus on the antihero protagonists of contemporary television drama (e.g., Vaage 2016). Undoubtedly, these morally corrupt characters make for fascinating case studies, but I still believe that the scope of cognition-based studies on viewer engagement with television characters needs to be extended to include more genres and formats. I regard this chapter as an initial step in that direction. Based on the aforementioned existing studies on animated characters and viewer engagement with television characters, it is safe to assume that the aesthetic qualities of animation and the narrative setup of the television medium factor into our engagement with animated television characters. Yet, it is still not exactly clear how we relate to animated television characters on a cognitive level. I believe that cognitive media theory is a powerful theoretical tool that can help us to gain a deeper understanding of the relationship between viewers and television characters from various genres, especially when it is combined with medium- and genre-specific studies from other disciplines.

Animated characters, animated performances

Perhaps the most obvious difference between live-action and animated characters is that in contrast to live-action characters, who are always bound to the body of an actor (although that body might be obscured in some way), animated characters do not require a physical body. Murray Smith (1995) has previously discussed this phenomenon in his investigation of the role of recognition in viewer engagement with fictional characters on film. He states that "recognition describes the spectator's construction of character: the perception of a set of textual elements, in film typically cohering around the image of a body, as an individuated and continuous human agent" (1995, 82). Smith further argues that the bodily attributes of a character are often closely tied to that character's traits. As Smith states, "the traits and occurrent states of characters are available to spectators principally through performative factors: the body, the face, the voice, and the actions performed through these physical attributes" (1995, 113). This aspect of viewer engagement is particularly noteworthy when studying viewer engagement with animated characters, since animated characters are typically modeled and perform after the exact liking of an animator. This means that in contrast to live-action performances, the creators of animated performances are usually in full control of even the smallest detail of a performance, such as, for example, the movement of a character's lips or the blinking of an eye. In addition, more than in live action, the physical attributes of an animated character can be easily altered to highlight certain character traits. I want to make clear that I am not referring to the depth of the characterization here but to the actual visual design of a character.

In the past, scholars have been fascinated with the viewer's ability to engage with comic and animated characters on an emotional level despite their often simplistic design. For example, Carl Plantinga notes:

> The very possibility of the audience's engagement with fictional characters rests in part on the human tendency to personify and respond to abstract, nonhuman entities, especially in the context of visual representations. Psychologists have demonstrated this in some intriguing experiments involving animated geometric representations. Subjects who are shown a short movie depicting triangles and circles on a surface nearly always interpret these movements as the interactions of intentional agents. The subjects attribute intentions to the triangles and circles, seeing their activity as self-directed. Small wonder, then, that audiences respond to animated characters such as Shrek or Snow White as though they were persons.
>
> (2009, 97–98)

Some of the differences between animated and live-action performances are rooted in the general differences between the two media that I have briefly outlined. For example, the performances of most animated characters are at least somewhat shaped by their design and their animation style. Nonetheless, as Donald Crafton points out in his seminal study on animation and performance, to most viewers, animated characters "still seem normal, like other screen actors" (2013, 17). Reflecting on his own reaction to animated characters, Crafton states:

> Watching them, I enjoy a powerful sensation of recognition and a potent sense of their presence. They are drawings, but are they also movie stars? This dissonance is the most fundamental conundrum. How can inanimate drawings or objects act, or perform at all?
>
> (2013, 17)

Crafton here voices his fascination with the spectator's cognitive ability to perceive animated and live-action characters in a similar way but also acknowledges that animated performances are created differently.

More importantly in the context of this chapter, Crafton distinguishes between two different modes of animated performances: embodied and figurative (2013, 22). Although most works of animation adhere to one of these two performance styles, they are not exclusive. For example, embodied performances might feature some elements of figurative performances and vice versa. Figurative performances prioritize "movement that conveys signifying gestures and pantomime typical of broad humor and slapstick rather than emotive personality, character nuance, and emotional expression" (Crafton 2013, 23). To further distinguish between figurative and embodied modes of performance, Crafton refers to Betty Boop, one of the most famous characters from early animation. According to Crafton, although Betty features some traces of embodiment, she is predominantly a figurative performer, since "her personality is an infectious composite of acquired details, more like a collection of poached traits than a complex expression of inner drives and motives" (2013, 27–28). Furthermore, narratives that primarily feature figurative performances typically do not provide the viewer with a deeper insight into a character's psyche. Instead, they rely more strongly on symbolism and repetition (Crafton 2013, 32).

In the 1930s, Disney established an animation style that was characterized by a high level of verisimilitude. According to Crafton, embodied animated performances are a direct result of the studio's approach to animation during that period of time. Crafton notes that most early embodied animated performances were based on what is today referred to as method acting – an acting technique that was first developed by Stanislavsky in the early 20th century. In contrast to figurative performances, which are typically extroverted, embodied acting is introverted. As Crafton states, "it is the philosophy and practice of creating imaginatively realized beings with individuality, depth, and internal complexity" (2013, 36). In a live-action context, the idea behind method acting is essentially that an actor internalizes the role they are playing to add depth and authenticity to their performance. Furthermore, particularly for star performers, method acting has become an effective way to shift the viewer's focus away from their own persona onto the character they are playing. And while some viewers might have a vague idea of what method acting in a live-action film encompasses (e.g., actors staying "in character" between takes), this is typically not the case for embodied animated performances. Crafton cites the character of Donald Duck as an example of embodied acting, since his behavior and his movements are generally internally motivated and consistent across different narratives. While Donald's often angry gestures might suggest that he operates in the figurative mode of performance, his movements are rarely gratuitous. In other words, Donald is not behaving in a certain way to generate a particular viewer response but rather, because that is who he is as a character.

At this point, I should note that embodied performances do not represent an evolution of figurative performances, since when discussing these two modes of performance in a television context, it might be tempting to link figurative performances to episodic television narratives and embodied performances to serial television narratives. This is due to the fact that Crafton's distinction between figurative and embodied animated performances somewhat resembles the way in which some television scholars distinguish between episodic and serial television narratives. For example, Mittell argues that episodic television programs are largely defined by a lack of narrative consequences and a reliance on repetitive plot elements (2015, 18). In contrast, serial television narratives are defined by an emphasis on narrative consequences and plotlines that accumulate over an extended period of time. Based on these definitions, it becomes clear how one might equate figurative animated performances, which accentuate the more immediate aspects of a performance (e.g., movement and action), with episodic television, and embodied performances, which are characterized by a sense of verisimilitude and internal complexity, with serial television narratives. However, I believe that such a categorization is too simplistic, since as Crafton notes, even early cinematic animated shorts, which were typically episodic in nature, often featured performances that were partially figurative and partially embodied.

That is to say, the line between figurative and embodied animated performances is not static but fluid. Of course, some works of animation might still adhere more strongly to one of these modes of performance, but others might switch back and forth between the two. Thus, instead of viewing figurative and embodied performances as two completely separate approaches to performance in animation, I regard them as two fluid modes of animated performance that highlight different aspects of a performance. In the context of this chapter, Crafton's performance model is valuable because it indicates how a work of animation might seek to elicit a particular viewer response at different points in the story. For example, according to Crafton, figurative performances are better equipped to elicit a visceral reaction (e.g., laughter, disgust) in the viewer, whereas typically, embodied performances generate more nuanced emotional responses (e.g., sympathy, antipathy). Yet, as I discuss in more detail in the second half of this chapter, the way in which these modes of animated performance seek to involve viewers on a cognitive level is also affected by the narrative context.

Embodied animated performances in *The Legend of Korra*

Nickelodeon's *The Legend of Korra* (referred to as *Korra* hereafter) is a prime example of serialized animated television. *Korra* is an American program that is heavily influenced by Eastern mythology. The Eastern influence is primarily apparent in the show's character design (which is based in Japanese animation) and the themes *Korra* explores (e.g., friendship, spirituality, destiny, and ecology). The series is a spin-off from the highly successful *Avatar: The Last Airbender* (Nickelodeon, 2005–2008, referred to as *Airbender* hereafter) and was created by Michael Dante DiMartino and Bryan Konietzko. *Korra* takes place in an ancient fictional universe in which the world has been divided into four nations that correspond to the four elements: air, fire, earth, and water. In this fictional universe, some people are born with the ability to control or "bend" an element, but only the avatar, whose responsibility it is to bring balance to the world, is able to control all four elements. The series follows Korra, a rebellious teenager from the water tribe, on her quest to become the new avatar. Other notable characters include Korra's friends Mako, Bolin, and Asami and her uncle and airbending master, Tenzin. Although the characters and their relationships progress throughout the series, each season is structured around a specific theme (Air, Spirits, Change, and Balance).

From its very first episode, *Korra* puts an emphasis on serial storytelling. For example, although the pilot episode of the show is largely concerned with introducing the main characters and establishing the story world, it also introduces a season-long story arc and resolves plotlines that originated in *Airbender*. As is typical of serial narratives, *Korra*'s storytelling emphasizes narrative consequences, which draws the viewer's attention to the characters' progression throughout the series. For example, a plotline that sees the villainous Zaheer poison Korra at the end of season three is not resolved at the beginning of season four but instead, becomes an important element of Korra's character arc. In particular, although Korra manages to defeat Zaheer, her encounter with him leaves her suffering from PTSD throughout most of the following season. With regard to viewer engagement, the ideal result of this emphasis on seriality is that viewers are not only invested in the present narrative events but also engage with the program by speculating about the long-term effects that a narrative event might have on the characters and their relationships. Furthermore, *Korra* frequently pairs its serial storytelling with embodied animated performances to deepen the viewer's understanding of and investment in the characters. Korra's character arc in the first season of the show is a prime example of this.

In the first episode of the series, members of the Order of the White Lotus travel to the Southern water tribe because they have heard rumors about a little girl who might be the new avatar. When they ask Korra's parents what makes them think that their daughter is the new avatar, they get their answer in the form of young Korra. She enters the room and immediately starts controlling all four elements while yelling: "I'm the avatar. You got to deal with it." Korra's introduction is only a short scene, but it perfectly encapsulates her character. She is presented as confident, hot-headed, stubborn, and funny. While Korra evolves over the course of the series, almost all of her struggles throughout the series can be traced back to this initial characterization. For example, this becomes obvious in "A Leaf in the Wind," in which the main plot revolves around Korra's inability to airbend.

Although the show uses Korra's inability to airbend to add some slapstick comedy to the episode, "A Leaf in the Wind" ultimately reinforces Korra's status as an embodied animated character when Tenzin suggests that Korra is unable to airbend as a result of her impulsive personality. As Tenzin states, "often the element that's the most difficult for the avatar to master is the one most opposite to his personality." It takes Korra until the final episode of the season to manage airbending, and when she finally does, the moment is presented as the culmination of a number of narrative elements. Korra first uses airbending to defeat Amon, the evil leader of an anti-bender separatist movement, which acts as the resolution of the main plotline of the season. At the same time, Korra's airbending ties in with her embodied animated performance, since she only manages to airbend as a result of having become more selfless over the course of the season. Thus, not only are Korra's first attempts at airbending visually stunning, but the scene is also closely tied to her character arc and adds to the resolution of season one's main storyline.

Similar examples of how *Korra* combines embodied animated performances and serial storytelling to add depth to the viewer's engagement with the characters can be found in the series' subsequent seasons. For example, in its final episode, *Korra* resolves the underlying tension between Korra and Asami by hinting at the beginning of a romantic relationship between the two young women. The revelation that Korra and Asami are in love subverts viewer expectations but also makes sense within the historical context of the series. To be more specific, over the course of the series, Korra and Asami have repeatedly competed for Mako's affection, but the show has also established that they like and respect each other. As a result, the reveal of their feelings for each other does not seem out of character and provides viewers with one of the main pleasures of serial narration: the resolution of a plotline that has slowly accumulated over time and signals character growth.

Thus far, I have argued that viewer engagement with *The Legend of Korra*'s characters is largely shaped by the program's serialized storytelling and its embodied animated performances. I have further indicated that the combination of these two narrative elements leads to what might be regarded as a nuanced emotional response. In other words, regardless of how viewers feel about *Korra*'s characters, their feelings towards them are likely the result of how the characters have developed over time.

However, the performances in *Korra* are not entirely devoid of figurative performance elements. *Korra* predominantly highlights the figurative elements of its performances during the meticulously choreographed action sequences. These action sequences take full advantage of the almost limitless possibilities of the animated medium. As television critic Matt Patches states in his review of the series' first season:

> When you have element-bending at your disposal, the possibilities are endless. Every episode features another ingenious use of adrenaline-infused animation; from police captain Lin Beifong's Spider-man-like attacks on Amon's airship fleet or an intimate battle between Korra and Amon's right-hand man, the electricity-enhanced Lieutenant, no show matches the intensity and grit of a *Legend of Korra* action sequence.
>
> (Patches 2012)

Patches here refers to how *Korra*'s action scenes frequently highlight the movements of the characters. This might suggest that for the duration of those scenes, *Korra* switches from embodied to figurative animated performances. However, I am convinced that even during these scenes, most of *Korra*'s performances remain embodied. Perhaps with the exception of some of the show's minor characters, some of whose performances can be categorized as figurative because they are primarily defined by their movements, the behavior of *Korra*'s main characters always remains internally motivated – even as they zip through the air in spectacular fashion. Ultimately, then, *The Legend of Korra* combines serial storytelling and embodied animated performances to evoke an intricate and nuanced viewer response. As previously discussed, Korra's fight scene with Amon represents the prime example of the type of character engagement *Korra* aims to accomplish: It delivers the visceral thrills of an action scene, but it also resolves some of the key plotlines of the first season in a way that is character-based.

The main focus of my analysis of *The Legend of Korra* has been on how the show's embodied animated performances in conjunction with a serial narrative structure shape the viewer's relationship with the characters. While one might expect that character engagement functions in the same way in most animated programs, I believe that this process is not only medium- or format-specific but is also determined by the distinct narrative setup of each program. *South Park* functions as a good example of this, since the show's combination of a simplistic animation style, figurative animated performances, and its playful approach to television storytelling lead to a type of character engagement that is distinctly different from *The Legend of Korra*.

Figurative animated performances and seriality in *South Park*

At the time of this writing, *South Park* has just finished its 21st season. This makes it the second longest-running animated television program in television history, only topped by *The Simpsons* (Fox, 1989–). The show, which follows the lives of four fourth graders in the fictional town of South Park, Colorado, was an instant hit when it first premiered in 1997. It became largely known for its crude sense of humor and quickly developed a cult following that turned into a worldwide phenomenon. Although the show's popularity has somewhat waned over the years, television critics still frequently praise *South Park* for its ability to reinvent itself. With regard to its animation style, tone, and narrative format, *South Park* provides a stark contrast to *The Legend of Korra*. While *Korra* is characterized by an intricate animation style and a kid-friendly atmosphere, and primarily focuses on serial storytelling, *South Park* is defined by a simplistic animation style and crude adolescent humor, and exists somewhere between episodic and serial storytelling. In addition, *South Park* almost exclusively features figurative animated performances.

As is typical of figurative performances, almost all of *South Park*'s performances prioritize movement and broad humor over internal complexity. This is particularly true for Kenny McCormick (Matt Stone), who has been killed countless times over the course of the show but never truly remains dead. Instead, after he has been killed, Kenny typically just shows up in the following episode without any explanation as to why he is still alive. In the context of this chapter, Kenny's death in "Cartman Gets an Anal Probe" functions as an example of how in its early incarnation, *South Park* was largely defined by figurative animated performances and an episodic narrative structure. Moreover, it illustrates some of the major differences between character engagement in *The Legend of Korra* and *South Park*.

South Park's pilot episode sees Kenny survive getting shot by aliens and trampled over by a herd of cows. Yet, he is finally killed when a police car runs over him. Furthermore, after his gruesome death, Kenny's bloody corpse is devoured by a pack of rats, who eventually manage to bite his head off and carry it away. The scene largely derives its black humor from how Kenny's figurative performance and the show's misleadingly kid-friendly animation style clash with extreme violence. For example, when Kenny gets shot by the aliens, his whole body rotates through the air and randomly lands in the middle of a nearby road. Even as Kenny flies through the air, he barely moves any of his extremities. In fact, the most notable change in Kenny's movements is that his eyes change from open to closed. Thus, even when faced with death, Kenny's movements remain restricted as a result of the inherent limitations of *South Park*'s animated style. *South Park* maintains this tension between child-friendly animation and over-the-top violence even after Kenny has been killed. While Kenny's dead body still resembles the two-dimensional shape of a crude paper cut-out, he now has a hole in his stomach that reveals his ribs. Moreover, when the rats eventually run away with Kenny's head, it slowly rolls out of the frame in a cartoonish way that further highlights the limitations of *South Park's* animated style. *South Park* ultimately frames Kenny's gruesome death as both shocking and amusing. The extreme nature of Kenny's death, the slapstick-y way in which his body moves during his death scene, and the lack of narrative consequences are primarily meant to elicit a visceral reaction (i.e., disgust, laughter) in the viewer.

What complicates character engagement in the later seasons of *South Park* is that although the show almost exclusively features figurative animated performances, these performances increasingly exist within a narrative framework that frequently oscillates between episodic and serial storytelling. That is to say, *South Park* encourages viewers to engage with the characters on a figurative level while also expecting them to occasionally entertain the possibility that they possess a deeper emotional complexity than their performances let on. To illustrate this argument, I want to briefly recount how *South Park*'s storytelling has changed over the years.

Over the course of its 21-season run, *South Park*'s storytelling has constantly evolved. When the show first premiered, it told one self-contained story per week. Thus, in the past, media scholars such as Ted Nannicelli and Jason Mittell have accurately referred to *South Park* as an example of episodic television storytelling. For example, Nannicelli describes *South Park* as "not typical serial in nature," arguing that "the lack of seriality in this case should make it uncontroversial to say that normally the object of our appreciative focus is the individual episode" (2017, 110). Mittell also refers to *South Park* as an example of self-contained television storytelling but states that it is "more playfully reflexive" than classic episodic television programs, since it acknowledges its "lack of even serialization" (2015, 23). It should be noted that Nannicelli's and Mittell's respective studies were published before *South Park*'s 19th season aired. This is significant because season 19 was the first time that the show entirely abandoned episodic storytelling in favor of a season-long story arc. Yet, even before *South Park* became fully serialized, the show has frequently experimented with its narrative format. For example, some of *South Park*'s plotlines already began to carry over between episodes in season four. Other significant examples of seriality throughout *South Park*'s history include the three-part "Imaginationland" saga in season 11 and the show's extended *Game of Thrones* spoof in season 17.

One of the main effects of *South Park*'s narrative flexibility is that the characters exist somewhere between stasis and character growth. While *South Park*'s recent switch from series to serial has, for some of the characters (e.g., Mr. Garrison, Randy Marsh, and Cartman), led to a more nuanced characterization, I argue that the show already partially employed the sort of accumulative character development that is commonly reserved for serial television when it was still operating as a series. One of the prime examples of what I am referring to here is Kenny's character arc throughout the program. One of the key episodes in Kenny's character development is "Kenny Dies," in which Kenny's death becomes the main catalyst of the story. The main plot of the episode revolves around Kenny being hospitalized for an unspecified terminal disease, which eventually leads to his death. In contrast to prior episodes, in which Kenny's death was played for laughs, this episode presents Kenny's death as a major event in the lives of the other characters. Given the satirical tone of *South Park*, the sudden self-seriousness with which Kenny's death is presented in "Kenny Dies" functions as a gag in itself. However, after "Kenny Dies," it took almost a year until the character appeared again. I want to clarify that I am not arguing that Kenny's death and sudden reappearance a year later are the same as the slow, accumulative character growth that is typical of television serials. Still, Kenny's semi-permanent death in "Kenny Dies" signals to the audience that *South Park*'s storytelling might not be as linear as some viewers might have previously assumed and encourages them to get used to the idea of narrative consequences.

Another episode that is crucial for Kenny's character development and on a more general level, *South Park*'s transformation from an episodic to a serial narrative is "Mysterion Rises." In this episode, it is revealed that Kenny is the super-hero vigilante Mysterion. In the context of this chapter, the revelation of Mysterion's superpower is particularly noteworthy: he is unable to die. Instead, any time Mysterion/Kenny dies, he magically wakes up in his bed unharmed, while the other citizens of *South Park* have no memory of his death. Of course, this explanation is an implausible "retcon" of prior seasons of the show, but it also encourages viewers to engage with Kenny on a deeper level. For example, the viewer's knowledge of Kenny's inability to die might somewhat inform their reaction to Kenny's death scenes in future episodes of the show. Kenny essentially started out as a running joke but developed into a fully fleshed-out character over the course of the series. However, as a result of *South Park*'s elusive narrative structure, the show's characters do not always develop in a linear way. To put it differently, despite the fact that, up until its two most recent seasons, *South Park* has primarily relied on episodic storytelling, many of its characters have a history that has slowly developed across an extensive number of self-contained episodes.

Furthermore, even before *South Park* became serialized, some plot developments had an impact on future episodes of the show. One of the main examples of such an event is the death of Chef in "The Return of Chef." After Isaac Hayes, the voice actor for Chef, publicly criticized *South Park*'s depiction of Scientology, the creators of the series used this episode to get rid of the character in a spectacular way. Since Hayes refused to lend his voice to Chef, the character's entire dialogue in "The Return of Chef" is pieced together from Hayes's previous vocal performances in the show. The plot of the episode revolves around Chef coming back to South Park after having been brainwashed by the so-called Super Adventure Club. The disturbing result of the Super Adventure Club's influence on Chef is that he is obsessed with wanting to have sex with the four main children. Over the course of the episode, the children desperately try to help Chef to return to his former self. However, they do not succeed, and the episode ends with him getting killed in an over-the-top violent way.

What is most notable about Kenny's character arc and the death of Chef in the context of this chapter is that both examples operate on multiple levels when it comes to viewer engagement. To be more specific, even as *South Park* increasingly employs narrative strategies that are typical of serial television, the program still relies on figurative animated performances, which as previously discussed, mainly aim to elicit instinctive reactions such as laugher, shock, or disgust in the viewer. At the same time, by employing narrative strategies that are typical of serial narration, *South Park* also encourages more nuanced forms of character engagement. How this works in practice becomes clear when looking in more detail at the portrayal of Chef's death.

Viewed in isolation, Chef's death does not significantly differ from other extreme visual gags that are featured on *South Park*. As Chef makes his way over a suspension bridge, lightning strikes and sets the bridge on fire. Although Chef tries to hold on to the bridge, he eventually catches fire, falls down the bridge, and is impaled by a tree. Immediately after getting impaled, Chef gets attacked by a mountain lion, who tries to rip his arm out. Meanwhile, his body is hit by misfired bullets from members of the Super Adventure Club, who are trying to save him from the wild animal. Finally, the mountain lion is joined by a grizzly bear, and, after fighting each other for a brief moment, the two animals tear Chef into pieces. The mountain lion rips Chef's entire face from his skull, while the grizzly bear bites off random body parts. Pointing out the similarities between Kenny's multiple deaths in the series and Chef's shocking demise, Stan, who has been witnessing the entire scene from the other side of the bridge, exclaims "Oh my God, they killed Chef!"

As with most of *South Park*'s visual gags, the extreme violence that is on display in this scene is softened by the show's simplistic animation style and Chef's figurative performance. The overly cartoonish way in which Chef helplessly waves his arms while his chubby, burning body bounces down the canyon provides a striking contrast to the image of his bloody, half-eaten corpse at the end of the scene. Earlier in this chapter, I have already discussed how *South Park* enables viewers to find pleasure in even its most extreme visual gags by amplifying the figurative elements of its performances. While this is also true for the death of Chef, this event also utilizes the viewer's long-term engagement with the character to add another layer to the audience's engagement.

The comedic tone of *South Park* makes it unlikely that viewers will be as emotionally affected by Chef's death as by the death of a beloved character in a television drama, but it is still likely to carry some emotional weight for long-time viewers of the program. In particular, not only does the revelation that Chef has suddenly turned into a brainwashed pedophile drastically subvert viewer expectations, but his death provides a surprising disruption of *South Park*'s typical lack of narrative consequences. Admittedly, the character arcs of most of the other characters on *South Park* are not as definitive as Chef's, yet many of them still have a rich history that has gradually developed over the course of 20 seasons. Some of these characters (e.g., Kenny) have developed throughout *South Park*'s entire history, across nonserialized seasons, whereas other characters have only recently shown signs of character growth since the show has become fully serialized (e.g., Gerald Broflovski). In addition, there are characters that fall somewhere in between, meaning that while they might have shown signs of character growth throughout the course of the series, their development has been accelerated by *South Park*'s embrace of serial storytelling (e.g., Randy and Cartman).

Conclusion

Over the course of this chapter, I have discussed to what degree the interplay between an animated television program's visual style, its performances, and its narrative framework can shape the viewer's engagement with the characters. I have argued that in the context of television narration, figurative and embodied animated performances can lead to unique engagement patterns. Crafton indicates that figurative animated performances are better suited to eliciting a visceral reaction in the viewer (e.g., laughter or disgust), whereas embodied animated performances are better suited to eliciting intricate emotional responses in the viewer (e.g., empathy or sympathy). Yet, my analysis of viewer engagement in *The Legend of Korra* and *South Park* has shown that this argument becomes more complicated if the performances are placed within a television context. The embodied animated performances and the serial storytelling in *Korra* encourage a nuanced emotional response, but the program also frequently features action scenes that emphasize figurative performance elements and thereby invites the audience to marvel at and be exhilarated by the movements of the characters.

In contrast, *South Park* employs figurative animated performances to elicit visceral responses in the viewer but does so within a narrative framework that gradually, over the course of 20 seasons, shifts from episodic to fully serialized. For example, Chef's death is remarkable for the way it combines a figurative animated performance with narrative consequences. It functions as one of *South Park*'s signature visual gags while also encouraging a deeper emotional response from long-time viewers of the show. Thus, the show uses a mode of performance that is primarily known for its effectiveness in eliciting an instinctive reaction from the audience but filters it through serial narration. By doing so, *South Park* adds a sense of embodiment to an otherwise strictly figurative performance and with that, highlights that figurative and embodied animated performances can lead to unique patterns of viewer engagement when they are placed within the context of television narration.

I want to conclude by stating that I do not consider this chapter to be a comprehensive study of viewer engagement with animated television characters. Rather, I regard it as an initial step in broadening the scope of cognition-based studies on viewer engagement with television characters to include a wider range of genres and engagement patterns. I believe that in order to gain a deeper understanding of the viewer/character relationship in contemporary television, future studies on viewer engagement with television characters should be both medium- and program-specific. This means that they should not only distinguish between viewer engagement with television characters and characters from other forms of storytelling, but they should also pay close attention to the unique narrative characteristics of individual television programs.

References

Bukatman, Scott. 2012. *The Poetics of Slumberland: Animated Spirits and the Animating Spirit*. Berkeley, CA: University of California Press.

Cholodenko, Alan. 2007. "Speculations on the Animatic Automaton." In *The Illusion of Life II: More Essays on Animation*, edited by Alan Cholodenko, 486–530. Sydney: Power Publications.

Crafton, Donald. 2013. *Shadow of a Mouse: Performance, Belief, and World-Making in Animation*. Berkeley, CA: University of California Press.

Harrison, Mark, and Carol A. Stabile, eds. 2003. *Prime Time Animation: Television Animation and American Culture*. New York: Routledge.

Mittell, Jason. 2004. *Genre and Television: From Cop Shows to Cartoons in American Culture*. New York: Routledge.

Mittell, Jason. 2015. *Complex TV: The Poetics of Contemporary Television Storytelling*. New York: New York University Press.

Nannicelli, Ted. 2017. *Appreciating the Art of Television: A Philosophical Perspective*. New York: Routledge.

Patches, Matt. 2012. "'Legend of Korra': The Most Dramatic Show on TV is a Nickelodeon Cartoon." *Hollywood.com*, June 12, 2012. http://www.hollywood.com/tv/legend-of-korra-the-most-dramatic-show-on-tv-is-a-nickelodeon-cartoon-57235927/.

Plantinga, Carl. 2009. *Moving Viewers: American Film and the Spectator's Experience*. Berkeley, CA: University of California Press.

Smith, Murray. 1995. *Engaging Characters: Fiction, Emotion, and the Cinema*. Oxford: Clarendon.

Vaage, Margrethe Bruun. 2016. *The Antihero in American Television*. New York: Routledge.

Wells, Paul. 1998. *Understanding Animation*. London: Routledge, 1998.

5 Seriality and expressiveness in *Mad Men*

Elliott Logan

Mad Men's (AMC, 2007–2015) fifth season finale, "The Phantom," closes on a moment that foregrounds the interruption of an otherwise continuing story and so seems to illustrate and support the narrative-centric accounts of seriality that predominate in television studies. To clarify the source of the sequence's effects and significance, however, we need to think about serial form in television drama beyond the sheerly narrative aspects routinely emphasized by television scholars. This is not to deny the importance of ongoing narrative structure in serial drama, which is indispensable to the designs and effects that are my focus in this chapter.[1] Instead, my aim is to show how meaningful points of continuity across episodes of *Mad Men* are formed not only through cause-and-effect narrative links but also – and more deeply – around the presentation and presence of the performers. In doing so, I hope to illuminate a dimension of artistry in serial drama that stands to be overlooked by views of seriality that are insensitive to human expressiveness onscreen.

The primacy of narrative and the ending of "The Phantom"

In the final scene of "The Phantom," Don Draper (Jon Hamm) sits at the bar of a cocktail lounge, where, keeping to himself, he orders an Old Fashioned and lights a cigarette. Our view of Don is colored by the concerns of the prior scene, in which he visits his wife Megan (Jessica Paré) on the set of the *Beauty and the Beast*–themed television commercial in which she is to star, a commercial being produced for one of Don's clients. Aspiring to become an actress, Megan has moved out of her position as a copywriter working under Don's supervision. That role was granted by Don's elevation of Megan from secretary, and her ensuing pursuit of independent professional success has developed into a source of tension in their marriage. Earlier in the episode, Megan accuses Don of wanting her to fail in order to prove her reliance on his gifts, while Don frames his resistance to her proposal as a mark of support for her independence. "You don't want it this way," he tells her. "You want to be somebody's discovery, not somebody's wife." Despite his protests in that scene, Don eventually grants Megan's wishes, putting her forward for the role, which is in the end given to her. (We might wonder whether, in doing so,

DOI: 10.4324/9781003188643-5

Don quells or capitulates to Megan's fears, both about herself and about him.) Don's gesture is meant to rebuild the couple's bond but may be read as re-affirming their lack of faith in one another. Thus, our doubts about the nature and quality of Don's commitment to Megan are in the air when, sitting at the bar, he is approached by a beautiful young woman, who asks him to light her cigarette. After Don obliges, she poses to him – on behalf of her equally young and glamorous friend, who catches Don's eye from the other end of the bar – a coy question: "Are you alone?" Don turns towards her and us. Jon Hamm's face extends neither special interest nor a sign of refusal. Before we can witness any definitive response, the image cuts to black. Both episode and season abruptly end.

The ending of "The Phantom" thus appears to support a common view of seriality in television fiction as a mode of essentially *narrative* part-whole composition. This view reflects the assumption that serial drama is not distinguished by its stylistic dimensions and their expressive affordances but by the segmentation of the story into sequential installments. Clear examples of this idea can be found in work that approaches television seriality through a particular model of film "poetics," which treats story events (what happens) and their presentation (how they are shown) as separable dimensions of a film's form.[2] Kristin Thompson, for example, aims to identify "storytelling techniques" that may differentiate television fiction from movie fiction, basing her comparison on Bordwell, Staiger, and Thompson's model of "the classical Hollywood cinema" (Thompson 2003, 18) In their description of the model, Bordwell, Staiger, and Thompson distinguish between story ("the events of the narrative in their presumed spatial, temporal, and causal relations") and plot ("the totality of formal and stylistic materials in the film") (1985, 12). The events of the film's story are thus given existence apart from their presentation in the "totality of formal and stylistic materials in the film"; the "totality" of form and style is not so total as to include the structuring of "spatial, temporal, and causal relations" between the events themselves. "In Hollywood cinema," they write,

> a specific sort of narrative causality operates as the dominant [formal system], making temporal and spatial systems vehicles for it. These systems do not always rest quietly under the sway of narrative logic, but in general the causal dominant creates a marked hierarchy of systems in the classical film. (1985, 12)

Note the many evocations of layering, together with the contrasts between passive and active relations ("vehicles for"; "rest quietly under the sway of"). These terms express the view that a film's sequential relating of events is an aspect of form independent of stylistic presentation. Moreover, it is the narrative structure of the classical Hollywood film that is considered to be fundamentally definitive of the form. Thus, in her account of television storytelling, Thompson brings into relief what she considers to be the specificity of television fiction against a model of Hollywood film that emphasizes not only the formal separateness, but also the primacy, of narrative structure treated as simply a series of events. What goes unexplored is the potential for the ongoing form of television drama to afford distinctive possibilities of stylistic expression.

This oversight is not an isolated case but is part of a wider tendency, which can be seen in a number of studies that approach seriality in television drama by drawing on similar sources from film studies. Michael Z. Newman (2006) and Jason Mittell (2006; 2015), for example, each propose a poetics of the period's prime-time serial drama that is informed by the work of Bordwell.[3] For both Newman and Mittell, what distinguishes serial television drama – in terms of both form and viewing experience – is accounted for primarily in regard to narrative structure. Consider how Newman's emphasis on the practice of television writers reduces our interest in a drama's characters to the skeletal framework of screenwriting vocabulary, such as in his discussion of character arcs. "The device that best ensures the [viewer's] commitment to the narrative," he writes, "is the character arc," which is "plot stated in terms of character. An arc is a character's journey from A through B, C, and D to E" (2006, 23). Mittell similarly describes the kind of viewer involvement encouraged by what he calls "narrative complexity" in television fiction. One of the values Mittell finds in narratively complex series is their self-reflexivity, which prompts the viewer to reflect on the work's mediation of the fictional world. The mode of narrative complexity does not provide an "unmediated window" onto that world, he writes, but "demands you pay attention to the window frame, asking you to reflect on how it provides partial access to the diegesis and how the panes of glass distort your vision of the unfolding action" (2006, 38). The metaphor of the window as framing device suggests a formal self-consciousness in the camera's selection and shaping of viewpoint. The examples Mittell provides, however, are based not in choices of style and presentation but in the structuring of events – the parceling-out of story information. He finds value in moments of "*narrative* special effect," which work by "calling attention to the constructed nature of the narration and asking us to marvel at how the *writers* pulled it off" (Mittell 2006, 35; emphasis added). In the work of Thompson, Newman, and Mittell, then, what we respond to in the fictional characters who populate a serial drama is made equivalent to a set of narrative turning-points – not as concrete happenings viewed on the screen but as nodes plotted out along a chart that hangs, in the space of our minds, on the wall of an imagined writers' room.

But like that of a movie, the fiction of a serial drama is *shown*. V.F. Perkins (1993) makes clear the critical implications of this fact about movies. "Since stories do not exist except as they are told," he writes, "and since film worlds can be discussed only as they are seen and shown, to discuss the opportunities available within the discipline of [movie] fiction must involve us in considerations of authorship and viewpoint" (1993, 70). The same extends to television fictions. If we are interested in the opportunities for significance afforded by the serial unfolding of television drama, we must attend to the relation between viewer and fiction made available by the presentation of its world onscreen. That is, how the color and significance of our experience is informed by the design and patterning of what we see and hear.[4]

On first viewing, the ending of "The Phantom" achieves part of its force by sharply reneging on its promise of resolution, leaving a tantalizing proposition to hang in the air around Don. On subsequent viewings, though, we know that the turn of Don's head in response to the woman's question – "Are you alone?" – will yield no definitive answer. We expect nothing more than the starkly imposed cut to black, over which we continue to hear Nancy Sinatra sing her beguiling James Bond theme "You Only Live Twice." If we continue to be magnetized by this moment in which the closing sequence culminates, then what is the source of the pull it exerts? Perhaps, it might be found in the way that although we are no longer surprised by the sudden ending, we remain kept in suspense by the promise of Don's future that is held out.

Our suspension in an interrupted moment is a crucial aspect of the experience this ending affords. But we should be cautious in assuming that it accounts for how the sequence's effects and significance are crafted in relation to the drama's serial form. This is because the sense that a fiction continues beyond the narrative's ending is not the sole preserve of serialized drama. Consider V.F. Perkins's remarks on endings in film from his study of *The Magnificent Ambersons* (Welles 1942). "In plot terms," Perkins writes,

> any point of conclusion is arbitrary, chosen. We may go out on a death or a birth. If we end, as so often, on a prospect of marriage we cannot leave with a guarantee of bliss, but we may be encouraged or forbidden to hope. The world does not end with the story's finish. It has a future and the future cannot be closed. So the key question remains at the completion of a movie story as it was throughout, that of the relation between event and viewpoint.
>
> (Perkins 1999, 71–72)

The world depicted in *The Magnificent Ambersons*, however, was created, recorded, and presented – and continues to be watched – with the knowledge that following the film's final moments, no more will be shown. *Mad Men*, by contrast, was made and is watched in the light of a different belief. The future within the fiction would not only, for a time in the wake of each episode's ending, lie open in the space of our minds – it would then also, episode by episode, come to be realized onscreen, filled in, up to a contingent, unknown point at which the series' world would no longer be further shown.

The ending of "The Phantom" achieves its persistently impressive force, I believe, through the particular way it acknowledges these conditions of serial form. The weight of the fictional world's accrued history – and its fragile, provisional significance – is expressed through the handling of performance. It thus stands to be overlooked if the episode's reflections on seriality are found only in its emphatic highlighting of narrative interruption and its promise of a continuing story. What is of most importance about *Mad Men*'s seriality bears only a weak relation to the "falling domino" logic of cause and effect, "A through B to C," "what happens next?" narrative sequencing. Matthew Weiner's design of the season's closing sequence hardly suggests a deep investment in connecting the parts of his vast fiction by a web of consequentially related events. Instead, the ending of "The Phantom" makes points of connection to earlier episodes and moments of the series through a range of expressive echoes and undercurrents, which sound and course through the views of *Mad Men*'s characters and world that the closing sequence presents.

Expressive echoes and the grip of belief

I want to focus on the way this expressive thread runs through two scenes from the closing sequence: Don's viewing of Megan's screen test, and his visit to her on the set of the *Beauty and the Beast* advertisement. Both are notable for the extent to which they organize moments of temporary, fragile coalescence – and of its undoing – around a set of stakes that rest on the readability of the human body. And each does so in ways that forge deep links with earlier scenes, moments, and images of *Mad Men*, to which the closing sequence of "The Phantom" might otherwise go unrelated.

Earlier parts of the episode have been careful to present Don and Megan's marriage as one that is increasingly beset by a wavering sense of belief in their bond, a rising doubt as to whether they truly possess the better images of one another that they profess to hold. For Don, the success or failure of belief – and of its various cousins, such as faith, trust, intimacy, and openness – is shown to be more than an issue of consciously held position or stated avowal. It is, rather, pictured as something like one's grip – newly vitalized or otherwise, slackened – on the readily assuring container of a certain bodily comportment towards others and the world. Tensions between sustained belief, stalking doubt, and loss of faith thus find a natural home in performance as both a stylistic element and a thematic concern. Performance, in fact, comes to provide a crucial focus for the overall stylistic organization of the two scenes, not merely within each separately but in ways that are linked across them. In the screen test scene, Don watches Megan present herself for audition on film. Then, in his visit to her on the set of the advertisement, he stands in the darkened space offstage and watches Megan take her place under the lights, where she readies herself for filming to begin. The crisis that has arisen within Don and Megan's marriage thus culminates in two scenes that are set up as self-conscious reflections on filmed performance. Moreover, these reflections are put forward in ways that form resonant connections with a range of earlier moments from the series. They include the title sequence, the opening scene of the pilot episode ("Smoke Gets in Your Eyes," 1.1), and the Carousel pitch from the final episode of the first season ("The Wheel," 1.13). Through the expressive presentation and presence of performance, then, an interpretive context is formed beyond the chained links of story causality that are so often a defining focus of serial drama criticism. It is a context that turns out to be crucial to the terms in which the seriality of *Mad Men* asks to be understood.

In the latter of Don and Megan's two searing arguments about her acting career in "The Phantom," Megan wonders aloud if her failure to gain any notice as an actress is because she is "terrible" and that Don's refusal to put her forward for the audition is in recognition of this. "But then," she says to him, somewhat rescuing herself from pity by gaining the acid strength of accusation, "how would you even know?" We can imagine that it was with Megan's words ringing in the space of his conscience that Don, alone after hours in the darkened office conference room, wound the flimsy thread of Megan's screen test through the wheels of the projector. But it is nevertheless difficult to say what exactly Don is looking for, or hoping to find, in the images that shine up on the screen before him. Whatever he sees there, it is linked with his eventual decision to acquiesce to Megan's wishes and put her forward for the role – only 30 seconds of narrative time separate Don's viewing of the screen test from his visit to Megan on the set of the advertisement. Whatever ground we have on which to make sense of Don's choice, it seems to take its elusive shape across the moments in which Don – watching Megan prepare for and move into her performance for the camera – briefly gains hold of something renewing in his relation to Megan, but then finds it mysteriously slipped from his grasp and replaced with a different kind of realization.

As the screen test reel runs noisily through the projector, we watch Don witness and respond to Megan while she undergoes a transformation before the camera and on the screen. When the projected image zooms in on Megan, isolating her in close-up, she smiles broadly at a person off-camera but then also seeks to hide her face in a modest display. The flash of Megan's smile and eyes projects an inviting guardedness, as if to freely welcome the attention her beauty earns, while keeping to a shy unavailability. We cut to Don, whose expression gently betrays a quiet smile of private recognition. The screen test image cuts jaggedly to a closer view of Megan in profile. We see her try to foster, through the bodily projection of acting, the belief that she inhabits a fictional world onscreen, an imagined reality existing in the off-camera space into which she gazes. Lowering her face and allowing it to be covered by her hair, as if to avoid the scrutiny of an unseen beholder, Megan works with the off-camera space to self-consciously construct a sense of inner privacy that had no great force only moments ago. She now tucks her hair behind her ear, to reveal her face, and looks up towards the imagined person offscreen to whose stare she is subject, acknowledging the pressure of their eyes upon her, but refusing to yield. As if in response to those eyes, Megan allows the beginning of a smile to play briefly across her face. But something is reserved; her mouth is pursed. The smile's withdrawal leaves just the shadow of a pout, the glimpse of a hardened look. Until now, the faint musical score that accompanies Don's watching has imparted, in its delicate piano keys, a sense of mysterious curiosity, its gradually rising chords welcoming and bringing home the pleasant familiarity expressed in Don's smile. But as Megan moves into her more distant mood, the pitch deepens, and as a sense of gravity quickly settles, the piano falls away, leaving in its wake the long notes of a fragile woodwind. On these plaintive tones, we cut back to Don in time to see his expression fade. What had been his evident pleasure dissolves into a stare of unmoored blankness. He appears to no longer see in the image passing before him what had, only an instant earlier, been such a ready source of affirmed feeling. The emptiness in Don's look is given further expression as the reel of the screen test runs out, and Megan's image vanishes into the burning white blank of the projector's light. This loss of object is tinged with a sense of meaningless chaos, as words scrawled in red ink on the tail of the print flicker indecipherably on the screen before Don. The final shot of the scene is a wide view of Don in profile leaning back in his chair. His cigarette burning down but forgotten, Don stares without fixation at the now-blank screen, in utter stillness. In his stasis, he yields what had earlier seemed strong belief. To my eye, the shot allows us to see Don's change of mind. It is pictured not as his arrival upon a newly clarified position of stated resolve but rather, as a kind of felt inner loss – as the fading, in an instant, of conviction.

The most immediate weight of the screen test scene, as I have described it, is felt in relation to a single storyline of "The Phantom," which in turn draws upon the thread of Don and Megan's marriage that has been gradually developing across *Mad Men*'s fifth season, together with the backdrop of the Jaguar signing and its aftermath. But in the views of Don that the scene presents, we are meant to also feel a weight – emergent in relationships between the performer and the camera – that has a different, more narratively distant source. By the time the scene begins, Don is already reclined in his seat, left arm outstretched beside him to hold his lit cigarette over the conference table ashtray. Matthew Weiner, the episode's director, does not then grant us Don's perspective by cutting to a view fully encompassed by the projector's screen. We are instead placed some way behind Don, watching as if from the back of the room. From this position, Don's posture is outlined for us against the backlight cast by the projector and reflected off its screen. The light traces Don in part as a shadow figure, his head tilted back in distanced consideration of the images before him and his arm casually resting open to one side, holding his own projection of easy but alert remove. Soon after, we cut to a closer shot, so that we are sitting just behind Don, his silhouette now reduced to a head and shoulder, made prominent in the right-hand side of the frame.

We might register in these shots a certain degree of care being taken to craft what are, by the end of *Mad Men*'s fifth season, familiar visual compositions. In his account of *Mad Men*'s opening title sequence, George Toles describes the way in which the silhouette stand-in for Don, despite tumbling in free-fall through the air,

> magically averts what seemed to be certain disaster. Don's silhouette reorganizes itself; he takes his final form with his back to us, resting on an office couch – arm outstretched on the rear cushion to perform relaxation

for whoever encounters him. He is the embodiment of focused composure: alert, ready to do business, ready to confront and prevail over muddle.

(2013, 148–149)

In *Mad Men*'s first episode ("Smoke Gets in Your Eyes"), this picture of "focused composure" is evoked again after the title sequence. At the end of the opening tracking shot through a cocktail bar, the camera settles in behind Don, who is seated with his face turned away from the viewer. We are shown the back of his head and of one shoulder, occupying the left-hand side of the frame. Don's face withheld from our view, his presence is here imbued with a sense of self-contained privacy. And so, in its views of Don, the screen test scene deliberately echoes the iconographic images by which the character was first introduced. It evokes not only the outline of Don presented at the close of *Mad Men*'s title sequence but also its echo in the opening shot of the pilot episode, in which we see Don for the first time, not as a graphic abstraction but rather, as flesh and blood, given human incarnation by the actor Jon Hamm.

These compositional echoes might be understood as sheer self-reflexive play with form, meant to consciously foreground the deliberately structured presentation of the fiction. Maybe they are intended to afford no more than the simple enjoyment of noticing. Yet, the resemblances of framing that I have pointed to are only part of a deeper, more thoroughgoing, and resonant set of connections between the ending of "The Phantom" and earlier scenes, moments, and images of *Mad Men*. More than incidental decorative touches, such echoes – which centrally issue from the presentation of the performers, from their expressive presence onscreen – form an altogether crucial focus for the design of the episode's closing sequence.

The point of framing Don in silhouette is not just to remind us of the character's iconographic pose from the title sequence and pilot episode. It also prepares us to register a more fundamental relationship between the opening of the series and the much later scene of Don watching Megan's screen test. *Mad Men* opens in a lively cocktail lounge where Don sits alone. Our initial view of him as self-contained in private composure is undercut by our first sight of his face, which reveals him to be mired in a state of anxious frustration as he scribbles down and crosses out words on a cocktail napkin. And we soon discover the object of his worry when he engages in conversation with the busboy, an older, Black gentleman, whose name, we soon learn, is Sam (Henry Afro-Bradley). Having asked Sam for a light, Don notices that he holds in his hand a particular brand of cigarette. "Old Gold man, huh?" asks Don. "Lucky Strike, here." Don then probes for the inner source of this stranger's brand allegiance, seeking some universal resonance that might answer his problem of how to advertise Lucky Strike cigarettes, their allure now clouded under the dark shadow of reports on the health effects of smoking. As Don tests the ground of Sam's commitment to Old Gold, he seizes and writes down a simple statement that Sam offers up – "I love smoking" – as though discovering a thought that he himself might have held all along. With this concentrated expression of belief in hand, Don closes off their conversation with a luminous smile of ease and newly found assurance. We cut to Don's view of the cocktail napkin on which he has written the words that struck him with such clarity. Quickly returned to a shot of Don's face, however, we find his assurance vanished. It seems as though, in the simplest turn of an instant (one masked from us by the cut to the napkin), what had held such promise is found, when externalized as an expression of Don's own hand, to have been nothing but vaporous, illusive – its clearing leaves behind just a face of confusion. Don's eyes flick and his jaw falls in unconscious signals of near-panic as he looks towards the other patrons drinking and smoking happily at the bar. He appears to seek in their faces something that would hold a return to the secure center of understanding that had so brilliantly arrived upon him but then so abruptly slipped away. And at the same time, we might see that in his view of these others, Don experiences a larger extension of the transient and evasive meaningfulness that has greeted him in his relation to the now lifeless words printed shabbily on the paper napkin. In the reverse shots of the bar's other clientele, we share in Don's obscure perspective of these distant strangers, sensing through the weight of the slow-motion image what remains an undefined significance. The opening scene ends on this note of the world's opacity, which has been shown to undo Don from within. Despite lacking any ties that would link them as part of an ongoing cause-and-effect narrative chain, the fifth season screen test scene and the opening of the pilot episode are thus closely related by the purposeful and fine crafting of expressive echoes, which have as their focus Don's embodiment of mysterious fluctuations in self-composure and belief.

Cohesion and collapse

Those echoes – especially of the title sequence – are nowhere felt more powerfully than in Don's visit to the studio set and his subsequent arrival in the cocktail bar of the episode's final moments. As the title sequence begins, the silhouetted figure that stands for Don is pictured as existing in some way apart from the world into which he appears to step. Again, Toles provides an apt description. "All the lavish trappings of [Don's] office domain," he writes, "fail to solidify and contain him. They gently scramble, dissolve, and sink beneath his feet before he begins his plummet" (2013, 148). Don's feet find solidity on an office floor that also holds his firmly placed briefcase. But what at first seems to be a fully dimensional space shifts into a flat surface that holds nothing and against which Don's silhouette is merely placed, or projected, as he falls downward in a different plane of reality.

This tension between the promise of a real, available world that one can inhabit and a fake or imagined, illusory vision that is beyond reach also runs throughout the presentation of Don's studio set visit with Megan. As Don regards a beaming Megan (his client standing more closely by her side), he is once more presented as a profile silhouette, this time cut out against the clear, bright glow of the set against which he stands. Despite the real tactility of the set's surfaces and objects – the lushness of its curtains and carpets, the hard sheen of the furniture and fittings – its every detail is picked out and glows flat under the insistent clarity of the soap operatic key light. It is a cartoon image brought near to life but kept within the artificiality of a sanitized fairy-tale. As Don and Megan stand together at the edge that marks the studio space from the set, a call for the cast and crew to take their positions interrupts the couple's pleasantries with Don's client. Before she takes her place, Megan embraces Don, whose back faces towards us. "You know I love you," she whispers and kisses him on the cheek; we sense that below the frame, she presses her hands into his. Megan then walks past her husband onto the set, as she does so passing between him and the camera; hence, Don has to turn to his right, fully around, in order to watch her go. Walking away from us into her position, Megan spins to her left and stops sharply in order to face out towards the on-set camera that waits ready to film, out there in the same dark space in which Don stands alone. Megan here takes her first real steps into the world of professional acting, steps prefaced by a grasping and insistent declaration of love for Don. Yet, she and Don find themselves, if they are to look towards one another, having to turn in opposite directions.

Don's presence here and Megan's responses to him are offered by both as expressions of closeness and devotion. Yet, more developed stylistic echoes of both the title sequence and the screen test scene suggest, in tension with what Don and Megan tell one another, the nature and depth of their profound separateness. As I have already pointed out, the design and lighting of the set for the *Beauty and the Beast* commercial makes it a world not unlike the office into which "Don" steps in the title sequence, one that presents an illusory surface image of tangible reality but resists any attempt to secure a convincing and sustainable grip. Megan at first stands with Don, also outside the set's theatrical artificiality, in the darkness of the studio surrounds. But in her "Beauty" costume, Megan is made vividly a part of the soon-to-be fictionalized world of the commercial set from which Don is so conspicuously marked apart. And as Megan finds her place on the set, she holds still in a delicate pose while final make-up is applied. No longer moving, she stands fixed in a tableau, appearing like an object of set dressing. So when Don looks at Megan in this moment, as she stands in a rectangle of light and prepares herself for presentation to the waiting camera, there lingers a trace of his watching her screen test; the boundary of light outlining the different spaces that Don and Megan occupy is linked to the barrier of the movie screen onto which she was projected. "Like the surface of a mirror," writes William Rothman, "the movie screen is a border between an image of reality and reality itself; it is also where the two touch" (2014, 121).

Notably, it is the empty space on the side of the studio camera (the camera that creates an "image of reality") into which Don strides as he walks away from Megan, who remains frozen behind him in her sealed box of light. Accompanying Don's walk, as if called up by it, is the opening timpani roll and sharply swelling violins of "You Only Live Twice." The pressured, high-octave anxiety of the opening bars is followed by a graceful, measured fall of the strings, which, as Don moves further and further away from Megan and towards us, echoes the fatal but harmless plummet of the title sequence. With each step – imbued by the fullness of the music – Don seems to gather density of purposeful containment as he lets himself slip from Megan's world and glide into another. As Don walks beyond the view of the camera, we cut to the interior of an oriental-themed cocktail bar, the décor harmonizing with the Japanese touches of the song and of the film from which it comes. As though without breaking his stride, Don walks into the room and down the few steps that lead from the foyer to his seat at the bar where the episode will end. Just as Don deftly takes the stair, the music slides, in perfect concert with the fall of his foot, into a new, changed movement, featuring the cheery pluck of simplified strings, freed from the bombastic drama of the preceding orchestral arrangement. There is a sense of landing on one's feet, of shaking off, as though it never happened, the fall from which one has recovered. While this sense is felt in part through the music's orchestration with Hamm's bodily command, it is also aligned, through Don's unbroken stride from the studio into the bar, with the power of filmic ellipsis, by which Don appears to seamlessly, magically leave behind one world, or state of being, for another.

In the screen test scene, Don's very view of his relation to others – and through them, to himself – is linked to the barrier of the movie screen as described by Rothman. This is in the way that his vision is associated with the light by which Megan's image is projected onto the screen before him. In an early wide shot showing him reclined in profile, Don, not yet captured by what he sees, drags deeply on his cigarette. He then blows with satisfying smoothness a cloud of smoke, which catches and spills like a slick across the arc of light shining from the projector. Don's placement in the frame is such that the smoke, as it glides away from him, reveals the projector's beam to issue as though from Don's own eyes, the machine's glare and his gaze coming together as one. It is this moment, more than any other, that draws the screen test scene into its close relation with the scene of Don's Carousel pitch from the final episode of season one ("The Wheel"). As Don delivers his pitch to the Kodak executives, the beam of the slide projector's lamp (at once tangible and spectral in the clouds of cigarette smoke) delivers up to Don a series of images in which are pictured past episodes and moments of his life spent with Betty and their young children.

The relationship crafted between these two scenes highlights the need to explore seriality in television drama through criticism that is responsive to more than narrative designs alone. As I have shown, the closing sequence of "The Phantom" is carefully handled to place its views of Don and Megan in relation to earlier parts of *Mad Men* that have no narrative importance to the later scenes, but which form an ambient echo that colors our experience and informs the sense we make of it. A satisfying account of the drama's serial form, then, would need to measure the significance and value to be found in these choices. The terms of that account would likely have little to do with matters of narrative causality – they would instead reflect and clarify *Mad Men*'s interest in serial drama as a medium able to study the fate of expressive gestures, and the bonds they form, over time. In the ending of "The Phantom," through its relation to the series' opening scene and the Carousel pitch, what is at stake here is pictured as nothing less than the continued inhabitation and survival of a shared world, or its collapse and abandonment.

Consider how, sealed in their visual recording, the permanence of the moments on display in the Carousel pitch is vividly encapsulated; they have passed – as they did then, in an instant – but they are nevertheless forever of Don's life, and seemingly brought back to him now. But as Toles notes in his reading of what Don sees while he shuttles these assembled pieces of his past through the slide projector, the images bring with them, in their renewed presence, a seemingly unbridgeable distance, an impenetrable barrier. "He recognizes himself as *literally* taking part [in the lives of his family]," Toles writes,

> being right in their midst, so in that sense he was *Don*, that unmistakable figure resurrected by the mechanically whirring time machine, *being there*. And yet, as many of us feel revisiting photos commemorating days of imagined felicity, there can be a wall as thick as stone separating us from our face and the role we assumed for the camera, to meet expectations. The aloneness, the apartness are faintly inscribed in the frozen visual record of that outing or ordinary bit of daily doing, like the "pain from an old wound."
>
> (2013, 170)

The sense of aloneness and apartness "inscribed" in the images does not emerge, however, from a straightforward gulf in time. "It is not simply the case of photographs transmitting the ache of distance from experiences that had once been undeniably possessed and *felt*," Toles writes; it is, rather, that "Don confronts his absence and exclusion *then*, in the time of pleasure, as though the images supplied a piercing burden of proof" (2013, 170). Despite their permanence, what is to be understood about the moments from Don's past that are pictured in the photographs, the significance that those moments hold for him, is not settled. What was once a moment of "undeniable possession" is now evidence of "absence and exclusion."

Don's experience there is echoed in a fleeting instant as he watches Megan walk past him to her place on the set of his commercial. Feeling the excitement of her new start, Megan has just pressed her hands into Don's, and having thanked her husband, whispered to him, "You know I love you." Megan then skips past Don, and he turns to watch her go. As he does, Jon Hamm furrows his eyes, re-focusing them, as if disturbed by a troubling but indistinct current of feeling that causes him to look again. In an echo of his watching her screen test, and even more distantly, his own life made part of the Carousel pitch, Don seems to briefly glimpse Megan as a familiar stranger, a view that must involve a sense of his own incomprehensibility. Don might feel, for a moment, adrift not only from Megan but also from the person he himself was, who thought he knew that he loved her. This glancing moment of subdued dislocation quickly fades – Don's expression frees itself, as if shrugging off a light déjà vu haze. And as Nancy Sinatra sings of double lives that go unlived in dreams, Don walks, with the distant air of his usual self-command, into the surrounding void.

Notes

1 Those designs are "significant only within [their] context of narrative and character development" (Perkins 1993, 79).
2 The two key resources here are Bordwell, Staiger, and Thompson (1985) and Chatman (1978).
3 Newman (2006, 26 n. 2) cites Bordwell (1989) and Bordwell (1988). Mittell (2006, 29) cites Bordwell (1985). Mittell's article provides the basis for his book (2015). The earlier publication is my focus here as part of a body of scholarship in the early to mid-2000s that shared a specific set of resources based in particular theories of film narration.
4 For this point in relation to film, see Perkins (1993, 140–141).

References

Bordwell, David. 1985. *Narration in the Fiction Film*. London: Methuen.
Bordwell, David. 1988. *Ozu and the Poetics of Cinema*. Princeton, NJ: Princeton University Press.
Bordwell, David. 1989. *Making Meaning: Inference and Rhetoric in the Interpretation of Cinema*. Harvard Film Studies. Cambridge: Harvard University Press.
Bordwell, David, Janet Staiger, and Kristen Thompson. 1985. *The Classical Hollywood Cinema: Film Style and Mode of Production to 1960*. New York: Columbia University Press.
Chatman, Seymour. 1978. *Story and Discourse: Narrative Structure in Fiction and Film*. Ithaca, NY: Cornell University Press.
Mittell, Jason. 2006. "Narrative Complexity in Contemporary American Television." *The Velvet Light Trap* 56: 29–40.
Mittell, Jason. 2015. *Complex TV: The Poetics of Contemporary Television Storytelling*. New York: NYU Press.
Newman, Michael Z. 2006. "From Beats to Arcs: Towards a Poetics of Television Narration." *The Velvet Light Trap* 58: 16–28.
Perkins, V.F. 1993. *Film as Film: Understanding and Judging Movies*. First Da Capo edition. Da Capo Press.
Perkins, V.F. 1999. *The Magnificent Ambersons*. BFI Film Classics. London: BFI.
Rothman, William. 2014. *Must We Kill the Thing We Love? Emersonian Perfectionism and the Films of Alfred Hitchcock*. Film and Culture. New York: Columbia University Press.
Thompson, Kristen. 2003. *Storytelling in Film and Television*. Cambridge: Harvard University Press.
Toles, George. 2013. "Don Draper and the Promises of Life." In *Television Aesthetics and Style*, edited by Jason Jacobs and Steven Peacock, 147–173. London: Bloomsbury Academic.

Part II

Audiences

6 From shots to storyworlds

The cognitive processes supporting the comprehension of serialized television

Jeffrey E. Saerys-Foy and Joseph P. Magliano

Consider a scene from the first episode of the HBO series *Westworld* (HBO 2016–), a serial television drama about a futuristic country western theme park populated by humanoid robots called hosts. Dolores (Evan Rachel Wood), a beautiful woman in a blue dress, walks up to a horse tied to a hitching post carrying a parcel. As she puts the parcel in a saddlebag, she drops a can, which rolls to the boots of the Man in Black (Ed Harris), who recently killed Teddy (James Marsden), the man she loves, in front of her and dragged her into a barn to have his way with her. He picks up the can and hands it to her. She smiles and accepts it graciously, and they have a brief, pleasant exchange:

Dolores: Mighty kind of you.
The Man in Black: Sweet. Not as sweet as you. I'm afraid I've got other plans tonight.
Dolores: Have a pleasant evening.

Dolores looks puzzled as the Man in Black tips his hat and walks off.

How do viewers understand this scene? How do they connect it to the rest of the episode and the other episodes in the season? There has been considerable research conducted on the cognitive processes that support narrative comprehension in stories, comics, and film (e.g., Graesser et al. 1994; McNamara and Magliano 2009). To our knowledge, none of this research focuses on serialized TV. Still, we contend that much of that research is germane to the study of serialized TV and could be brought to bear to answer these questions.

In this chapter, we draw on research from cognitive psychology to explore how people understand the rich storyworlds that are the hallmark of serialized TV. We begin by discussing how people comprehend narratives across different media by constructing mental models. Next, we provide an overview of cognitive processes that contribute to mental model construction. We then illustrate how these processes play out at multiple levels, from comprehending scenes to seasons, by analyzing the first season of *Westworld*, which has a multilayered plot spanning many locations, timelines, and characters set within a richly developed world that displays the complexity of serialized television (Mittell 2006, 33–38). We will also draw connections between concepts from

DOI: 10.4324/9781003188643-6

cognitive psychology and the literature on serialized television. This analysis will also allow us to expand upon current psychological approaches to comprehension, which have focused on the level of events, to discuss how viewers comprehend the world in which the events occur. We will anchor our analysis in the scene that we used to open this chapter, which we will refer to as *the Can Scene*.

We want to provide a basic summary of some key points of the first season of *Westworld* so that readers have enough background to interpret our analysis. We are going to focus on Dolores, a host who plays the role of country damsel, and her adventure with William. When William arrives at the park with his brother-in-law, he plays the role of the good guy, rescuing women and staying faithful to his wife. Dolores stumbles upon William and his brother-in-law after her parents are killed by criminals, and they travel through the park and fall in love. William becomes convinced that Dolores is different from the other hosts. At the end of the season, Dolores disappears, and William searches for her throughout the park, only to find her back in Sweetwater where they first met with no memory of their adventure, at which point he realizes that she was just going through her programmed routines. Decades later, William revisits the park as a villain, the Man in Black, and he mercilessly tortures and kills the hosts on his mission to unlock the secret of the park. The story is richer than this summary conveys, but we hope this brief description will provide sufficient background knowledge to help readers understand our analysis.

Cognitive processes supporting comprehension

In this section, we discuss the nature of comprehension as conceptualized in discourse psychology. Much of this research has focused on text rather than visual narratives. As such, we discuss the implications of processing across different media.

Mental models

Much of the research on the cognitive processes supporting narrative comprehension has focused on understanding the processes that give rise to a durable memory representation, called *a mental model* (e.g., Zwaan and Radvansky 1998, 162–185), which provides the underlying basis for comprehension in general (McNamara and Magliano 2009). Mental models consist of a network of connected propositions reflecting content that was conveyed and inferences that were generated.

Discourse psychologists distinguish between three potential types of knowledge that could be represented in a mental model. The *surface form* refers to memory for the explicit details of what was presented (van Dijk and Kintsch 1983), which in the context of serialized TV would include the images and sounds. In the Can Scene, for example, the surface form would include the exact words of the conversation (i.e., "Sweet. Not as sweet as you"), the composition of the shots, and the shot sequences. Memory for surface form is short lived (Schmalhofer and Glavanov 1986). The *textbase* refers to memory for the gist of the events that were explicitly conveyed (van Dijk and Kintsch 1983, 11). In the context of the Can Scene, the *textbase* would consist of a summary of the behaviors that were explicitly depicted (e.g., the can dropped and the Man in Black picked it up; Graesser et al. 1999). Memory for the textbase is more durable than for the surface form (Schmalhofer and Glavanov 1986). Finally, mental models contain the *situation model*, which includes inferences that establish how events are related in terms of who is involved, their goals and beliefs, and how the events are connected in space, time, and causality (Zwaan and Radvansky 1998). The situation model is the most durable part of a mental model for a narrative (Schmalhofer and Glavanov 1986).

Scenes can be construed as a series of images and sounds that comprise the surface form, and it is up to the viewer to build a mental model that reflects the events that are conveyed and how they relate to one another (Zwaan and Radvansky 1998). This mental modeling occurs at different levels. Mental models for scenes are hierarchically structured around characters, their goals, actions to achieve those goals, and how these are causally related (Suh and Trabasso 1993; Zwaan and Radvansky 1998). Scenes are also connected together to form mental models of events within and across episodes to form story and character arcs (Newman 2006).

Front-end and back-end processes supporting mental models

Magliano et al. (2013) provided a framework for comprehending visual narratives (both filmed and illustrated) that makes a distinction between front-end processes, which are responsible for information extraction and attentional selection, and back-end processes, which support mental model construction. Front-end processes are different depending on the nature of the information. To process language, one needs to access the appropriate meaning of words, their relationship, and ultimately, the underlying meaning of sentences. In contrast, front-end processes that support the visual content are those that enable one to understand complex scenes (e.g., object recognition, action recognition, and inferring the gist of the scene).

Front-end processes support knowledge activation, which is important for information extraction in the front-end and mental model construction in the back-end. Knowledge activation is a passive, stimulus-driven process (Myers and O'Brien 1998). Content from the shot that is being viewed and heard acts as retrieval cues that activate semantically related knowledge. Related content becomes activated in working memory and can potentially contribute to information extraction. Prior knowledge also supports the construction of the textbase and the inferences that support the situation model. Even the most mundane events could not be understood without the activation of prior knowledge. We can use this knowledge to recognize the actions that are depicted (e.g., William hands the can to Dolores) and generate inferences (e.g., The man picking up the can is the same person who previously attacked Dolores) to explain why those events are happening (e.g., Graesser et al. 1994). Activated knowledge can come from different sources, such as general knowledge of the world, episodic memory (i.e., memory for events) from the show or personal experiences, and genre knowledge.

Whereas front-end processes vary across media, back-end processes are consistent across media (e.g., text and TV) because mental models are the basis for comprehension (McNamara and Magliano 2009). Magliano et al. (2013) specified three types of back-end processes. The first is event segmentation, which involves understanding the boundaries between events (e.g., Kurby and Zacks 2008). Consider the Can Scene: the sequence involves the can falling from the bag and rolling to the Man in Black, who picks it up and hands it back to Dolores. Event segmentation processes enable the viewer to understand the Can Scene as a whole and the boundaries between the smaller actions that comprise it. When processing filmed narratives, event boundaries tend to be perceived as a function of the extent to which the film depicts continuities and shifts in time, space, causality, and the goals of characters (e.g., Magliano et al. 2001; Magliano and Zacks 2011).

A second back-end process is inference generation. There are two classes of inferences that are emphasized by theories of comprehension (McNamara and Magliano 2009). *Bridging* inferences serve to establish how two or more events are connected. They are deemed necessary for establishing a coherent mental model (e.g., Graesser et al. 1994). For example, when viewers see the Man in Black pick up the can, they can infer that he is the same person who attacked and ravished Dolores at the beginning of the episode. *Knowledge-based* inferences involve the use of background knowledge to elaborate upon the narrative content. For example, viewers may predict that William plans to harm Dolores when he shows up in the Can Scene.

The final back-end process is updating, which involves integrating the products of front-end processes and inferences into the mental model for the narrative that is being processed, and in the context of serialized TV shows, the scene within the episode that is being viewed. For example, when viewers learn that the Man in Black is William, they have to update and merge their mental models for these characters to reflect this revelation. These back-end processes are iterative and coordinated (Radvansky 2012). For example, event segmentation informs inference generation, which in turn informs updating.

Front-end processes can affect back-end processes in terms of both how they are accomplished and their quality (Hutson et al. 2018; Magliano et al. 2013). Attentional selection in filmed events appears to be heavily constrained by factors that tend to capture attention (Hutson et al. 2017; Loschky et al. 2018; Smith 2012), such as movement in a shot, and cinematic conventions, such as continuity editing (Smith 2012). For example, viewers will fixate on the can rolling across the ground because of its movement. As a result of these features, viewers tend to look at the same regions of the screen at the same time, even when viewers have dramatically different mental models (Hutson et al. 2018; Loschky et al. 2015).

Storyworld models

Extended narratives like those found in serialized TV present a wealth of information, and viewers cannot remember all of it, let alone access all potentially relevant information for a particular scene (cf. Dixon and Bortolussi 2018). However, people are very good at detecting patterns and extracting rules (e.g., Bower et al. 1979), and this allows them to construct general descriptions of relevant aspects of the storyworld that go beyond specific events. Others have explored the idea of storyworlds (e.g., see Bell and Ryan 2019 for a range of approaches based on Possible World Theory), but this topic has not received much attention within psychological research, which has primarily focused on events. We argue that viewers construct a mental model, which we will refer to as a *storyworld model,* that contains general information about the world (cf. Foy and Gerrig 2014). Here, we will discuss three elements that we believe would be part of a storyworld model – rules, embedded worlds, and characters – and how these elements play a role in comprehension.

Rules. Though fictional worlds are not bound by the rules of the real world, they are generally bound by world-specific rules. Psychological studies suggest that viewers may mentally represent the rules of storyworlds (Filik 2008; Foy and Gerrig 2014; Nieuwland and van Berkum 2006). Foy and Gerrig (2014) showed that viewers generalized characteristics (e.g., the ability to fly) from individuals (e.g., Superman) to other characters of the same type (e.g., an unfamiliar alien from Krypton), suggesting that they attached these characteristics to groups rather than individuals. Nieuwland and van Berkum (2006) showed that people adjust to the constraints of a narrative as it unfolds.

Viewers construct the rules of a storyworld through a number of sources. Because viewers know that *Westworld* is set in a Wild West–themed park, they have prior knowledge that allows them to expect cowboys with six-shooters, bank robberies, and other genre hallmarks. Many rules in the storyworld are culled together from different sources within the narrative, some explicit and some implicit. For example, viewers learn that hosts follow the commands of programmers by seeing it happen, such as in Episode 1, when Dr. Ford (Anthony Hopkins) tells a host to put himself away, and the host promptly climbs into a body bag. Viewers also hear programmers refer to the fact that hosts are programmed to follow commands. Not only do these rules allow viewers to comprehend new events, but, as we will discuss later, violations of these rules are crucial to the show's plot.

Embedded worlds. *Westworld* contains worlds that are situated within the main narrative, which Chan et al. (2018) called embedded worlds (see also Ryan 1985, 721). These can take many forms, such as a dream sequence, characters telling stories, and interwoven narratives. Sometimes worlds cross over into each other, and sometimes they remain compartmentalized. For example, in *The Princess Bride* (1987), the fantastic adventure story about Westley and Buttercup is described in a book being read to the narrator by his grandfather, and these worlds never cross. Characters may also have different perspectives, such that they seem to inhabit different worlds, which may also be a form of embedding (Ryan 1985, 722–732). The plot of *Westworld* is built on embedded worlds. The hosts view the park as a real Country and Western world, whereas the guests know that it is a theme park. These embedded worlds shape interactions between characters and how viewers respond.

Character models. Research has shown that comprehenders represent multiple types of information about specific characters, such as emotional states (e.g., Gillioz and Gygax 2017), goals (e.g., Zwaan and Radvansky 1998), and traits (Rapp et al. 2001). Smith (1995) argued that viewers understand characters in films using a "person schema," which is a set of assumptions about characters based on viewers' knowledge of real people, such as that they have a physical body, emotions, goals, and other characteristics that are typical of real people. This person schema serves as a foundation on which people can understand characters by updating it to reflect information about the traits of specific characters, such as physical characteristics, social roles, character types, and other information. Like Gerrig (2010), we will explore how memory-based processes allow viewers to construct mental models of characters that are dynamic, reflecting the way that characters change over time, including the processes of categorization and individuation (Schneider 2001). For serialized TV, which provides rich sensory information, some of this representation may include surface-level details (e.g., an image of Dolores' dress), but mental representations of characters in general will also consist of schematic information (Dixon and Bortolussi 2018) with an emphasis on dispositions and motivation (Schneider 2001).

In summary, cognitive psychologists characterize narrative comprehension as involving the construction of mental models that consist of networks of information that convey spatial, temporal, and causal relationships between different narrative elements. The surface form provides the input for constructing a durable representation known as a situation model. Understanding visual narratives involves a coordination of front-end and back-end processes and the construction of storyworld models.

Understanding the Can Scene: From shots to scenes to episodes

In this section, we discuss how the cognitive processes described earlier are involved in (1) connecting shots to understand the events in the Can Scene, (2) relating the Can Scene to preceding events, and (3) understanding the story arc in the first episode.

From shot to scenes

The Can Scene contains 16 shots (which gives a mean of 2.5 seconds per camera shot) and demonstrates a full range of shot scales, with relatively tight shot scales reserved for the exchange between Dolores and William. Shots and shot sequences influence the viewer in at least two ways. First, cinematic features (e.g., shot scale, composition, and editing) direct visual attention to important segments of the screen (Hutson et al. 2017; Loschky et al. 2015; Smith, 2012). Cinematic features can also activate prior knowledge stored in a situation model, which can create endogenous force (i.e., features internal to the viewer) that directs visual attention to important segments of the screen (Loschky et al. 2018).

To illustrate, consider the fact that the Can Scene depicts events that take place in a complex street scene. How do viewers know where to look on the frame, particularly in the long shots that depict a cacophony of events? The second shot of this sequence is a low-angle long shot, with Dolores framed center-screen left and her movements directed at screen left as the shot continues. Viewers should initially fixate on Dolores at the outset, because people initially fixate at the center of the screen when a new shot starts (Loschky et al. 2015; Smith 2012). Additionally, foregrounded movement on a screen attracts attention (Mital et al. 2011), so her movements towards screen left should continue to attract fixations as the shot progresses. Also, Dolores, William, and Teddy have been previously introduced to the viewer in the prior scene; therefore, they should be represented in the mental model as main characters, creating an endogenous force such that viewers are more likely to look at these characters than other characters (Loschky et al. 2018). Thus, a combination of cinematic features and prior knowledge supports front-end processes by directing viewers' attention to important information.

Second, cinematic features may also support the creation of a situation model for the events that are depicted. Filming and editing typically follow conventions (e.g., continuity editing) that are intended to convey temporally, spatially, and causally continuous (or discontinuous) events (Bordwell 1985). In explaining how this is the case, Bordwell (1985) draws upon the classic distinction in literary theory between the *syuzhet* and the *fabula*. The syuzhet corresponds to explicit content in a narrative, which involves the surface form, and the fabula corresponds to the situation model. The cinematic features can be construed as processing instructions for constructing a situation model in the fabula. Specifically, Bordwell (1985) argues that consistent, repeated patterns of the syuzhet in film help give rise to schematic knowledge that informs the viewer how to understand the implied spatial, temporal, and causal relationships that are part of the fabula.

The Can Scene exemplifies Bordwell's argument. The shot sequence that depicts the can falling never actually shows it fall. The first shot is a close-up of Dolores as she looks down and screen right to center, which co-occurs with a sound that matches that of a can falling (which requires prior knowledge to recognize). The next shot is a high-angle medium shot of the can rolling from the bottom of the screen to the top of the screen, where two boots are shown. There is no overlap in the visual images across shots. Instead, viewers connect the shots together based on the conventions of continuity editing (Bordwell

1985). For example, Dolores' head movement and the rolling of the can across the screen in the next shot convey a continuity of motion that helps the viewer connect the two shots in space and time (Bordwell 1985; Bordwell et al. 2017; Smith 2012).

Continuity editing conventions also support the back-end process of segmentation, which is part of the fabula, by providing information about the extent to which actions are continuous or form a new scene (Bordwell 1985; Magliano et al. 2001; Magliano and Zacks 2011). However, other narrative conventions may also support event segmentation. One way that writers structure scenes is by using beats. There are different definitions of beats, but a key feature is that they represent a point of change (Atkins 2019). They can be small, such as a pause that represents a shift in an action (e.g., when the can stops at someone's feet), shifts in the arc within the scene (e.g., when the man picking up the can turns out to be William), and significant shifts in the story (e.g., when William says goodbye to Dolores). Viewers can segment events of the Can Scene at different levels. On a coarse-grained level, it can be viewed as a whole, coherent scene centering around William saying goodbye to Dolores. At a finer grain, it can be viewed as a set of smaller events (e.g., Dolores approaches the horse, Dolores drops the can, etc.). This segmentation will be influenced by aspects of the situation model (i.e., changes in space, character entrances and exits, or changes in characters' actions; Magliano et al. 2001; Magliano and Zacks 2011), and we speculate that beats may also contribute to fine-grained event segmentation.

This scene also shows how cinematic conventions in the syuzhet may support inferences about what characters know, think, and feel (Bálint and Rooney 2019; Clinton et al. 2017). For example, the Can Scene makes use of a point-of-view shot sequence involving Dolores as the can falls. Clinton et al. (2017) showed that the use of point-of-view shots and other perspective-taking conventions increased the strength of perceived character emotions within a scene. Interestingly, when the films were shown without sound, the effect of the use of perspective shots was weaker. As such, the conventions in conjunction with content support inference generation, presumably because the conventions direct attention to content that supports the activation of important knowledge (Magliano et al. 2019). The use of close-up shots (and shot scales that afford seeing the facial expression of the actors) in particular may be important for inferring the mental states of the characters (Bálint and Rooney 2019). In the Can Scene, the perspective shots anchor viewers onto Dolores' perspective by making her facial expressions explicit to the viewer, making salient her appreciation and puzzlement as William walks away. Inferring cognitive and affective states of characters is an important part of comprehension because these states explain behavior (Graesser et al. 1994). Thus, Dolores' reaction, as we will discuss in the next section, reinforces viewers' knowledge about Dolores, allowing them to understand subsequent events.

In sum, cinematic features of scenes provide processing instructions for the construction of situation models. These features can be construed as part of the syuzhet, and they affect processing in two ways. First, they help direct viewers' attention to specific parts of the screen, and second, they support how the events are situationally understood in the fabula.

Connecting scenes into episodes

The Can Scene occurs about 20 minutes into the first episode of the series, so viewers must understand it within the context of what they have already seen. It is at the end of a sequence of events that repeat, with significant variations, a sequence from the beginning of the episode. Viewers are particularly sensitive to discrepancies between events in different versions of a narrative (Magliano et al. 2018), and they are likely sensitive to the differences in scenes that are repeated throughout the show. Shortly before the Can Scene, Dolores leaves a store and walks towards her horse. As she leaves the store, she is spotted through a window by Teddy, who is in a saloon across the street. Both times, Teddy exits the saloon to follow Dolores. The first time viewers see this sequence, Teddy picks up the can instead of William. The second time, visitors stop Teddy as he exits the saloon, preventing him from picking up the can. Surface cues (e.g., movement, Dolores' blue dress) guide viewers' attention towards important information. The overlap between the surface cues and situational features (e.g., the setting, characters, and their actions) across sequences serves as a cue that activates viewers' prior knowledge about the first time they saw Teddy follow Dolores, supporting back-end processes (Myers and O'Brien 1998), and likely supports a range of inferences (Graesser et al. 1994). For example, Teddy is dressed in exactly the same clothes and repeats his behavior down to the words he exchanges with other characters in the saloon. These similarities provide retrieval cues that activate the situation model of the prior scene, which in turn allows viewers to draw a bridging inference that it is the same character in both scenes, connecting these scenes together in the mental model. Viewers can also draw a knowledge-based inference predicting that Dolores will drop the can again.

Part of why this seemingly innocuous interaction (William picks up a can and hands it to Dolores) is engaging is because of how it is situated within the rest of the episode. Viewers watched in horror as William killed Teddy and dragged Dolores into a barn to have his way with her. William's appearance serves as a memory cue that activates viewers' memories for these events. Based on this prior knowledge, it would be reasonable for viewers to expect Dolores to be horrified when she sees William. However, viewers infer that Dolores does not fear the Man in Black because she and the other hosts have been programmed to forget previous experiences, though they may worry about what William will do.

Episodes within serialized television exhibit a structure with a beginning, middle, and ending, but the ending often does not provide complete closure; instead, episodes often end by opening up a conflict that will carry through to subsequent episodes (Newman 2006). We will discuss how back-end processes allow viewers to understand the whole first episode by exploring how they comprehend Dolores' character arc through constructing a storyworld model that includes information about the rules of the world, embedded stories, and characters within the world.

The Can Scene (and its lead-up) is the first time viewers see Dolores and other hosts repeat their behaviors down to the dialogue, word for word, as though they'd never done them before. Viewers have not been informed to expect this, and humans don't typically repeat their behaviors quite so exactly. However, Dolores and Teddy serve as memory cues activating viewers' prior knowledge. Viewers know that they are hosts, so they can infer that the hosts are programmed to repeat their behaviors (referred to as loops). Additionally, earlier in the episode, Teddy shoots William to protect himself and Dolores, but the shots have no effect, and Bernard's (the lead programmer, played by Jeffrey Wright) voice overlays the scene, saying "What if I told you that you can't hurt the newcomers?" These two rules, that hosts repeat their behaviors without remembering them and that they cannot harm guests, are represented as general rules of the world rather than as being part of a specific event, and they help viewers understand subsequent events, such as when the host Walter (Steven Ogg) malfunctions and goes on a shooting spree in which he kills other hosts but doesn't harm any guests. Viewers understand that Walter's programming prevented him from hurting the guests.

According to Porter et al. (2002), continuity across episodes gives viewers the illusion of character, which, along with a continuous story, is another defining feature of serialized TV. We would extend this statement to episodes as well. As the episode continues, viewers continue to build a mental model of Dolores. Through the opening narration, viewers learn that Dolores believes she is a real person living in the Wild West. A half hour into the episode, viewers see Dolores painting wild horses by the river. A young boy – a guest – approaches her and says, "You're one of them, aren't you? You're not real." Dolores looks puzzled and says that she has to go. From this, viewers learn that Dolores is programmed not to recognize signs of the world beyond the park, a trait that she shares with the other hosts. Additionally, viewers learn more about Dolores as an individual, such as that she paints as a hobby. Viewers' character model of Dolores will include both category information (i.e., information about hosts) and individual information (Schneider 2001).

After leaving the riverside, Dolores returns home to find her father (Louis Herthum), Peter Abernathy, sitting outside, holding a polaroid of a young woman in a city in the outside world. He says, "I found this in the field today" and shows it to Dolores, to which she responds, "Doesn't look like anything to me." Viewers know that Dolores and Peter do not see the same thing when they look at the picture. To understand this scene, viewers need to understand their conflicting perspectives. However, viewers cannot represent all the perspectives of characters in a story, because this presents an overload of information (Dixon and Bortolussi 2018). To deal with this overload, Dixon and Bortolussi (2018) argue that viewers construct gist-level representations of characters' perspectives. As discussed earlier, surface features may make characters' perspectives more salient by supporting knowledge activation. According to van Krieken (2018), perceptual verbs (e.g., see, hear) and cognition verbs (e.g., think) cue readers to take the perspective of a character. Here, the dialogue in which Peter and Dolores express what they see, along with a perspective shot and close-ups, supports viewers' understanding of the characters' perspectives. In this scene, viewers see a perspective shot of the polaroid followed by a close-up of Dolores' face as she responds, foregrounding her lack of response to the photo.

Dolores' and Peter's conflicting perspectives on the photo illustrate the role of coherence breaks – inconsistencies – within the story in the plot of *Westworld*. That Dolores can't see the polaroid is consistent with viewers' knowledge, but Peter's ability to see it is inconsistent with Dolores' response and with what viewers know about the hosts. Coherence breaks like this may prompt viewers to generate inferences that make them fit with prior knowledge (Hakala and O'Brien 1995) and call attention to characters' perspectives (Foy et al. 2017). Prior to this scene, viewers learned that the hosts had been updated and one of them, the sheriff, had malfunctioned as a result of the updates. If this prior knowledge is accessible, viewers might infer that Peter is malfunctioning, a conclusion that is bolstered the next morning when Dolores discovers Peter talking strangely before lapsing into what looks like a stroke. During this scene, the similarity in Peter's behavior and the sheriff's behavior serves as a memory cue that connects these scenes together, allowing viewers to integrate information about these changes into their mental models of these characters (Gerrig 2010).

Though Peter is decommissioned as a result of this malfunction, Dolores seems to be functioning as usual. The next day opens with Dolores' voice repeating her monologue from the opening of the episode over the recurring shot of her waking up that also occurred at the beginning of the episode, and she walks out to the porch wearing the same blue dress, holding the same bag of painting supplies. The shots and actions are identical, activating viewers' memory of prior story loops (Gerrig 2010). She repeats her usual conversation ("Good morning, Daddy. Sleep well?") completely oblivious to the fact that Peter has been replaced by a different host sporting a curly black mustache, smoking a cob pipe (Bradford Tatum). Dolores' behavior is perfectly consistent with her character model and the rules of the world, indicating that she is perfectly intact, unaware that anything has changed.

Shortly afterwards, the plot arc of the episode ends when viewers see that all is not normal. The first episode ends with a shot of Dolores killing a fly as she serenely looks out into the prairie, which violates the rule that hosts do no harm (and her claim that she would never hurt a thing). Foy et al. (2018) found that readers adjust their character models to accommodate inconsistencies in characters' behaviors, but the adjustments are specific, leaving other aspects of the character intact. When Dolores kills the fly, viewers likely attribute this to the update that caused other hosts to malfunction. Only some of the hosts are reacting to the update, suggesting that Dolores' ability to harm does not generalize to all hosts. Unlike the other hosts, which seriously malfunctioned and needed to be decommissioned, Dolores seems otherwise normal. Nonetheless, this shot brings Dolores' arc within the episode to a close by indicating that the routine in *Westworld* is going to change; in doing so, it prevents full closure in the story within the episode and opens up the beginning of Dolores' transformation, which over the course of the season, will transform the whole park (Mittell 2006).

As viewers watch the events of the episode unfold, they must piece together the order of events. Prior research has shown that people detect shifts in time (e.g., Zwaan 1996) and construct the order of events in simple stories (Claus and Kelter 2006), but little psychological research has explored how they do so. Viewers infer that William attacked Dolores and Teddy before the Can Scene because it was shown earlier. This illustrates the Strong Iconicity Assumption, which is the assumption that events are presented in the order in which they occurred unless otherwise noted (Zwaan 1996). It would be coherent for viewers to assume that William attacked Dolores after the Can Scene. If she hadn't been attacked yet, it would make sense for her not to recognize William and to be grateful when he hands her the can. Nonetheless, this interpretation likely never occurs to viewers because of the Strong Iconicity Assumption. For the most part, the events of the first episode are coherent in the order in which they unfold, allowing viewers to use the Strong Iconicity Assumption throughout. Subsequent episodes unfold in a nonlinear manner, and we will discuss how viewers construct the timeline across episodes in the next section.

In sum, viewers understand and represent the Can Scene in terms of how it is semantically related to the prior events of the episodes and infer relationships between it and future scenes. The basic processes delineated in the study of narrative comprehension in the psychological sciences may help explain how this scene is understood, as well as scenes in serialized TV in general.

From episode to serialized TV

Television shows can range from being fully episodic, with plots that are entirely wrapped up in each episode, to fully serialized (Mittell 2006). While episodic shows have continuity in characters, viewers may not connect their mental models together across episodes if they lack causal relationships (Kurby et al. 2005). In contrast, because there are causal connections across episodes in serialized television (e.g., unachieved goals), viewers are likely to integrate representations of events to form story arcs that span the series. In this section, we will explore how back-end processes supporting the construction of situation models and storyworld models allow viewers to understand the first season of *Westworld* by focusing on Dolores' and William's development.

Making connections across texts and episodes is challenging because retrieval processes deteriorate over time (Myers and O'Brien 1998), which makes it more difficult to generate bridging and knowledge-based inferences.

Serialized TV uses multiple strategies to support comprehension, such as showing selected clips from previous episodes, which act as memory cues to retrieve prior knowledge, before a new episode begins (Mittell 2010). Before the second episode, viewers see fragments of Dolores' interactions with Teddy, and the clips end with her killing the fly, activating this information in their situation model so that it is available to support inferences.

Additionally, *Westworld* makes extensive use of overlap in surface features, such as consistency in characters' appearance (e.g., attire, hair), repeated shot structures, and the use of familiar settings (e.g., the saloon) across episodes, allowing these to serve as strong retrieval cues. Earlier iterations of these features are important for laying the foundation of a mental model. The first shot of the second episode shows a close-up of Dolores waking up to begin her loop, mirroring a shot that viewers saw twice in the first episode, and this overlap activates viewers' character model for Dolores. There is a subtle difference in this shot, though, which is that it is darker than previous versions. The next shot shows Dolores walking outside in the middle of the night, which is a deviation from her normal loop and therefore, from the rules that constrain her behavior. Later in the episode, viewers see Dolores walking through town. Though the shot structure is different (the camera follows Dolores from the side), viewers likely infer that she is going through the segment of her loop in which she drops the can, because they have seen her repeat this behavior before, and it is likely integrated into their character model for Dolores. Thus, viewers can draw inferences because information about her loop was activated by the shot of her waking up and clips from the Can Scene that preceded the episode. As she walks towards her horse, though, she stops, and the camera shows a close-up of her face as she turns around. Next, viewers see a perspective shot with the street covered in dead bodies, and a few seconds later, everything returns to normal. The differences in the shot structures in which the Can Scene is conveyed over episodes may be important cues to viewers that instances may be different from what has transpired in early episodes or have important significance in the story arc. In this case, the perspective shot allows viewers to understand that Dolores is hallucinating – perhaps remembering the violent bank robbery from the first episode. This event likely requires viewers to update the character model for Dolores, because these deviations from her routine form coherence breaks that allow inferences about her character development (Gerrig 2010). Viewers may infer that she is beginning to remember previous experiences, which violates the rules that hosts are programmed to forget everything outside their previous loop, allowing her character to be further individuated (Schneider 2001).

The second episode ends, significantly, with young William meeting Dolores for the first time when he picks up the can for her, marking the beginning of their storyline. In the third episode, Dolores shoots the outlaws who kill her parents and runs into the prairie, where she encounters William and a posse. Subsequently, William and Dolores go on a journey together. Throughout this journey, Dolores exhibits unusual behaviors in which she violates the rules of the park, allowing viewers to learn more about her (Gerrig 2010). When she and William are threatened by the Confederados in Episode 5, she shoots them, a behavior that is unlike that of the defenseless country damsel who did nothing when William attacked in the first episode. During a train ride, she paints the place on a canvas covering freight (Episode 7). Later, after narrowly escaping death, Dolores and William find a river that looks like her painting (Episode 8), reinforcing her ability to remember prior experiences. These behaviors are coherence breaks, because they differ from what viewers would expect based on their character model of Dolores and the rules of the world. As more of these behaviors occur, though, William and the viewer become convinced that Dolores is unique – that she is different from other hosts – and that she is choosing her own behaviors. Both viewers and William begin to believe that she really loves him and update their character models accordingly.

This belief, though, turns out to be an embedded world within the actual world of the story. Later, Dolores disappears; William finds her when he returns to Sweetwater, where she looks directly at him without remembering him and goes through her routine of dropping the can, which is picked up by another man. Through the use of perspective shots and close-ups, viewers see the scene through William's perspective. He sees that he got lost in Dolores' narrative, convinced that she really loved him when she was just going through her loop. Viewers infer that the loss of this embedded world, the one in which Dolores is special and loves William, plays a role in William's transformation into the villainous Man in Black. It is not coincidental that this realization occurs during a repeat of the Can Scene. The scene itself serves as a memory cue, activating previous times it has occurred (Gerrig 2010), including when young William (in a white hat) and old William (in a black hat) picked up the can. The repetition reinforces the perspective that Dolores has been going through her pre-programmed behaviors the whole time, just like the other hosts.

As this discussion illustrates, one of the central questions that drive the season is the status of the hosts – whether they are human or not – and this question is at the center of Dolores' character arc. It has implications for whether viewers of *Westworld* consider the hosts to be mere objects or characters, which likely affects how viewers affectively react to and engage with the hosts (Smith 1995). Evaluating the hosts as characters is not an absolute or discrete assessment (Smith et al. 1974). The hosts have some features of personhood at the outset that would lead to the activation of person schemas (e.g., emotions), but they have other features that downplay their personhood (e.g., pre-programmed behaviors). They are not conveyed as sentient, but over the course of the first season, viewers gain evidence that Dolores is becoming sentient, and their perceptions of her personhood change throughout the season.

Shows like *Westworld*, which contains frequent flashbacks and interweaves multiple timelines, exemplify the distinction syuzhet and fabula from Russian Formalism (Erlich 1965). The timeline within a fictional story is usually relative, because it is not anchored against externally verifiable events and usually does not contain precise information about time (i.e., hour, day, or month; see

Fludernik 2003). *Westworld* provides a few explicit markers (i.e., that there was a serious incident before the park opened 30 years ago), but mostly, information about time is implicit.

How, then, do viewers construct a timeline of events in the story? When watching the first season for the first time, some viewers believe that many of the events are shown in chronological order, and that young William's and the Man in Black's storylines are happening at the same time. When the viewer is introduced to William in Episode 2, there is no indication that he is a younger version of the Man in Black. Viewers see the Man in Black going through the park trying to find a maze interspersed with William's adventure with Dolores, indicating that they are happening at the same time. Using the Strong Iconicity Assumption, viewers assume that the Man in Black arrives first because he shows up in the first episode, whereas William shows up in the second episode.

The writers go to great lengths to ensure that this timeline is coherent; any violations of this timeline would likely trigger inferential processing, tipping viewers off to the possibility that events are not unfolding in chronological order. For example, during Episode 3, Dolores has flashbacks of encounters with the Man in Black. Later in the episode, she runs into young William. Based on the Strong Iconicity Assumption (i.e., the order of events shown as part of the syuzhet/textbase reflects the order in which they should be represented within the fabula/mental model), the order of the shots suggests that these events are in the same timeline. This timeline is coherent with what viewers have learned so far, illustrating how shot order and coherence can be used to hide plot twists. The show also takes advantage of other cues to obscure the twist. The Man in Black is set up as the villain, walking around in black, ruthlessly torturing and killing hosts. William, on the other hand, is set up as a good guy, rescuing women and acting like a gentleman. Thus, their character models also reinforce the idea that they are different characters. At the end of the season, it is revealed that William and the Man in Black are the same person. Viewers can draw upon information about timeline in their mental models, such as that young William went to the park for the first time 30 years before his return as the Man in Black. They are also likely to connect elements of their mental models of William and the Man in Black together using causal information. Viewers can bridge their character models of William and the Man in Black coherently by inferring that William's disillusionment with Dolores helped transform him into the villainous Man in Black. The show also provides numerous visual cues to help viewers construct timeline, such as changes in location (e.g., whether the church at Escalante is buried or not) and character appearance. For example, viewers can use skin texture and clothing to distinguish between events that are current and those that happened 30 years in the past.

Other viewers foresaw the twist. Timelines are constructed inferentially using sensory input and prior knowledge. People vary in their knowledge of serialized TV conventions, from shot construction to storytelling techniques (e.g., foreshadowing). Experts can use their knowledge to remember information more efficiently and notice patterns (Bedard and Chi 1992), detect subtle changes across scenes (Werner and Thies 2000), and generate inferences (e.g., Graves and Fredericksen 1991). For example, professional TV critic Sepinwall (October 16, 2016), noticed subtle differences across shots, cueing him to infer that William and the Man in Black might be on different timelines. One cue that he noted was that the train station where guests arrive looked different when William and Teddy arrived during the first episode (in the Man in Black's timeline). The surface overlap would have activated his memory for prior scenes in the train station, and the discrepancy formed a coherence break, leading to an inference about timelines. Later, after Episode 5, Sepinwall (October 30, 2016) connects a scene where William learns about the park's financial difficulties with a later scene where the Man in Black asserts that he saved the park from financial ruin. Thus, he formed a bridging inference that William is the Man in Black, which reinforced the separate timelines.

Many other viewers caught the twist as well. Avid serialized TV viewers are likely familiar with the storytelling conventions used to construct and conceal plot twists. Since *Westworld* is streaming, viewers may watch an episode multiple times, allowing them to build up their knowledge to make new connections and detect patterns. Additionally, people may engage in online discussions of TV shows, allowing them to share insights and develop and test new theories.

As this section illustrates, the same front-end and back-end processes that allow viewers to understand shots and episodes also allow them to understand story arcs across episodes. TV shows provide a range of cues to activate relevant prior knowledge (e.g., repeating shot structures, characters' appearances), allowing viewers to draw inferences that allow the construction of situation models for the events that are portrayed. These same processes allow viewers to construct storyworld models representing elements that occur across events, such as gist-level information about characters and the rules of the world, facilitating comprehension across episodes.

Conclusion

In this chapter, we discussed how viewers understand serialized TV by constructing mental representations of the events in the narrative by making connections across shots, scenes, and episodes. We discussed front-end and back-end processes that support the ability to understand events from the level of the shots to the series. Front-end processes involve factors that direct attention and enable viewers to process the features of shots. Through the back-end processes, viewers access information in memory, allowing them to use prior knowledge to draw inferences to fill in gaps and enrich their mental model. Serialized TV, which features complex story arcs that unfold over several episodes, poses unique questions that have yet to be explored within the field of comprehension. We speculated that viewers use a combination of surface cues and causal knowledge to infer the chronology of events. We have argued that viewers construct general descriptions of rules and characters within the narrative world that extend beyond specific situations, allowing them to construct gist-level mental representations that describe the storyworld and understand the rich narratives that characterize serialized TV.

References

Atkins, David. 2019. Phone call with first author, April 4, 2019.

Bálint, Katalin E., and Brendan Rooney. 2019. "Narrative Sequence Position of Close-Ups Influences Cognitive and Affective Processing and Facilitates Theory of Mind." *Art and Perception* 7, no. 1: 27–51. doi:10.1163/22134913-20191095.

Bedard, Jean, and Michelene TH Chi. 1992. "Expertise." *Current Directions in Psychological Science* 1, no. 4: 135–139.

Bell, Alice, and Marie-Laure Ryan. 2019. *Possible Worlds Theory and Contemporary Narratology.* London; Lincoln: University of Nebraska Press.

Bordwell, David. 1985. *Narration in the Fiction Film.* Madison, WI: University of Wisconsin Press.

Bordwell, David, et al. 2017. *Film Art: An Introduction.* New York: McGraw-Hill Education.

Bower, Gordon H, et al. 1979. "Scripts in Memory for Text." *Cognitive Psychology* 11, no. 2: 177–220. doi:10.1016/0010-0285(79)90009-4.

Chan, Greta C., Jeffrey E. Foy, and Joseph P. Magliano. 2018. "Factors That Affect Crossover between Multiple Worlds within a Narrative." *Discourse Processes* 55, no. 8: 666–685.

Claus, Berry, and Stephanie Kelter. 2006. "Comprehending Narratives Containing Flashbacks: Evidence for Temporally Organized Representations." *Journal of Experimental Psychology: Learning, Memory, and Cognition* 32, no. 5: 1031–1044.

Clinton, James A., et al. 2017. "The Role of Cinematic Techniques in Understanding Character Affect." *Scientific Study of Literature* 7, no. 2: 177–202. doi:10.1075/ssol.16019.cli.

Dixon, Peter, and Marisa Bortolussi. 2018. "Readers' Processing of Perceptual Perspective and Stance." *Discourse Processes* 56, no. 7: 1–17.

Erlich, Victor. 1965. *Russian Formalism: History Doctrine*, 4th ed. Vol. 4. Berlin: Mouton De Gruyter.

Filik, Ruth. 2008. "Contextual Override of Pragmatic Anomalies: Evidence from Eye Movements." *Cognition* 106, no. 2: 1038–1046.

Fludernik, Monika. 2003. "Chronology, Time, Tense and Experientiality in Narrative." *Language and Literature* 12, no. 2: 117–134.

Foy, Jeffrey E., and Paul C. LoCasto. 2018. "Minimal Departure, Maximal Departure, and the Cognitive Mechanisms Underpinning the Mental Representation of Fiction". Presented at the International Conference for Narrative.

Foy, Jeffrey E., and Richard J. Gerrig. 2014. "Flying to Neverland: How Readers Tacitly Judge Norms during Comprehension." *Memory & Cognition* 42, no. 8: 1250–1259.

Foy, Jeffrey E., Paul C. LoCasto, Stephen W. Briner, and Samantha Dyar. 2017. "Would a Madman Have Been So Wise as This?" The Effects of Source Credibility and Message Credibility on Validation." *Memory & Cognition* 45, no. 2: 281–295.

Gerrig, Richard J. 2010. "A Moment-by-moment Perspective on Readers' Experiences of Characters." In *Characters in Fictional Worlds: Understanding Imaginary Beings in Literature,*

Film, and Other Media, edited by Jens Eder, Jannidis Fotis, and Ralf Schneider, 357–376. Berlin: de Gruyter.

Gillioz, Christelle, and Pascal M. Gygax. 2017. "Specificity of Emotion Inferences as a Function of Emotional Contextual Support." *Discourse Processes* 54, no. 1: 1–18.

Graesser, Arthur C., Cheryl Bowers, Brent Olde, and Victoria Pomeroy. 1999. "Who Said What? Source Memory for Narrator and Character Agents in Literary Short Stories." *Journal of Educational Psychology* 91, no. 2: 284–300.

Graesser, Arthur C., Murray Singer, and Tom Trabasso. 1994. "Constructing Inferences during Narrative Text Comprehension." *Psychological Review* 101, no. 3: 371–395.

Graves, Barbara, and Carl H. Frederiksen. 1991. "Literary Expertise in the Description of a Fictional Narrative." Poetics 20, no. 1: 1–26.

Hakala, Christopher M., and Edward J. O'Brien. 1995. "Strategies for Resolving Coherence Breaks in Reading." *Discourse Processes* 20, no. 2: 167–185.

Hutson, John P., Joseph P. Magliano, and Lester C. Loschky. 2018. "Understanding Moment-to-Moment Processing of Visual Narratives." *Cognitive Science* 42, no. 8: 2999–3033.

Hutson, John P., Tim J. Smith, Joseph P. Magliano, and Lester C. Loschky. 2017. "What is The Role of the Film Viewer? The Effects of Narrative Comprehension and Viewing Task on Gaze Control in Film." *Cognitive Research: Principles and Implications* 2, no. 1: 46.

Kurby, Christopher A., M. À. Britt, and Joseph P. Magliano. 2005. "The Role of Top-down and Bottom-up Processes in between-text Integration." *Reading Psychology* 26, no. 4–5: 335–362.

Kurby, Christopher A., and Jeffrey M. Zacks. 2008. "Segmentation in the Perception and Memory of Events." *Trends in Cognitive Sciences* 12, no. 2: 72–79.

Loschky, Lester C., John P. Hutson, Maverick E. Smith, Tim J. Smith, and Joseph P. Magliano. 2018. "Viewing Static Visual Narratives Through the Lens of the Scene Perception and Event Comprehension Theory (SPECT)." In *Empirical* Comics Res*earch: Digital, M*u*ltimodal, and* Cognitive Metho*ds*, edited by Alexander Dunst, Jochen Laubrock, Janina Wildfeuer, 217–238. New York: Routledge.

Loschky, Lester C., Adam M. Larson, Joseph P. Magliano, and Tim J. Smith. 2015. "What Would Jaws Do? The Tyranny of Film and the Relationship between Gaze and Higher-level Narrative Film Comprehension." *PloS One* 10, no. 11: e0142474.

Magliano, J. P., K. Higgs, and J. Clinton. 2019. "Sources of Complexity in Comprehension Across Modalities of Narrative Experience." In *Cognition and Narrative Complexity*, edited by M. Grishokova and M. Poulaki, P., 149–173. Lincoln, NE: University of Nebraska Press.

Magliano, Joseph P., James A. Clinton, Edward J. O'Brien, and David Neil Rapp. 2018. "Detecting Differences between Adapted Narratives: Implication of Order of Modality on Exposure." In *Empirical Approaches to Comics Research: Digital, Multimodal, and Cognitive Methods*, edited by Alexander Dunst, Jochen Laubrock, Janina Wildfeuer, 284–304. New York: Routledge.

Magliano, Joseph P., Lester C. Loschky, James A. Clinton, and Adam M. Larson. 2013. "Is Reading the Same as Viewing?" In *Unraveling the Behavioral, Neurobiological and Genetic Components of Reading Comprehension*, edited by B. Miller, L.C. and P. McCardle, 78–90. Baltimore: Paul Brooks Publishing.

Magliano, Joseph P., Jason Miller, and Rolf A. Zwaan. 2001. "Indexing Space and Time in Film Understanding." *Applied Cognitive Psychology: The Official Journal of the Society for Applied Research in Memory and Cognition* 15, no. 5: 533–545.

Magliano, Joseph P., and Jeffrey M. Zacks. 2011. "The Impact of Continuity Editing in Narrative Film on Event Segmentation." *Cognitive Science* 35, no. 8: 1489–517.

McNamara, Danielle S., and Joe Magliano. 2009. "Toward a Comprehensive Model of Comprehension." *Psychology of Learning and Motivation* 51: 297–384.

Mital, Parag K., Tim J. Smith, Robin L. Hill, and John M. Henderson. 2011. "Clustering of Gaze during Dynamic Scene Viewing is Predicted by Motion." *Cognitive Computation* 3, no. 1: 5–24.

Mittell, Jason. 2006. "Narrative Complexity in Contemporary American Television." *The Velvet Light Trap* 58, no. 1: 29–40.

Mittell, Jason. 2010. "Previously on: Prime Time Serials and the Mechanics of Memory." In *Intermediality and Storytelling*, edited by Marina Grishakova and Marie-Laure Ryan, 78–98. Berlin, New York: De Gruyter.

Myers, Jerome L., and Edward J. O'Brien. 1998. Accessing the Discourse Representation during Reading. *Discourse Processes* 26, no. 2–3: 131–157.

Newman, Michael Z. 2006. "From Beats to Arcs: Toward a Poetics of Television Narrative." *The Velvet Light Trap* 58, no. 1: 16–28.

Nieuwland, Mante S., and Jos J. A. Van Berkum. 2006. "When Peanuts Fall in Love: N400 Evidence for the Power of Discourse." *Journal of Cognitive Neuroscience* 18, no. 7: 1098–1111.

Porter, Michael J., Deborah L. Larson, Allison Harthcock, and Kelly Berg Nellis. 2002. "Re (de) Fining Narrative Events Examining Television Narrative Structure." *Journal of Popular Film and Television* 30, no. 1: 23–30.

Radvansky, Gabriel A. 2012. "Across the Event Horizon." *Current Directions in Psychological Science* 21, no. 4: 269–272.

Rapp, David N., Richard J. Gerrig, and Deborah A. Prentice. 2001. "Readers' Trait-based Models of Characters in Narrative Comprehension." *Journal of Memory and Language* 45, no. 4: 737–750.

Ryan, Marie-Laure. 1985. "The Modal Structure of Narrative Universes." *Poetics Today* 6, no. 4: 717–755.

Schmalhofer, Franz, and Doris Glavanov. 1986. "Three Components of Understanding a Programmer's Manual: Verbatim, Propositional, and Situational Representations." *Journal of Memory and Language* 25, no. 3 (06): 279–294.

Schneider, Ralf. 2001. "Toward a Cognitive Theory of Literary Character: The Dynamics of Mental-Model Construction." *Style* 35, no. 4: 607–639.

Sepinwall, Alan. 2016. "Review: In 'The Stray,' 'Westworld' Asks How Much the Robots Really Remember." *Uproxx*. October 16, 2016. https://uproxx.com/sepinwall/review-in-the-stray-westworld-asks-how-much-the-robots-really-remember-2/

Sepinwall, Alan. 2016. "Review: How 'Westworld' May Be Acting Too Clever for Its Own Good." October 30, 2016. *Uproxx*. https://uproxx.com/sepinwall/review-how-westworld-may-be-acting-too-clever-for-its-own-good/

Smith, Edward E., Edward J. Shoben, and Lance J. Rips. 1974. "Structure and Process in Semantic Memory: A Featural Model for Semantic Decisions." *Psychological Review* 81, no. 3: 214.

Smith, Murray. 1995. *Engaging Characters: Fiction, Emotion, and the Cinema*. Oxford: Clarendon Press.

Smith, Tim J. 2012. "The Attentional Theory of Cinematic Continuity." *Projections: The Journal for Movies and Mind* 6, no. 1: 1–27.

Suh, Soyoung, and Tom Trabasso. 1993. "Inferences during Reading: Converging Evidence from Discourse Analysis, Talk-Aloud Protocols, and Recognition Priming." *Journal of Memory and Language* 32, no. 3 (06): 279–300.

van Dijk, Teun A., and Walter Kintsch. 1983. *Strategies of Discourse Comprehension*. San Diego, CA: Academic Press.

van Krieken, Kobie. 2018. "Ambiguous Perspective in Narrative Discourse: Effects of Viewpoint Markers and Verb Tense on Readers' Interpretation of Represented Perceptions." *Discourse Processes* 55, no. 8 (Nov): 771–786.

Werner, Steffen, and Bjorn Thies. 2000. "Is" Change Blindness" Attenuated by Domain-specific Expertise? An Expert-novices Comparison of Change Detection in Football Images." *Visual Cognition* 7, no. 1–3: 163–173.

Zwaan, Rolf A. 1996. "Processing Narrative Time Shifts." *Journal of Experimental Psychology: Learning, Memory, and Cognition* 22, no. 5: 1196–207.

Zwaan, Rolf A., and Gabriel A. Radvansky. 1998. "Situation Models in Language Comprehension and Memory." *Psychological Bulletin* 123, no. 2: 162–185.

7 Beliefs, desires, and emotions

A theory of emotions and some implications for the understanding of viewer reactions to TV serials

Rainer Reisenzein

As Nannicelli and Taberham (2014, 5) have pointed out, the investigation of emotions in film viewing has in recent years become "one of cognitive film theory's most central and lively research projects" (see also M. Smith 2017). Indeed, there are good reasons why emotions should be considered by film theorists (by which I mean to include theorists of TV series) (Reisenzein 2018). The most basic reason is, simply, that emotions play an important role in human psychology and that understanding humans therefore means, in an important part, to understand their emotions. This also applies to films: Although typically fictional, the events depicted in films often elicit emotions (if perhaps emotions of a special kind) in the viewers; indeed, many scenes are created with the explicit purpose of inducing particular emotions, such as fear or surprise. Explaining how viewers react to films – one of the central goals of cognitive film theory (e.g., Plantinga 2002) – therefore comprises explaining their emotional reactions to films.

To achieve this goal, one needs a theory of emotions, that is, a theory that describes in general terms how different emotions are caused and what effects they have. More precisely, to explain viewers' emotional reactions to a particular film scene or a particular kind of aesthetic device (e.g., the plot twist; Pérez and Reisenzein 2020), one needs to know (1) how different emotions generally arise in humans in response to eliciting events and (2) what the specific elicitors were in the given case (the specific scene) or class of cases (e.g., plot twists). Answering the second question requires an analysis of the content of the specific film scene, or class of film scenes, as well as of the cultural context in which the films are made and viewed. These are tasks for film scholars and students of culture. In contrast, answering the first question is a task for psychology or more generally, cognitive science (which includes the theoretical branch of cognitive media studies).

In this chapter, I try to give an answer (or better, *another* answer) to the first question by summarizing a theory of emotions – a computational interpretation of the belief-desire theory of emotion – proposed in previous writings (e.g., Reisenzein 2001; 2009a; 2009b). The potential usefulness of this theory as a framework for studying emotional reactions to TV series is then briefly illustrated by a theory-guided analysis of the emotional reactions of viewers to

DOI: 10.4324/9781003188643-7

the death of Jon Snow, one of the main protagonists of the TV serial *Game of Thrones* (see also Pérez and Reisenzein 2020).

A computational belief-desire theory of emotions

The belief-desire theory of emotion

The starting point of the computational emotion model to be described was the cognitive-motivational or belief-desire theory of emotions (BDTE), originally developed by philosophers (e.g., Green 1992). BDTE is a member of the class of cognitive emotion theories that have played a pivotal role in discussions of emotions in psychology and philosophy since the 1960s (see Reisenzein 2017). However, BDTE differs from classical cognitive emotion theory in a number of foundational assumptions, which allow it to escape the central objection that has been raised against the classical theory – that it "overintellectualizes" the emotions.

The most important difference between BDTE and classical cognitive emotion theory concerns the theories' assumptions about the mental preconditions of emotions, the cognitions (and desires) required for having emotions. The classical view on this issue is the *cognitive-evaluative* theory of emotion, called *appraisal theory* in psychology (Arnold 1960; Lazarus 1966; Scherer, 2001; see Ellsworth and Scherer 2003 for a review) and *judgment theory* in philosophy (e.g., Solomon 1976; Nussbaum 2001). Some version of appraisal theory has been used – at least for explaining the elicitation of emotions – in most previous analyses of emotional reactions to films (e.g., Carroll 1990; Grodal 1997; Plantinga and Smith 1999; M. Smith 1995, 2017; G. M. Smith 2003; Tan 1996).[1]

Appraisal theory assumes that to have an emotion about a state of affairs *p*, one must have certain cognitions – paradigmatically, beliefs – about *p*, called appraisals (Arnold 1960; Lazarus 1966). Appraisal beliefs are of two kinds, factual and evaluative (Arnold 1960). To illustrate, Mary is happy that Mr. Schroiber was elected as chancellor if she (firmly) believes that this state of affairs *p* is the case (factual belief) and if she evaluates *p* as good for her (evaluative belief); whereas Mary is unhappy that *p* if she believes *p* and evaluates *p* as bad for her. Each emotion (happiness, unhappiness, hope, fear, etc.) is characterized by a unique set of factual and evaluative beliefs – a unique pattern of appraisals – which are necessary as well as, under normal circumstances, sufficient for the emotion to occur. Arnold (1960) interprets the proposed cognitive preconditions of emotions as their *causes* and accordingly takes the emotion itself to be a separate mental state (specifically, an action tendency to approach or withdraw; see also Frijda 1986; Tan 1996). In contrast, Lazarus (1991) assumes that appraisals are *components* of the emotional state, and Solomon (1976) straightforwardly *identifies* emotions with appraisals.

In contrast to the cognitive-evaluative theory of emotion, BDTE is a *cognitive-motivational* theory (e.g. Green, 1992; Miceli & Castelfranchi, 2015; Reisenzein, 2009a): It assumes that emotions depend not only on beliefs (cognitive or informational states) but also on *desires* (motivational states). For example, according to BDTE, Mary feels happy that Schroiber was elected as chancellor (*p*) if she desires *p* and comes to believe that *p* is the case; she feels unhappy that *p* if she is averse to *p* (i.e., desires *not-p*) and comes to believe *p*. As Arnold (1960) did in the case appraisal theory, I favor a causalist reading of the belief-desire theory of emotion, according to which beliefs and desires are the causes of the emotion, which is a separate mental state (arguments for the causalist position are presented in Reisenzein 2012a). Unlike Arnold, however, I assume that this separate state is not an action tendency but a nonpropositional signal experienced as an emotional feeling (see later for more detail).

Two clarifications may be helpful at this point. First, the proponents of BDTE share the widely held view that beliefs and desires are fundamentally different kinds of mental states that cannot be reduced to one another (e.g., Green 1992). In particular, desires cannot be reduced to evaluative beliefs: To desire that an event should happen is not the same as to believe that it would be good if the event occurred. Second, most psychological appraisal theorists do not deny that desires (which they call *motives*, *concerns*, or [having] *goals*) are also important for emotions. However, they regard desires only as *indirect* causes of emotions: They are the standards (or at least one kind of standards) against which events are compared to determine whether they are good or bad. The effect of desires on emotions is thus indirect, as this effect is mediated by evaluative beliefs. In contrast, BDTE claims that desires and factual beliefs are both *direct* causes of emotion. In the computational model of BDTE described later, this idea is explicated by assuming that hedonic emotions (those characterized by pleasure or displeasure) are the products of an unconscious comparison process in which newly acquired beliefs are compared with desires. In an extension of BDTE proposed in Reisenzein (2009a), a parallel assumption is made for surprise: Surprise is the direct result of an unconscious comparison of newly acquired beliefs with pre-existing beliefs.

BDTE has an important implication: It entails that the cognitions that are at the core of appraisal theory – evaluative beliefs – are in fact *not necessary* for emotions; what *are* necessary are only factual beliefs and desires. Evaluative beliefs can influence emotions only indirectly, by giving rise to desires (e.g., reading a positive book review by a trustworthy reviewer, I start to desire to read the book). Emotions, however, can directly cause evaluative beliefs (e.g., I judge a book as bad because I dislike it).

Why should one prefer BDTE to appraisal theory? One should do so because this allows one to escape, or at least to strongly mitigate, the central criticism that has been raised against the appraisal theory of emotions, that it overintellectualizes the emotions (e.g., Zajonc 1980; Griffith 1997). This critique is based on two main objections to appraisal theory that together seek to repudiate its basic postulate: (1) Appraisals are not necessary for emotions, and (2) appraisals are not sufficient for emotions.

To support the first objection, the critics of appraisal theory have argued, for example, that phobics feel afraid even though they firmly believe that the objects of their fear (e.g., spiders or heights) pose no threat; and that fear and other emotions can be evoked by subliminally presented stimuli, which, it was assumed, prevents their recognition and, as a consequence, an appraisal of their value (e.g., Öhman and Soares 1994). Recent empirical evidence actually justifies doubts about these claims (see Reisenzein 2019). However, other arguments also speak against the assumption that appraisals are necessary for emotions. A particularly strong (in my view) objection is the following (Reisenzein 2009a): Some of the core appraisals postulated by appraisal theorists, such as "*p* is motive-congruent" (offered as the meaning of "*p* is good for me") and "*p* is unexpected," are actually *meta*cognitions, as they are beliefs about the relation of *p* to one's desires and beliefs, respectively; hence, appraisal theory implies that emotions presuppose not just cognitions but also metacognitions. This implication is not only unsupported by introspection; it is also implausible on evolutionary, developmental, and computational grounds (Reisenzein 2009a). We do not need metacognitions to be happy about *p* or surprised about *p*. BDTE avoids these problems, because it assumes that emotions require neither evaluative appraisals nor (other) metacognitions. All that is needed are factual beliefs and desires. BDTE agrees with appraisal theory, however, that *factual beliefs* are needed for emotions. But this assumption should not be given up lightly. For example, as discussed later, it seems necessary to distinguish "serious" emotions from "fantasy feelings" (Meinong, 1910).

The second objection to appraisal theory, that appraisals are not sufficient for emotions, has been less extensively discussed (e.g., Arnold 1960; Green 1992; Solomon 1976). It is, however, no less serious, particularly because everyday examples provide ample support for it. For example, one generally values one's health highly; nevertheless, the thought that one is healthy (factual belief) and that this is a good thing (evaluative belief) usually fails to evoke a feeling of joy. BDTE can explain this phenomenon: Evaluative beliefs are not sufficient for emotions, either alone or together with factual beliefs; a desire needs to be present as well. However, not everything that is positively evaluated is also desired at the same time. In particular, one does not desire states of affairs that one believes to already obtain (as already pointed out by Meinong 1894). This is why the thought that one is healthy, and that this is a good thing, usually fails to evoke joy: The desire to be healthy has long been fulfilled.

Before proceeding, note that the version of BDTE that I endorse does not claim to be able to explain all mental states that may be subsumed under the category "emotion" in common sense. For example, BDTE cannot explain sensory pleasures and displeasures (e.g., the pleasant feeling evoked by the smell of a rose), and it probably cannot account for disgust either (Reisenzein 2009b). This, however, should not be regarded as a weakness but as a strength of the theory, because it points to necessary, theoretically motivated subdivisions of the object domain of emotion theory. However, BDTE seeks to account for all emotions that are directed at propositional objects, that is, actual and possible states of affairs *p*, such as happiness and unhappiness about *p* (see earlier), hoping and fearing *p*, surprise about *p*, etc. These feelings cover the majority of the emotions distinguished in everyday language (Ortony et al. 1988).

According to the proposed causal interpretation of BDTE, all "propositional" emotions are reactions to the actual or potential fulfillment (e.g., joy or hope) or actual or potential frustration (e.g., sorrow or fear) of desires plus, in some cases (e.g., surprise, relief, disappointment), the confirmation or disconfirmation of beliefs (Reisenzein 2009a, 2009b). To support this claim, I invite the readers of this chapter to consider the following belief-desire analyses of emotions and ask themselves whether they find them plausible:

- Mary feels happy that *p* if she desires *p* and believes *p*; she feels unhappy that *p* if she is averse to *p* and believes *p*.
- Mary *hopes* that *p* if she desires *p* but is uncertain about *p* (i.e., her subjective probability that *p* is the case is between 0 and 1); Mary *fears* that *p* if she is averse to *p* (desires *not-p*) and is uncertain about *p*.
- Mary is *surprised* that *p* if she up to now believed *not-p* and now comes to believe *p*.
- Mary is *disappointed* that *not-p* if she desires *p* and up to now believed *p*, but now comes to believe *not-p*; Mary is *relieved* that *not-p* if she is averse to *p* (desires *not-p*) and up to now believed *p*, but now comes to believe not-*p*.

Emotional reactions to the fortunes of others (e.g., joy for another and pity) can be similarly analyzed; specifically, they can be analyzed as forms of happiness or unhappiness about, respectively, a desired or undesired state of affairs that concerns the positive or negative fate of another person (Reisenzein 2015; see also Ortony et al. 1988; Castelfranchi and Miceli 2009). "Moral emotions" (e.g., pride, guilt, and indignation) can be incorporated into BDTE by assuming that the content of the fulfilled or frustrated desire in these cases is the compliance of oneself or another person with a social or moral norm (Reisenzein 2015). This covers the main classes of propositional emotions (see Ortony et al. 1988).

In addition to accounting for the *qualitative distinctions* among emotions (happiness, fear, pity, etc.), BDTE also provides for a parsimonious explanation of the *intensity* of emotions: The intensity of an emotion directed at a state of affairs *p* is a joint function of the strength of the belief that *p* and the strength of the desire for *p* or (for negative emotions) the aversion against *p* (the desire for *not-p*). For example, happiness about *p* is felt if one desires *p* and firmly believes *p*; given that this is the case, the intensity of happiness about *p* is a monotonically increasing function of the strength of the desire for *p*. Analogous quantitative "emotion laws" have been formulated for several other emotions (see Reisenzein 2009a). Experimental evidence supports these emotion laws (e.g., Gratch et al. 2009; Mellers et al. 1997; Junge and Reisenzein 2013).

A computational model for BDTE

Like most emotion theories, the belief-desire theory of emotion is formulated on the "intentional level" (in Dennett's, 1971, sense) of system analysis familiar from common-sense psychology; in fact, BDTE is an explication of a core part of the implicit theory of emotions contained in folk psychology (Heider 1958). In taking BDTE as the starting point for the construction of a computational model of emotion, I accepted this piece of common-sense psychology as basically correct. I thus endorse a *compatibilist view* of the relation between folk and scientific psychology.

Seen from this compatibilist perspective, the aim of modern (i.e., post-behavioristic) cognitive psychology can be described as *supplementing* the analysis of experience and behavior on the intentional level (i.e., using concepts such as *belief, desire, intention, joy, hope*, etc.) with an analysis of these phenomena at the "design level" (Dennett 1971), the level of the causal mechanisms that underlie them. The basic assumption of cognitive psychology in this project is that mental processes are computations with internal representations, analogous to information processing in computers. Accordingly, the goal of cognitive psychology is to "reverse-engineer," or reconstruct, the mental representations and computations that underlie experience and behavior. If the computational theory of the mind is correct,[2] then knowing these mental representations and computations would allow us to understand *in full detail* how experience and behavior are generated, at least in general terms. In any case, the adoption of the "design stance," i.e.. thinking in terms of representations and computations, can be a highly valuable tool for clarifying psychological theories as well as the phenomena these theories are about (Currie 1995; Fodor 1975; 1987; Nicholls and Stich 2003; Weinberg and Meskin 2006). These considerations also apply to emotions. In fact, I believe that some of the basic questions of emotion theory can only be answered if one moves beyond the intentional level of system analysis to the level of the cognitive architecture, i.e., the level of mental representations and the algorithms that process them.

Devising a computational model for the belief-desire theory of emotions requires making assumptions about the representational-computational system that subserves the mental states (beliefs and desires) assumed to generate emotions in BDTE. The cognitive architecture that I have adopted as the basis of the computational model for BDTE (henceforth abbreviated CBDTE) is in one respect entirely "classical": I assume that its core consists of a propositional representation system, a "language of thought" (Fodor 1975; 1987). A specific instantiation of a propositional representation system is the theory of mental schemas (e.g., Rumelhart 1984; Schank 1977) used in a model of surprise that antedated CBDTE (Reisenzein et al. 2012).

The assumption that the representational system underlying beliefs and desires is propositional is emphatically not meant to deny the existence of non-propositional mental codes, such as sensory, imagistic, or motor codes (e.g., Barsalou 1999; Anderson and Lebiere 1998; Power and Dalgleish 2016). The mind certainly has room for more than one representational code. In fact, the assumption of CBDTE that emotions are nonconceptual, sensation-like representations *implies* the existence of at least one nonlinguistic mental code – a sensory code reserved for affect. Still, CBDTE insists that a language of thought is required propositional emotions, i. e. for emotional reactions to believed and imagined states of affairs. There are several reasons for making this assumption (Reisenzein 2009a; Reisenzein and Junge 2012).

First, a language of thought provides for a plausible and transparent computational analysis of beliefs and desires (see later). Second, other proposed representation systems (e.g., image-like representations or sub-symbolic distributed representations of the neural network type) either are unable to represent the (potentially highly complex) propositional contents of beliefs and desires or achieve this only by incorporating crucial features of propositional representation systems and, thus, by becoming languages of thought themselves.[3] Third, as discussed in more detail later, a major class of emotion-evoking stimuli consists of verbal communications; to represent the information conveyed by these communications, the expressive power of the mental code used for this purpose must be no less than that of the natural language in which the verbal messages are formulated. Because the nature of a representational system is ultimately defined by what it can express, this seems to imply that the mental code in question is itself a language. Last but not least, nearly all existing, worked-out computational models of emotion assume a propositional representation system (see Marsella et al. 2010; Reisenzein et al. 2013).

If one combines the assumption that the representational format of the contents of beliefs and desires is propositional with the basic postulate of cognitive science, that mental processes are computations with internal representations, then one immediately obtains Fodor's (1987) thesis that the mental states of *believing* and *desiring* are special modes of processing propositional representations, that is, sentences in the language of thought. To use Fodor's well-known metaphor (see also Nichols and Stich 2003), believing that a state of affairs *p* is the case consists, computationally speaking, of having a token of a sentence *s* that represents *p* in a special memory store (the "belief store"), whereas desiring *p* consists of having a token of a sentence *s* that represents *p* in another memory store (the "desire store"). For example, prior to Schroiber's election, Mary desired victory for Schroiber in the election but believed that he would not win it. On the computational level, this means that prior to Schroiber's election, Mary's desire store contained among others the sentence "Schroiber will win the election," and her belief store contained the sentence "Schroiber will not win the election."

CBDTE also follows Fodor (1975) in assuming that at least the central part of the language of thought is not learned but innate. However, going beyond Fodor, CBDTE assumes that the innate components of the propositional representation system also include a set of "hardwired" procedures for the maintenance of the system, especially for the updating of beliefs and desires on the basis of newly acquired information (beliefs) (Reisenzein 2009a). At the core of these mechanisms are two comparator devices, a *belief-belief comparator* (BBC) and a *belief-desire comparator* (BDC).

The BBC compares newly acquired beliefs with pre-existing beliefs, whereas the BDC compares them with pre-existing desires. Computationally speaking, using again Fodor's "store" metaphor, the BBC and BDC compare the mentalese sentence tokens s_{new} in a further store, reserved for newly acquired beliefs, with the sentences s_{old} currently in the stores for pre-existing beliefs and desires. If either a match (s_{new} is identical to s_{old}) or a mismatch (s_{new} is identical to *not*-s_{old}) is detected, the comparators generate an output that signals the detection of the match or mismatch to the rest of the cognitive system.

CBDTE assumes that the BBC and BDC *operate on a pre-conscious level*, without and even against the person's intentions. The person only becomes aware of their results. Furthermore, the output of the comparator mechanisms is assumed to be *nonpropositional and nonconceptual* – an assumption that is of crucial importance for understanding the nature of emotions. What this means is that the outputs of the comparator mechanisms are not sentences in the language of thought (which express that a belief or desire match or mismatch has occurred); rather, they are signals that vary in kind and intensity but have no internal structure. Hence, they are analogous to sensations, such as sensations of tone or temperature (Wundt 1896). These signals carry information about the degree of (un-)expectedness and (un-)desiredness of the propositional contents of newly acquired beliefs, but they do not represent these contents themselves. In our example, Mary's BBC detects that the sentence s_{new} representing "Schroiber wins the election," contradicts the content s_{old} of a pre-existing belief; and Mary's BDC detects that s_{new} matches the content s_{old} of an existing desire. As a consequence, Mary's BBC outputs the information that a belief-belief mismatch has been detected, meaning that one of Mary's beliefs has been disconfirmed by new information; whereas Mary's BDC outputs information that a belief-desire match has been detected, meaning that one of Mary's desires has been fulfilled.[4]

According to CBDTE, the output signals of the comparator mechanisms cause a set of hardwired effects in the cognitive system that serve to prepare the agent to deal with the detected belief and desire matches and mismatches. First, attention is automatically focused on the content of the newly acquired belief that gave rise to match or mismatch – in Mary's case, Schroiber's unexpected but desired election victory. This is a precondition for the in-depth analysis of the emotion-eliciting events. Second, some minimal, immediate updating of the belief-desire system takes place automatically: Sentences representing the content of disconfirmed beliefs are deleted from the belief store, and sentences representing the contents of fulfilled desires are deleted from the desire store. Third, if the BBC and BDC output signals exceed a certain threshold of intensity, they give rise, directly or indirectly (e.g., by activating subcortical structures), to unique conscious feeling qualities: the feelings of surprise and expectancy confirmation (BBC) and the feelings of pleasure and displeasure (BDC). The function of these feelings is assumed to be the same as the function proposed by consciousness theorists such as Baars (1988) for conscious experiences in general: To make important information available system-wide and thereby, enable it to exert global control. Furthermore, CBDTE assumes that the simultaneous experience of an emotional feeling and the focusing of attention on the content of the belief that caused it give rise to the subjective impression that the feeling is directed at the object of this belief (Reisenzein 2009a). In addition to the described effects, the outputs of the comparators may also cause physiological arousal and facial expressions under certain circumstances, but in agreement with the now available empirical evidence, the link of emotions to expression and physiology is assumed to be comparatively weak, as well as context-dependent (see Reisenzein 2019).

Note that the effective inputs to the belief-desire and belief-belief comparators are exactly the belief-desires constellations that according to BDTE, give rise to emotions; and that their outputs, when conscious, are emotional feelings. This suggests that the BBC and BDC are identical to the mechanisms that generate propositional emotions, and that emotions are simply the outputs of these mechanisms. This is exactly what CBDTE claims.

Readers may miss another adaptive effect of emotions proposed by some emotion theorists (e.g., Arnold 1960; Frijda 1986; Lazarus 1991): The elicitation of emotion-specific action tendencies (e.g., the desire to flee or avoid a feared object, or the desire to help a person for whom one feels pity). In fact, Arnold and Frijda even *identify* emotions with these action tendencies, and some cognitive film theorists have followed them in this assumption (e.g., Tan 1996; G. M. Smith 2003). But this assumption is too strong: Emotions, for several reasons, cannot be identified with action tendencies (see Reisenzein 1996). Furthermore, although it is true that some (but not all) emotions are associated with specific action tendencies, I am unconvinced that these associations are due to hardwired links between emotions and actions. They can be more parsimoniously explained as the result of the attention-directing and informational effects of emotion: The focusing of attention on an emotion-eliciting event implies that this event is given priority in information processing (Frijda 1986), and the prioritized processing of the event will often comprise the generation of an appropriate action goal. For example, focusing attention on a possible danger often stimulates the motivational system to generate a prevention goal. In addition, the processing of an emotion-evoking event can activate basic desires. For example, the analysis of surprising events often reveals a knowledge gap, which is a natural elicitor of curiosity (Loewenstein 1994); and the experience of unpleasant feelings often activates a hedonistic motive to abolish these feelings (see Baumeister et al. 2007).

To summarize, the proposed computational model of the belief-desire theory of emotion assumes that emotions are the results of computations in a propositional representation system that supports beliefs and desires. The core of the belief-desire system is innate, and this innate core includes a set of hardwired monitoring-and-updating mechanisms, whose central components are the BBC and the BDC. These mechanisms are comparable to sensory transducers, such as the sense organs for color, sound, touch, and bodily changes, in at least two respects: First, analogous to the function of the sense organs, the function of the comparator mechanisms is to detect system-critical information and communicate it to the cognitive system; second, the immediate products of the comparator mechanisms are nonpropositional, sensation-like signals. However, instead of sensing the world (at least directly), the "internal transducers" sense the current state and state changes of the belief-desire system as it deals with new information. Hence, a central assumption of CBDTE is that, in addition to sense organs that inform us about the state of the outside world and those that inform us about the state of our bodies, there are also sensors that monitor our mind or more precisely, our representational system. Emotions are elicited whenever these "internal sensors," the BBC and the BDC, detect a match or mismatch between newly acquired and pre-existing beliefs, or between newly acquired beliefs and pre-existing desires.

According to CBDTE, emotions are thus intimately related to the updating of the belief-desire system. In fact, this relationship could not be closer: According to the theory, the comparison devices that make up the core of the updating mechanisms – the BBC and the BDC – *are simultaneously the basic emotion-generating mechanisms*. Corresponding to this, CBDTE assumes that the *evolutionary function* of the emotion mechanisms is *not* to solve domain-specific problems, as several evolutionary emotion theorists have proposed (e.g., McDougall 1908/1960; Ekman 1992; Tooby & Cosmides, 1990). Rather, their function is to solve the domain-general problems of (1) detecting matches and mismatches of newly acquired beliefs with existing beliefs and desires and (2) globally preparing the cognitive-motivational system to deal with them once they have been detected. Related to this, CBDTE does not support a distinction between "basic" and "nonbasic" emotions: All emotions covered by the theory, however complex or culturally determined they might be in other respects, are equally basic in the sense that they are all products of innate, hardwired emotion mechanisms, the BBC and the BDC.

Fantasy feelings, emotion inferences, and the role of language for emotions

As argued in Reisenzein (2009a, 2009b, 2012a), CBDTE solves, resolves, or at least gives clear answers to several long-standing questions of emotion psychology. Here, I would like to focus on three issues that are of particular importance for understanding emotional reactions to films and TV series: fantasy emotions, the inference of the emotions of other people, and the role of public language for emotions.

Fantasy emotions. CBDTE has been extended to "fantasy emotions" (Meinong 1910), i.e., emotional reactions to fictional events, including imagined events and events portrayed in films and novels (Reisenzein 2012b, 2012c). This extension was inspired by Meinong's (1910) theory of fantasy feelings, which anticipates the now popular theory that fantasy feelings are based on a special kind of propositional attitudes similar to, but weaker than, belief (see Schroeder and Matheson 2006).

Meinong called these special cognitive attitudes *assumptions*. In the extension of CBDTE to fantasy feelings proposed in Reisenzein (2012b, 2012c), I started from the assumption that fantasy feelings are based on *desire-assumption* pairs rather than *desire-belief* pairs. For example, Mary experiences fantasy joy about Schroiber's election as chancellor if she desires this state of affairs and assumes that it is the case (hence, I assumed that genuine desires are needed even for fantasy feelings).

To implement this idea on the design level, the CBDTE architecture was enriched by a mental store for assumptions, corresponding to the "possible worlds box" of Nichols and Stich (2003), and the assumption store was equipped with hardwired comparator mechanisms analogous to those proposed for the belief store, the BBC and the BDC: an assumption-assumption comparator (AAC) and an assumption-desire comparator (ADC). The AAC compares newly made assumptions with existing assumptions, whereas the ADC compares newly made assumptions with existing desires. Fantasy emotions arise when the AAC or the ADC detect an agreement or a conflict between a newly made assumption (AAC) and an existing assumption or a desire (ADC), respectively. Furthermore, analogous to the case of "serious" emotions, attention is then focused on the eliciting events, and the assumption store is updated. In contrast to serious emotions, however, no updating of the desire store occurs (and the belief store is, of course, not updated either). In the example, although Mary feels fantasy joy if she imagines that Schroiber has been elected, her desire for Schroiber's election is unchanged by this imagination, as is her belief that Schroiber has not yet been elected. Thus, the emotion mechanisms responsible for fantasy emotions do not change beliefs and desires in a direct way. However, their outputs can, by being cognized, influence beliefs and desires indirectly. For example, if Mary notices that she feels regret when she imagines that her postcode is drawn in the postcode lottery, this belief can evoke a desire to buy a ticket (cf. Zeelenberg and Pieters 2007). The main original function of the mechanisms for fantasy emotions was, probably, to allow us to predict the emotions of others as well as one's own (as in the example given).

If this theory of fantasy feeling is correct, emotional reactions to fiction are generated by mechanisms different from, albeit to a large degree parallel to, those that produce "serious" emotions.[5]

Inference of emotions in others. Many of the emotions experienced in everyday life are evoked by the actions and fortunes of others (e.g., Ortony et al. 1988). How we react emotionally to these events depends in part on how responsible for them we hold the involved persons to be, which in turn depends on attributions of intent, foresight, controllability, etc. (see, e.g., Weiner 1995). In addition, our emotional reactions to events that affect others also depend on the estimated emotional impact of these events on others.

To explain and predict emotional reactions to social events, it is therefore necessary to model how humans infer others' mental states. The two main theories of this process are that others' mental states are inferred using an implicit folk-psychological theory and that they are inferred using mental simulation (see Shanton and Goldman 2010). In recent years, there has been a growing consensus that both processes are involved in mental state inference (Shanton and Goldman 2010).

Regarding the special case of inferring other people's *emotions*, CBDTE provides for both possibilities: The inference of emotions by a mental simulation process is addressed by the theory of fantasy emotions described earlier, whereas theory-guided emotion inference can be modeled using a simplified, or coarsened, version of the noncomputational part of the CBDTE (i.e., the belief-desire theory that formed its starting point) as a model of the implicit emotion theory of common-sense psychology. This is possible because, as mentioned, the belief-desire theory is an explication of the common-sense theory of (propositional) emotions. A parallel approach has been proposed by Weiner (1995) in emotion psychology and by Pyanadath and Marsella (2005) in affective computing.

Language and emotion. To clarify the role of language – more precisely, verbal communications – for emotions, Reisenzein and Junge (2012) combined CBDTE with three largely uncontested assumptions about homo sapiens: (1) Humans are a highly social species (Richerson and Boyd 2005); (2) they use language as their main communication system; (3) they transmit huge amounts of cultural beliefs and norms from one generation to the next, again primarily via language.

This investigation yielded four main conclusions about the role of language for emotions, all of which seem to be well in accord with the facts:

1. Verbal communications are a major class of emotion elicitors, i.e., inducers of the beliefs that proximately evoke emotions according to CBDTE. For example, Mary acquired the belief that Schroiber won the election, and as a result felt happy, when she watched the news: The news reporter said "Schroiber has won the election"; this utterance was translated by Mary's linguistic module into the language of thought; there, the sentence was integrated with other relevant verbal information and information acquired by sensory perception, resulting in Mary's belief that Schroiber had won. Mary's emotion mechanisms then automatically compared this belief with Mary's pre-existing beliefs and desires, detected a mismatch in the first and a match in the second case, and generated feelings of surprise and pleasure.
2. Verbal communications are also a central source of the pre-existing beliefs, and indirectly also the desires, with which newly acquired beliefs are compared in the emotion-generation process. For example, Mary's desire that Schroiber should win the election, and her belief that he probably would not win it, were acquired by verbal communication: Mary learned about Schroiber, his political program, and his chances of being elected from watching the news and reading the newspapers; on the basis of this information, she came to believe that Schroiber's election, although unlikely, would be in her interest; as a result, she began to desire Schroiber's election.

   Of course, emotion-relevant beliefs and desires can also be acquired by direct perception. But even in these cases, what one perceives is frequently accompanied by verbal information that is of crucial importance for how one interprets the perceived events (see Lazarus 1966). Furthermore, considering that language, as humans' central medium of communication, is also the central medium of cultural transmission, it even seems possible that *most* of our beliefs – and indirectly also, most of our desires (because all desires but the basic ones are acquired by acquiring belief about new ways of fulfilling already existing desires) – have been acquired through verbal communication. If so, there is perhaps no case of emotion generation in adult humans that is not to some degree influenced, at least indirectly and historically, by verbal communications. Even the fear of spiders may have been culturally transmitted (see Davey 1994).

3. The beliefs that proximately cause an emotion are in many cases the results of a goal-directed epistemic process that is not restricted to the person's head but extends into the social environment to include other agents as sources of knowledge, information gatherers, hypothesis testers, and inference aids (Reisenzein 2001). In fact, in some cases, most of the work needed to compute emotion-evoking beliefs is delegated to others: Physicians are consulted to determine the causes of physical complaints, detectives are hired to collect information on the partner's faithfulness, etc. Language is what makes these social computations possible in the first place.
4. Unlike what is suggested by the inordinate research attention devoted by psychologists to nonverbal emotion expressions (e.g., facial and vocal expressions, physiological reactions), it is actually verbal communications that are humans' most important, because most sophisticated and versatile, means of communicating emotions.[6] Verbal communications have two significant advantages for emotion communication. First, emotions are normally accessible to introspection in the form of feelings; verbal reports can therefore provide direct information about them. Second, compared with spontaneous nonverbal expressions, verbal communications about emotions can be deployed in a much more flexible way and can transmit much more, as well as more specific, information. Spontaneous nonverbal emotion expressions can only convey information about currently present emotion episodes, they have limited recipient specificity, and the information they convey is restricted to a small number of quality and intensity distinctions. In contrast, verbal communications of emotion are not bound to the time of occurrence of the emotion episode, can be addressed to specific recipients, and can convey essentially any information about the emotion and its context that is available to the sender. This includes (1) precise information about the quality and intensity of the emotion, (2) information about the object of the emotion and its mental and situational context, (3) information about the causes and implications of the emotion-evoking event, and (4) information about ways of dealing with it or with the emotion it has caused. If one is interested in communicating these kinds of information, one not only *can* but *needs* to use language.

> The nonverbal communication of emotions seems to be mainly useful for two purposes: To accompany verbal communications about a different topic (e.g., to give immediate feedback of approval or disapproval in a cooperative discussion situation) and to convince others that one really feels the emotion that one purports to have and thus, really has the desires and beliefs that ground it (see Reisenzein 2015; Reisenzein and Junge 2012).

An analysis of emotional reactions to Jon Snow's death in *Game of Thrones*

Pérez and Reisenzein (2020) applied a cognitive theory of surprise that antedated CBDTE (see Reisenzein et al. 2012) to the explanation of viewer reactions to plot twists, using as their model case the death of Jon Snow in *Game of Thrones* (*GoT*). The surprise model is generally consistent with CBDTE, but this theory goes far beyond surprise to cover all propositional emotions. For this reason, CBDTE can serve as a framework for a more comprehensive analysis of the emotional reactions of viewers to Jon Snow's death. Indeed, the analysis of Twitter comments and YouTube videos of viewer reactions indicated that *GoT* fans responded to Snow's death not only with surprise but also with hedonic emotions such as sorrow and anger (see Pérez and Reisenzein 2020).

The creation of viewer beliefs and desires

During the 50 episodes of *GoT* that preceded Jon's death in the last episode of season 5, the typical *GoT* fan built up the expectation that Jon Snow would live to the end of the series. This expectation seems to have been based on three pieces of information (Pérez and Reisenzein 2020): (1) the gradual recognition that Jon Snow belonged to a core group of characters who were kept alive while numerous others died; (2) the perception that Jon Snow became increasingly important during the series, coupled with the apparently widespread "metanarrative" knowledge that important characters of a series usually survive; and (3) a popular fan theory about the true identity of Jon Snow, which made him the prime candidate for becoming the new king on the Iron Throne. Hence, in agreement with my above-described conclusions about the role of language for belief acquisition, the belief that was disconfirmed in Episode 5 – that Jon would live to the end of the series – was based not only on personal viewing experiences but also on a theory about the origin and likely future of Jon Snow devised by other *GoT* fans and communicated on the internet, as well as on general assumptions of viewers about typical character roles, presumably also acquired in part by personal experiences and in part by communication from others.

By the last episode of season 5, many *GoT* fans had also acquired the desire to see Jon Snow live to the end of the series. This "character desire" (see

Currie 1999) seems to have been based on at least two sources. First, many fans wanted Jon to live because they believed that only he could bring the saga to a satisfactory and meaningful conclusion (Pérez and Reisenzein 2020). Second, as revealed by a survey among *GoT* fans (see Pérez and Reisenzein 2020), most fans had developed an attachment to Jon; they liked him. Attachments to characters in TV series seem to develop just like attachments to people in real life: Others are liked if they display valued traits (e.g., bravery and generosity in Jon Snow's case). For many fans, the attachment to Jon possibly even went beyond mere liking: Jon had become one of their – if virtual – friends (cf. Blanchet and Vaage 2012). As they began to like Jon, and even more so as Jon became their friend, the *GoT* fans developed the desire to see him do well, which implied, minimally, that he should stay alive. If we accept Aristotle's theory of friendship, we can even be more specific: The fan friends of Jon wished him well for his sake and not for their own, i.e., they desired to see him do well *for altruistic reasons*. As argued in Reisenzein (2015), altruistic desires seem to be necessary for experiencing pity and joy for others.

Emotional reactions to Jon Snow's death

The belief acquired in the last episode of season 5, that Jon Snow was dead, was thus incongruent with both the beliefs and the desires of probably the majority of *GoT* fans. As a consequence, their emotion mechanisms generated surprise and displeasure signals, which coalesced into a feeling of shock. Those *GoT* fans who had become Jon's friends and thus altruistically desired his survival should also have felt pity for him. Furthermore, to the degree that the treacherous attack on Jon by his comrades, in particular by his personal steward Olly, violated social or moral norms that the viewers cared about, the killing should have caused indignation and anger against the murderers (see Reisenzein 2015; Ortony et al. 1988). Some viewers apparently also felt angry at the makers of *GoT* for "killing" Jon and thereby robbing them of a favorite character and the saga of a meaningful resolution (Pérez and Reisenzein 2020).

The effects of viewer emotions

CBDTE predicts that the surprise and displeasure signals caused by Jon Snow's death propagated through the viewers' cognitive system and focused their attention on the eliciting event. This, in turn, instigated processes of event analysis that focused on the reasons for Jon's death and the implications of this event for the continuation of the saga (for evidence, see Pérez and Reisenzein 2020). In addition, CBDTE predicts that the displeasure caused by Jon's death would create a hedonistic desire to reduce it. Because emotion management by intervening in the fictional world was impossible in the case of *GoT*, the only thing that the viewers could do to reduce their suffering (apart from trying not to think about the evoking event anymore) was to try to manipulate their beliefs or desires, for example by denying that death was final in Jon's case. This is indeed what happened. A new theory was soon born on the internet: Jon will, in one form or other, be resurrected. *GoT* fans who believed in this theory could appease their sadness about Jon's death by the hope evoked by the prospect of future desire-satisfaction. Jokes about the killing scene found in comments to YouTube videos of the scene could also be interpreted as attempts to cope with the negative emotions evoked by Jon's death (cf. Kuiper 2012).

Consistent with the conclusions drawn in the first part of the chapter about the role of language in the communication of emotions, the emotions of *GoT* fans did not remain private affairs of individual viewers. Rather, the feelings of surprise, sadness, and anger caused by the death of Jon Snow were communicated to other *GoT* fans on internet forums both verbally and by using pictograms (emojis). Likewise, the individual viewers' attempts to explain Jon's death and to predict the future course of the saga merged on the fan forums into a joint project of explanation, prediction, and emotion management (Pérez and Reisenzein 2020).

The emotions of Jon Snow

As is true for events involving other people in real life, the emotions evoked in viewers of social events depicted in films depend in part on the mental states (beliefs, desires, emotions, etc.) attributed to the protagonists. For a full understanding of viewers' emotional reactions to films, these mental state inferences must therefore be taken into consideration.

In the case of Jon Snow's assassination in *GoT*, inferences about Jon's emotions during the attack could have increased the intensity of their altruistic sorrow for Jon. Indeed, knowledgeable viewers of the scene probably realized not only that Jon might die; they also inferred – as part of largely automatic cognitive processes of scene interpretation – what Jon thought and felt. These viewers knew that Jon was the commander of the Nights' Watch, who could demand respect and trust from his comrades, and that he did not suspect that they planned to kill him. From this, it was easy to infer that Jon was most likely at least as surprised and shocked by the attack on him as were the viewers themselves. Furthermore, the viewers could plausibly assume that Jon, after he had received the first blow, realized that he might die, and that he experienced fear as a consequence. Likewise, the viewers could infer with high likelihood that Jon felt disappointed by the breach of trust of his comrades, most of all his personal steward Olly. The pity that the viewers felt for Jon (see earlier) may have been in part based on these inferred emotions. That is, they may have felt sorry for Jon not only because he had to die, but also because he was suffering in the process, not only physically but also emotionally, by experiencing shock, fear, and disappointment.

Conclusion

The proposed theory-guided analysis of emotional reactions to Jon Snow's death is incomplete as well as partly speculative, mainly because not enough is known about how elaborated the situation models of the *GoT* fans really were. This question could be clarified, and the proposed analysis could be empirically tested, with a retrospective survey of *GoT* fans.[7]

Notes

1 A detailed comparison of the similarities and differences of these previous analyses of filmic emotions with the belief-desire analysis proposed here must be left to another occasion. However, as will become evident, the belief-desire model of emotion described in the following differs significantly from appraisal theory in its assumptions about the proximate causes of emotion, the nature of emotion, and the consequences of emotion. In particular, emotions are assumed to be caused by factual beliefs and desires rather than by factual and evaluative beliefs, and they are taken to be sensation-like, nonpropositional signals rather than action tendencies or syndromes of responses. These differences carry over to the analysis of filmic emotions.

2 The details of the computational theory of the mind are the topic of a large and ongoing research program in psychology and cognitive neuroscience. While many important aspects of this theory are still under discussion (e.g., the questions of how many and which representational codes there are; how modular versus holistic the mind is; and which computational structures and processes are inborn and which are acquired), the great majority of experimental psychologists and cognitive neuroscientists remain convinced that the basic assumption of the computational approach is correct: The mind is a computational-representational system. This belief is substantiated, on the one hand, by the undeniable successes of the computational approach in psychology and artificial intelligence (see e.g., Anderson and Lebiere 1998; Reisenzein et al. 2013) and on the other hand, by the fact that the computational-representational theory (broadly understood) is so far the only detailed proposal of how the mind actually works. Also, the computational theory of the mind is highly compatible with evolutionary psychology and with neuroscience: Evolutionary psychology is concerned with the evolved architecture of the mind; from the perspective of the computational theory, these are the inborn information-processing mechanisms (see Tooby and Cosmides 1990). Cognitive neuroscientists attempt to gain insight into the information-processing mechanisms of humans from studying their neurophysiological correlates.

3 For example, Mary can not only be happy that *Schroiber won the election* (= *p*); she can, with equal ease, be happy that *Peter was pleased about p* or that *Peter acknowledged that she correctly predicted p*. A language-like representation system can handle such complex, hierarchically nested propositions with ease. In contrast, it is at best uncertain whether other proposed systems of mental representation can do likewise. Iconic (image-like) representations, as traditionally conceived of, are unable to represent propositional contents (Fodor 1975). And although more recently proposed imagistic representation systems – specifically, the perceptual symbol systems proposed by Barsalou (1999) – are to some extent able to handle propositions (though see Machery 2006), it appears that this is so precisely because they incorporate crucial features of propositional representation systems. In line with this conclusion, Barsalou (1999, 595) himself has pointed out that "perceptual symbol systems … too are propositional systems." Indeed, it seems to me that a perceptual symbol system that is able to represent propositions of arbitrary complexity is essentially just a propositional representation system with a partly iconic symbol set (i.e., a subset of the symbols resemble what they represent).

4 In the case of fear and hope, the BDC detects a possible or probable, rather than a certain, mismatch between what is desired or undesired and what is or could be the case, and generates special signals experienced as hope and fear, respectively.

5 The "special attitude" theory of fantasy feelings is not uncontested, however (see Buckwalter and Tullmann 2017). The most plausible alternative is that fantasy emotions,

like "serious" emotions, are based on beliefs, but beliefs whose propositional contents are modified by a fiction operator (e.g., Matravers 1991; Neill 1993). For example, Mary experiences fantasy joy about Schroiber's election in the TV series *The Chancellor* if she desires that he is elected *in the series* and believes that this is true *in the series*. To incorporate this proposal into CBDTE, no special mechanisms for fantasy emotions have to be added; instead, the modeled propositional representation system would have to be expanded to include an appropriate fiction operator. For the analysis of viewers' emotional reactions to specific scenes in films or TV series (see the second part of this chapter), it is, however, immaterial whether fantasy emotions are based on assumptions or beliefs with modified contents.

6 From the perspective of CBDTE, communications of emotions to others inform them about the occurrence of a belief or desire match or mismatch in the communicating agent and indirectly, a (possible) change in the world that gave rise to this match or mismatch.

7 The survey study proposed in this chapter has meanwhile been conducted by Lorenz and Reisenzein (2021, in prep.).

References

Anderson, J.R., and C. Lebiere. 1998. *The* Atomic Components of Thou*ght*. Mawah, NJ: Erlbaum.

Arnold, M.B. 1960. *Emotion and Personality*. New York: Columbia University Press.

Baars, B.J. 1988. *A Cognitive Theory of Consciousness*. Cambridge, MA: Cambridge University.

Barsalou, L.W. 1999. "Perceptual Symbol Systems." *Behavioral and Brain Sciences* 22: 577–660.

Baumeister, R.F., K.D. Vohs, C.N. DeWall, and L. Zhang. 2007. "How Emotion Shapes Behavior: Feedback, Anticipation, and Reflection, Rather Than Direct Causation." *Personality and Social Psychology Review* 11: 167–203.

Blanchet, R., and M. Bruun Vaage. 2012. "Don, Peggy, and Other Fictional Friends? Engaging with Characters in Television Series." *Projections: The Journal for Movies and Mind* 6, no. 2: 18–41.

Buckwalter, W., and K. Tullmann. 2017. "The Genuine Attitude View of Fictional Belief." In *Art and Belief*, edited by E. Sullivan-Bissett, H. Bradley, and P. Noordhof, 194–209. Oxford: Oxford University Press.

Carroll, N. 1990. *The Philosophy of Horror*. New York and London: Routledge.

Castelfranchi, C., and M. Miceli. 2009. "The Cognitive–motivational Compound of Emotional Experience." *Emotion Review* 1: 223–231.

Currie, G. 1999. "Narrative Desires." In *Passionate Views: Film, Cognition, and Emotion*, edited by C. Plantinga and G.M. Smith, 183–200. Baltimore, MD: Johns Hopkins University Press.

Currie, G. 1995. "Imagination and Simulation: Aesthetics Meets Cognitive Science." In *Mental Simulation*, edited by M. Davies and T. Stone, 151–169. Oxford: Blackwell.

Davey, G.C.L., 1994. "The 'Disgusting' Spider: The Role of Disease and Illness in the Perpetuation of Fear of Spiders." *Society and Animals* 2: 17–25.

Dennett, D.C. 1971. "Intentional Systems." *Journal of Philosophy* 68: 87–106.

Ekman, P. 1992. "An Argument for Basic Emotions." *Cognition & Emotion* 6: 169–200.

Ellsworth, P.C., and K.R. Scherer. 2003. "Appraisal Processes in Emotion." In *Handbook of Affective Sciences*, edited by R.J. Davidson, K.R. Scherer, and H.H. Goldsmith, 572–595. Oxford: Oxford University Press.

Fodor, J.A. 1975. *The Language of Thought*. New York: Crowell.

Fodor, J.A. 1987. *Psychosemantics: The Problem of Meaning in the Philosophy of Mind*. Cambridge, MA: MIT Press.

Frijda, N.H. 1986. *The Emotions*. Cambridge: Cambridge University Press.

Gratch, J., S. Marsella, N. Wang, and B. Stankovic. 2009. "Assessing the Validity of Appraisal–based Models of Emotion." *Proceedings of the 3rd International Conference on Affective Computing and Intelligent Interaction*.

Green, O.H. 1992. *The Emotions: A Philosophical Theory*. Dordrecht: Kluwer.

Griffith, P.E. 1997. *What Emotions Really Are*. Chicago, IL: University of Chicago Press.

Grodal, T. 1997. *Moving Pictures: A New Theory of Film Genres, Feelings, and Cognition*. Oxford: Oxford University Press.

Heider, F. 1958. *The Psychology of Interpersonal Relations*. New York: Wiley.

Junge, M., and R. Reisenzein 2013. "Indirect Scaling Methods for Testing Quantitative Emotion Theories." *Cognition and Emotion* 27: 1247–1275.

Kuiper, N.A. 2012. "Humor and Resiliency: Towards a Process Model of Coping and Growth." *Europe's Journal of Psychology* 8: 475–491.

Lazarus, R.S. 1966. *Psychological Stress and the Coping Process*. New York: McGraw–Hill.

Lazarus, R.S. 1991. *Emotion and Adaptation*. New York: Oxford University Press.

Loewenstein, G. 1994. "The Psychology of Curiosity: A Review and Reinterpretation." *Psychological Bulletin* 116: 75–98.

Lorenz, V. A., and Reisenzein, R. 2021. "Emotional Reactions to Jon Snow's Death in *Game of Thrones:* An Empirical Test of the Belief-Desire Theory of Emotion." Manuscript in preparation, University of Greifswald.

Machery, E. 2006. "Two Dogmas of Neo-empiricism." *Philosophy Compass* 1: 398–412.

Marsella, S., J. Gratch, and P. Petta 2010. "Computational Models of Emotion." In *Blueprint for Affective Computing*, edited by K. Scherer, T. Bänziger, and E. Roesch, 21–46. Oxford: Oxford University Press.

Matravers, Derek. 1991. "Who's Afraid of Virginia Woolf?" *Ratio* 4: 25–37.

McDougall, W. 1908. *An Introduction to Social Psychology*. London: Methuen.

Meinong, A. 1894. *Psychologisch-ethische Untersuchungen zur Werttheorie*. [*Psychological-ethical investigations in value theory*]. Graz: Leuschner & Lubensky.

Meinong, A. 1910. *Über Annahmen* [*On Assumptions*]. 2nd ed. Leipzig, Germany: Barth.

Mellers, B.A., A. Schwartz, K. Ho, and I. Ritov. 1997. "Decision Affect Theory: Emotional Reactions to the Outcomes of Risky Options." *Psychological Science* 8: 423–429.

Miceli, M., and C. Castelfranchi. 2015. *Expectancy and Emotion*. Oxford: Oxford University Press.

Nannicelli, Ted, and Paul Taberham, eds. 2014. *Cognitive Media Theory*. New York & London: Routledge.

Neill, A. 1993. "Fiction and the Emotions." *American Philosophical Quarterly* 30: 1–13.

Nichols, S., and S. Stich. 2003. *Mindreading: An Integrated Account of Pretense, Self–Awareness and Understanding Other Minds*. Oxford: Oxford University Press.

Nussbaum, M.C. 2001. *Upheavals of Thought: The Intelligence of Emotions*. Cambridge: Cambridge University Press.

Öhman, A., and J.J.F. Soares. 1994. "'Unconscious Anxiety': Phobic Responses to Masked Stimuli." *Journal of Abnormal Psychology* 103: 231–240.

Ortony, A., G.L. Clore, and A. Collins. 1988. *The Cognitive Structure of Emotions*. New York: Cambridge University Press.

Pérez, H., and R. Reisenzein. 2020. "On John Snow's Death: Plot Twist and Global Fandom in Game of Thrones." *Culture and Psychology* 26: 384–400.

Plantinga, C. 2002. "Cognitive Film Theory: An Insider's Appraisal." *Cinémas: Journal of Film Studies* 12: 15–37.

Plantinga, C., and G.M. Smith, eds. 1999. *Passionate Views: Film, Cognition, and Emotion.* Baltimore: John Hopkins University Press.

Power, M., and T. Dalgleish. 2016. *Cognition and Emotion: From Order to Disorder.* Hove: Psychology Press.

Pynadath, D.V., and S. Marsella. 2005. PsychSim: Modeling Theory of Mind with Decision–Theoretic Agents. *International Joint Conference on Artificial Intelligence 2005*, 1181–1186.

Reisenzein, R., 1996. Emotional Action Generation. In *Processes of the Molar Regulation of Behavior*, edited by W. Battmann and S. Dutke. Lengerich: Pabst Science Publishers, 151–165.

Reisenzein, R. 2001. "Appraisal Processes Conceptualized from a Schema-Theoretic Perspective: Contributions to a Process Analysis of Emotions." In *Appraisal Processes in Emotion: Theory, Methods, Research*, edited by K.R. Scherer, A. Schorr, and T. Johnstone, 187–20. Oxford: Oxford University Press.

Reisenzein, R. 2009a. "Emotional Experience in the Computational Belief–desire Theory of Emotion." *Emotion Review* 1: 214–222.

Reisenzein, R. 2009b. "Emotions as Metarepresentational States of Mind: Naturalizing the Belief-Desire Theory of Emotion." *Cognitive Systems Research* 10: 6–20.

Reisenzein, R. 2012a. "What is an Emotion in the Belief-Desire Theory of Emotion?" In *The Goals of Cognition: Essays in Honor of Cristiano Castelfranchi*, edited by F. Paglieri, L. Tummolini, R. Falcone, and M. Miceli, 181–211. London: College Publications.

Reisenzein, R. 2012b. "Fantasiegefühle aus der Sicht der kognitiv–motivationalen Theorie der Emotion [Fantasy Emotions from the Perspective of the Cognitive-motivational Theory of Emotion]." In *Emotionen in Literatur und Film*, edited by S. Poppe, 31–63. Würzburg: Königshausen & Neumann.

Reisenzein, R. 2012c. "Extending the Belief-Desire Theory of Emotions to Fantasy Emotions." Proceedings of the 11th International Conference on Cognitive Modeling (ICCM), edited by N. Rußwinkel, U. Drewitz, and H. van Rijn, 313–314.

Reisenzein, R. 2015. "Social Emotions from the Perspective of the Computational Belief–Desire Theory of Emotion." In *Cognitive Foundations of Group Attitudes and Social Interaction (Studies in the Philosophy of Sociality, Vol. 5)*, edited by A. Herzig and E. Lorini, 153–176. Berlin: Springer.

Reisenzein, R. 2017. "Cognitive Theory of Emotion." In *Encyclopedia of Personality and Individual Differences*, edited by V. Zeigler-Hill and T.K. Shackleford, 1–11. Cham: Springer. doi:10.1007/978-3-319-28099-8_496-1

Reisenzein, R. 2018. "Naturalized Aesthetics and Emotion Theory." *Projections: The Journal for Movies and Mind* 12, no. 2: 76–85.

Reisenzein, R. 2019. "Cognition and Emotion: A Plea for Theory." *Cognition and Emotion* 33: 109–118.

Reisenzein, R., E. Hudlicka, M. Dastani, J. Gratch, K. Hindriks, E. Lorini, and J.-J.C. Meyer. 2013. "Computational Modeling of Emotion: Toward Improving the Inter-and Intradisciplinary Exchange." *IEEE Transactions on Affective Computing* 4: 246–266.

Reisenzein, R., and M. Junge. 2012. "Language and Emotion from the Perspective of the Computational Belief–Desire Theory of Emotion." In *Dynamicity in Emotion Concepts (Lodz Studies in Language 27)*, edited by P.A. Wilson, 37–59. Frankfurt am Main: Peter Lang.

Reisenzein, R., W.-U. Meyer, and M. Niepel. 2012. "Surprise." In *Encyclopedia of Human Behavior*, edited by V.S. Ramachandran, 564–570. Amsterdam: Academic Press.

Richerson, P.J., and R. Boyd. 2005. *Not by Genes Alone. How Culture Transformed Human Evolution*. Chicago, IL: University of Chicago Press.

Rumelhart, D.E. 1984. "Schema and the Cognitive System." In *Handbook of* Social Cog*nition*, edited by R.S. Wyer and T.K. Srull, Vol. 1, 161–188. Hillsdale, NJ: Lawrence Erlbaum Associates.

Schank, R.C. 1977. *Scripts, Plans, Goals and Understanding*. New York: Wiley.

Scherer, K.R. 2001. "Appraisal Considered as a Process of Multilevel Sequential Checking." In *Appraisal Processes in Emotion: Theory, Methods, Research*, edited by K.R. Scherer, A. Schorr, and T. Johnstone, 92–120. Oxford: Oxford University Press.

Schroeder, T., and C. Matheson. 2006. "Imagination and Emotion." In *Architecture of the Imagination: New Essays on Pretence, Possibility, and Fiction*, edited by S. Nichols, 19–39. Oxford: Oxford University Press.

Shanton, K., and A. Goldman. 2010. "Simulation Theory." *Wiley Interdisciplinary Reviews: Cognitive Science* 1: 527–538.

Smith, G. M. 2003. *Film Structure and the Emotion System*. Cambridge: Cambridge University Press.

Smith, M. 1995. *Engaging Characters: Fiction, Emotion, and the Cinema*. Oxford: Clarendon Press.

Smith, M. 2017. *Film, Art, and the Third Culture: A Naturalized Aesthetics of Film*. Oxford: Oxford University Press.

Solomon, R.C. 1976. *The Passions*. Garden City, NY: Anchor Press/Doubleday.

Tan, E.S. 1996. *Emotion and the Structure of Narrative Film: Film as an Emotion Machine*. Mahwah: Lawrence Erlbaum.

Tooby, J. and L. Cosmides. 1990. The Past Explains the Present: Emotional Adaptations and the Structure of Ancestral Environments. *Ethology and Sociobiology* 11: 375–424.

Weinberg, J.M., and A. Meskin. 2006. "Puzzling Over the Imagination: Philosophical Problems, Architectural Solutions." In *The Architecture of the Imagination: New Essays on Pretence, Possibility, and Fiction*, edited by Shuan Nichols, 175–202. Oxford: Oxford University Press.

Weiner, B. 1995. *Judgments of Responsibility. A Foundation for a Theory of Social Conduct*. New York: Guilford.

Wundt, W. 1896. *Grundriss der Psychologie [Outlines of Psychology]*. Leipzig: Engelmann.

Zajonc, R.B. 1980. "Feeling and Thinking: Preferences Need No Inferences." *American Psychologist* 35: 151–175.

Zeelenberg, M., and Pieters, R. 2007. "A Theory of Regret Regulation 1.0." *Journal of Consumer Psychology* 17: 3–18.

Part III

Poetics

8 Reaching through time

On seriality, temporality, and twofoldness

Murray Smith

> [The *Trainspotting* characters] spend the first film, as you do when you're in your teens or your twenties – [as if] time's irrelevant, you just don't give a hoot about it. You do not care about it. And then you get a bit older, and you realise it's time that doesn't care about you – that's actually the way the equation works.
>
> Danny Boyle, on *T2* (2017)

Returning to Leith after a 20-year hiatus, Renton visits his old mate Sick Boy – still fuming with resentment at Renton's departure with the proceeds of their heroin deal all those years earlier. This is their second encounter during Renton's visit – the first having quickly descended into a vicious bar brawl. Renton is filling Sick Boy in on the factors leading to his return home after the two decades of self-imposed exile – among them the episode of "acute coronary insufficiency," which we witness Renton endure in *T2*'s opening sequence. Renton now has a stent in his left coronary artery:

> Good as new apparently, good as new. Should last another thirty years, they said, but they didn't say what to do with those thirty years. Two or three, fine, I'll take that, I can cope with that – I can think of enough things to do to piss away what remains. But thirty – what am I supposed to do with that?!

Thirty years is indeed a long time – let's say, half a lifetime if we are lucky; a third of a lifetime if we are very fortunate (assuming that living a long life helps us live, or find, a good life). Renton may be no model citizen, but at least one aspect of his exasperation at the prospect of sticking around for several decades more taps into something everyone can grasp. We're all used to forming and executing plans on the scale of seconds, minutes, hours, days, weeks, months, even a few years. I can reach for the salt, set the timer to record the final of the Champions League later that day, book the online shop for next week, plan to visit my brother in a few months' time, and embark on that degree program, which if I follow it through, will make my CV look a bit healthier.

DOI: 10.4324/9781003188643-8

But the further things stretch out – the longer the envelope of time that we try to structure through planning – the more demanding it becomes. We can be confident the salt will still be on the table in a few more seconds, that the Champions League final will go ahead this evening, that Sainsburys will still be delivering groceries next week – and that I'll still want to add some salt to my chips, watch the game, and have the food supply at each of those moments. But beyond that – who knows? Maybe there'll be a pandemic. The problem is particularly acute in relation to our own selves. What will I be like in five years? Maybe I won't want the same things that I want now. Sometimes we struggle to envisage how things will be in a month or a year, and the further we look ahead, the murkier it gets.

It is not easy, then, to reach through time, to shape our destinies through planning, or – as Renton also discovers on his return to Edinburgh – to revisit and reflect on our former lives and selves, figuring out who we were and what we've become. ("And you may ask yourself: How did I get here?") The worlds of feature filmmaking and television production are particularly apt domains in which to explore the relationship between agency, identity, and extended temporality for two reasons. First, feature filmmaking and television production typically require the coordination of many different agents across time and space; and this is most emphatically true of serial television production, where program makers frequently sustain coordination among a large cast and crew for years and sometimes decades. So, the particular character and demands of film and television production – and above all, serial production – dramatize the challenges of the *longue durée*, of agency over time, in a particularly vivid fashion. But film and television simultaneously afford an arena of *reflection upon* the problem of agency and extended temporality. And the fact that a condition of (especially) serial production is the prolonged, and often indefinite, duration of creation makes it especially fertile ground for reflection on time, human agency, and human experience. In other words, the underlying character of serial production makes it apt to be thematized in the works so produced.

Time, seriality, medium

The framing of the current volume brings two further questions into view concerning the capacity of narrative to represent time. The first concerns the distinction between self-contained and serial narrative form; the second that between televisual and cinematic narrative – or more broadly, the differences among various media with respect to narrative and time. In order to address the first of these questions – the principal focus of the current chapter – I need to clear the ground with regard to the second question. What might we say about the relationship between cinema, television, and related media with respect to time and narrative?

Seventy years on from the rise of television as a commercial rival to cinema, there might be some temptation to do away with the distinction between the two media altogether. Feature films still typically begin their exhibition lives via a (more or less) exclusive theatrical run, but most will quickly make their way onto broadcast television, online platforms, and disc, and from then on, exist in this multiform fashion. If we don't catch a film in its usually brief theatrical run upon initial release, the chances are we'll connect with it in a televisual or mobile-screen environment. In this sense, all audiovisual works, even the grandest of cinematic projects, seem destined to become grist for the mill of television schedules and online streaming platforms.

But the humble television has now been displaced by the home cinema system, and every generation of smartphone boasts a higher-resolution screen than the last one, now easily combined with Bluetooth earbuds, blocking out domestic distractions and allowing an immersive engagement rivaling cinematic screening norms in at least some respects. Remember, too, that many multiplex screens are small and poorly designed, and cinemas are routinely polluted by pockets of smartphone illumination and the (not so) occasional ringing phone. Add to all of this the fact that above- and below-the-line personnel frequently and more or less freely move between feature film and television production, and the case for maintaining the distinction between cinema and television seems weak indeed. All screen stories now swim in an undifferentiated media sphere, and clinging on to the distinction between cinema and television seems like nothing more than an act of sentimental nostalgia.

Not so fast! The worlds of cinema, television, and the internet may be thoroughly enmeshed in these and other ways, but in fact, the preceding description depends on making distinctions between cinema, television, and other modes of audiovisual production and consumption. The emergence of "convergence culture" has led not to the flattening of distinctions among audiovisual media, but rather their complication.[1] Instead of eliminating the distinction between cinema and television, we need to refine it in two ways: Recognizing, on the one hand, the way the film and television industries work in an integrated fashion, while on the other hand, acknowledging the diverse and proliferating types of screen media production and consumption, old and new, not adequately captured by a simple distinction between cinema and television. We will see such complexity emerging across the case studies I'll examine later in this chapter. But before we come to those case studies, we still need to consider the first of the questions posed at the beginning of this section, the question concerning the way in which time is represented in self-contained and serial narrative works, in relation to the distinction, however complex, between cinema and television.

So, how is time – and in particular, temporal duration – represented in film and televisual narrative? To begin with, we need to acknowledge three different layers of time that any narrative will bind and bring into a relationship. First, there is a narrative's *represented* time: The time represented by or "in" the narrative (the days or weeks or years across which the story takes place; we can make a further distinction here between "story duration" and "plot duration"). Second, there is *representational* time: The duration of the representation itself (the minutes or hours or days that define the work, assuming it has a fixed duration; the run time or "screen duration" of a narrative film).[2] Think of these two kinds of time – represented and representational – as together comprising what I will simply call *narrative* time. With just these parameters, a vast world of permutations opens up, as the history of storytelling and the libraries of scholarship on time and narrative together testify. And yet, there is a third layer of time, less commented upon, that we need to accommodate: The *lived* time in which narrative works – creating narrative time by conjoining represented and representational time – sit.

If it seems as if there is no distinction to be made between the screen duration (in my terms, representational time) of a moving image work and what I am calling lived time, serial narrative works point up the need for the distinction: One season of a television serial might have a screen duration of, say, 13 hours, and yet, its broadcast will likely be distributed over many weeks. Even if all episodes of the show are made available simultaneously online, for even the most hardcore binge viewer, there will almost certainly be some disparity between the run time of the season and the lived duration across which the episodes were viewed. And if we move up to the level of seasons, the distinction between representational time and lived time becomes clearer still: Seasons are made available according to a rhythm – usually an annual cycle – creating a temporal pattern of consumption distinct from the run of time of the seasons combined. True, nowadays, complete shows eventually become available as "box sets" for continuous viewing, but such consumption, while possible, is not the norm. The gradual release of narrative episodes over an extended period, punctuated by substantial pauses while future episodes are devised and completed, is a part of the fabric of serial television, not a mere contingency of production. The eventual availability of the box set stands out against this fundamental, constitutive norm of serial television production and appreciation.

Narratives, as I've suggested in the introduction, generally articulate time at the scale of human experience, a scale ranging from seconds – experience in the present moment – to lifetimes. But time stretches far beyond that scale, and there are works that seek to represent "deep time": Time on a much larger scale, from generational to evolutionary, geological, epochal, and cosmological timeframes. The Clock of the Long Now, for example, is a clock designed to last for 10,000 years and to be understood and appreciated as a device lasting and measuring time for such a duration. Meanwhile, in the town of Halberstadt, Germany, a performance of John Cage's *As Slow as Possible*, begun in 2001, is due to finish in 2640. It should not surprise us that neither of these works is a narrative – precisely because narratives, tuned to the rhythms of human existence, are ill-suited to render supra-human durations and processes.[3]

Serial narrative form occupies a middle ground, allowing the representation of "in the moment" existence like any type of narrative, but enabling such representation to be connected with existence in time stretching out, sometimes indefinitely, into the past and future. This is perhaps most evident in its capacity to represent, and so augment our understanding of, *generational* time. Across its many component parts, for example, Edgar Reitz's *Heimat* (1984–2013) tells the story of the Simon family, and the fictional village of Schabbach, across six generations, from the 1840s through to the first decade of the new millennium.[4] Serial narratives also work with time in a distinctive way insofar as they create a channel of narrative time running parallel to – or better, threaded through – lived time rather than a delimited pocket of narrative time framed by the flow of lived time. Serial narrative form enables a distinctive type of connection between personal time and the longer durations that frame it.

Seen in this light, we can think of serial narrative form as an aspect of *the extended mind* – that is, as a technology which amplifies our capacity to think about time, by scaffolding our "brainbound" minds with external supports in the form of serial narrative works. Similarly, works like the Clock of the Long Now and Cage's *As Slow as Possible* extend our capacity to comprehend supra-humanly extended timescales and durations. Just as our ability to think mathematically is strengthened by environmental aids – from the abacus to the modern computer – and our musical cognition is expanded and empowered both by instrumentation and notation, so our ability to grasp the nature and effects of time, especially at scale, is much enhanced by external representational tools like clocks, musical performances, and (serial) narrative works.[5]

Within the domain of serial narrative, we can discern a wide array of possibilities according to the different ways in which the duration of represented time, and the rhythm according to which that block of represented time, is sampled – the frequency, the regularity, and thus, the predictability with which the represented time of the work is made available to us within and across lived time. Soap operas, for example, create a kind of continuous story time running parallel with lived time: The represented time of the soap opera story world is sampled frequently, regularly, and hence, predictably. Even if it does not exactly mirror the duration and speed of lived time, its gradual and parallel unfolding binds it closely to such time. Serial television dramas often work with a more compressed and selective, but still regular and predictable, sampling of represented, storyworld time – although it should be said that there is enormous variety here. The predictability of representational time within serial television works (serial episodes produced to a fixed screen duration) and their steady release across lived time (episodes and seasons being made available at a regular and predictable rate) are *not* matched by the same level of uniformity and predictability in their sampling of represented time (within or across different shows). A further variety of serial narrative form – one that we witness mostly in cinema or in works that straddle cinema and television – involves a highly compressed, selective, intermittent, and consequently unpredictable sampling of represented time. I return to this form later.

Time, place, and personhood

Before turning to this possibility, however, I want to begin not with a work of serial film or television production but with a work from the neighboring domain of photography: artist Tom Phillips's *20 Sites n Years* long-form documentary project. I do so for two reasons. First, the example will underline the point that while there might be a natural kinship between the medium of television and serial form, such form is hardly restricted to television. In addition to the historical precursors of televisual seriality in popular literary fiction and cinema, contemporary serial projects are evident in a wide range of media beyond television. Second, *20 Sites* will bring still other parameters of seriality into focus – chiefly, the fictional or non-fictional character of a work, the extent to which its treatment of time is narrativized, and the extent to which the moment-to-moment passage of time is rendered through motion. Through a series of steps, taking these parameters into account, we will make our way from *20 Sites* through various intermediate examples to clear cases of serial narrative form in film and television.

Beginning in 1973, Phillips chose 20 locations roughly marking out a circle (with a radius of half a mile) around his home between Camberwell and Peckham, south London, photographing these sites on an annual basis. The accumulating series of photos thereby tracks the changes in the landscape – mostly gradual, occasionally dramatic – of this part of London year by year. The project creates an annual time-slice, insofar as each set of photos from a given year can be treated as a group representing that moment in the history of the neighborhood, as well as an annually punctuated record of change through time – much the like rings laid down within tree trunks marking patterns of growth over time. Notably, Phillips established the project with the intention that it should be continued into the future, in the first instance by family and friends, for as long as possible, and as far as possible using the same equipment, and the same vantage points, as the original set of photos. As of 2021, 48 years from its inception, the project is ongoing.[6]

As the total set of photos continues to grow, so viewers face an ever-expanding set of comparative options, most saliently between photos of the same location as captured in different years. Phillips's website provides slideshows based on these locations, moving the viewer through the years as the photos record their appearance at annual intervals; this form of presentation places the work on the very cusp of motion picture form. *20 Sites* thereby tracks the impact of time above all on *place*. Although human figures are visible in many of the photos, they are never the primary subject, which remains the location: in relation to location 1 – 102 Grove Park, London SE5, Phillips's home at the time when the project was inaugurated – the artist writes: "This restrained image does not, or should not, feature people."[7] But of course, these urban locations reflect the presence of humans through and through: in part because Phillips's system involves the shooting of a new annual batch of photos within a narrow window each year (May 24 to June 2), the series tends not to play up purely natural changes (like those produced by the seasons) but rather, the effects of human behavior on the landscape.

Taking a step closer to moving image production, *Smoke* (1995) – a collaboration between writer Paul Auster and director Wayne Wang – embeds a fictional variant on Phillips's *20 Sites*. In the film, Brooklyn cigar store owner Auggie Wren, played by Harvey Keitel, takes photos of the exterior of his store at 8am every morning, recording its changing appearance over time (though at a much faster rate than in *20 Sites*: once a day rather than once a year). Within *Smoke*, however, this photographic motif plays a secondary role, embellishing the primary focus of the film – the story of Auggie and some of his customers over one summer – rather than acting as the centerpiece of the film. The difference of emphasis, relative to *20 Sites*, is captured by the fact that one of the main storylines in the film – concerning recently widowed writer Paul Benjamin (William Hurt) – is triggered when Benjamin sees his deceased wife in one of Auggie's photos. In this way, and as of course is much more conventional, individual human presence and character – rather than landscape and location – are put in the foreground of the film. In other words, unlike *20 Sites*, *Smoke* is a narrative!

For a closer, filmic equivalent to *20 Sites*, we would need to look to the avant-garde genre of the landscape film. James Benning's *27 Years Later* (2007), for example, juxtaposes shots from his noted earlier film *One Way Boogie Woogie* (1977) with parallel takes of the same locations shot roughly 25 years later. While the two Benning films record just two time slices, and with a much larger gap between them than we find between Phillips's photos, Benning exhibits the same interest in the effects of time on place, and the same attention to holding constant most of the parameters of shooting (camera position and framing, lens type, film stock, and so forth), other than the moment at which it occurs.

Following the trail of *Smoke*, however, it is in feature filmmaking and serial television production that we find the most sustained exploration of time and personhood, rather than time and place. While most of the volume in your hands is focused squarely on serial television, in what follows I will focus on two sets of cases slightly offset from this main focus: cinematic sequels, and serial works that straddle the worlds of feature film and serial television production. And through these cases, I'll consider three themes in particular: The effort to reach back through time to reflect on its passage; the complementary effort to reach forward through time by committing to plans for the future; and the upshot of both activities, in the context of serial form, for character and characterization.

Richard Linklater's fascination with the relationship between film and time is well established. In both the *Before* trilogy – *Before Sunrise* (1995), *Before Sunset* (2004), *Before Midnight* (2013) – and in his *Boyhood* (2014), Linklater has forged an approach to filmmaking akin to longitudinal non-fictional projects, in some ways resembling Phillips's *20 Sites* but still more closely related to the BBC productions *Up* (starting with *Seven Up!* in 1964, through to *63 Up* in 2019, the last film in the series made prior to director Michael Apted's death in January 2021) and *Child of Our Time* (starting in 2000), each of which tracks the growth and development of a group of children across the years and decades.[8] As with these non-fictional projects, the three *Before* films track the biographical journeys of their fictional protagonists, Jesse and Celine, from their first encounter in a train traveling from Budapest to Vienna early on June 16, 1994, to their reunion in Paris nine years later, and on to a family vacation – Jesse and Celine are now married with children – in Greece a further nine years ahead.[9]

While sharing an interest in tracking the development of individuals and their relationships over time, *Boyhood* takes a very different form. Where the *Before* trilogy displays intermittent and dispersed temporal form – 3 day-long samples from a span of 18 years – *Boyhood*, by contrast, works with radically compressed temporality (12 years of story duration being represented in 165 minutes of screen time). And this difference points to a contrast between *Boyhood* and the *Before* trilogy of considerable importance in the current context. The thematic focus on time in the *Before* films is plain from the outset, as is the potential for one or more sequels; after all, *Before Sunrise* leaves us wondering whether Jesse and Celine will follow through on their pact to meet exactly six months from the moment of their parting, at the same place, on platform 9 of Vienna's Hauptbahnhof station at 6 pm on December 16, 1994. (We discover in *Before Sunset* that neither keeps up their end of the bargain – but also, of course, that they do find their way back to each other eventually.) Neither the second nor the third film in the trilogy, however, arose from a pre-commitment – parallel to the fictional commitment made, though not fulfilled, by Jesse and Celine – to revisit the stories of the two characters at particular intervals (or even a looser promise to get back to them at some indefinite point). Instead, at least in terms of their public statements on the occasion of the release of each film, Linklater and his collaborators have left us with nothing more than a vague "We'll see."

The production of *Boyhood* was quite different. Linklater began shooting the film in 2001, planning to develop the story and shoot more scenes at annual intervals, thereby exploiting the natural aging of the cast. The annual cycle of shooting continued through to 2013. The project thus resembles serial television production in its combination of a commitment to future production on a planned schedule, with a flexible and open attitude towards the exact content of the developing narrative. But the outcome is distinctly cinematic: A feature film, close to three hours in duration, tracking the fortunes of Mason (Ellar Coltrane) and Samantha Evans (Lorelei Linklater), and their divorced parents Mason Snr (Ethan Hawke) and Olivia (Patricia Arquette), as the children grow from childhood through adolescence to early adulthood. *Boyhood* is thus unique in the way it combines the temporally extended scale of serial television production with the (relative) compactness, and the self-contained character, of the feature film as an output.

The shock of the old

The year 2017 saw the release of three remarkable sequels – remarkable in the first instance for the size of the gap between the production and release of the original works and the appearance of the sequels: *Blade Runner 2049* was released 35 years after *Blade Runner* in 1982; *Twin Peaks: The Return*, 26 years after the initial broadcast of the second season of *Twin Peaks* in 1991; and *T2*, 21 years after *Trainspotting* in 1996. In each case, the gaps in the represented story times of the films are comparable, if not identical (the action in *Blade Runner 2049*, for example, begins 30 years after the close of the story in *Blade Runner*). To put the length of these gaps into some perspective, consider the fact that if we stepped back through film history, taking generational strides of 35-year durations, a mere three steps would take us back virtually to the dawn of film history: the first step taking us from 2017 to 1982, the second to 1947, and the third to 1912. So these are, by the measure of human memory and human experience, large temporal gaps.[10]

It comes as no surprise, therefore, that all three films, in their different ways, play with what we might term "the shock of the old." Perhaps the mother of all such shock effects – at least in the context of contemporary mainstream filmmaking – comes in the closing seconds of *The Force Awakens* (2015), when Mark Hamill turns to the camera and draws back the hood of his cloak to reveal his unkempt and weather-beaten visage, some 32 years after we last witnessed the youthful version of it in the world of *Star Wars*, in *The Return of the Jedi* (1983).[11] *Blade Runner 2049* creates a similar jolt when Harrison Ford surfaces in the last third of the film as the now aged and reclusive Deckard. By contrast, in this respect, *T2* comes out of the blocks fast, immediately confronting us with the contrast between the apparently fit, but actually ailing, middle-aged Renton, grinding out the miles on a gym treadmill, and his smiling, slender, youthful self, striding purposefully across Waterloo Bridge in the early morning sunlight. (Recall Boyle's remark on the *Trainspotting* characters: "When you're in your teens or your twenties … time's irrelevant, you just don't give a hoot about it … And then you get a bit older, and you realise it's time that doesn't care about you – that's actually the way the equation works.") In all these cases, the potency of the representation of the physical aging of the characters depends to a large extent on the transparent, indexical nature of the medium of film – on the fact that we are actually seeing, through these films, the aging of the actors playing the characters. And the same is true of *Boyhood*, which uses that same capacity of film to record the growth into adulthood of its young actor-protagonists and the passage of their older co-stars into middle age.[12]

Boyle and his collaborators reach back through time to create the juxtaposition of the two Rentons, inserting fragments of a shot from the final scene of *Trainspotting* into the opening sequence of *T2*. The play with time here is particularly intricate: Each time the sequence cuts to these brief insert shots, we have the impression that Renton is walking towards the camera, and indeed he is. But with each new fragment, we cut to an *earlier*, not a later, portion of the original shot. This becomes apparent when we recall that in the original shot, Renton gradually moves out of focus, and occupies more of the frame, as he approaches the camera; while in *T2*, with each cut back to the shot, Renton is in sharper focus and seen in a slightly longer framing. This backwards-stepping structure recalls in miniature *Memento* (2000) and adumbrates the narrative to come: following his collapse on the treadmill, Renton will return to his homeland, just as he was fleeing from it at the end of *Trainspotting*.[13]

Blade Runner 2049 and *T2* are straightforwardly cinematic works, though even in these two cases, we need to add a couple of footnotes. First, in both cases, the films to which they act as sequels were adaptations of novels, and *T2* contains some material adapted from both Irvine Welsh's *Trainspotting* (1993) and the first of his sequels to that novel, *Porno* (2002). Second, both sequels had been preceded by other works continuing the narratives of the original films in noncinematic contexts. Welsh published two further novels focusing on the *Trainspotting* characters prior to the release of *T2* – *Skagboys* (2012) and *The Blade Artist* (2016) – while *Blade Runner 2049* was also trailed in the months preceding its release by three short films, dramatizing events taking place between the original film and the sequel, available and most easily seen by viewers on YouTube.[14] *Twin Peaks: The Return*, from one point of view, is just as straightforwardly a work of serial television, produced and distributed by Showtime and taking the basic form of a television serial, episodes being released on a weekly basis between May 21 and September 3, 2017 (with just a couple of early episodes being given advance online release). And of course, the show is, precisely, a return – to the world of *Twin Peaks* and to many of that world's characters, first seen in seasons one and two of *Twin Peaks*, produced and broadcast by ABC across 1990–1991.

But Lynch began his career as a painter and sculptor, and made his reputation as a feature director, before his move into television production with *Twin Peaks*, and he continually shuttles between the worlds of the gallery, the big screen, and the (still relatively!) small screen. One chapter in the unfolding story of *Twin Peaks*, 1992's *Fire Walk with Me*, took the form of a feature film; *Mulholland Drive* began as a pilot for a television serial, but was transformed into a feature. Lynch has stated that he conceives of *The Return* not as a series of episodes but as a single, long-form work, notwithstanding its release format. *Cahiers du cinéma* and *Sight & Sound* both accorded *The Return* high honors – naming it, respectively, the first- and second-best *film* of 2017. None of this erases the fact that *The Return* is a television serial, but it does point to the complexities of the relations among cinema, television, and adjacent media, which go beyond the literal status of any given work. Lynch brings to bear his painterly and cinematic sensibility in the domain of television, and we fail to register something important about all three seasons of *Twin Peaks* if we simply insist, flat-footedly, that they are televisual works.

How does *The Return* work with the shock of the old and, in general, with the long gap between the broadcast of *Twin Peaks* season two (in 1991) and three (in 2017)? Three strategies stand out. First and most obviously, there are the *resurrections* of characters from the first two seasons; a quarter-century may have passed, but *The Return* ensures that we regularly encounter first-generation denizens of *Twin Peaks*. Second, there are *remembrances*, in the form of a number of end-credit dedications to deceased actors and other personnel.

Some of these dedications are to actors, such as Miguel Ferrer (playing FBI Agent Albert Rosenfield) and Warren Frost (as Dr. Hayward), who lived long enough to appear in footage shot for the new season. Others only appear in *The Return* via interpolated footage from the earlier seasons: Frank Silva (Bob) had died in 1995, and Jack Nance (Pete Martell) in 1996, while David Bowie, who would die in January 2016, agreed that footage of him playing FBI Agent Phillip Jeffries in *Fire Walk with Me* could be used in the new season on condition that his voice be dubbed over by an authentic Louisiana actor (Nathan Frizzell being cast to voice this role). The dedications to Silva, Ferrer, Frost, Bowie, and Nance appear at the conclusion of, respectively, episodes 2, 3, 7, 14, and 17 of *The Return*.

One of the most striking and complex of the strategies by which *The Return* renders the shock of the old – the sometimes brutal effects of the passage of time – bears chiefly on Agent Cooper, as played by Kyle MacLachlan. Except that there is a problem in describing MacLachlan's appearance in the third season in these terms. MacLachlan does appear as Agent Cooper, but he also appears as Cooper's nameless doppelgänger *and* as the character Dougie Jones, a benign, idiotic double, counterbalancing the sinister doppelgänger. What's more, in the final episode of the season, Cooper is left a note – apparently from Diane, but signed off by "Linda" – addressing him as "Richard" (names mysteriously invoked by The Fireman as a warning to Cooper while he is still trapped in the Black Lodge in the first episode of the season).

In this way, *The Return* plays a complex game with character *recognition* – with the process by which we individuate and reidentify characters across a narrative. Taken as a whole, *The Return* affords us both character recognition and *re*-recognition – a major expectation and pleasure of any serial work – whereby we not only individuate and reidentify characters within the scope of *The Return* but also reidentify characters from the earlier seasons. The strategies of resurrection and remembrance noted earlier highlight such re-recognition. But in relation to Agent Cooper, the show confronts us with a kind of *disfigured* recognition, combining continuity at the level of the body – MacLachlan's face and body easily reidentifiable from the earlier seasons – with discontinuity at the level of the person, that same, single body embodying three very different characters. MacLachlan's good-natured and clean-cut Cooper is now rent between the dead-eyed, soulless doppelgänger, in one direction, and the smiling, empty-headed Dougie Jones, in the other direction.

Seriality, character, twofoldness

The Return points to the way in which serial form brings to the fore certain possibilities in character engagement that are, if not impossible to achieve in shorter and more contained works, certainly more readily accomplished in long-form works. As we have just seen through the case of *The Return*, our recognition of characters can be stretched and stressed by serial narratives. But seriality may also have an important bearing on the evolution of a character across a narrative – that is, not on our ability to individuate and track a character as a particular, continuous agent across a narrative, but on our cognizance of change within a continuous agent.[15] Whether the development of a character manifests change in the character, or whether the perception of change arises from the delayed revelation of certain aspects of a character, it is clear that serial form affords a larger canvas on which to play out this evolution.[16] Walter White's gradual transformation in *Breaking Bad* from beaten-down, stressed-out, terminally ill, emasculated husband and high school teacher to murderous drug king-pin must count as one of the clearest examples of such development. This example also illustrates and underlines the utility of serial form as a vehicle for antiheroic protagonists, and the moral complexity necessary for sustaining such figures, at once attractive and repellent: surely it is no coincidence that the current surge in serial television production has been realized in significant part through such dramas, from *The Sopranos* (1999–2007) to *Dexter* (2006–13) to *Mad Men* (2007–15) to *Breaking Bad* (2008–13) to *Ray Donovan* (2013–22) and *Ozark* (2017–22).

The antiheroic character structure most obviously bears on matters of *allegiance* – on the manner, that is, in which a narrative work shapes our attitudes towards its characters, above all in terms of the morality of their actions and attitudes. Allegiance is distinct from *alignment*, which describes our epistemic rather than ethical positioning with regard to characters, as it is created through spatial attachment and subjective access. But while we should not collapse allegiance with alignment, it's important to recall that alignment plays a crucial role here: What we learn about a character through alignment, and when we learn it, is fundamental to the evolution of our attitude towards – and degree of allegiance with – that character.[17]

The dynamics of alignment within serial works are significant in further ways as well. Jason Gendler has written of the "rich inferential world" of *Mad Men*, pointing to the complex web of implications cumulatively emerging within individual episodes as well as the extended development of the narrative across episodes and seasons.[18] Shifting the focus from work and character to the spectator, Robert Blanchet and Margrethe Bruun Vaage have examined the distinctive "parasocial attachments" made possible by long-form, serial works, including a kind of "friendship" with the complex, richly developed fictional agents sustained by shows such as *Mad Men* and *The Sopranos*. (For the skeptics, one piece of relevant testimony: A.W. Eaton begins her essay on *The Sopranos* by declaring that she misses Tony Soprano!)[19]

Across the various cases we've examined, we can see that another important feature of character is made salient and inflected by serial form: the twofoldness of character, that is, the fact that our engagement with and appreciation of characters is constituted by a conjoint awareness of their mimetic-representational and artifactual dimensions.[20] A character, in other words, is at once an artifact *and* an imaginary person – recognized as such, and made to be recognized as such. In *Blade Runner 2049*, the fleeting appearance of a new replicant clone of Rachael – almost identical with Rachael as incarnated by Sean Young in 1982 – further highlights Deckard/Harrison Ford's aged countenance. "Her eyes were green," notes Deckard laconically; the clone replicant is summarily executed. There's no going back. The effect of the clone on Deckard is echoed by the effect of the CGI simulation of Rachael on us, a further troubling reminder of the temporal gulf separating the original film and the sequel. But the key point here is that the scene lays bare the artifactual fold of character, for the Rachael we see here is an artifact several times over, within and without the storyworld: a clone of a replicant whose memories were implanted, originally fabricated by Philip K. Dick and elaborated by a succession of screenwriters and directors.

In *The Return*, by contrast, the twofoldness of character is made plain by the fission to which Kyle MacLachlan-as-Agent-Cooper is subjected – that single agent splintering into Cooper's doppelgänger, Dougie Jones, and Cooper himself – a process foregrounding the embodiment of a character by an actor. (Lynch also plays up the twofoldness of character with the most intriguing of his end-credit remembrances: Catherine Coulson, who died in 2015, receives a dedication at the end of episode 1; while the character she played, Margaret Lanterman, aka The Log Lady, is remembered at the end of episode 15.) The scission of Kyle MacLachlan's Agent Cooper into three characters departs from the background, default norm that one character will be embodied by one actor. *Heimat*, another work zigzagging between the worlds of cinema and television, also departs from this norm, if less violently, casting Marita Breuer initially in the role of Maria Simon and many years later as her husband Paul's paternal grandmother, Margarethe Simon; somewhat more conventionally, Maria's youngest son Hermann is played by five actors, in part to represent different phases of his life and in part according to the contingencies of casting for different series within the overall work.[21]

Boyhood, we've noted, pulls in the opposite direction, disdaining the conventional exception to the one actor–one character norm associated with coming-of-age dramas, in which a single character is played by two or more actors as that character matures and ages (as exemplified by the case of Hermann Simon in *Heimat*). Instead, *Boyhood* goes "beneath" convention by representing the growth of Mason Jnr and Samantha Evans – and the aging of their parents – through the natural aging of the actors playing these roles, a strategy made possible by Linklater's unique creative and shooting strategy for the film. Once again, we see how *Boyhood* resembles those long-form documentary works, such as the *Up* series, which document the passage through life of real individuals. The effect is paradoxical. On the one hand, it is clear that *Boyhood* reaches for a kind of realism, drawing real actor and fictional agent – the two folds of motion picture character – as closely together as possible. On the other hand, the strength and pervasiveness of the coming-of-age convention throws Linklater's strategy into relief as a highly self-conscious one, at once realist *and* formalist.

The twofoldness of character in *Boyhood* is also manifest in the casting of stars Patricia Arquette and Ethan Hawke as the (divorced) parents of Mason

Jnr and Samantha: In addition to the fact that both of them, by virtue of being stars, bring with them their star personae and performance histories, in Hawke's case, there is his significant creative relationship with Linklater and the resonances between Hawke's Mason Snr in *Boyhood* and Hawke's Jesse in the *Before* trilogy of films (two of which, *Before Sunset* and *Before Midnight*, were shot and released while the *Boyhood* project was ongoing). Along with *Boyhood*'s "compressed serial" form of production, these factors consolidate the link between the film and serial narrative more generally.

The twofoldness of character is apparent in serial television production in a host of other ways both within and between shows. Consider the phenomenon of multiple incarnations of the same underlying character in different shows. Swedish detective Kurt Wallander, originally the invention of novelist Henning Mankell, now has no fewer than four incarnations, as embodied by Rolf Lassgård, Krister Henriksson, Kenneth Branagh, and Adam Pålsson. The most recent of these shows – Netflix's *Young Wallander* (2020–), featuring Pålsson – to some extent falls under the "coming-of-age" principle insofar as the show focuses on an earlier slice of Wallander's life than do the other adaptations (all of which feature Wallander in some phase of middle age). But the example can't be fully assimilated to that principle, since this young Wallander is young in the present day, not in the earlier period implied by the novels or the earlier adaptations. Taken together, the Wallander shows indicate how readily we accommodate the idea of multiple incarnations of and variations on a single underlying character – an accommodation, I argue, only possible due to our basic apprehension of the twofoldness of character.[22]

One further example to drive the point home: The Netflix drama *Narcos* (2015–17) depicts a partly fictionalized history of Columbia in the 1980s and 1990s, focusing on the efforts of the DEA, alongside the Columbian government and the CIA, to combat the narcotics trade. While each episode of the show begins with a statement underlining the fictionalized character of the history being presented,[23] the creators of *Narcos* are also at pains to play up the fact that the narrative tracks, at least in broad strokes, the real history of Columbia and the United States in the period depicted. One strategy for playing up these connections with the reality of the history being dramatized involves the systematic use of documentary footage of many of the figures involved: DEA agent Steve Murphy (the narrator of seasons 1 and 2), various Columbian politicians (as well as soldiers, policeman, and ordinary citizens), and not least, Pablo Escobar – photos and footage of whom are scattered throughout the opening credit sequence of the first two seasons. The transparent force of film and photography – in this case, embodied in the documentary footage of figures integral to the history being dramatized – is evident once again.

The final episode of season 2 takes this strategy a step further. Following the capture and killing of Escobar, we cut to a bar where Murphy's DEA partner – agent Javier Peña – recently taken off the case, is shown brooding in a bar (Figure 8.1). But the scene in the bar opens with a tracking shot initially framing not Peña but two older men toasting Escobar's defeat (Figure 8.2). Attentive

Figure 8.1 *Narcos* (Netflix 2015–2017). The aftermath of Escobar's capture – Javier Peña, as played by Pedro Pascal, ruminates in a bar.

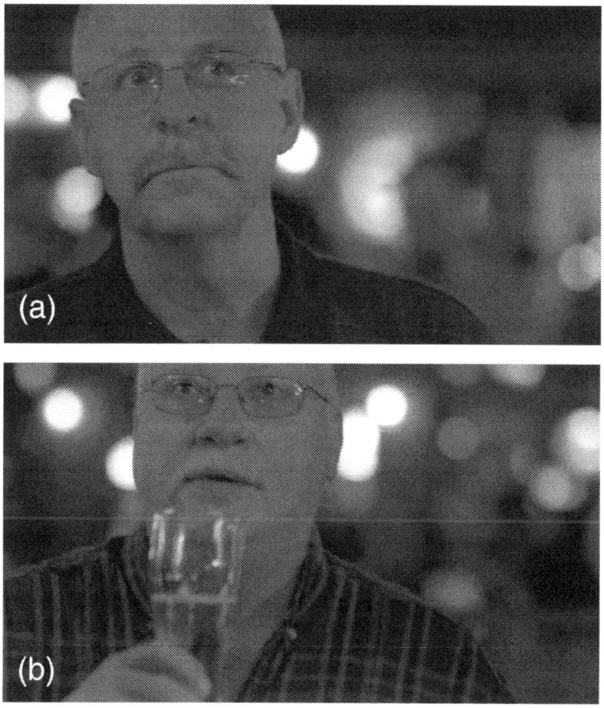

Figure 8.2 *Narcos* (Netflix 2015–2017). (a) The real Steve Murphy and (b) Javier Peña in the bar.

viewers will recognize these men as the real Steve Murphy and Javier Peña, seen as younger men in documentary photos in the opening credit sequence of every episode (Figure 8.3). At this point, then, the show not merely interleaves documentary footage of the real historical figures in among the staged,

Figure 8.3 *Narcos* (Netflix 2015–2017). The real Murphy and Peña during their DEA tenure in Columbia.

dramatized scenes that constitute the fabric of the show, but allows a pair of these figures to cross the boundary between those two kinds of footage. In the very same episode, and in the diegetic spaces created in the episode, then, Murphy and Peña are present both in their fictional incarnations – as played by Boyd Holbrook and Pedro Pascal, respectively – and as their older, real selves.

The point, however, is not that this gesture is in any way disruptive, undermining our ability to engage with the show on its ordinary terms as a tense and thrilling historical crime drama. After all, the appearance of the real Murphy and Peña within the staged spaces of the show is in essence nothing more than a joint cameo appearance by the two men, complicated only by the co-presence of their younger selves as played by Holbrook and Pascal. The point, rather, is that this play with character enriches the show, layering its dramatization of history with further complexity, without undermining our absorption in the story it tells. And this play with character is possible because it exploits the underlying twofoldness of character: our understanding that characters are artifacts, even when they are based on historical figures.[24]

Notes

1 On the idea of "convergence culture," see Jenkins (2006).

2 The analysis of film temporality in terms of story, plot, and screen duration is due to David Bordwell, Kristin Thompson, and Jeff Smith, *Film Art: An Introduction* (12th edition, 2020).

3 I discuss the Clock of the Long Now and *As Slow as Possible* in more detail in my 2021, 85–6.

4 The work as a whole is comprised of *Heimat – A German Chronicle* (1984); *The Second Heimat – Chronicle of a Generation* (1992); *Heimat 3 – A Chronicle of Endings and Beginnings* (2004); *Heimat Fragments* (2006); and *The Other Heimat – Chronicle of a Vision* (2013).
5 In Smith 2017, chapter 7, I argue that narrative representation extends the mind more generally, particularly in relation to empathy and the imagination.
6 See the slideshows of the photographic series for each location on Phillips's website: www.tomphillips.co.uk/works/20-sites-n-years/20-slideshows. Phillips' intentions are recorded under "Technical Specs" on the website, among them:

> Artist 1 intends that the pictures should be taken by his family and their descendants, if they are willing, and that the work should thus go on indefinitely: the services of their friends may be enrolled or even from time to time that of professional photographers. Continuity is the most important factor.

20 Sites n Years is also the subject of a film by Jake Auerbach, released in 2016.
7 "20 Slideshows: 01. 102 Grove Park. C. 10.20 am.The Central point," at www.tomphillips.co.uk/works/20-sites-n-years/20-slideshows.
8 *Seven Up!* was directed by Paul Almond; all subsequent episodes, filmed at intervals of seven years, were directed by Apted, who became closely identified with the series. *Child of Our Time*, hosted by medical scientist Robert Winston, comprises 11 series, beginning in 2000 and running up to 2017, with a further single-episode special in 2020 (the year in which, of course, the millennial children turned 20).
9 For more on Linklater's *Before* trilogy, see my 2021, in many ways a companion piece to the present chapter.
10 A new season of the television sitcom *Roseanne* appeared in 2018, 21 years after the broadcast of season 9 in 1997. Although related to the examples under consideration, as a sitcom, *Roseanne* presents a somewhat different type of case. The expectation was that once restarted, new seasons would continue to be produced – an 11th season had been approved, until the show was abruptly canceled by ABC as a result of Roseanne Barr's racist tweeting.
11 Hamill had, of course, appeared in other films and television shows; the shock here depends on his long absence from and reappearance within the universe of *Star Wars*.
12 Boyle makes this claim in Film4 (2017). The classic analysis of the dimension of film at stake here is to be found in Bazin (1967); the contemporary argument in terms of "transparency" is due to Walton (1984). Leigh Singer observes that while in *Trainspotting* the freeze frames in the opening sequence are labeled with the characters' names, in *T2* it is the *actors'* names that are imprinted on the equivalent opening freeze frames. This device serves to play up the role of our perception of the actors' aging in our apprehension of the characters' aging. See Singer (2017).
13 For more on the relationship between *T2* and *Trainspotting*, see the "Afterword" in my 2002/2021.
14 In order of release across August and September 2017 (prior to the release of *Blade Runner 2049* in October of that year): *2036: Nexus Dawn* and *2048: Nowhere to Run*, live action shorts both directed by Luke Scott, and the anime short *Blade Runner Black Out 2022*, directed by Shinichirō Watanabe.
15 The idea that the same object may persist across time and through change raises complex metaphysical questions, which I don't tackle here. See the debate, for example, between "perdurantists" and "endurantists"; relevant overviews are provided by Gallois (2016) and Hawley (2020).
16 David Bordwell (2008, 117–120) discusses the difference between character change – implied, sometimes misleadingly, by the notion of a "character arc" – and the delayed revelation of aspects of a character.
17 The concepts of recognition, alignment, and allegiance are set out in my *Engaging Characters: Fiction, Emotion, and the* Cinema (1995), second, revised edition forthcoming 2021.

18 Gendler (2016) notes, however, that

> While it is easy to assume that serial narratives routinely call upon accumulated character knowledge in order to enrich viewer inferences, somewhat surprisingly, most episodes in *Mad Men* season five [the principal focus of the article] are actually largely enriched through episodic rather than serial information.
>
> (article abstract)

19 Blanchet and Bruun Vaage (2012). Eaton writes: "Several years after the end of the HBO series *The Sopranos*, I still miss the characters. In particular, I miss the protagonist, Tony, who feels like an old friend" (Eaton 2012, 281).

20 I set out the case for the twofoldness of character in Smith (2011). See also the new Introduction to the second edition of Smith (1995), forthcoming 2021.

21 At different stages of his childhood, youth, and adulthood, Hermann Simon is played by Jens Werkheiser (episodes 6 and 7), Frank Kleid (episode 8), Jörg Richter (episodes 9 and 11), and Peter Harting (episodes 10 and 11) in *Heimat*. In *The Second Heimat* and *Heimat 3*, the adult Hermann is played by Henry Arnold.

22 Of course, the exact sense in which the Wallander of all of these works might be thought of as the "same character," or perhaps as the distinct descendants of a single original character, is a complex question, which I leave aside here. All I assume is that whatever the correct metaphysical account, psychologically we regard these characters as, if not identical, nonetheless closely bound together in a distinctive way. For discussion, see Reicher (2010).

23 "This dramatisation is inspired by true events. However, certain scenes, characters, names, businesses, incidents, locations and events have been fictionalised for dramatic purposes."

24 My thanks to Ted Nannicelli and Héctor Pérez for their feedback, and for their infinite patience with me as I brought this chapter to completion.

References

Bazin, André. 1967. *What is Cinema? Vol 1*. Berkeley, CA: University of California Press.

Blanchet, Robert, and Margrethe Bruun Vaage. 2012. "Don, Peggy, and Other Fictional Friends? Engaging with Characters in Television Series." *Projections* 6, no. 2: 18–41.

Bordwell, David. 2008. "Three Dimensions of Film Narrative." In *Poetics of Cinema*. Routledge: New York.

Bordwell, David, Kristin Thompson, and Jeff Smith. 2020. *Film Art: An Introduction*, 12th ed. New York: McGraw-Hill.

Eaton, A.W. 2012. "Robust Immoralism." *Journal of Aesthetics and Art Criticism* 70, no. 3: 281–92.

Film4. 2017. "The Cast of *Trainspotting* Reunited: *T2 Trainspotting* Film4 Interview Special." https://www.youtube.com/watch?v=9AdgBq2Mp2Q

Gallois, André. 2016. "Identity Over Time." *Stanford Encyclopaedia of Philosophy*. https://plato.stanford.edu/entries/identity-time/#5

Gendler, Jason. 2016. "The Rich Inferential World of *Mad Men*: Serialized Television and Character Interiority." *Projections* 10, no, 1: 39–62.

Hawley, Katherine. 2020. "Temporal Parts." *Stanford Encyclopaedia of Philosophy*. https://plato.stanford.edu/entries/temporal-parts/

Jenkins, Henry. 2006. *Convergence Culture: Where Old and New Media Collide*. New York: New York University Press.

Reicher, Maria E. 2010. "The Ontology of Fictional Characters." In *Characters in Fictional Worlds*, edited by Jens Eder, Fotis Jannidis, and Ralf Schneider. Berlin: De Gruyter. 111–133.

Singer, Leigh. "Trainspotting/T2 Trainspotting: Judgment Days." Video Essay. https://www.youtube.com/watch?v=P0pwOWrn0Xw

Smith, Murray. (1995) Revised second edition forthcoming 2021. *Engaging Characters: Fiction, Emotion, and the Cinema*. Oxford: Clarendon Press.

Smith, Murray. (2002) 2021. *Trainspotting*. London: BFI Modern Classics/Bloomsbury.

Smith, Murray. 2011. "On the Twofoldness of Character." *New Literary History* 42, no. 2: 277–294.

Smith, Murray. 2017. *Film, Art, and the Third Culture: A Naturalized Aesthetics of Film*. Oxford. Oxford University Press.

Smith, Murray. 2021. "Epic Intimacy." In *Before Sunrise, Before Sunset, Before Midnight: A Philosophical Exploration*, edited by Hans Maes and Katrien Schaubroeck. New York: Routledge. 83–101.

Walton, Kendall. 1984. "Transparent Pictures: On the Nature of Photographic Realism." *Critical Inquiry* 11, no. 2: 246–277.

9 Five theses on the difficulty of ending Quality TV series

Margrethe Bruun Vaage

Achieving closure in any narrative form is no mean feat. Spectators of contemporary television series – in particular, of the type often labeled Quality TV – anticipate the ending with great expectations. As Jason Mittell points out in his taxonomy of endings in contemporary American series, or what he discusses as "complex TV," only some television series have a planned finale. Others are canceled, and the spectator must do with "stoppage" (Mittell 2015, 319). Nevertheless, the denigration of serial fiction is as old as the form itself (Hayward 1997), and in order for a series to be perceived as art, perhaps its seriality must be controlled by the promise of an ending, as Michael Z. Newman and Elana Levine (2012) argue in their critical discussion of the celebratory reception of American Quality TV in the press and the academy.[1] They point out that the discourse on American Quality TV has involved distancing these series from regular TV, and in particular, the feminine connotations of soaps. They claim that one distancing strategy is to emphasize the ending, and how a Quality TV series' finite form renders it different from the deferral of closure in soaps (Ibid., 80ff). The Quality TV series' end thus plays a central role in ongoing discussions about the demarcation between so-called regular and Quality TV, and what, if anything, differentiates the two.

Newman and Levine may be right in seeing the emphasis on endings in the Quality TV discourse as part of an effort by the TV industry, fans, and critics alike to distinguish Quality TV from regular TV, and as such, to distinguish the taste of those who produce and consume these series. As Newman and Levine also point out, the "rise of conspicuous showrunner-*auteurs* inserts into television discourse a number of tropes of authorship familiar from older, already legitimated and aestheticized cultural forms" (2012, 45). Jane Feuer concurs that being "'authored' is perhaps the most important factor distinguishing quality drama from ordinary TV" (2005a, 30).[2] The creators of traditional sitcoms and soaps would not be emphasized as *auteurs* to the same degree as creators of Quality TV series tend to be, even though soap opera fans, for example, are highly aware of the creator as well, as will become evident in the very last section. The cult of the creator in Quality TV discourse can be seen as part of an effort to elevate these series' status to art, as *auteurism* helped lift the Hollywood film director from a position of relative anonymity to celebrated

DOI: 10.4324/9781003188643-9

artist, and their films from entertainment to art. Building on these observations, I argue that it is at the end of a Quality TV series in particular that we expect the author to step forward, so to speak, and through aesthetic choices clarify the intentions behind the series. The ending is especially important for one's search for authorial comments and intentions. This is arguably true of the ending of every narrative, but there is additional pressure on the author of Quality TV due to auteurism and also due to the series' long duration, as I show in the very last section in this chapter.

Unfortunately, this increased attention to the end of Quality TV series coincides with formal features that make satisfying endings difficult to achieve. In his overview of series creators' reflections on endings, Lee Harrington (2013) demonstrates that the creators are aware that criticism of the ending is inevitable. This chapter sketches five reasons why it is difficult to design a satisfying ending. There is the need to give the series an ending (which can be an open ending, as in art film, as we shall see) due to the demands of art and authorship as well as its long duration. However, bringing the series to a close is intrinsically difficult due to the Quality TV series' narrative form: Its ensemble casts and multiple plotlines, genre hybridity, complex moralities, position in between art and commerce, and elicitation of close ties with the characters all add to the difficulty of ending these series satisfactorily. None of these problems is unique to American Quality TV, but because all of these factors tend to co-occur in these series, the ending is particularly difficult and adds to the burden of authorial presence. The endings of Quality TV series are haunted by contradicting demands.

I use the terms "Quality TV" and "complex TV" and take these to point to the same phenomenon in contemporary television. However, arguably, the notions emphasize different aspects of this trend: The notion Quality TV draws our attention to the discourse on a series and its cultural status, whereas complex TV is used to analyze the series' narrative and stylistic characteristics and the engagement it invites from spectators. I have tried to use the notions accordingly. In television studies, the notion of Quality TV points to the quest in the television industry to appeal to a so-called "quality" demographic of the audience (highly educated, urban, affluent viewers) coupled with the critical reception of series that succeeded in doing exactly this.[3] What interests me here are the implications of this discourse in terms of expectations of endings. By using the notion of Quality TV, I do not mean to suggest that these series are better than other programs on television.[4] I concentrate on American Quality TV without implying that Quality TV is restricted to an American context, and on serials without claiming that Quality TV must be serial. The ending of episodic series deserves a study of its own.

Second, due to space concerns, I will limit my discussion to the very end of the entire series and will not explore at length the numerous other, smaller endings of TV series, such as episode endings and seasonal endings. Although I will touch upon such endings too, I will not offer even the briefest of theories about the relation between these various types of ending.

Finally, I suggest that the audience's expectations of, and search for, authorial intentions peak at the very end of Quality TV series and that this can be tied to the hype around the creator or showrunner as an element of auteurism in the Quality TV discourse. Critics might argue that there are numerous problems with this, among them the collective production of television series. It is beyond the scope of the present chapter to discuss this. I do not argue that we should, or necessarily even do, turn to the actual creator(s) when trying to settle the meaning of any given series. Some fans look for statements from the creator, but often, the author can be seen as a construct, a voice we look for in the series. This is an intricate narratological and philosophical problem, and I will not attempt to solve it here.[5]

Ensemble casts and multiple plotlines

A good place to start is with a characterization of narrative closure. Closure is achieved when all the questions saliently posed by the narrative are answered, argues Noël Carroll (2007). For a complex serial, this immediately poses a problem. Complex serials are typically ensemble-cast series with multiple plotlines, and they saliently pose a plethora of questions. Some complex serials have a main character, whose arc we want to see completed in some sense or another. However, in many series, the difference between main and supporting characters is difficult to maintain. Many have noted the difficulty of ending a story with multiple characters and plotlines (e.g., Azcona 2010; Bordwell 2006; Hayward 1997, 57; MacDowell 2013, 87).

On the other hand, as Jane Feuer (1984, 2005b) argues, the fully serialized, multiple-plotline and ensemble-cast soap opera can be said to excel at seasonal endings, although it is per definition a narrative form that defies closure. The lingering on close-up shots of emotionally expressive faces accompanied by dramatic music can give a feeling of closure even if most questions in the narrative are left unanswered. A seasonal ending is different from a series finale. Nevertheless, Feuer's point is still relevant. Richard Neupert (1995) emphasizes how endings can be created by either closure in the story or closure in the discourse, i.e., through completeness of theme or by use of various (stylistic or narrative) closure devices. James MacDowell concurs in his study of the Hollywood happy ending: Closure devices "go a long way towards closing the film on the level of form" (2013, 67). We have come to accept these closure devices as endings due to frequent use: bracketing (where a film's end echoes its opening), the camera receding from the characters, lovers kissing, a book or curtains closing (MacDowell 2013, 65). These devices become "aesthetic signifiers of finality" (MacDowell 2013, 65).

One technique that features with some regularity in television series is the use of montage sequences. The use of montage in *The Wire* and *Sons of Anarchy*'s season endings may give closure at the level of form, although the questions saliently posed by the narrative are left unanswered. However, whereas the montage endings of *The Wire* might be said to be aesthetically praiseworthy, the use of the same device in *Sons of Anarchy* appears less motivated. A central argument in *The Wire* is that the institutions (the drug trade, the dysfunctional features of the police department, etc.) perpetuate themselves – this is a narrative about cyclicity (Mittell 2009; Nannicelli 2009). There is no end to this tragedy, merely repetition. The montage sequences in *The Wire* are not only (episodic, seasonal, and finale) closure devices but a way for the creator(s) to step forward. The sequences make sense thematically and highlight the author's argument. The montages in *Sons of Anarchy* do not fulfill the same dual function and feel trite as the series nears its end. On the other hand, in this latter case, there is a main character who meets his fate in the series finale, answering a major question in this series (will Jax be able to escape the trajectory set out for him by his criminal biker background and make the club he is running legit?). I will return to the morality of this ending later. Here, the point is that it would be dissatisfying if montage sequences became the norm for series finales. The spectator expects more from the series finale, unless the montage sequence also makes sense as story resolution and/or as the author's voice.

There is a more deep-seated problem facing the complex serial. MacDowell argues in relation to the romantic comedy (romcom) *Sleepless in Seattle* that in order to explain why the formation of a couple at the end of the film feels like closure, one needs to turn to the film's point of view. He labels the film a dual-focus narrative: Near equal attention is given to the two main characters Sam and Annie, which "helps to persuade us that a final couple constitutes an appropriate end-point" (MacDowell 2013, 77). He turns to films with multiple characters and plotlines, and questions whether their alignment with multiple characters would make closure possible. In *Sleepless in Seattle*, Sam and Annie finally unite in the end, but MacDowell asks how this ending would be perceived if equal narrative attention had been given to the ex-fiancé Walter, whom Annie dumped unscrupulously, or Sam's ex-girlfriend Victoria, who is conveniently whisked off. Had *Sleepless in Seattle* been a television series, we would probably have been aligned with Walter and Victoria too, and their stories would also have had to be wrapped up somehow. MacDowell quotes Deborah Thomas, who points out that "so-called happy endings … are rarely happy for everyone" (2013, 85). María del Mar Azcona argues that endings of multi-protagonist films can be difficult because "the wider the perspective, the more difficult it becomes to ascribe an absolute meaning, or to describe in a coherent and unified way a set of events or their narrative resolutions" (quoted in MacDowell 2013, 87). Discussing *Best Years* as one such film, MacDowell explains that uniting one couple cannot give closure because its world

> has been constructed to serve not just one main purpose (say, bringing together a couple), but several, having been simultaneously a portrait of returning veterans, a romantic narrative about coping with disability, an exploration of a marriage, a courtship plot, and so on.
>
> (2013, 88)

An underlying problem here is that multi-protagonist stories tend to make use of tropes and narrative patterns from different genres, including varying genre conventions for what counts as closure, a point to which I turn shortly.

One way to address this problem is to give multi-protagonist and multi-plot serials one main plot that evolves in inter-seasonal arcs that involve all main characters in one way or another, such as the fight for the throne in *Game of Thrones*.[6] However, ending this serial would then predictably narrow its focus to this one story-arc and as such, be in danger of abandoning the proper multi-plot narrative structure that perhaps, as one of many factors, made the series appealing in the first place.[7] Be that as it may, it is also worth noting that if an ensemble-cast series succeeds in resolving all the main characters' plotlines at once, the feeling of closure is bound to be strong. Frank Kermode (2000) sees endings in stories as essentially related to death as the ultimate ending in real life. Perhaps this can explain why the ending of *Six Feet Under* is arguably one of the most elegant and rewarding finales in American Quality TV: in flash-forwards, we see all the main characters' dying moments, preceded by an inter-title with their names, birth year, and year of death, as we have seen one character after another be introduced and die in episode openings over the course of the series. And since this is a series about a family of undertakers, death has thematically played a central role all along. It would not work for every serial, but in this particular case, following all the central characters briefly to their dying moments is a beautiful and effective way of achieving closure, and a case where the end of an ensemble-cast, multi-plot serial is more closed, both in story and in discourse, and as such, more emotionally satisfying than a single protagonist stand-alone narrative can perhaps be.

Complex morality

Elsewhere, I have explored antihero series (Vaage 2016), a prominent trend in American Quality TV. Mittell observes that "[o]ne common trait shared by many complex television series is the narrative prominence of unsympathetic, morally questionable, or villainous figures, nearly always male" (2015, 142). Amanda Lotz (2014) labels them "cable guys" due to their prominence on American cable TV. As pointed out by others too, the spectator of an antihero series is left feeling conflicted: should she like or dislike a character such as Tony Soprano or Walter White? Discussing the morality in *The Sopranos*, Noël Carroll argues that "Tony clearly occurs in a narrative context where he is unblinkingly framed as a character whom the audience should regard as evil" (2013, 372). To back up this claim, he discusses how one character, Dr. Krakower, condemns Tony. Suggesting that the spectator is meant to like Tony is to commit the narrative fallacy, Carroll argues – failing to see the character's place in the narrative. However, Tony's place in the narrative is not so easily pinned down. Why should we take Dr. Krakower to be the creator's mouthpiece? A.W. Eaton (2013) makes a similar point. I argue (Vaage 2016, 111) that settling the question of this story's perspective on Tony and his immorality requires careful analysis and cannot be done by pointing to a brief episode where one single character condemns him. Now, there is good reason to emphasize the end when looking for authorial perspectives: It is typically at the end of a story that we expect the story's moral to be revealed. This is evident in the Production Code, for example, in which a film's ending carries special weight: Gangster films were allowed to pass only if the main immoral character, for whom we have been rooting, is punished in the end. Virtue must triumph, and the film's morality is restored (MacDonald 2013, 36). Martin Zeller-Jacques (2014) makes a similar point in his discussion of the ending of *The Sopranos*. Although one might add that this does vary depending on context and genre conventions, overall, we tend to expect an ending to clarify the moral of the story.

Although *The Sopranos* does challenge the spectator's sympathy for Tony radically in the build-up to the finale, the final episode ends ambiguously, and I discuss it as an open ending later. As I point out in my discussion of the antihero, the spectator is increasingly reminded of the immoral nature of this character, especially towards the end of the series. One typical outcome is that the antihero loses his family and/or loved ones and then dies, sometimes by his own choice, as do Jax Teller in *Sons of Anarchy*, or involuntarily, as in Nucky Thompson's death in *Boardwalk Empire*. Not all antiheroes die: Vic Mackey in *The Shield* is turned into an office rat, his own personal hell, but he survives his transgression. Not all antiheroes are clearly punished: The nameless main character in *Banshee* merely rides into the sunset on his motorcycle, and Dexter becomes a lumberjack (in what was perhaps one of the least successful antihero series endings). Although antihero series playfully invite the spectator to like their immoral leads and enjoy their transgressions, in the end the antihero is usually punished, or at the very least, the spectator's sympathy for him is undermined or questioned (Vaage 2016, 54, 112, 184).

HBO was an innovator and trendsetter, and other cable companies, and then networks, followed suit. It is interesting that at the end of these immoral stories, and even in the age of dark cable dramas, morality is restored. American cable TV is not under censorship, there is no Production Code in operation, and in the case of HBO, there are no advertisers to offend. HBO series cater to an educated, adult audience who seemingly like edgy topics. Indeed, Quality TV established itself as a brand by being dark and transgressive. According to Robert Thompson, right from its emergence in the 1980s, quality TV had "grim and thought-provoking subject matter [that] clashed with the simple and happy world presented on most TV" (1996, 35). Robin Nelson points out how what he labels "high-end TV" "explores a risky, 'edgy' television which flouts the historic tendency for small-screen fictions to be conservative, particularly in the USA" (2007, 3). It seems unlikely that questioning our allegiance to the antihero is imposed on the creator when he or she is creating a product that is marketed as pushing boundaries. Why, then, is the thwarted morality of the antihero story usually revised in the end?

One explanation could be that the creator cashes in on the puzzling nature of the spectator's sympathy with this immoral character. The spectator has been encouraged to like the antihero, but now this treacherous story and its narrator actually see him as irredeemably bad, intentionally pulling the rug from under the gullible fan. The finale might leave the spectator pondering whether the sympathy she felt was warranted. Indeed, although we are encouraged to like the antihero, the very end is perhaps intended to leave us in a state of relative moral clarity: It was intriguing to engage with this character, he gave us a power rush and the thrill of the illicit, but now, in the end, I the creator and we the spectators agree that the antihero is bad. An antihero story will offer the thrill of transgression and then feelings of moral righteousness at the end.

However, one other reason for undermining our sympathy with the antihero in the end might be that the end carries special rhetorical weight, and the author feels the need to step forward and clarify his or her own view on the story. The moral clarity sketched earlier is arguably the intended response to an antihero series, but actual spectator responses are typically far more muddled, as evident in Emily Nussbaum's (2014) discussion of the bad fan: The bad fan is the fan who only likes the antihero and fails to grasp that he is also supposed to dislike him. Creator Vince Gilligan pointed out repeatedly that he was surprised by the audience's stubborn sympathy for the antihero Walter White in *Breaking Bad* (see Vaage 2016, 39). Antihero series flirt heavily with immorality, and perhaps the creator feels the weight of moral responsibility and clarifies in the end that the antihero is morally bad. This brings us back to the rhetorical force of an ending: Had the antihero not been questioned towards the end, and the spectator's sympathy for him not been put to the test, would this not have reflected badly on the creator? Even in fiction, and even in the free market of commercial entertainment, and even in dark cable dramas to boot, in the end, there seems to be a mutual need for the author to clarify his or her actual moral views to the public as socially acceptable.

Genre hybridity

MacDowell points out that the degree to which an ending appears closed depends on the film's genre. In a romcom, a couple uniting feels like an ending in spite of being the beginning of a relationship. We have learned intertextually that this is how such films end. He continues:

> Other genres have comparable generic conventions that may act to in some sense "close" what might otherwise appear "open," such as the cowboy riding off to an unspecified future in the Western, or the final "it's still out there" scare in the horror film. Both these kinds of ending might appear unresolved in other contexts, but their familiarity as closural [*sic*] tropes ensures that they are felt to be less so in the genres which gave rise to them.
>
> (2013, 69)

The idea that closure is achieved when questions are answered must therefore be qualified: Genres teach us which questions we should ask. Asking how Annie and Sam will cope after their initial meeting in *Sleepless in Seattle* is not relevant.

In applying this to Quality TV, one problem is that these series are typically characterized by genre hybridity (Dunleavy 2009, 215; Nelson 2007, 26; Thompson 1996, 15).[8] Which devices give closure in a series where genres are mixed? Competing generic conventions may give rise to contradictory expectations. Adding to the difficulty here is that an ending is expected to mesh with the narrative logic of a series. In his overview of the discourses in use in popular, critical, and academic writing on endings, Zeller-Jacques (2014) argues that we assume that there is an ideal way to end a series, according to its own narrative logic, and we assess the finale by evaluating how justified it appears in relation to that logic. Zeller-Jacques found that this discourse is closely tied to ideas of authorship: When evaluating the ending in this way, we search for the creator's plan. One example Zeller-Jacques points to is the TV critic Alan Sepinwall's praise of *The Sopranos* finale backed up by the following observation: It "fits perfectly with everything Chase has done on this show before" (Sepinwall quoted in Zeller-Jacques 2014, 123). Others vehemently disagreed, and again, I return to this finale later. For now, suffice it to say that the difficulty facing a TV series that is a mix of genres is that each genre's logic may dictate a different ending.

Let us look at the finale of *The Good Wife*, and the infamous slap, as an example. *The Good Wife* starts out as an episodic procedural with a case-of-the-week structure. Increasingly, it merges episodic and serial forms and grows more complex in its characterization and plotlines, more playful and unpredictable in an operational aesthetic, as Mittell (2015) sees as typical of complex TV. It is a serialized procedural – the story of Alicia as she matures as a lawyer and an independent career woman. It is also the story of her love life, and for many seasons, it was a will-they-or-won't-they story about her relationship with Will, naturally leading to more of a romcom ending – up until, that is, Will dies in the penultimate season. A new love interest is introduced in the final season, but will this new couple do as a final couple? Then, there is Alicia's politician husband Peter; the series is also a family melodrama about their relationship, as emphasized in its title. *The Good Wife* is a mix of genres, and a satisfying ending is going to be difficult to achieve.

The creators' choices left the series' fan base perplexed. In order to give a feeling of closure in line with romcom conventions, they bring Will back to life momentarily as Alicia imagines discussing her options with him in several sequences. There had been no use of imaginary communication with dead people in the series previously, and although their final hug has its bittersweet merits, Alicia's lengthy interaction with him is in breach of the narrative logic of the series and its realism.

The creators commit another mistake in the final sequence, in which Alicia's business partner Diane slaps Alicia after she has appeared with her husband Peter in a press conference. Diane has the right to be angry, as Alicia has betrayed her trust and made a strategic choice in defending their client that severely tainted Diane's husband. The slap suggests that Alicia has become over-zealous in her defense of clients and that she has grown cynical and unscrupulous. Alicia has been portrayed as a trailblazer, as someone to admire, but now this is undermined. This is an unexpected turn. Further confusion is added when exploring the slap as making use of bracketing, a well-known closure device (Neupert 1995, 22). The slap mirrors Alicia's slapping her cheating husband Peter after a press conference in the series' pilot episode. This first slap marks the end of Alicia as the good wife – the series' title is paradoxical. She goes back to work, she builds a career, and she frees herself from her husband. However, the slap in the finale seems to suggest that Alicia should be condemned. The slap confuses *The Good Wife* with an antihero narrative, suggesting that we should question our allegiance to her. However, her trespass does not seem beyond reproach, and the series has not developed such a critical view of Alicia in the run-up to the finale. Again, the ending is in breach of the narrative logic of the series and denies the spectator an ending dictated by either of its genre components. To add to these problems, the slap carries rhetorical weight because it is the end point. A similar event mid-season would not be perceived as articulating the main message in this story to the same degree. The slap arguably makes the spectator search for authorial intentions, but it is not clear exactly what it is supposed to mean.

Zeller-Jacques (2014) points to yet another way we assess endings, namely, by pointing to industrial reasons, e.g., a cliff-hanger paving the way for a spin-off series, sequel, or feature film. He does not equate this with explaining away the ending – or not appreciating it – but it is tempting to see this as a discourse of dissatisfaction. Paving the way for a spin-off feels like a lack of closure. The slap can probably be explained by wanting to create a spin-off series with Diane as the lead (*The Good Fight*), but it still feels like a let-down as the ending of *The Good Wife,* which is Alicia's story. To be fair, a genre hybrid like *The Good Wife* was always going to be difficult to wrap up.

Open or closed endings

The ending of *The Good Wife* is relatively open and ambiguous: It is not clear whether Alicia will resume a relationship with her current love interest or how her relationship with Diane is affected. In defense of this series' creators, one could say that they do what creators of Quality TV series should do, namely, avoid closed endings. In my preceding assessment of the series' ending, I assumed that the natural ending would be a merging between the endings dictated by its genre components. However, as argued by Robert Thompson, among others, quality TV is perhaps "simply television's version of the 'art film'" (1996, 16).[9] According to this view, Quality TV can be seen as art narration rather than classical narration. David Bordwell explains how art film narration is characterized by ambiguity, also in its endings: the end must be open, perhaps arbitrary – reasserting ambiguity as the dominant principle in the film (2008, 151ff). Neupert labels a film a *closed text* if the story is resolved and the discourse is closed (1995, 35ff). Most commercial films are closed texts. In contrast, art film narration is characterized by open endings: Most radically, art films can be what Neupert labels *open texts*, in which the story is unresolved and the discourse, too, is open.

If Quality TV is television's version of art narration, such series should typically be open texts: The endings should be open and ambiguous, with a lack of story resolution and traditional closure devices.[10] However, Quality TV series do often aim for some kind of closure or resolution. Indeed, some of the most celebrated endings are closed in both story and discourse, such as in *Six Feet Under*. Antihero series are also typically closed texts. Think of the grand finale of *Sons of Anarchy*, in which the police chase Jax Teller on his bike in what almost appears as a parade set up to honor him as he rides to his death.[11] There is also the highly controversial closed ending of *Lost* (see Mittell 2015, 323).

The finale of *The Sopranos* is one of the most notoriously open endings. In line with art film narration, there is no story resolution. A number of stylistic and narrative cues might point to one ending or another, but their significance is open to interpretation (see Mittell 2015, 334–338). Spectators may turn to the creator for an explanation: Mittell discusses how one might attribute the finale's sudden cut to black "to a distinct message from David Chase," e.g., "many took the ending as a direct attack on viewers' desire for closure" (2015, 335). Indeed, Bordwell points out that authorial presence is a guiding principle in art film narration: "art cinema uses a concept of authorship to unify the text" (2008, 154). He explains that the difference between classical storytelling and art film narration is that in the former "the puzzle is one of *story*: who did it? How? Why?" whereas in "the art cinema, the puzzle is one of *plot*; who is telling this story? How is this story being told? Why is this story being told this way?" (Bordwell 2008, 155, emphasis original).[12] In line with this, open endings will make the spectator search for authorial intentions.

However, for the creators of Quality TV series, the problem is that open, ambiguous endings tend not to fare too well with the audience. Quality TV stands between art and commerce: It might aspire to be art and rely on notions of authorship to gain cultural status, but it is also a commercial product, one that – perhaps increasingly – has become the new mass art, appealing now to a much wider range of spectators than the so-called quality demographics to which it was initially designed to appeal. Art film narration has perhaps never appealed to wider audiences. The audience of *The Sopranos* was puzzled and surprised by its open art narration ending. Adding to the difficulty of ending Quality TV series, then, is their radical hybridity, their position in between art and popular culture, which seems to dictate both open and closed endings.

One illustrative example here is the *Mad Men* finale. This series relied on the ambiguity of art film narration to a high degree throughout, but the ending is closed. It is not the ending of Don Draper's story that interests me most here but rather, the end to the story about the series' female lead, Peggy Olsson. Peggy is given a closed ending borrowed from the romcom in the form of a union with her long-term co-worker Stan. *Mad Men* has never been a romcom. Most couples in this series are relentlessly unhappy, a far cry from the romcom's celebration of romantic love.[13] Although there are narrative events leading up to a union between Peggy and Stan, the final season has not been a dual narrative with this as its natural outcome. As MacDowell points out, the suspense in a romcom is not whether or not the two main characters will get each other: We know they will. The question is how and when (MacDowell 2013, 72). There was no such certainty about Peggy and Stan, and the abrupt realization that they are in love during a phone call is surprising, making the happy ending anxious. One is bound to ask what happens next – is this good for Peggy? Or to turn to authorial intentions: Is this what a happy ending for Peggy should look like?

One can argue that the ending to Peggy's character arc is unmotivated. Bordwell writes about unmotivated happy endings that "this strategy introduces a problem of authorial attitude akin to irony but much more disruptive" (1982, 6). The ending to Peggy's story calls attention to itself as an expression of the author's attitudes. Peggy takes on a special role in *Mad Men* as the character who changes the most over the course of the narrative. She represents the new woman, independent and with her own career. It is tempting to read Peggy's ending as a statement about this type of woman. One might have hoped to see her a powerful executive, but Peggy is still fighting for respect among bigoted co-workers, and Don is still her boss. However, Peggy is getting there: Her staying at MacCann's is a well-considered choice and a stepping stone. Be that as it may, what marks the end of Peggy's character arc is not career progression: Peggy finds love. On the one hand, this is disappointingly traditional. But there is a potentially progressive message, as Stan is her subordinate. He chooses to declare his love for his female boss. As such, Stan comes to represent a modern man, a man who does not fear strong women, and this makes him fairly unique in this series. Don, for example, is attracted to strong, independent women as lovers (Rachel Menken, Dr Faye Miller), but chooses the much more easily manageable younger women (Betty the model, Megan the secretary) as long-term partners. In the first season, Peggy has an affair with her co-worker Pete, who seems attracted to her as the underdog but rejects her when she is gaining confidence and status (e.g., when she is dancing seductively after her first copyediting success in episode 8, he sneers at her that "I don't like you like this"). Peggy and Stan are portrayed as happy together in a final montage sequence. Peggy is working at her desk and Stan massages her shoulders, seemingly supporting her as a career-driven workaholic. Turning to authorial intentions, Peggy's ending does make sense as a message about a new kind of relationship in a new era, but such ruminations are created by its weak motivation narratively. It is a paradoxically closed ending to an ambiguous story, leading back yet again to the search for authorial intentions.

Ending stories and endings in real life

I disliked the *Mad Men* finale on a first-time viewing but thought it was a good ending when re-watching the last season years later. This resonates with a finding in Helen Taylor's (1989) study of *Gone with the Wind*. She investigated audience responses to this story's ambiguous ending ("Frankly, my dear, I don't give a damn") and found that viewers' reactions differed at various stages in life. The TV series' role in, and resemblance to, real life as it is lived merits some final comments by way of conclusion.

In a much-quoted passage, Christian Metz muses that a "narrative has a beginning and an ending, a fact that ... distinguishes it from the rest of the world" (1968, 17). MacDowell points to the tension between the "endlessness of reality and the necessary endedness of narrative" and concludes that every ending in a story is unrealistic to some extent (2013, 112). In television series, the end is often postponed for a long time, and thus, Kristin Thompson (2003) suggests that we must rethink how important an ending or closure is for a narrative. Whereas an ending has traditionally been seen as an essential part of a narrative, the television series spectator will have learned to cope with uncertainty for months, sometimes years. Nonetheless, as has been pointed out already, Quality TV series is expected to come to a proper end eventually. Perhaps, the ending of a television series heightens the sense of artificiality, because long-term narration is so enmeshed in everyday life. We have engaged with these characters for so long. Robert Blanchet and I (2012) argue that our relation to characters in television series resembles real-life personal relationships, making them feel like fictional friends.[14] If we are right in this prediction – that there is a significant difference between engaging with a character in a film for two hours and with characters in television series for months and years – one can also predict that, everything else being equal, the ending of a television series is bound to be more painful for the spectator than the ending of a film.

The power of serial fiction to trigger close relationships between readers/spectators and fictional characters has been found disturbing by critics: Fans have been accused of failing to differentiate between what is fictional and what is real (see Hayward 1997, 37, 67). However, Jennifer Hayward (1997) shows that fans' engagement with serials such as soaps is highly reflexive. They take a playful attitude towards the characters and the actors who play them, often engaging paratextually in order to predict what the creators have planned. Mittell discusses such paratextual engagement as one of the defining features of complex TV, which according to him, makes "active audience behavior even more of a mainstream practice" (Mittell 2015, 36). However, as demonstrated by Hayward, this kind of behavior is found in fans' engagement with other kinds of serial fiction as well. We can say that serial fiction elicits strong parasocial relations but also a high degree of meta-textual awareness.

Endings sever these parasocial ties. However, this need not be seen as artificial, as there are parallels in real life. *Pace* Metz as quoted earlier, real life is not free from endings. People die or leave; relationships end. The finale of a TV series is perhaps best compared to a farewell party for old friends, or even a break-up. These natural endings pose some of life's most challenging circumstances – mourning the loss of a partner, dealing with the major transition of the death of a loved one, or the smaller yet still painful change when a close friend moves far away. In real life, these events are profoundly existential: We reflect, reconsider, and take stock. We try to find meaning in it all. The ending of a television series is not as painful as the ending of a real-life relationship. Nevertheless, on a smaller scale, the end can activate some of the same emotions. How convenient, then, that we can actually turn to its maker: Someone has designed this, and we can scrutinize the intentions behind it for meaning and clarity.

Zeller-Jacques (2014) argues that we expect an ending to enable us to see previous events in a new light whereby everything makes sense. He points to Peter Brooks, who sees the desire for an ending as tied to "the active quest of the reader for those shaping ends that, terminating the dynamic process of reading, promise to bestow meaning and significance on the beginning and the middle" (Brooks quoted in Zeller-Jacques 2014, 115). Applying this idea to serial fiction, one can argue that this desire is bound to be strong, perhaps even stronger than in relation to stand-alone works of fiction such as film: We have invested so much time with these characters and this creator, and now we hope to learn something significant, for there to be a moral or message, a beautiful plan that will assuage the pain of letting these cherished characters go.[15] Our natural inclination to question the meaning of it all when going through periods of loss arguably leads to an increased search for authorial presence at the end of television series. Regardless of whether one sees the ending as essentially artificially imposed and unrealistic, or as realistically motivated because relationships end in real life too, the effect is the same: The end makes us turn to the story's maker, hoping for help in making sense and reassurance that it was worthwhile. One can predict that the longer we have invested in a story, the stronger this desire will be.

So, to end where we started, wrapping up a story is always difficult. In this chapter, I have argued that ending a Quality TV series can be even more difficult than ending other narratives due to the pressure the discourse on these series puts on the author, who is seen as instrumental in order to bestow the series with status as art, coinciding with a number of formal features that complicate closure.[16]

Notes

1 I follow Newman and Levine in capitalizing the notion of Quality TV to highlight that these are series that "target a narrow, upscale audience and that are widely viewed as high quality by these viewers as well as by many critics and scholars. We do not use the term as our own designation of value", as Newman and Levine put it (2012: 172n3).

2 For further discussion, see e.g., Dunleavy (2018: 71ff) and Nochimson (2019).

3 See Thompson (1996). For further discussion see e.g., Dunleavy (2009: 132ff), Dunleavy (2018: 43ff) and Newman and Levine (2012).
4 For discussion, see Cardwell (2007).
5 See Nannicelli (2017) for further discussion.
6 See Pérez and Reisenzein (2019) for a discussion of Jon Snow's death and its appraisal by fans due to the implications for the resolution of the saga.
7 It is beyond the scope of this chapter to analyze the recently released *Game of Thrones* finale, but in line with the predictions I make, it was highly controversial. Thanks to Michael Clark for discussions.
8 This is in no way to deny that other types of series are genre hybrids as well – genre hybridity is not a necessary and sufficient condition for Quality TV.
9 See also Thompson (2003, 106ff).
10 However, Jane Feuer (1984) has argued that closure in prime-time soaps such as *Dynasty* and *Dallas* can be seen as progressive by leaving contradictions unresolved and exposed. The ambiguous ending should not be seen as restricted to art narration. Indeed, in the discussion of progressive, ambiguous endings, film and television scholars have made use of a great range of film and television genres and modes, often re-reading seemingly closed, happy endings to find undercurrents of ideological subversion. I will leave out such a discussion of progressive stories here and focus on ambiguous endings as a narrative element most typical of art narration.
11 My student Ami Samways made this observation in her insightful discussion of this series.
12 Mittell (2015) suggests that such a focus on the storytelling is typical in the reception of complex TV overall and labels this an operational aesthetic triggering forensic fandom, whereby fans explore storytelling mechanisms in great detail. I argue elsewhere (Vaage 2017) that his claim that one must engage in forensic fandom is exaggerated. Nevertheless, when a complex TV series ends, I think most spectators will experience the last, or the last few, episodes through the lens of an operational aesthetic and expect to appreciate the way the story is told.
13 See MacDowell (2013, 133ff) for a careful discussion of the romcom and romantic love.
14 See also Vaage (2014).
15 Or, alternatively, some new information that will make us want to re-watch the entire series, which is arguably tied to a search for authorial intentions, too, as argued by Zeller-Jacques in relation to re-watchability and how the ending can "reengage viewers' narrative desire by revealing the hand of an author at work throughout the text" (2014, 124).
16 This chapter was presented as a paper at The Aesthetics of Television Serials conference in Gandia in November 2017, and I thank all the participants for comments and questions. I'm also grateful to the two editors for helpful suggestions. Finally, thanks to students in the module FI622: Television Series at the University of Kent over the years for excellent discussions of television endings.

References

Azcona, María del Mar. 2010. *The Multi-Protagonist Film*. Chichester: Wiley-Blackwell.

Blanchet, Robert, and Margrethe Bruun Vaage. 2012. "Don, Peggy and Other Fictional Friends? Engaging with Characters in Television Series." *Projections* 6, no. 2: 18–41.

Bordwell, David. 1982. "Happily Ever After, Part II." *The Velvet Light Trap* 19: 2–7.

Bordwell, David. 2006. *The Way Hollywood Tells It: Story and Style in Modern Movies*. Berkeley, CA: University of California Press.

Bordwell, David. 2008. *Poetics of Cinema*. New York: Routledge.

Cardwell, Sarah. 2007. "Is Quality Television Any Good? Generic Distinctions, Evaluations and the Troubling Matter of Critical Judgement." In *Quality TV: Contemporary American*

Television and Beyond, edited by Janet McCabe and Kim Akass, 19–34. London: I.B. Tauris.

Carroll, Noël. 2007. "Narrative Closure." *Philosophical Studies* 135, no. 1: 1–15.

Carroll, Noël. 2013. "Rough Heroes: A Response to A.W. Eaton." *The Journal of Aesthetics and Art Criticism* 71, no. 4: 371–376.

Dunleavy, Trisha. 2009. *Television Drama. Form, Agency, Innovation*. New York: Palgrave Macmillan.

Dunleavy, Trisha. 2018. *Complex Serial Drama and Multiplatform Television*. New York: Routledge.

Eaton, A.W. 2013. "Reply to Carroll: The Artistic Value of A Particular Kind of Moral Flaw." *The Journal of Aesthetics and Art Criticism* 71, no. 4: 376–380.

Feuer, Jane. 1984. "Melodrama, Serial Form and Television Today." *Screen* 25, no. 1: 4–17.

Feuer, Jane. 2005a. "The Lack of Influence of Thirtysomething." In *Contemporary Television Series*, edited by Michael Hammond and Lucy Mazdon, 27–36. Edinburgh: Edinburgh University Press.

Feuer, Jane. 2005b. "Discovering the Art of Television's Endings." *Flow*. https://www.flowjournal.org/2005/06/mash-desperate-housewives-er-huff-judging-amy-mary-tyler-moore-genre-televisuality-season-finale/.

Harrington, C. Lee. 2013. "The Ars Moriendi of US Serial Television: Towards A Good Textual Death." *International Journal of Cultural Studies* 16, no. 6: 579–595.

Hayward, Jennifer. 1997. *Consuming Pleasures: Active Audiences and Serial Fictions from Dickens to Soap Opera*. Lexington, KY: University Press of Kentucky.

Kermode, Frank. 2000. *The Sense of an Ending. Studies in the Theory of Fiction with a New Epilogue*. New York: Oxford University Press.

Lotz, Amanda D. 2014. *Cable Guys: Television and Masculinities in The Twenty-First Century*. New York: New York University Press.

MacDowell, James. 2013. *Happy Endings in Hollywood Cinema. Cliché, Convention and the Final Couple*. Edinburgh: Edinburgh University Press.

Metz, Christian. 1968. *Film Language: A Semiotics of Cinema*. New York: Oxford University Press.

Mittell, Jason 2009. "All in The Game: *The Wire*, Serial Storytelling and Procedural Logic." In *Third Person: Authoring and Exploring Vast Narratives*, edited by Pat Harrigan and Noah Wardrip-Fruin, 429–438. Cambridge, MA: MIT Press.

Mittell, Jason. 2015. *Complex TV. The Poetics of Contemporary Television Storytelling*. New York: New York University Press.

Nannicelli, Ted. 2009. "It's All Connected: Televisual Narrative Complexity." In *The Wire: Urban Decay and American Television*, edited by Tiffany Potter and C.W. Marshall, 190–202. London: Continuum.

Nannicelli, Ted. 2017. *Appreciating the Art of Television: A Philosophical Perspective*. New York: Routledge.

Nelson, Robert. 2007. *State of Play. Contemporary "High-End" TV Drama*. Manchester: Manchester University Press.

Neupert, Richard. 1995. *The End: Narration and Closure in the Cinema*. Detroit: Wayne State University Press.

Newman, Michael Z., and Elana Levine. 2012. *Legitimating Television. Media Convergence and Cultural Studies*. New York: Routledge.

Nochimson, Martha P. 2019. *Television Rewired. The Rise of the Auteur Series*. Austin: University of Texas Press.

Nussbaum, Emily. 2014. "The Great Divide: Norman Lear, Archie Bunker, and the Rise of the Bad Fan." *The New Yorker*. http://www.newyorker.com/magazine/2014/04/07/the-great-divide-3.

Pérez, Héctor J., and Rainer Reisenzein. 2019. "On Jon Snow's Death: Plot Twist and Global Fandom in *Game of Thrones*." *Culture and Psychology*, 26, no. 3: 384–400.

Taylor, Helen. 1989. *Scarlett's Women: Gone with the Wind and Its Female Fans*. New Brunswick: Rutgers University Press.

Thompson, Kristin. 2003. *Storytelling in Film and Television*. Cambridge, MA: Harvard University Press.

Thompson, Robert J. 1996. *Television's Second Golden Age. From Hill Street Blues to ER*. New York: Syracuse University Press.

Vaage, Margrethe Bruun. 2014. "Blinded by Familiarity: Partiality, Morality and Engagement in Television Series." In *Cognitive Media Theory*, edited by Ted Nannicelli and Paul Taberham, 268–284. New York: Routledge.

Vaage, Margrethe Bruun. 2016. *The Antihero in American Television*. New York: Routledge.

Vaage, Margrethe Bruun. 2017. "Review of Jason Mittell's *Complex TV: The Poetics of Contemporary Television Storytelling*." *Projections* 11, no. 2: 105–109.

Zeller-Jacques, Martin. 2014. "Don't Stop Believing: Textual Excess and Discourses of Satisfaction in the Finale of *The Sopranos*." In *Melodrama in Contemporary Film and Television*, edited by Michael Stewart, 114–134. Basingstoke: Palgrave Macmillan.

10 Pop music in television serials

Priming, authorial commentary, and musical memory

Birger Langkjær

I am sitting in a café one morning writing this chapter. Background music from hidden loudspeakers adds to my coffee/writing experience, and suddenly, The Handsome Family's "Far from Any Road" can be heard from the otherwise anonymous playlist. If anyone in the room notices this apart from me (most are engaged with laptops and smartphones), I am pretty sure that it will not remind them about The Handsome Family and their musical portfolio. Rather, it will remind them about the first season of *True Detective* (HBO 2014–), the show that gave the song prominence.

This chapter centers on popular music in TV series, mainly U.S. series, and in particular, on how pop songs work as part of serial storytelling. I will focus on title themes, underscoring, and diegetic music in different forms. My main argument is that while music in TV series has traditionally invoked principal generic expectations about the fiction worlds of those series, the soundtracks of contemporary serials often add and emphasize something extra apart from core generic content. Maybe not far from any road, but at least not the usual road. Popular musical styles in general and the vocal pop song in particular play a central role in this. Another argument is that pop songs can add meaning and authorial commentary to characters, actions, and events in playful ways and extend the boundaries of the fictional worlds by various means. Finally, pop songs have a role to play in making scenes and episodes in a show stand out as memorable.

More specifically, I will first outline how title tunes, most prominent in the opening of each episode, can invoke major generic expectations about the show. Historically, this generic forecasting is the default priming function of title tunes. Second, I intend to show how title tunes in contemporary musical styles and in the form of pop songs tend to emphasize, or musically announce, what is special about the show and its fiction world rather than signaling its core generic features. Third, I will show how different within-scene underscoring by pop songs often makes authorial commentaries on characters and plot. Fourth, the series *Girls* (HBO 2012–2017) will be my key example of how diegetic pop songs can also add meaning and create memorable musical moments in surprising ways through what cognitive psychology terms "expectancy violations" (Bower 1976; Maki 1990).

DOI: 10.4324/9781003188643-10

Priming the show and its genre: Title tunes

In general, a title sequence is a signature for its show, or – in the words of Gérard Genette – a paratext (Genette 1997). It is a preliminary entry into a fiction world. In line with its condensed form and its placement at the beginning of each episode, the title sequence and its title tune work to prime the viewer for the forthcoming episode.

Phillip Tagg identifies three communicative functions of the title tune: The Reveille, the Preparatory, and the Mnemonic functions (Tagg 1979, 84). The Reveille function is to signpost that something is happening and to call the viewer, who may be doing other things, to the screen. The Preparatory function is to designate that something specific is going to happen (*Kojak* (CBS 1973–1978) rather than, for example, the news). The Mnemonic function is to raise expectations about the new episode. These expectations "will be increased while waiting for the action to commence, during which time the music will set the emotional scene for the ensuing story" (Tagg 1979, 84).

Elaborating on Tagg's claims, Caroline Davidson compares title sequences to trailers: "Functioning as a trailer for the coming attraction, [title sequences] seek to convert the distracted potential viewer into a repeat viewer/consumer and use arresting images and notable music to achieve this" (Davidson 2013a, 147–148).[1]

Davidson does not specify whether she refers to trailers in general or to film trailers in particular as a model of the title sequence. One difference between a film trailer and a title sequence, though, is that a film trailer is an announcement of *a single narrative in its entirety* (Kernan 2004; Jensen 2014), whereas a title sequence invites the viewer into the fiction world as such, of which what follows is just one episode. It does not give a preview of specific actions to come but of the *kind* of actions to come and more to the point, the kind of storyworld in which they take place.

Priming by title sequences, setting up the viewer's mind, and attuning her emotionally include activating generic expectations about forthcoming narrative content. And music can play a vital part in establishing such viewer expectations. As shown by Tagg and Clarida (2003), stylistic features in music are very efficient in fostering audience recognition of televisual genres, as viewers relate specific musical styles to particular fiction genres. In addition, audiences are surprisingly good at identifying musical styles in an instant. Gjerdingen and Perrott (2008) reported an experiment in which they had participants listen to excerpts from ten different musical genres (nine of them nonclassical music). Even when participants only heard 250 milliseconds of music, they identified the music genre much more frequently than would be expected by chance. A quarter of a second is not enough time to identify melody or rhythm, and the authors therefore suggest that participants identify the music genre by its timbre; the sound of the music, so to speak: For example, the perceived "twang" of country or "the enormous acoustic energy in extreme low frequencies" in rap music and hip-hop (Gjerdingen and Perrot 2008, 98). As musical styles connect to televisual genres, the generic priming of a show through the style of its title tune is instant.

Theorists of film music often describe music in terms of its ability to create mood and emotions (Prendergast 1992; Gorbman 1987; Carroll 1988). This ability is also central to Tagg's description of the Mnemonic function of television music (Tagg 1979). Furthermore, detailed analysis (Cook 1998), general descriptions (Chion 1994), and experimental research (Thayer and Levenson 1983; Marshall and Cohen 1988) often focus on music in audiovisual media as a simultaneous interaction between music and visuals. In other words, these approaches mainly focus on music/image interactions on the fly and the viewer emotions they trigger on a moment-to-moment basis rather than on cognitive and emotional effects distributed over time. When accompanying an audiovisual narrative, however, the emotional tone of the music turns out not just to color our perception on the fly but also to have thorough consequences for our expectations about future events and our remembrance of past events. Marilyn Boltz (2001) has demonstrated how the affective value of accompanying music influences and steers visual attention and subsequent memory for objects, events, and character intentions in a scene. In addition, Boltz, Schulkind, and Kantra (1991) have investigated how forecasting music, that is, music that comes before a pivotal scene, frames audience expectations about future outcomes due to the music's affective value. In other words, they found that music coming before a dramatic scene primes the recipients' forecasting of future events in terms of good or bad outcomes. Expanding on the idea of music as priming, Tan, Spackman, and Bezdec (2007) found evidence for how music can trigger "both forward and backward affective priming" of how an audience perceives character emotions (Tan et al. 2007, 146). For the present purpose, at least, it seems to be established in the experimental music psychology literature that music in combination with a visual scene can prime our expectations for future events and influence our recall of earlier scenes.

Historically, title tunes of early U.S. television series were used to prime their audiences to expect the story to follow certain basic genre prototypes. For example, Ronald Rodman has pointed out how serial crime fiction in the 1950s often used jazz but that title tunes differentiated themselves in relation to the subgenre of the show in question. Accordingly, they could use smooth jazz for detective series to underline the urban setting or military brass sounds for police dramas to indicate police authority (Rodman 2010, 235–236). These musical styles are preparatory in terms of viewer expectancies of the series genre and the kind of experience to come. Classic crime serials such as *Dragnet* (NBC 1951–1959) and *Peter Gunn* (NBC/ABC 1958–1961) have title tunes that prime audiences to look out for criminal intent in the narrative (Walther Schumann's title brass/timpani theme for *Dragnet* is actually titled "Danger Ahead"!). Thereby, they instruct their historical audiences to expect certain things. This priming, however, is more generic than specific. Nonetheless, the emphasis on generic features of the fiction world through musical style becomes more complex in the 1980s and later as series begin to blend genres (such as crime and melodrama or dramedies). Genre hybrid series can use their title tunes to emphasize one genre-feature rather than another. The title theme of *Hill Street Blues* (NBC 1981–1987), for example, is a soft rock ballad that emphasizes a kind of first-person emotionalism (expressing gentle sadness), while the visual shots depict police cars on duty in the city and police officers in workplace situations. In this way, the music highlights one generic path rather than another, giving emotional depth to a police drama in which the police force are also ordinary people with an emotional life and living ordinary lives.

Signaling what is special: Musical styles, the pop song, and the particularity of the show

Whereas title tunes for TV series originally formed audience expectations in terms of genre, there is a tendency since the 1980s in U.S. serial fiction to have the title tune emphasize aspects of a show that are complementary rather than identical to its core genres. In addition, forms of popular music have been pivotal to this historical change.

Miami Vice (NBC 1984–1989) and *Twin Peaks* (ABC 1990–1991) may count as examples. *Miami Vice* was different from previous cop shows, and Jan Hammer's intense and drum/percussion-based up-tempo rock was one of its defining features. Its electronic drum beat and use of the rock idiom – in combination with a frantic visual montage – represents a pure energy outburst rather than expressing any particular emotional register related to "crime" or "melodrama." In this way, the title tune expresses a distinguishing feature of the show apart from its generic content. Although very different in musical style, the musical emphasis on something other than the main genre is also characteristic of *Twin Peaks* (see also Kalinak 1995). In fact, it is hard to hear from Badalamenti's music that it is a police series involving the FBI trying to solve a murder case: "The slow, repetitious quality of the theme opens a fantasy, a dream-like, melancholy narrative world, which (incidentally) does nothing to suggest that the program is a police drama" (Rodman 2010, 285). Compare the upbeat tempo, freewheeling guitars, and hectic drumming, opening in a machine-gun style, to a fast-edited montage of action sequences and Florida scenery in *Miami Vice* with the slow-paced, flowing, bass melody of *Twin Peaks* accompanying views of birds, trees, mountains, and a flowing river connected by long dissolves. These two title sequences and their music invite their audiences to expect and adapt to very different narrative modes, either to expect unrestrained character action or to immerse themselves in a tense, yet contemplative, perceptual mode. Neither of their music styles indicates their main genre. Rather, their music indicates the way in which the shows are cop shows or, maybe more to the point, what they are besides cop shows. Even though the music is generic in terms of style (as any music will be), its style does not signal the basic genre of the shows (crime fiction). Rather, the musical style evokes something particular about the show apart from its TV generic content.

This tendency towards emphasizing something particular to the show apart from its central genre has continued in recent series. A show such as *Mad Men* (AMC 2007–2015) also features an unusual title sequence. Its title tune, "A Beautiful Mine" from the album *Magnificent City* (2006), is a collaboration between RJD2 and Aceyalone. Paradoxically, it is instrumental hip-hop minimalism priming an early 1960s world, so the obvious question is: How can contemporary music prime a historical world? The answer is that the music points neither to the historical world of the fiction nor to its genre. Rather, it establishes particular aspects of the fiction world related to its character depiction. More specifically, the music opens with a repetitiously falling string motif and flute-glissandos, which lead to an erratic, syncopated, unpredictable drum break figure. As the rhythm becomes an (almost) regular drum and bass beat, the whirling and falling melodies now contrast with the steady rhythm and simultaneously, accent the motif of falling in the visuals. This uneasy musical minimalism creates an ambiguous tension that portrays aspects of characters and the special fiction world of *Mad Men* more than it indicates its genre or period.

The previous examples have all been of instrumental music, most of it specifically composed for the series (*Mad Men* excluded, although the music is an edited version). Since the 1990s, though, many shows have featured title tunes, which are regular pop songs with a verse/refrain structure and vocals. The energized rock song by The Rembrandts to *Friends* (NBC 1994–2004) with the refrain "I'll be there for you" indicates both the upbeat comedy and the central theme of friendship. Likewise, the sing-along rock intro to *Ally McBeal* (Fox 1997–2002) by Vonda Shepard in a simple chord progression and the refrain "I've been searchin' my soul," which indicates a more serious aspect, is fused with the slapstick comedy depicted in the visual montage. Together, music, lyrics, and visuals cue the show as a dramedy, yet leaning towards comedy. These tunes have other ear-catching qualities than traditional title tunes, due not least to their song-based melodies (the viewer may not only listen but also sing along) and their lyrics. The lyrics give an extra layer of meaning, and especially the refrain often becomes a motivic one-liner for the show's core theme (such as friendship or soul searching). Other shows, however, tend to use pre-existing pop songs in ways that are more ambiguous and emphasize what is special about the show besides its generic core content. This is the case in shows such as *The Sopranos*, *The Wire*, *True Blood*, *True Detective*, and the BBC series *Peaky Blinders*.

In the title sequence of *True Detective*, the female vocal in the original The Handsome Family version of "Far from Any Road" appears in a reduced form due to editing. This makes the male vocal the main narrator. The deep (Cash-like) voice with plenty of reverb is accompanied by guitar and a horse-imitating rhythm (plus a regular cowbell on each beat) at a slow pace. The vocal delivery enhances the storytelling quality of the show as the singer begins an uncanny and mythic narrative of a desert with bones and rattlesnakes, obviously a no man's land. The song and its Gothic-horror style of storytelling set the macabre tone of what to come, while its country-style delivery designates a southern element. Nothing of this indicates a police/detective plot. Rather, it primes us to a morbid, death-fascinated, and macabre tale that takes place somewhere in the American south. It does not so much prime the show as a detective show but rather, forecasts the way in which it is a detective show.

Several other shows use songs for the opening sequences: *The Sopranos* (HBO 1999–2007) opens with Alabama 3's "Woke Up This Morning (The Chosen One Mix)," a song somehow hipper than its characters yet with gloomy lyrics and musically flowing along the small visual odyssey of Tony Soprano driving away from the city of New York towards New Jersey. *The Wire* (HBO 2002–2008) features Tom Waits's "Way Down in the Hole," which lends raw, yet playful, coolness to the series and is performed by five different singers/groups, one version for each season: Blind Boys of Alabama, Tom Waits, The Neville Brothers, DoMaJe, and Steve Earle. Another example of how to sidestep genre clichés is *True Blood* (HBO 2008–2014), which is a story about vampires. Nevertheless, Jace Everett's title song "Bad Things" is a cheeky love song in a bluesy country-rock style that anchors the non-naturalistic fiction world of vampires in a somehow more ordinary and naturalistic context. Due to this genre context, the sexual implications of the repeated song lyrics, "I wanna do bad things with you," are imbued with ambiguous significance.

Other series feature pop songs as title tunes, which appear to be historically idiosyncratic in comparison to the fiction world they announce (as was the case with *Mad Men*). For example, The Brian Jonestown Massacre – a psychedelic 1960s pastiche from a 1990s band – opened *Boardwalk Empire* (2010–2014), a

Figure 10.1 "Far From Any Road" by The Handsome Family primes our expectations to the show and its series of macabre murders in the Southern swamps. Rust Cohle (Matthew McConoughey) and Marty Hart (Woody Harrelson) at the first murder scene. *True Detective* (2012, HBO)

series about the prohibition era of the 1920s and 1930s. This also counts for the 1995 number "Red Right Hand" performed by Nick Cave and the Bad Seeds to *Peaky Blinders* (BBC 2013–), a series that takes place around 1919 among gangsters in Birmingham, England. Nonetheless, the strange and crooked Cave ballad has enigmas in the lyrics and fate-invoking bells that make it fit a world of murders and mysteries back in time, a thematic lead that Nick Cave and the Bad Seeds followed up with the album *Murder Ballads* (1996). In these cases, the music is not there to indicate a period through using its historical musical style. The music is not historically mimetic but about evoking themes, establishing moods, and making the audience adopt the right attitude for the fiction world to come.

It seems to me that what landmark shows such as *Miami Vice* and *Twin Peaks* did in their title sequences has become a central (yet not exclusive) norm since the 1990s, especially with subscription-based digital platforms. The approach is to create a signature in music (and visuals) that uses musical characterization in ways that bear less on core generic norms related to audiovisual genre content and more on musical style, evoking what makes their fiction worlds particular apart from their generic content. Recently, pre-existing pop songs have been especially productive in creating odd or particular musical openings for their shows. The title tune has become a true signature tune for what is special about the fiction world a show provides; not any show but *that* show.

The pop song as underscoring and authorial commentary

The previous pages have focused on title tunes at the beginning of the show. Needless to say, however, serial fiction also has music within the specific narrative of each episode, and along with the development of title tunes, the within-episode underscoring has also given more prominence to pop songs.

To begin with, we need to differentiate two forms of pop music on television, which I have already dealt with in the previous examples but not defined on a principal level. Jeff Smith (1998) distinguishes between pop scores and compilation scores in the movies. Pop scores are scores in a popular (and contemporary) musical style; however, they do not follow the verse/refrain structure of the song form but adapt freely to changes in the drama. Compilation scores in movies, on the other hand, are a series of nondiegetic musical numbers in a song form that appear throughout a film. In other words, there are two kinds of nondiegetic pop music: pop scores and pop songs.

In fact, many scores for TV series throughout television history are not classical symphonic scores but pop scores. As mentioned beforehand, the early police shows *Dragnet*, with music by Walther Schuman, and *Peter Gunn*, with music by Henry Mancini, both use nondiegetic jazz in a pop score fashion. The pop song form, on the other hand, has traditionally appeared as diegetic music from record players, radios, or live bands in the story to inject popular tunes into the soundtrack that are more or less contemporary with the show in which they appear. In this way, it has been standard procedure to combine nondiegetic pop scores and diegetic pop songs. What has changed since the 1990s is that the song form also becomes nondiegetic. Thus, the classical practice of combining pop scores and diegetic pop songs has transformed into a more hybrid practice in which both pop scores and pop songs can appear as nondiegetic.

However, a nondiegetic pop song tends to foreground itself more than a pop score for at least two reasons. First, this kind of underscoring has the metrics of a pop number, that is, a tight song structure running for less than three minutes, its main features being the order and frequency of verses and chorus within a framework of musical openings, bridges, and closure. Second, these songs usually feature lyrics that add a narrator-component to the song, a higher-order language level that specifies the song's musical expressivity in terms of a singer (the narrator) and a song-narrative (the story). This combination of a song's predictable pattern of repetition and its narrative lyrics contributes to marking the music as an entity in its own right, which makes it an effective instrument for different forms of authorial commentary.

Miami Vice not only foregrounded its rock-based title tune throughout its title sequence and during extensive MTV-like montage sequences; it also used and foregrounded pop songs in the ongoing plot. In the pilot episode, part II, Phil Collins's "In the Air Tonight," a slow ballad, plays out loudly to a scene in which Crocket and Tubbs, the odd cop buddy-couple, drive at night in an open car to catch some drug criminals and get revenge. Moschini describes the music's role with reference to its lyrics: "Phil Collins's angle of narration coincides with that of the leading characters" (Moschini 2011, 195). Thus, the song lyrics function on a meta-communicative level by giving the viewer access to the characters' state of mind, though I hasten to add that Moschini, to some degree, exaggerates the fit between lyrics and characters. In addition, he leaves out any mention of musical qualities other than the lyrics.

To begin with, in and of themselves, the lyrics are not that specific. Song lyrics are often what reception aesthetics (or "reception theory") within literary theory would describe as open texts with plenty of "gaps" (see, for example, Iser 1978), which to a certain extent allow the reader to fill in their own interpretation. In the scene from *Miami Vice* underscored by "In the Air Tonight," the refrain goes: "I could feel it, something in the air that night, oh lord." One might ask: Who is the "I," and what is coming? These obvious "gaps" are for the listener to fill in. The verses hint at a revenge story, as in the opening line of the first verse: "Well if you told me you were drowning, I would not lend a hand." The lyrics, however, are not very precise and leave it open for the viewer to hear all kinds of meanings that resonate with the broader audiovisual lyricism of the sequence. In addition, the "I" and the "you" in the lyrics are also emphasized during an intermittent scene in which the music continues as Crocket calls his ex-wife to make sure their past love was real. This fluctuating contextualization makes the song appear to be about different things as it plays. That is, the narrative of the lyrics and the song as an entity disperses itself into two narratives due to the changing contexts it accompanies. Furthermore, the scene obviously does not play for action but works as a kind of preparatory access to the characters' emotional state or mood. Phil Collins's thin and high-pitched voice sounds in a "big" musical space of floating synthesizer-harmonics, some distorted guitar sound, and the drum sound. In combination with the urban nocturnal visuals that emphasize abstract features (close-ups of turning wheels, the graphics of light and shadow, and the reflections of water, glass, and steel surfaces), the music expresses a decisive but melancholic state of mind. The music has a central placement, yet together with the visuals and the spare dialogue, it plays with the narrative in two ways simultaneously. It emphasizes the fictional world both from within (fictional characters' states of mind) and from the outside (the series as an aesthetic artifact).[2]

Miami Vice also uses pop songs as overt, and often ironic, authorial commentary on the action. In the pilot episode, part I, a witness is secretly murdered on a beach in sunny daylight. The killer is a man dressed in women's clothing in order to get under the radar of the police. Up to the killing, the camera follows the killer via close-ups of the back of his hand (and his face, partly disclosed behind a big hat) up to the moment when he picks up a gun and points it at his victim. This murder scene is nondiegetically accompanied by Cyndi Lauper's "Girls Just Want to Have Fun," a happy-going song with lyrics about girls who do not want to be constrained by their boyfriends (or parents) but want to "walk in the sun" and "have fun." This girlish, yet girl-empowering, narrative in the song's lyrics becomes ambiguous as it plays out to the fatal gender masquerade. Simultaneously, the song's upbeat and positive determination provides a twist due to the murderous scheme evolving. As in the previous example, the nondiegetic pop song has a double function in this scene. It emphasizes the determination of the killer (and the inevitability of the outcome) and in addition, it instantiates an ironic playfulness to the narrative. The music adds an extra layer of authorial commentary to the fiction world due to its double function of invoking both diegetic events and their mode of telling, fiction and artifact alike.

Other series use pop music to blur the distinction between subjective and intersubjective spaces in the fictional world or to make fuzzy the difference between diegetic and nondiegetic elements. British series such as Dennis Potter's *The Singing Detective* (BBC 1986) and *Lipstick on Your Collar* (Channel 4 1993) indulge in parallel, subjective realities with musical numbers that both provide cultural-historical commentary and invoke the fantasy life of their main characters. On U.S. television, *Ally McBeal* (Fox 1997–2002) used pop music in uncharted territory by creating parallel universes as it "revels in soundtrack games" (Brown 2001, 275).

In *Ally McBeal*, these games were often clearly marked as fantasies of the main character Ally, such as the baby she both dreams about and hallucinates as it dances to Blue Swede's "Hooked on a Feeling" (mainly accompanied by the "Ooga-Chaka" vocal opening). Part of this parallel universe is also intersubjective, in the sense that all the main characters sometimes hear and participate in collective dance routines in the spacious unisex toilet. In this way, the alternative reality is not restricted to the music/dance scenes as was the case with the Dennis Potter shows. In fact, the characters are conscious of the importance of music to their self-esteem and identities, and overtly discuss and reflect upon the music. In *Ally McBeal*, most characters have their own pop musical themes. John Cage needs (various) songs by Barry White to boost his masculine self-confidence, and in season 3, Billy Thomas turns into a male chauvinist hardliner, repeatedly making self-assuring entrances at the office to a nondiegetic rendering of Mighty Sam McClain's "New Man in Town." Further, the residential singer, Vonda Shepard, and her band at the nightclub, to which all the characters usually go after work, perform cover versions of a series of pop hits that provide Greek chorus–style commentaries to each episode's main theme and actions.

Pop songs may also be central to crafting ambiguous character portraits. In the pilot of *The Sopranos* (HBO 1999–2007), Tony Soprano drives his car after a man who is trying to escape on foot. A nondiegetic rendering of the late 1950s vocal ensemble Dion and the Belmonts' doo-wop hit "I Wonder Why" dominates the soundtrack. The scene ends as Tony hits the man with the car (on the musical beat!), gets out, and beats him up, while the vocals go "Wop, wop …." This is what we might call the *A Clockwork Orange* effect, having the violent protagonist accompanied by a piece of music that is not violent by nature but is played along with a character's violent acts. In this case, the pop song also provides a double characterization that aligns with Tony's Janus-faced character throughout the show. On the one hand, Tony is the type of person who likes that kind of oldies' pop music (emphasizing him as an ordinary, nostalgic person of a certain age); on the other hand, the music contrasts with his non-ordinary and transgressive acts of violence. By the odd combination of nostalgic doo-wop music and cynical violence, the series simultaneously creates a bond and a distance between main character and viewer that makes Tony appear both appealing and appalling.[3]

The previous examples have highlighted different functions of nondiegetic pop songs within dramatic scenes. They can enhance emotional aspects of a scene or express a character's mind, they can make authorial comments on actions, or they can enable ambiguous characterizations of events and characters. Other series, such as *Big Little Lies* (HBO 2017–) and *SKAM* (NRK 2015–2017), use diegetic pop music as personal soundtracks related to characters who listen to music. This provides the characters with a kind of authorial power and has interesting effects. In season 3 of the Norwegian series *SKAM*, for example, the main character Isak moves through the school yard hiding from others' glances, with his hoodie making only part of his face visible, while he (and the series audience) listen to a loud rendition of NAS's "You Can Hate Me Now." What makes this music a surprise to the audience is that this season focuses on Isak falling in love with another boy from his school. In this context, the homophobic hip-hop stands out, yet the music's aggressive energy makes sense as a protective shield against the gazes of others. Throughout the four seasons of the series, *SKAM* frequently re-contextualizes music in ways that challenge the original meaning of the music (see Ligaard 2017). This is often done as a commentary on characters or the series' main themes, or to empower characters who make statements through their song choices.

Diegetic pop songs can also enter the fiction world in estranged forms, as in the first season of *Westworld* (HBO 2017–), where hits by Radiohead, among others, sneak into the diegetic music, such as the piano player at the bar where the prostitute Maude is in charge. Even though this music appears in disguise and without lyrics, it is, nevertheless, a way to make audiences recall specific songs, including their lyrics, as part of setting the mode of the scene and, essential to *Westworld*, to emphasize repetitions and loops in the narrative.

Pop scores have co-existed with both diegetic and nondiegetic pop songs in television series on a wide scale since the 1990s. Pop scores and underscoring through song compilations is not an either/or in TV series. This makes hybrid scoring the current norm, something to expect. Yet, the structural salience of the pop song due to its song form, its melodic/rhythmic catchiness, and its lyrics makes it a special vehicle for intricate soundtrack games that make music central to invoking viewer interest on a scene-by-scene level as well as in its overall narrative execution.

Most pop songs used in television series are not composed for the series but pre-exist in other music-cultural contexts prior to entering a specific show. This might seem to be an "unoriginal" move (Prendergast 1992). Nonetheless, and in accordance with previous examples, I intend to expand on the idea that the use of pre-existing music can be highly important in the urge to make a show stand out as special, as original. *Girls* will be my prime example and cognitive "expectancy violations" related to the use of music (Boltz et al. 1991) my guiding explanatory framework.

Memorable music moments due to expectancy violations: The case of *Girls*

The HBO series *Girls* (2012–2017) has, among other things, been praised for its use of pop songs. Online magazines such as *Vulture*, *Billboard*, *Soundvenue*, *Much*, and many others have made lists of what they consider to be the most memorable "musical moments" in *Girls* (for example, *Billboard*; "Girls": The Top 10 Awkward, Amazing Musical Moments | Billboard). The phrase "musical moments" implies that it is not the music in and of itself but rather, the new quality of the specific combination of music and the scene in which it occurs that is central to these lists.

I will suggest that what makes these moments memorable is the fact that while the appearance of music in each sequence might be expected, the actual choice of music represents a surprise. The surprise is an effect of what cognitive psychology terms "expectancy violations." Several experimental studies have shown that people do not necessarily remember the ordinary moments, whereas surprise incidents tend to increase memory for the specific event. Boltz, Schulkind, and Kantra (1991) have investigated this mechanism in experimental setups where music forecasts a future scene due to its affective value and the scene turns out differently than expected. They found that expectations generated by music that were violated in a later scene enhanced viewers' memory of that scene (see also Boltz et al. 2009). *Girls* often uses music to violate expectations, though it does so in different ways.

Girls contains simple underscoring that underlines dramatic scenes and/or makes transitions between scenes in non-surprising ways. These could include offbeat chords on an acoustic guitar to emphasize light comedy, or melancholic passages on piano/guitar. Pop music also appears as diegetic background in bars, at parties, and in apartments characterizing the places and types of situations. These uses of pop music follow standard procedures in film and television. At moments, however, the music can move to the foreground.

One such moment happens at the very opening of each episode as what we may term a scheduled surprise, because *Girls* has no recurrent title tune. Instead, it begins each episode *in medias res* with a scene that embodies one of the episode's main plotlines. At the end of the opening scene, a song enters the soundtrack. As the song continues, the title "GIRLS" fills the screen (both letters and background in new colors each time), but this quickly gives way to the second scene. This opening music differs for each episode, but it always, in some way, relates to the specific theme of the opening scene. The music functions as an authorial commentary on the opening scene and as a transitory device for getting us into the next scene. This form of opening constitutes an internal norm of the show, something to expect.[4] Yet, the actual choice of music, and the way it works as a musical comment, comes as a surprise. In addition, the ending of each episode mirrors this opening pattern as another – uniquely occurring – musical number plays and wraps up the final scene in a sort of commentary.

In episode 3 of the first season of *Girls*, Hannah has found out that she has HPV, that her present boyfriend has lied to her about it, and that her ex-boyfriend has turned out to be gay. In addition, he admits that he also knew about his sexual orientation when they were in a relationship. In the final scene of the episode, she is in her room with her laptop trying to write a tweet on the theme of betrayal. The moody ballad "Get Well Soon," softly sung by Sarabeth Tucek and accompanied by acoustic guitar, appears to match Hannah's mood, functions as a mood-enhancing accompaniment to the viewer, and forecasts the episode's ending, as it functions to anticipate a narrative closure on a sad note. Accordingly, we see Hannah write: "My life has been a lie, my ex-boyfriend dates a guy." Yet, the song abruptly ends, and instead, Robyn's "Dancing On My Own" fades up, possibly, we may infer, from Hannah's playlist. Her concentrated facial expression changes as she bites her thumb in a kind of flirty way and makes small rhythmic movements with her head as if the music had triggered something else besides her self-pitying blue mood. Finally, she deletes what she was about to tweet and decides instead to quote the response of one of the other girls, the flamboyant bohemian Jessica, on the fact that she has HPV: "All adventurous women do." This is also the title of the episode. When her flat-mate Marnie comes home, she hears the music and enters Hannah's room, where she finds Hannah dancing "on her own." While dancing (and somehow in a funny way trying to imitate Robyn's dance moves), Hannah tells Marnie about her ex-boyfriend's revelations, and Marnie joins her dance, both of them smiling and giving themselves to the dance before Hannah puts her arms around Marnie from behind in a sisterly embrace.

What is surprising about this final scene of the episode is that previous events add up to a sad ending. In addition, the Sarabeth Tucek song seems to confirm our expectations of an unhappy ending. Yet, the tweet Hannah finally decides to write recasts her HPV diagnosis in a positive light: It is no longer a disgraceful disease given to her by a cheating boyfriend but a badge of honor for those self-confident women embracing an adventurous life. In this way, the Tucek song falsely forecasts an unhappy ending. But what does the song by Robyn do?

At first, Robyn's dance hit may sound like an odd choice for an upbeat ending, as its lyrics is about a singer-I abandoned by the one she loves. Nevertheless, in the narrative context of *Girls*, the lyrics appear to celebrate Hannah's self-enjoyment of being "on my own." This self-enjoyment is also enhanced by the hard-drifting beat under Robyn's vocal. In this way, Hannah adapts to the energizing movement of the rhythm, but as she is not the singer-I, she has an onlooker's position on the lyrics: She is not *in* the song world but looking at it analogously to her own life while embracing its beat. It is a second-order appreciation of the narrative of "being alone" in the lyrics (in the same way as the experience of something sad in fiction can give way to positive feelings) and a first-order direct appreciation of the musical energy. The music monumentalizes something ephemeral, a sudden but fleeting transition of mind. The scene is also a transformation by dance that celebrates an including and comforting sisterhood. In *Girls*, shaken self-confidence or a crisis in one relationship often leads to the strengthening of other relationships.

Figure 10.2 "All adventurous women do." Lena Dunham as Hannah Horvath comes to terms with her HPV and past boyfriend listening to Robyn's "Dancing on My Own." *Girls* (2012, HBO)

Girls is abundant in such scenes, in which music changes (and is changed by) the mood and the direction of the scene in terms of how the character perceives her situation. This often happens in the very last scene of an episode, giving it a final twist just before curtain fall. However, a main point is that the scene also imbues the meaning of the music with new significance. The dramatic context gets something out of the music that was not obviously there to begin with but emerges due to the combination of a song and a dramatic scene. In episode 4 of season 2, Jessica comes home after a break-up with her husband, while Hannah sits in the bathtub singing Oasis's "Wonderwall" (*a capella*). Jessica – surprisingly – undresses and joins Hannah in the bathtub, sniffing and crying, while Hannah silently watches her with empathy. Despite nudity and intimacy, there is no hint of eroticism, which is somewhat underlined when Jessica, still crying and sobbing, snots in the water. This makes Hannah complain, and suddenly, they both laugh. As the camera tracks backwards, Oasis's studio recording of the song is heard. Thereby, two different renderings of the same song frame a scene-changing moment in which something sad turns into a positive reconciliation.

Episode 1 of season 6 varies this surprise-device. Hannah is at a female surfers' camp to write an article but soon – and kind of against character – starts an affair with one of the male surfing instructors. Leading up to the affair is an evening when Hannah and the instructor sit at the campfire at the beach and hear someone with a guitar playing and singing Tal Bachman's feel-good song "She's So High," energetic in its guitar accompaniment and happily longing in its vocals' frequent falsetto. In its sing-along campfire rendition, the song seems very different from Hannah's style and taste, but nevertheless, it charms her into a love story with the surfer-instructor. The beach-babe TV series cliché makes an odd fit with Hannah's character, but –due not least to its foregrounded musical moment of mood or attitude change – it makes the music and the situation memorable. *Girls* makes this use of pop musical numbers an internal norm. It makes the viewer expect such turnarounds in moods and emotional consequences of actions and events on characters, yet these scenes come as surprises in terms of their "when" and "what." In these instances, pop songs are central devices.

In conclusion

Title tunes are musical framing devices that tune the viewer into and out of the show. In the opening sequence, the tune calls the viewer to fictional adventures and primes her for the kind of fiction world she is about to engage in. The title tune played at the end, on the other hand, is a remembering device celebrating the fresh memory of the show the viewer has just seen yet already with a nostalgic air of the past. It does not as much celebrate the specific episode you have just seen; rather, it replays broader show-related emotions.

A trend within contemporary series is to have a recurrent title tune that opens and identifies the show at the beginning of each episode, yet the credit music at the end varies. *The Sopranos* did just that consistently, and *Girls* varied both its opening music and its ending. In these cases, the final music is not so much a celebration of the show as such but a musical endnote that is specifically related to that episode. In opposition to series that always end their episodes with the same tune, the one-time use of a musical number emphasizes the particular episodic identity rather than the broad narrative outline across episodes and seasons. This chimes with a remark by Jason Mittell on complex serial narration, which he – despite seasonal story arcs – finds often have a surprising emphasis on episodic closure (Mittell 2015).

As this chapter has argued, current trends of music in serial television fictions function to make the show unique, adding a fiction world particularity to its generic constituents. This emphasis on discriminating aspects of each series is easily compatible with popular music, which may express all kinds of attitudes and emotional stances. Series can combine specific pop music that comes with a history of its own and a dramatic moment in an odd blend that makes the scene particular, turning a scene into "that" memorable scene.

In these ways, serial fiction is now pushing to let audiences re-memorize parts of the portfolio of popular music from its inception in the early 20th century until today in new contexts. In any case, popular music affords a supplementary reservoir, forms of virtual worlds and genres through music style and vocal storytelling, which blends well with and extends contemporary serial fiction worlds, often in interesting and memorable ways.

Notes

1 Both Tagg and Davidson obviously understand how title tunes function within the communication situation of classic television broadcasting. This is characterized by, among other things, its scheduled program flow (Ellis 1982) and the presumption that viewers may do other things than actually watching the television while it is on (Altman 1986). The soundtrack, including title tunes, breaks into the household flow, as it calls attention to and informs about ongoing and upcoming events on TV (Altman 1986). However, Davidson has also made a pilot study that indicates how digital platforms and binge watching may encourage some viewers to skip these sequences after watching a couple of episodes (Davidson 2013b). Digital distribution and 24/7 access to serial fictions may reduce the importance of Tagg's first two concepts, the Reveille and Preparatory functions, whereas the Mnemonic function is in line with how I use the term "priming" in this chapter.
2 See a similar distinction in Tan 1994 and Plantinga 2009.
3 Murray Smith has analyzed this ambiguousness of the Tony Soprano character within a broader theory on how audiences engage with fictional characters (Smith 2011). See related argument in Vaage (2015).
4 David Bordwell has frequently, and in various contexts, dealt with how films both follow external (generic) norms and create internal norms that are specific to a single film; see, for example, Bordwell (2007). Obviously, both kinds of norm are of central importance to create expectancies (and surprises) in terms of style and narrative.

References

Altman, Rick. 1986. "Television/Sound". In *Studies in Entertainment. Critical Approaches to Mass Culture* edited by Tania Modleski. Bloomington, Indiana: Indiana University Press.

Boltz, Marilyn G., Brittany Ebendorf, and Benjamin Field. 2009. "Audiovisual Interactions: The Impact of Visual Information on Music Perception and Memory." *Music Perception: An interdisciplinary Journal* 27, no. 1: 43–59.

Boltz, Marilyn G. 2001. "Musical Soundtracks as a Schematic Influence on the Cognitive Processing of Filmed Events." *Music perception: An Interdisciplinary Journal* 18, no. 4: 427–454.

Bolz, Marilyn G., Matthew Schulkind, and Suzanne Kantra. 1991. "Effects of Background Music on the Remembering of Filmed Events." *Memory & Cognition* 19, no. 6: 593–606.

Bordwell, David. 2007. *Poetics of Cinema*. London: Routledge.

Bower, Gordon H. 1976. "Experiments on Story Understanding and Recall." *Quarterly Journal of Experimental Psychology* 28: 511–528.

Brown, Julie. 2001. "Ally McBeal's Postmodern Soundtrack." *Journal of the Royal Musical Association* 126, no. 2: 275–303. Al

Carroll, Noël. 1988. *Mystifying Movies*. New York: Columbia University Press.

Chion, Michel. 1994. *Audio-Vision. Sound on Screen*. New York: Columbia University Press.

Cook, Nicholas. 1998. *Analyzing Musical Multimedia*. Oxford: Oxford University Press.

Davidson, Annette. 2013a. "Title Sequences for Contemporary Television Series." In *The Oxford Handbook of New Audiovisual Aesthetics*, edited by John Richardson, Claudia Gorbman, and Carol Vernallis, 146–167. Oxford: Oxford University Press.

Davidson, Annette. 2013b. "The Show Starts Here: Viewer's Interaction with Recent Television Serials' Main Title Sequences." *SoundEffects* 3, no. 1+2: 6–22.

Donnelly, K. J. 2002. "Tracking British Television: Pop Music as Stock Soundtrack to the Small Screen." *Popular Music* 21, no. 3: 331–343.

Ellis, John. 1982. *Visible Fictions. Cinema, Television, Video*. London: Routledge.

Genette, Gèrard. 1997. *Paratexts. Thresholds of Interpretation*. Cambridge: University of Cambridge Press.

Gjerdingen, Robert O., and David Perrott. 2008. "Scanning the Dial: The Rapid Recognition of Music Genres." *Journal of New Music Research* 37, no. 2: 93–100.

Gorbman, Claudia. 1987. *Unheard Melodies. Narrative Film Music*. Bloomington, IN: Indiana University Press.

Iser, Wolfgang. 1978. *The Act of Reading. A Theory of Aesthetic Response*. Baltimore: The John Hopkins University Press.

Jensen, Charlotte Sun. 2014. "Reduced Narration, Intensified Emotion. The Film Trailer." *Projections* 8, no. 1: 105–125.

Kalinak, Kathryn. 1995. "Disturbing the Guests with This Racket": Music and *Twin Peaks*. In *Full of Secrets: Critical Approaches to Twin Peaks*, edited by David Lavery, 82–92. Detroit: Wayne State University Press.

Kernan, Lisa. 2004. *Coming Attractions. Reading American Movie Trailers*. Austin, TX: University of Texas Press.

Ligaard, Eva Elise. 2017. ""Hva hører du på?" Refleksioner over "SKAM-musikken"". *NTIK*, Årg. 6, no. 2/3: 54–59.

Maki, R. H. 1990. "Memory for Script Actions: Effects of Relevance and Detail Expectancy." *Memory and Cognition* 18: 5–14.

Marshall, Sandra K., and Annabel J. Cohen. 1988. "Effects of Musical Soundtracks on Attitudes toward Animated Geometric Figures." *Music Perception* 6, no. 1: 95–112.

Mittell, Jason. 2015. *Complex TV. The Poetics of Contemporary Television Storytelling*. New York: New York University Press.

Moschini, Ilaria. 2011. "Music and Series: The Verbalizing Role of Soundtrack Lyrics From Tv Series to User-generated Narrations." *Visual Communication* 10, no. 2: 193–208.

Plantinga, Carl. 2009. *Moving Viewers. American Cinema and the Spectator's Experience.* Oakland, CA: University of California Press.

Prendergast, Roy. 1992. *Film Music – A Neglected Art.* New York: Norton.

Rodman, Ronald. 2010. *Tuning In: American Narrative Television Music.* Oxford: Oxford University Press.

Smith, Jeff. 1998. *The Sounds of Commerce. Marketing Popular Film Music.* NY: Columbia University Press.

Smith, Murray. 2011. "Just What Is It That Makes Tony Soprano Such an Appealing, Attractive Murderer?" In *Ethics at the Cinema*, edited by Ward E. Jones and Samanta Vice. Oxford: Oxford University Press: 66–90.

Tagg, Phillip. 1979. *KOJAK –50 Seconds of Television Music [Toward the Analysis of Affect in Popular Music].* Göteborg Studies from the Dept. of Musicology, University of Göteborg.

Tagg, Phillip, and Bob Clarida. 2003. *Ten Little Title Tunes: Towards a Musicology of the Mass Media.* New York: The Mass Media Music Scholars' Press.

Tan, Ed S. 1994. *Emotion and the Structure of Narrative Film: The Film as an Emotion Machine.* London: Routledge.

Tan, Siu-Lan, Matthew P. Spackman, and Matthew A. Bezdek. 2007. "Viewers' Interpretations of Film Characters' Emotions: Effects of Presenting Film Music Before and After a Character is Shown." *Music Perception: An Interdisciplinary Journal* 25, no. 2: 135–152.

Thayer, J., and R. Levenson. 1983. "Effects of Music on Psychophysiological Responses to a Stressful Film." *Psychomusicology* 3: 44–54.

Vaage, Margrethe Bruun. 2015. *The Antihero in American Television.* London: Routledge.

11 *Twin Peaks* and the performative poetics of complex television

Aaron Taylor

How might we describe an actor's contribution to the aesthetics of the storytelling mode known as "complex television?" Coinciding with the success of specialty cable channels in the 1990s, and further enabled by new online dissemination tactics in the 2000s, the conventional formal paradigms of American broadcast television have been expanded to include an arguably greater degree – or at least, a different kind – of structural complexity. Consequently, there is growing scholarly interest in charting the formal parameters of this category of televisual programming as well as analyzing its ensuing cognitive demands. And yet, one of this mode's most striking manifestations of complexity is frequently overlooked: Its intricate performative dimensions as manifested by the actors populating its various landmark programs.[1] What is being offered here are some initial notes towards the development of a broader performative poetics of complex TV.

These preliminary musings will be exemplified via a case study of the most broadly canonized example of complex TV to date: *Twin Peaks* (1990–1991, 2017). As a series, *Twin Peaks* is typically regarded as the enabling agent of complex TV's programmatic emergence in the 1990s. Moreover, its 2017 revival was almost instantly greeted with hyperbolic critical proclamations that its formal audaciousness could enable an even greater degree of aesthetic intricacy within a historically conservative production culture (Peterson 2017). The innovations of the series have broadly been catalogued, but interestingly, discussions of its affective and narratological "weirdness" rarely contend closely with how its highly influential oddity is crafted through the specific performance choices and broader methodological strategies of its actors. It is profitable, then, to investigate how the choices and strategies adopted by *Twin Peaks*' recurring performers might stand in for broader formal developments in complex TV as a whole. The series is an ideal case study due to its influential aesthetics as well as its distinctive serial history – i.e., the markedly long interval between its second and third "seasons," which concomitantly is matched by the passing of 25 years in diegetic time. Such an expansive gap is poignantly bridged by the recurrence of familiar performance signs by markedly aged actors. In this regard, *The Return* has some commonalities with "the 2016 relaunch of *The X-Files* …[which] draws on the idiolect of detectives Mulder and Scully – and the familiarity that the majority of the audience has with the characters they

DOI: 10.4324/9781003188643-11

perform – as shorthand for understanding the new episodes, some fourteen years after the original show ended" (Drake 2016, 9).

Through close analyses of instructive moments from the series, then, I will offer considerations of three relevant areas – *character elasticity*, *encipherment*, and *modal mixing* – which, in turn, will help situate complex televisual performance in relation to matters involving time, space, knowledge, and genre.

Performative poetics of complex television

For the purposes of this chapter, I will be working more or less in accordance with Jason Mittell's influential definition of complex television. For Mittell, complex TV "redefin[es] the boundary between episodic and serial forms, with a heightened degree of self-consciousness in storytelling mechanics, and demanding intensified viewer engagement focused on both diegetic pleasures and formal awareness" (2015, 53). This latter component – the deliberate prompting of our enjoyment of a series' narratological workings – is dubbed complex TV's "*operational aesthetics*" (Mittell 2015, 42). It is this self-conscious facet of complex TV that I would like to accentuate with regard to performance, with corresponding attention also paid to what intertwining episodic and serial narrative strategies might mean for the actors tasked with portraying the intricate characters prized by both categories.

Before proceeding further, I should address possible objections that *Twin Peaks* is far more serialized than it is discretely episodic. However, I would assert that its narrative complexity issues from the compounding number of subplots in the second and third seasons. Many of these have only a tangential relation to the "main" storylines, resulting in a highly digressive, stuttering, sometimes minutely progressing overall structure.[2]

For the purposes of this volume, my suggestions regarding televisual performance are also prompted by the minimal attention paid to the material specificity of performance in cognitive film theory. Despite the abundance of worthy narratological treatises on characterization in the moving image, cognitivist media studies often overlook performance as such and instead, tend to focus on fictional beings in the abstract – as features of a filmic text. As Philip Drake reminds us, "performance is fundamentally different from representation and … all media texts are essentially performative, constructing particular relationships between performer and audience" (2016, 6). What remains underacknowledged is just this very *performativity*. Instead, the tendency has been for cognitivist scholars to discuss characterization abstractly, in a disembodied fashion. What is neglected is the actor's embodied, performative iteration, which actually brings characters into fictive being for an apprehending audience.

One strain of this neglect is an inherited, quasi-structuralist legacy of treating characters as pure textual functions within a narratological system. Here, a character is less a possible person than a feature of a textual framework. By subordinating character-types to functional "spheres of action," structuralist theorists insist on describing characters as *actants* (Greimas 1983; Propp 1968,

79–83). An actant occupies a role that is structurally necessary to the integrity of the narrative. Correspondingly, she *must* embody the traits and perform the actions that her role necessitates. An example of this inherited structuralism is Kristin Thompson's neo-formalist description of character behavior as being (1) inherently motivated by the demands of the narrative; (2) the impetus for story momentum; and (3) in need of consistency and reiteration (2003, 21–22, 27–28). But at no time does Thompson provide the particularities of what an actor is actually doing to contribute to characterization – i.e., just exactly how it is that the performer enacts the narrative's structurally required action.

Another strain of disregard is the legacy of focusing on the emotional and/or moral solicitations prompted by fictional beings but without acknowledging how an actor's specific performance choices might prompt affective engagement or ethical considerations. Mittell's landmark study of complex TV, for example, is perhaps the most broadly ambitious attempt to analyze the form's challenging configuration of characters. However, even this invaluable study does not consider how performance is instrumental to such narratological complexity. In a 45-page chapter on characters – including an extended discussion of our moral allegiance with antiheroes – there are a number of references to particular performances. And yet, very little is included in the way of providing the mimetic specifics of what actors are doing expressively with their bodies (Mittell 2015, 118–163). In short, our apprehension of complex TV is necessarily incomplete without further concentrated attention being paid to its performative dimensions.

Héctor J. Pérez has identified an essential path forward for cognitivist scholars interested in situating the actor's body as a device for filmic or televisual narration. For Pérez:

> the narration of the acting body engages all of our cognitive resources to the maximum in our reaction to gestures, adding narrative meta-awareness, which entails consciousness of being immersed in an aesthetic experience, to the whole range of motorsensory responses of bodily narration and new appeals to the imagination through empathy.
>
> (2015, 25)

The majority of cognitive film theory that contends with character either overlooks the artistic dimension of a performer's movements and expressions or tends to itemize them in the most abstract of terms. Typically absent is a technical consideration of actors' skill – how we react to their gestures, become conscious of the aesthetic experience they provide, and/or respond empathically to the affective, motorsensory dimensions of their expressive bodies at work.

I take seriously, then, Elliott Logan's important assertion that our apprehension of TV characters cannot be categorically disentwined from our appreciation of the actors who embody them (2015, 28). Thus, the conceptual ideas I am introducing here are offered in the spirit of satisfying Logan's charge to television scholars that we articulate "those qualities of the work, and our experience of it, that develop and find their significance in matters of duration and gradual accretion handled through repetition and variation" (2015, 35). Our apprehension of acting, then, is a matter of attuning our consciousness to a narrating body in action – within a single moment, across time, and in relation to the camera's delimited spaces.[3] In sum, as a cognitivist scholar, I do not wish to propose categorical terms that perpetuate the abstraction of televisual characters from the expressive bodies that enable these fictional beings to materialize in the first place. The terms I proffer are, I hope, sensitive to and adequate descriptors of the material specificities of actors' expressive labor as manifested in agglomerated instances across the unfolding of a complex television series, during distinctive if not iconic singular moments, and occurring within specially delimited spaces.

Character elasticity

First, in its approach to characterization, complex TV is noteworthy for its incorporation of both "novelistic" density and comparably relative stasis or flatness. A delicate balance is struck between a character's gradual development and the necessity to retain some fundamental consistency that coheres with a series' conceptual identity (Mittell 2015, 123–124). For an actor, then, the challenge is to incorporate this incrementally compounding thickness into their performance choices while still telegraphing a certain core integrity of personality. Call this *character elasticity*. Actors in *Twin Peaks* approach this task via an overarching performative rhetoric that combines unidimensional characterization with a paradoxical depth of feeling. One of the distinct pleasures of the show is witnessing intentionally flat representatives of various film and TV genres manifest shockingly intense emotions.

As a way of signaling episodic TV's need for character consistency, *Twin Peaks* offers a veritable parade of types: FBI detectives, small-town cops, juvenile delinquents, femmes fatales, crooked businessmen, gangsters, prom queens, etc. With a few notable exceptions, almost none of the characters undergo dramatic departures from these generic roles, even in the quarter-century gap between seasons. Transformations are so rare as to be supernaturally literal – as when principal protagonist FBI Agent Dale Cooper (Kyle MacLachlan) is replaced by an evil doppelgänger during season two's cliffhanger. Other figures – especially comic ones – are defined by behaviors that have minimal variance and that attain their respective affective intentions through telegraphed repetition. The stunned, soft-spoken intonation of Officer Andy Brennan (Harry Goaz) is one such example, as is the chipmunkish chittering of his receptionist wife, Lucy (Kimmy Robertson) – to say nothing of the molasses-paced, Brando-inspired mumblings of their son, Wally (Michael Cera), in S03E04.

At its most pronounced, this stasis is articulated through reiterations of single traits that make near-automatons of their performers. *The Return* is full of such figures: the endearing vacancy of Candie (Amy Shiels), a perpetually distracted Las Vegas showgirl, comes to mind. But season three's most sustained exemplar of stasis is Dougie Jones, the second, near-mindless replicant of Cooper who replaces the missing FBI agent (and is also played by MacLachlan). This schlubby salesman shuffles about in his oversized pea-green suit, capable only of repeating short catchphrases like an actor brain-damaged by his imprisonment in a sitcom that ran well past a merciful cancellation date. In one fan-favorite scene (S03E03), Dougie magically hits jackpot after jackpot in the same casino in which Candie performs, each time mimicking an earlier winner's cry of "Hell-o-OH-ohhh!!!".[4] Kyle MacLachlan's tripled vowel is triply poignant: as a comic delight, a veiled reminder of Cooper's own triplicated identity, and an aural expression of TV characters' structurally necessary repetitions. Again and again, Dougie sits before the slot machines – arms open in guileless expectation – and each time he thrusts himself back from the deluge of unexpected riches, like a television viewer awaiting the illusion of the first time but yet still surprised by the manifestation of that which is anticipated. Season three infuriatingly withholds the return of our beloved Cooper for 16 long episodes – partly as an act of authorial sadism against those making a nostalgia-driven return trip to Twin Peaks. Each and every moment of Dougie's somnambulism, then, contains a kernel of expectation: "Maybe he'll snap out of it *now*," we think. MacLachlan's repetitive turn in the casino is a reflexive tease, speaking to our own hope against hope for the shock of an instant reward: The return of comforting, episodic reliability amidst serialized change.

To be clear, the husk that is Dougie is not the replacement of a character who was made complex through our gradual exposure to him in the previous two seasons. For Cooper is also a comparably simple fellow – despite his unusually sunny openness to sensory stimulation (his chorus of "*Damn* fine coffee" became a national catchphrase in 1990). Dougie is a clown who has replaced a damn fine G-man, and yet his body sluggishly exudes wilted versions of Cooper's beloved idiolects. Witness Cooper's trademarked can-do thumbs up – snapped smartly into action 13 times across seasons one and two – attenuated by Dougie's laboriously ascending digit (S03E04). Or, take note of Cooper's

Figure 11.1 *Twin Peaks*, S03E05 (Showtime, 2017).

one-handed grip on a coffee mug – nose cruising appreciatively across its surface (S01E02) – that is replaced by Dougie's two-handed snorfling of a latté, like a cartoon character lifted off its feet by a heavenly aroma (S03E05). As Dougie manifests frustratingly weakened, lethargic reminders of Cooper's snap and verve, MacLachlan, too, signals the requirement for complex TV characters to exhibit a residual consistency even when paradoxically faced with the expectation of change. They are not often permitted the boundless capacity for change enjoyed by serialized characters, but neither can they relax into the constancy granted by episodic television's familiar patterns.

Twin Peaks' interest in types and their elasticity is not just horizontally oriented across serial temporality but is also vertically expansive. For as mentioned earlier, the thin surfaces of the generic, cartooned figures populating the series are belied by their seemingly boundless depth of feeling. The first two seasons are rightly famous for their frequent scenes of extraordinary emotion – particularly instances of unseemly grief.[5] Characters shriek, weep, and simply disintegrate into a psychic pain that overwhelms their bodies. Confronted with the news of Laura Palmer's death, for example, a bumpkin cop dissolves into a puddle, a loving mother uproots elegant tresses, a high school principal blubs into a PA system, the nice girl-next-door wails at her school desk, and a genteel business lawyer becomes a public spectacle (all in S01E01).

Fascinatingly, some of these instances manage to be blackly humorous while still confronting us with a grief that cannot be refuted or contained – as when Laura's father, Leland (Ray Wise), hurls himself on her coffin as it descends into the grave, only to be tossed up and down by a broken hydraulic system. Lacey speaks of the fluid combination of melodramatic and comic modes of acting on the show. "*Twin Peaks* may play with the comic absurdity of the melodramatic, yet it also requires that we are, if not thrilled, then at least disturbed by the excesses of melodramatic performance" (Lacey 2016, 128). I would suggest that such disturbance is at least partly explicable in terms of our expectations of TV types; we simply do not imagine that such mirages are the wellsprings of genuine emotion. Indeed, perhaps, they seem to feel much more than we might under similar circumstances *because* they are characters, not people.

While crying is also always a showcasing of actorly talent, what Ray Wise manifests in one of *Twin Peaks*' climactic moments cannot usefully be described as declamatory ostensiveness – a virtuoso display of technical skill or presentational performance (Naremore 1988, 34–45). When Leland confesses to the murder of his daughter's suspected killer (S02E04), it is not an excess of emotion he channels but a terrible torrent of anguish that distends any conventionalized image of paternity. In this scene, iconic televisual fathers who know best are exposed as guises for fathers who feel far too much.[6]

Wise is framed in a shallow-focused medium close-up, while behind him, Warren Frost appraises him, arms folded – both a diegetic participant in Leland's interrogation and a nondiegetic audience to Wise's artistry. Leland delivers his confession to Sherriff Truman out of frame and thus looks both up at and through his interrogator. The camera delimits a space, then, that simultaneously invokes the interrogation lamp essential to hackneyed scenes of perp-sweating and the spotlight essential to theatrical scenes of performative display. He considers Truman's question – "Leland, did you kill Jacques Renault?" – as if dazed, and slightly frowning, a lawyer considering withholding crucial information. But with an upturned cock of his head and the mere ghost of a smile, he answers Truman matter-of-factly: "He killed my Laura." And with that, Leland is undone by sorrow once again. Wise's frightening eyes begin to spill over with tears. Correcting Cooper's placating reference to "grief," Leland strives to describe "absolute loss" instead, and in so doing, his attention is taken beyond his interrogators, into a private realm in which sadness is felt at a molecular level. His hands gesture inwards to this inaccessible place, but then are redirected towards his ears – as if to stop up the sounds of his "screaming cells." No quietude is to be obtained, and his heaving, frustrated breaths propel his consciousness back towards his captors – hands now beseeching as he unburdens himself of his guilt in lieu of his torment. "Yes, I killed him" is

Figure 11.2 Twin Peaks, S02E04 (ABC, 1990).

a declaration ensconced in high, juddering sobs that take to pieces what might otherwise have been an assertion of vengeful triumph. All the while, Wise's mad, consuming pain is coming to a head in perfect unison with the upward modulations of "Laura Palmer's Theme" – often employed in other scenes of expansive feeling – and as Leland spirals into an admission of violence, so too does the musical score modulate downwards. It darkens entirely into ominous synth tones just as his beseeching hands are clenched into murderous fists that seem to drive Leland's pitiable sobs of "Yes!" into near-demonic exultations. This family man has become feral and fearsome in the intensity of his pain.

Wise's masterclass on weeping is in keeping with other scenes in which clichéd figures achieve a kind of density through the intensity of their crying. It is not quite accurate to assert that these characters "often move between depth and surface, moments of 'truth' and more mannered moments" (Abbott 2015, 182). And it is certainly not the case that hoodlums-made-good like Bobby Briggs (Dana Ashbrook) or hapless high school principals like Bill Hastings (Matthew Lillard) are made more "real" through their protracted scenes of copious weeping over their respective lost loves (S03E04 and S03E09). Indeed, their excessive grief "arouses anxiety because of its inappropriateness" and is a symptom of the constructive "embarrassment" that the series evokes in viewers (Thompson 2003, 124). Call it a kind of cognitive dissonance, whereby we might shrink from these wailing specters whose emotional elasticity does not exactly stretch credulity but rather, our capacity to apprehend these characters as representatives of stable, one-dimensional sociological or structural categories. In short, complex televisual performance can complicate classical, literary distinctions between surface and depth, consistency and change.

Encipherment

How, then, do we draw near to such beings? That is, what kind of sympathetic relationships might viewers form with complex televisual characters, and how might actors facilitate these affiliations? Conventional television of the network era is said to foster a closeness to its audience by virtue of an emphasis on "faces, reactions, explorations of emotions" often situated within interior spaces (Newcomb 1974, 245–246, 248). As our exposure to these private dramas is durative across serialized time (rather than restricted to an isolated fictive instance), it is often consequently claimed that we form "parasocial" relationships with the virtual "friends" whom we ritualistically invite into our own homes and everyday lives (Horton and Wohl 1956). Unlike dramatic characters, whose lives are more tautly circumscribed by the classical dictates of closure, televisual characters – like us – have unwritten futures. This provisionality is said to encourage predictive speculation and the recognition of similarities between our own situations and theirs, rather than the various forms of identification that film is said to foster (Caughie 2012, 57).

Conversely, Mittell claims that in complex TV of the post-network era, traditional character allegiance and parasocial closeness have given way to "operational allegiance," whereby "we are engaged with the character's construction, attuned to how the performance is presented" (Mittell 2015, 163). Spending time with the inhabitants of *Twin Peaks*, then, is a less a matter of feeling along with them than of feeling our way around them, puzzling over the intricate networks between individuals. Its cult appeal issues from "its complexity, its density, its technical precision and virtuosity, its consistency and yet its ability to continually pose problems for interpretation" (Jenkins 1995, 55). This intricacy is not simply the product of showrunners David Lynch and Mark Frost's extravagant narrative designs; it is also the outcome of performance strategies that often refute relationships predicated upon sympathetic or empathetic alignment. Let us call this tactic *performative encipherment*.

To better appreciate this alternative mode of hedonic engagement, it is helpful to draw some lessons from soap operas. We should recall that the first two seasons of *Twin Peaks* owed their popularity to their generic affiliation with the daytime and prime-time soap operas of the 1980s. These seasons inherited from soaps a purposeful investment in analytical and interpretive play. "Soap structure encourages accumulating knowledge of character relationships [and] subplot complications," argues Jennifer Hayward, "not as a set of 'keys' that will eventually buy narrative resolution, but as a part of an intricate game with no teleological purpose" (1997, 153). Hayward's description of soap opera story complexity should remind us that the soapy pleasures pertaining to character and performance also can derive from putatively feminine social competencies: "reading faces, interpreting relationships, contemplating the impact of events on feelings" (Newman and Levine 2012, 91).

The utility of these social competencies for a poetics of complex TV performance should be clear: They inform our sense of the meaningfulness of an actor's expressions, postures, gestures, movements, and vocalizations. In one sense, "the danger in studying strategies of performance … is that it presumes that what is going on in the actors' minds is going to be evident in the way that they perform," and literally speaking, "there is no way we can truly know an actor's mental processes" (Butler 2018, 68). But in another, more constructive sense during the viewing process, we *are* required to attend to the expressive subtleties of an actor's creative physicalizing in order to infer all sorts of narratively salient information about the minds of the *characters* they portray.[7] Without these competencies, much narrative action would simply be insensible.

A standard soap tactic, for example, might be taken from *The Young and the Restless* (1973–). Here, we might draw on any number of tumultuous encounters between supercouple Nikki (Melody Thomas Scott) and Victor Newman (Eric Braeden), which are often composed in shallow-focused two-shots featuring the former in the background and the latter tightly framed in the foreground (or vice versa depending on the power dynamic at work). As the camera rack focuses on Victor informing Nikki that he suspects her, say, of resuming her old alcoholic habits (or, perhaps, having an affair with his rival, Deacon Sharpe), we in turn shift our attention to Nikki as we observe her hidden reaction to Victor's barb. A widening of eyes and momentary arresting of Nikki's normally alert visage might signify her dismay at being found out before a shift to a flirtatious smile or flinty glare denotes her chosen method of regaining composure and mounting a counteraction. In either case, Scott intentionally orchestrates our sense of Nikki's experience and narratively salient characteristics via bodily signals, and we are able to intuit Nikki's state of mind through observation even though we obviously don't and can't have direct access to her feeling-state. What soaps underline, then, is that the inferences we make about others' motives – often based on external expressive signifiers – "allow people to comprehend the meaning of events and better understand how the different aspects of an individual's personality fit together" (Reeder and Trafimow 2005, 107).

Contrarily, though, complex television occasionally distinguishes itself from such generic tactics by a pronounced tendency to undermine our ability to successfully intuit the feeling-states of characters and predict future behaviors. While such obfuscations are ordinarily undertaken for the purposes of suspense, we are not simply speaking of an actor's expressive withholding or performed performance, which is diegetically intended to misdirect or deceive characters and audiences alike – the stuff of so much domestic melodrama or crime thrillers.

Rather, the encipherment addressed here refers to an actor's deliberate efforts to stymie our efforts at mind-reading and motive-attribution in alignment with a show's purposeful operational aesthetics. Such obfuscation prompts our own playful acts of speculative world-building as well as our evaluative preoccupation with narrative construction.

On the subject of world-building, we refer to complex TV's solicitations for us to imaginatively expand upon the directly represented parameters of a diegetic world. Viewing communities contribute to this enlargement through paratextual activities: wiki-building, cartographic mappings, amateur creative production, and – perhaps most frequently – fan theorizing (see Mittell 2015, 261–291). One aesthetic strategy employed by complex TV series to encourage such participatory work is the deliberate and recurring tropic use of the chronic enigma. "Ongoing or unresolved mysteries about [a series'] characters, character relationships, or aspects of their invented worlds" generate this extensive ludic activity and cultic appeal, as "there is a sense in which what we see on screen is only a part of a much wider narrative world, always implying further events and developments" (Hills 2005, 190). Rather than employ a highly communicative narrational system, then, complex TV strategically withholds information, only releasing salient narrative details sporadically across a series. And perversely, such clues or selective revelations tend to open even wider expanses of the unknown than viewers had initially anticipated.

Lost (2004–2010) is a paradigmatic series in this respect, with every small disclosure about its mysterious island's secrets only spreading further rhizomatic, conspiratorial tendrils. Actors on *Lost* play a key role in advancing its enticing enigmas – particularly those tasked with portraying deceitful characters who know more than they let on, or who literally aren't who we thought they were. Their performance choices, then, involve a degree of *withholding* – the omittance of outward signs of what would otherwise be communicative markers of character motivation, feeling, or moral alignment. Concurrently, the encipherment of their characters also involves a strategic *expressive ambiguity* – rendering opaque their bodies' signifying capacities through counter-intuitive line readings, playing against a scene's explicit mood or intention, or permitting unmotivated/untargeted exhibitions of feeling to emerge. In Mittell's words, "since interiority is a restricted area of access, we must infer characters' morality and beliefs on the basis of exterior markers, including their appearance, behaviors, and interactions" (2015, 134). But with performative encipherment, this inferential activity is subverted, and our speculations are often merely provisional. So, rather than encourage the intimacy and parasociality so instrumental to the serialized melodrama of soap operas, actors in complex TV construct objects of scrutiny and decipherment in their stead.

Twin Peaks offers even more radical instances of withholding and expressive ambiguity that prompts operational allegiance, imaginative world-building, and a cognitive preoccupation with narrative construction. Compare, for example, two further instances of soap-inflected hysteria, both ably undertaken by Grace Zabriskie in her role as Sarah Palmer – mother of Laura and wife of Leland. Zabriskie's work is exemplary in that Sarah is a minor character, appearing in only 23 scenes throughout the entire run of the series, but Zabriskie's remarkable performance choices ensure that Sarah's moments are always memorable ones. Her enciphering work prompts our speculative activity – self-reflections regarding our proximity to her traumatized grief and later, collective hypothesizing about just who it is we are apprehending.

In a scene that follows her harrowing response to the news of Laura's death (in S01E01), Sarah is tranquilized by Doc Hayward and interviewed by Sherriff Truman. We already have been discomfited by a scene of her frenzied grieving over the telephone, which seemed to exceed all boundaries of conventional, televisual propriety (see Lacey 2016, 129–130). But rather than allow the interview to devolve into comfortable, generically familiar territory (poli ce-gently-question-grieving-mother), Zabriskie permits Sarah's traumatized subjectivity to circumnavigate the soporific effects of the drug, confronting us with astonishingly genuine (not melodramatically conventionalized) psychic torment. Cutting from the iconic photo of Laura as Prom Queen, over which we hear dreadful shrieks, to a close-up of Sarah's animal sobs oozing away into dull moans, Sarah melts backwards into upholstered oblivion. Struggling to answer Truman's questions through a narcotic fog, her slurred but factual replies about times, final exchanges, etc. are punctuated by sharp, audible pangs of sorrow that transmute the facticity of her words into hiccoughing gasps and wrench her slackened features back into a clenched agony. Noise from above

Figure 11.3 *Twin Peaks*, S01E01 (ABC, 1990).

startles her, and a close-up highlights her enormous, horrified eyes and her panicked whisper, "*Who's* upstairs?" This chilling moment slackens into dull mollification. "I can tell from the sounds that it isn't her," she slurs to Truman and bravely forces a malformed smile. But neither Truman nor the viewers are let off that easily. This social gesture erodes quickly as smile devolves into spastic grimace, then relaxes into anaesthetized impassiveness, only to return again as a bestial contortion of pain she is compelled to hide from her onlookers with the screen of her hand.

During moments such as these, Sarah is provided with an emotional and personal expansiveness that far exceeds her minimal screen time. Zabriskie's work provides us with an occasion to undertake the following cognitive activities: (1) we *imaginatively enlarge* Sarah's world (i.e., we might intuit the scope of her relationships with Laura and Leland), (2) *make conjectures* about her character (i.e., we might infer a fierce, primal devotion to her loved ones), and/or (3) *consider our own embodied position* in relation to Sarah's (i.e., our possible discomfiture at her distress might issue from our proximity to such raw emotion). Moreover, her expressive ambiguity fuels *participatory speculation*. For although the identity of Laura's murderer was a carefully guarded secret – kept even from the show's cast members – Zabriskie's brief telegraphing of Sarah's terror ("*Who's* upstairs?") is retroactively read as a moment of poignancy by fans eager to project deductive theories and ascribe motivation onto enciphered character action.[8] For at that moment, Laura's murderer *is*, in fact, upstairs, although his identity is kept secret at this early stage of the series. Given that the series would also vaguely hint at the possibility that Sarah is a psychic medium of sorts, fans read into Sarah's enciphered terror not just a moment of disoriented panic but an unconscious intuition that one of the men upstairs is not who he appears to be (LostIntheMovies 2015).

This is not a matter of "reading too much into" body language but of responding to deliberately abstruse performance strategies designed to engage us in speculative play. As Mittell reminds us,

> through a long-term investment in a series, viewers accrue knowledge and experiences about characters that allow us to posit our own version of their interiority, especially within the gaps between episodes, when we are left to think about what we have seen and consider our own relationship to characters.
>
> (2015, 132)

As indicated, it is not that we project upon Sarah an interiority that is otherwise underdeveloped but that Zabriskie's enciphering strategies enable other types of imaginative interaction with *Twin Peaks* as a serialized fiction. The gaps referred to by Mittell are particularly worthy of note here. For in the 25 years between the events of seasons 2 and 3, Sarah undergoes a literally indescribable transformation from shattered victim of domestic trauma to herself becoming the host for a monstrous, extra-dimensional being. The precise nature of her metamorphosis has spawned uncountable numbers of fan-theory explanations within dozens of subreddits, which are further prompted by the suppressive abstruseness of Zabriskie's performance.

In another histrionic set piece from S03E12, Sarah undergoes a schizoid episode in a liquor store, which establishes a performative rhyme with her breakdown in the series' pilot episode.[9] As before, the impression here is the leakage of an uncontainable, unbearable interiority. Like her daughter, Sarah, too, is "full of secrets," and Zabriskie's withholding tactics and expressive ambiguity in this scene augment *Twin Peaks*' many undecipherable mysteries.

Performances in this complex television series help facilitate "ludic hypothesizing across serialized gaps in the narrative," whereby "the richness of … performance opens up a wide range of different thoughts we imagine [a character] might be suppressing" (Mittell 2015, 161). And who can say what exactly it is that Sarah is suppressing, or how much of her humanity remains beneath her grotesquely churning features? As she cryptically puts it to a concerned Deputy Chief Hawk, "It's a goddamn bad story."

Mixing modalities

Our final performative strategy corresponds to the propensity for complex television to traffic in a pronounced degree of categorical hybridity. In Mittell's account of complex TV's operational aesthetics, viewers are frequently tasked with apprehending sophisticated linkages between familiar production traditions and narrative genres. "Complex television is a site of tremendous genre mixing," he asserts, "where conventions and assumptions from a range of programming categories come together and are interwoven, merged, and reformed" (2015, 233). Certainly, a number of pioneering series in the 1990s instituted such hybridization as a storytelling norm, including *The X-Files* (SF/police procedural), *Buffy the Vampire Slayer* (horror/comedy), and *The Sopranos* (crime/domestic melodrama). *Twin Peaks* is certainly one of these urtexts, with arguably the most radical degree of hybridity. Suffice to say, such admixtures of storytelling categories present particular challenges to actors. Their expressive bodies are expected to serve as corporeal shorthand for certain genre conventions as well as functioning as the embodied, unifying loci of otherwise disparate narrative traditions.

Moreover, an actor's performance choices can also serve as indexical signs with curiously doubled referents. On the one hand, they instantiate necessary fictional properties (e.g., a character's traits), but on the other, they can simultaneously conjure up associations with extratextual circumstances surrounding a series' production. In other words, an actor in a complex TV series sometimes "characterizes" (i.e., portrays a fictional being) while concurrently denoting that this creative construction is unfolding before us. We can refer to an actor's contribution to the blending of genres, and this doubled reference to character and creative laborer, as *modal mixing* – a combination or layering of extra-diegetic material.

Speaking first to the means by which actors contribute to a complex TV program's strategic blending of genres, it is crucial to recognize that genres have an *empeopling* function: they ensure that diegetic orders are populated by sets of unified types that lend their storyworlds structural cohesiveness. In turn, we can attest that the social utility of a genre involves establishing particularized fandoms that cohere around the shared recognition and accreditation of familiar personages. Just as, say, film noir gathers its hard-boiled identity around a roster of hard-bitten faces (Bacall, Bogart, Garfield, Grahame, Widmark, Windsor), so, too, is this taste category propagated by admiring viewers who declare their shared affinity for noir's memorable mugs. In Drake's words, "individual performers become associated with a repertoire of performance signs: their 'idiolect,' the performance signs strongly associated with a particular actor" (2016, 9). So, too, are these idiolects incorporated into a genre's semantic and syntactic configurations, and absorbed into audiences' ritualized modes of apprehension.

It is not the occasion here to fully extrapolate the structural and social functionality of performance as it pertains to the "genre-fying" of narrative categories and production trends. However, we can simply say that actors do play a key role in the cohering of television genres and their respective interpretive communities. In concrete terms, the incorporation and absorption of generic idiolects is neatly and memorably dramatized in S02E01 of *Twin Peaks*.[10] Here, the usually demure girl-next-door, Donna Hayward (Lara Flynn Boyle), briefly experiments with a femme fatale persona by simply donning Laura's old sunglasses, smoking sensuously, and breathily engaging in pulpy repartee with her incarcerated biker-beau, James Hurley (James Marshall). These noirish shadings are further bolstered by Angelo Badalamenti's slinky "Freshly Squeezed" theme – one of the show's iconic, lounge-lizard motifs. And so, with the help of a few key accoutrements and jazzy inflections, Boyle flits readily from one generic role to another, and audiences are quick to recognize and accredit her noirish self-interpellation.

While Donna's dabbling in genre stereotypes is out of character, fictionally speaking, it is absolutely of a piece with *Twin Peaks*' broader tendencies to combine genres in collagist fashion. But rather than invoking postmodernism or surrealism as explanatory discourses for the series' abrasive generic juxtapositions, it should be noted here instead that aggressive generic hybridity is a tactic endemic in complex TV's broader operational aesthetic.[11] In the aforementioned early exemplars of this mode, actors were also required to alternate rapidly between clashing generic modes in situations that demanded a concomitantly self-conscious emotional reactivity from viewers. A demonic threat in *Buffy* – like the punkish Spike (James Marsters) – might quickly undercut its own horror with a sardonic jibe. Or the simmering fury of crime boss patriarch Tony (James Gandolfini) could abruptly melt into familial tenderness in *The Sopranos*. Other actors might serve as anchors for these jarring shifts or weld together generic disparateness through staid performance motifs. Thus, *The X-Files*' science-fictional monstrosities gain both credence and affect via the deadpan expressivity of David Duchovny's unflappable Agent Fox Mulder. Similarly, not only was Kyle MacLachlan cast as Agent Dale Cooper due to his ability to "think on screen," but Lynch also praised him for his ability to "connect different worlds" (Lynch and Rodley 2005, 141).

The primary difference with *Twin Peaks*, then, is its lack of concern with establishing diegetic motivation for the shifts between generically specific moods or styles. By contrast, in the complex melodrama *This Is Us* (2016–), Justin Hartley plays Kevin Pearson, a disgruntled actor starring in a terrible sitcom, "The Manny." In S01E01, Kevin gives a "realistic" turn during the taping of a dramatically serious moment, but the take is rejected by the ratings-obsessed writer-showrunner, prompting Kevin to quit the show in a rage. Here, Kevin's "inappropriate" emotional realism is vetoed for its tonal inappropriateness to "The Manny." Conversely, as Lacey asserts, "if the tendency in most television drama is for the transition between [realistic and expositional acting] to be seamless, in *Twin Peaks* it is often sudden and disorienting" (2006, 131). It is definitely the case that on *Twin Peaks*, certain "personalities and acting styles deliberately clash with the more 'serious' sensibility of [other] characters" (Creeber 2004, 50). These clashes create a cognitive dissonance attributable to generic idiolects working at cross-purposes. We've cited already the seriocomic scene of the malfunctioning hydraulic lift at Laura's funeral. And even the chilling pall cast by Sarah's liquor-store meltdown is incongruously warmed by the comic flatness of the comparatively under-skilled young actors playing the cashiers who watch her freak out (Zoe McLane and Johnny Ochsner). Their verisimilarly challenged gawping does not quite pass for "worried discomfort," and thus, the black cloud of Zabriskie's skillful hysteria is quickly dispelled by their sunny amateurism.

The suggestion here is that *Twin Peaks*' mixed modalities prompt our recognition that other elements might direct a scene's movement beyond narrative-driven dictates – predominantly, mood. Linda Williams's (1991) influential work on "body genres" is useful to invoke here. In horror, melodrama, and pornography, we witness "the spectacle of a body caught in the grip of intense sensation or emotion," and these "ecstatic excesses" are said to prompt viewers' own emotional mimicry (Williams 1991, 4). While *Twin Peaks* is celebrated for performative instances of intense horror and melodrama – in which the affect of a moment might be said to overwhelm its narrative functionality – it also features spontaneous instances of ecstatic excess that privilege the musically motivated body. We can speak of performance here in its literal, presentational sense, as characters occasionally break into song and dance with minimal narrative pretext. In S01E03, Audrey Horne (Sherilynn Fenn) allows the bliss of a jazzy juke at the RR Diner to carry her (and us) away.[12] The oozing shuffle executed by the Arm (Michael J. Anderson) in S01E02 surreally mirrors the zigzag pattern on the Red Room's floor upon which he grooves.[13] And

Leland's merry rendition of "Mairzy Doates" in S02E01 compels the unctuous Horne brothers – Ben (Richard Beymer) and Jerry (David Patrick Kelly) – to execute an impressive soft-shoe and a clumsy rendition of the Worm, respectively.[14] In particular, Beymer's graceful stepping transports us back to his star-making turn in *West Side Story* (1961) – especially since his fellow Jet, Russ Tamblyn, also resides in Twin Peaks (as psychiatrist Dr. Jacoby). Dancing in *Twin Peaks*, then, "signals not only the contingency and instability of the media text in relation to the demands of diegesis, narrative and the progressive unfolding of knowledge, but also foregrounds [a] propensity for time-shifting folds of sensation" (Thain 2016).

Other moments of musical excess are decidedly of the "backstage musical" variety. The Bang Bang Bar, for example, is frequently the locus of diegetically motivated musical performances. Julee Cruise's ethereal singing is privileged in season 1, and each episode of season 3 features a performance by a real-world celebrity musician. But unlike the brief appearances by non-fictional guest artists in other television series – say, the various bands who perform in *Buffy*'s fictional nightclub, the Bronze – each live number at the Bang Bang Bar is played out in its entirety. These become moments of pure musical spectacle, with performance literally foregrounded as such. As their sets unfold in real time, the musical artists become oddly unintegrated from the diegesis – even while other actors paradoxically portray bar patrons who either watch the musicians perform or execute little dramas as the songs play. The musicians' "non-matrixed" performances might be said to rupture diegetic integrity, just as the "received acting" of the bar patrons (played by extras) and the "complex acting" of the named characters work to recuperate it (see Kirby 1972). Moreover, several of these performers have direct connections to David Lynch (Rebekah Del Rio, Trent Reznor, Riley Lynch) or literally reprise earlier "numbers" from the series' first two seasons (both James Marshall and Sherilyn Fenn re-perform an earlier song and dance, respectively). And so, these musical spectacles do not only contribute to inter-episodic continuity; they also contain pronounced allusive and intertextual functions, which are in keeping with the series' operational aesthetic.

This referential dimension of performance brings us to our last aspect of modal mixing: Actors' doubled reference to the characters they portray as well as to the medium of their own expressive bodies. Complex TV can occasionally create an explicit interplay between textual and extratextual facets of a program. Because our apprehension of a complex TV narrative is often filtered through a preoccupation with the sensibilities of its showrunner, it is not simply that actors signal their own acting as such but also that their work can indexically point towards a larger creative overseer. While stars are certainly creative agents in their own right, "any attitudes the actors express are ultimately situated in a context over which someone else has ultimate control" (Nannicelli 2017, 27). Actors, therefore, might exemplify the patented preoccupations of certain showrunners. Performers in the *West Wing* (1999–2006), for example, immortalized the Aaron Sorkin walk-and-talk, and *Deadwood*'s actors (2004–2006) made plausible David Milch's poetic profanity.

What Lynch enables, however, in the revival of *Twin Peaks* is a reflexivity that far exceeds the stylization of these other complex series. Rather, the doubled modalities in season 3 never quite cohere as they do in most complex TV. Typically, an author-function might overshadow our apprehension of a scene, but it doesn't really overtake the diegesis completely. Ian McShane's elegant baritone is the perfect instrument for Milch's graceful vulgarities in *Deadwood*, but it is still the irascible (and fictional) Al Swearengen we directly apprehend cursing so beautifully (despite the fact that it is, indeed, Shane who is uttering words written by Milch). However, what are we to make of the temporal contexts Lynch orchestrates for his performers in *Twin Peaks* – specifically season 3's notoriously interminable long takes? And further, how are we to apprehend the expressive labor unfolding in these glacially paced scenes when Lynch himself appears in them as his fictional alter-ego, FBI Deputy Director Gordon Cole? The suggestion here is that these long takes facilitate performances that prompt viewers to oscillate between two levels of consciousness: An apprehension of the unfolding diegesis, but also the associative linking of extratextual elements pertaining to the series' production.

Frequently, scenes in season 3 play out in static long shots that run for several lengthy minutes. Little seems to happen in terms of significant story action. A man sweeps the floor of the Bang Bang Bar for two and a half minutes in S03E07. Dr. Jacoby spray-paints shovels for what feels like an eternity in S03E03. Candie stalks a pesky fly for 5% of S03E10's running time. To some extent, Lynch is wreaking havoc with complex TV's already fraught tensions between episodic and serialized logics, in which a broader story develops incrementally within self-contained narrative units. But he also grants his performers a dramatic frame with a spatio-temporal integrity that is exceedingly rare in television. Actors are left to their own devices, and their improvisational work represents a fascinating negotiation of undramatized time. Consequently, viewers are compelled to graft explanatory micronarratives onto these instances of "dead" time. We track subtle shifts in an actor's physicality and, through free association, imaginatively project character motivation onto a narratively ambiguous scene. At the same time, we might also import extratextual associations based on our knowledge of Lynch's creative practices in order to formulate a "story" around the scene's production – attributing motivation to performers at the level of collaborative interplay and authorial intent.

S03E09's two-minute smoke break, for example, contains multitudes.[15] Acerbic former FBI operative Diane Evans (Laura Dern) smokes broodily outside a morgue and is joined, after a spell, by Gordon Cole and Agent Tammy Preston (Chrysta Bell). Gordon stands between the two women, eyeing up Diane's cigarette longingly and casting furtive looks at Tammy, who shifts uncomfortably from one stilted position to another. All the while, Diane alternates between insouciant puffs and withering glances at the disapproving,

Figure 11.4 *Twin Peaks*, S03E09 (Showtime, 2017).

younger agent. Tension builds over a long minute before Gordon caves and asks his old friend for one nostalgic drag, much to Tammy's dismay. The gentle humor of the scene arises entirely from the thoughts we project into the characters' heads during this silent comedy of manners. But we might also be tickled by considering the scene as a story of actor–director relationships. For both Dern and Bell are referred to as figures of inspiration for Lynch, and so, Lynch's ping-ponging glances between them are not without considerable directorial affection and bemusement. In addition, we might intuit a rivalry between diva and ingenue, since Dern's partnership with Lynch extends much further back than Bell's ("We used to smoke together way back when, remember?" Gordon asks). Indeed, it isn't difficult to imagine that the discomfort Bell displays (fidgeting, rocking, unconsciously posturing) is not feigned. Unlike Dern – a veteran film actor – Bell is a rookie and doesn't seem to have internalized the stillness and relaxation the medium requires of performers. And thus, Diane's pointedly pissy glare is also the teasing, mock-judgmental sizing-up of a young upstart by an older pro.

Through the mixing of modalities, enciphering performance choices, and elastic characterizations, actors in complex TV make important contributions to the category's distinctive blending of episodic and serial forms and its pronounced operational aesthetic. These strategies are offered here as contributions towards the development of a more comprehensive performative poetics for this televisual mode. By adjusting their expressive acts to the requirements of intricately structured storytelling, these actors involve us in challenging and creative responses to the works in which they appear. Blurring, mystifying, and stretching small- screen conventions, they enlarge television's opportunities for enacting its own memorable idiosyncrasies.

Notes

1 For a few noteworthy studies of televisual performance, see Butler (2018, 54–88); Caughie (2000); Drake (2016); Logan (2016); Lury (1995); and Pearson (2010).
2 The main storylines can be allocated to specific seasons. The first involves FBI Agent Dale Cooper's initial investigation of the murder of Laura Palmer (a small-town prom queen). Season two features Cooper's efforts to penetrate the Black Lodge – a dimension that spawned an evil force responsible for Laura's death. Season three revolves around Cooper's return from the Black Lodge, where he has been imprisoned for 25 years. Prominently featured are the exploits of a comically bumbling *tulpa* (a thoughtform duplicate) and a malevolent doppelgänger that have replaced him.
3 For an account of blending episodic and serial knowledge, see Gendler (2016). For an excellent consideration of the relationship between TV actors' bodies and the camera, see Donaldson (2013).
4 Cinema Garmonbozia,"Twin Peaks – Coop's HELLO-O-O Compilation," *YouTube*, May 24, 2017, www.youtube.com/watch?v=tl3OCzcEMFY.
5 For extensive examples, see Tyrone Slothrop, "*Twin Peaks* – Screaming and Crying – Season 1," *YouTube*, May 20, 2017, www.youtube.com/watch?v=iWBDzJixlJg; and Tyrone Slothrop, "Twin Peaks – Screaming and Crying – Season 2," *YouTube*, June 23, 2017, www.youtube.com/watch?v=vRJOpuY4eeU.
6 Theairinthebranches, "Leland Confesses to Renault Murder," *YouTube*, March 6, 2009, www.youtube.com/watch?v=ulMSwnktFi4.
7 And certainly, attending to actor interviews and certain craft discourses might also belie Butler's claim here about actors' unknown mental processes.
8 For Lynch and Frost's secretive tendencies, see Gross (1990) and Jacobs (2017).
9 Alexei Mercurio, "Sarah Palmer at grocery store," *YouTube*, May 20, 2020, www.youtube.com/watch?v=UIQiEVKa3nU.
10 girlfrmars, "Donna Hayward (33) – Twin Peaks S02E01," *YouTube*, September 2, 2020, www.youtube.com/watch?v=cU9nGupwbL0.
11 For a few examples that label *Twin Peaks*' generic blending as postmodernist or surrealist, see Abbott (2005, 183); Creeber (2004, 49–50); and Thompson (2003,129).
12 ASD, "Audrey's Dance," *YouTube*, December 20, 2013, www.youtube.com/watch?v=4b64KyEFVhg.
13 Cristian Stean, "Twin Peaks Dance of the Little Man," *YouTube*, March 18, 2013, www.youtube.com/watch?v=h0YI_eHg3Aw.
14 Smica_lica, "Twin Peaks Leland Palmers 'Mairzy Doats' with Horne brothers, *YouTube*, July 19, 2017, www.youtube.com/watch?v=z-lUIao3cJ4.
15 Jones Jack, Chrysta Bell, David Lynch, Laura Dern - Epic Twin Peaks scene," *YouTube*, July 29, 2017, www.youtube.com/watch?v=8L9Yp3mlVVs.

References

Abbott, Stacey. 2015. "'Doing Weird Things for the Sake of Being Weird': Directing *Twin Peaks*." In *Return to Twin Peaks*, edited by Jeffrey Weinstock and Catherine Spooner, 175–192. New York: Palgrave Macmillan.

Butler, Jeremy G. 2018. *Television: Visual Storytelling and Screen Culture*, 5th ed. New York: Routledge.

Caughie, John. 2000. "What Do Actors Do When They Act?" In *British Television Drama: Past Present Future*, edited by Jonathan Bignell, Stephen Lacey, and Madeline MacMurraugh-Kavanagh, 162–174. London: Palgrave.

Caughie, John. 2012. "Television and Serial Fictions." In *The Cambridge Companion to Popular Fiction*, edited by David Glover and Scott McCracken, 50–67. Cambridge: Cambridge University Press.

Creeber, Glen. 2004. *Serial Television: Big Drama on the Small Screen*. London: BFI.

Donaldson, Lucy Fife. 2013. "Camera and Performer: Energetic Engagement with *The Shield*." In *Television Aesthetics and Style*, edited by Jason Jacobs and Steven Peacock, 209–218. London: Bloomsbury.

Drake, Philip. 2016. "Reframing Television Performance." *Journal of Film and Video* 68, no. 3–4: 6–17.

Gendler, Jason. 2016. "The Rich Inferential World of *Mad Men*: Serialized Television and Character Interiority." *Projections* 10, no.1: 39–62.

Greimas, A.J. 1983. *Structural Semantics: An Attempt at a Method*. Translated by Daniele McDowell, Ronald Schleifer, and Alan Veli. Lincoln, NE: University of Nebraska Press.

Gross, Terry. 1990. "Interview with Ray Wise." *Fresh Air*, National Public Radio, December 12, 1990. Transcript available at https://www.sheepproductions.com/tps/people/rwinterv.txt

Hayward, Jennifer. 1997. *Consuming Pleasures*. Lexington, KY: University Press of Kentucky.

Hills, Matt. 2005. "Cult TV, Quality and the Role of the Episode Programme Guide." In *The Contemporary Television Series*, edited by Michael Hammond and Lucy Mazdon, 190–206. Edinburgh: Edinburgh University Press.

Horton, Donald, and Richard Wohl. 1956. "Mass Communication and Parasocial Interaction: Observation on Intimacy at a Distance." *Psychiatry* 19: 215–229.

Jacobs, Matthew. 2017. "Naomi Watts Had to Go to David Lynch's House to Read Her *Twin Peaks* Scripts." *Huffington Post*, May 19, 2017. https://www.huffingtonpost.ca/entry/naomi-watts-twin- peaks_us_591f28cee4b094cdba53d0d4.

Jenkins, Henry. 1995. "'Do You Enjoy Making the Rest of Us Feel Stupid?' alt.tv.twinpeaks, the Trickster Author, and Viewer Mastery." In *Full of Secrets: Critical Approaches to Twin Peaks*, edited by David Lavery, 51–69. Detroit: Wayne State University Press.

Kirby, Michael. 1972. "On Acting and Not-Acting." *The Drama Review* 16, no. 1: 3–15.

Lacey, Stephen. 2016. "Just Plain *Odd*: Some Thoughts on Performance Styles in *Twin Peaks*." *Cinema Journal* 55, no. 3: 126–130.

Logan, Elliott. 2015. "How Do We Write about Performance in Serial Television?" *Series* 1, no. 1: 27–38.

Logan, Elliott. 2016. *Breaking Bad and Dignity*. Basingstoke: Palgrave Macmillan, 2016.

LostInTheMovies. 2015. Comment on "Weird Personal Coincidences While Watching Twin Peaks?" *Twin Peaks*. Reddit, September 2, 2015. https://www.reddit.com/r/twinpeaks/comments/3jedeq/weird_personal_coincidences_while_watc hing_twin/.

Lury, Karen. 1995. "Television Performance: Being, Acting and 'Corpsing.'" *New Formations* 27: 114–127.

Lynch, David, and Chris Rodley. 2005. *Lynch on Lynch*. London: Faber and Faber.

Mittell, Jason. 2015. *Complex TV*. New York: New York University Press.

Nannicelli, Ted. 2017. *Appreciating the Art of Television: A Philosophical Perspective*. New York: Routledge.

Naremore, James. 1988. *Acting in the Cinema*. Berkeley, CA: University of California Press.

Newcomb, Horace. 1974. *TV: The Most Popular Art*. Garden City: Anchor Books.

Pearson, Roberta. 2010. "The Multiple Determinants of Television Acting." In *Genre and Performance: Film and Television*, edited by Christine Cornea, 166–183. Manchester: Manchester University Press.

Newman, Michael Z., and Elana Levine. 2012. *Legitimating Television*. London: Routledge.

Pérez, Héctor J. 2015. "The Three Bodies of Narration: A Cognitivist Poetics of the Actor's Performance." Translated by Martin Boyd. *L'Atalante* 19: 17–26.

Peterson, Price. 2017. "Twin Peaks: Anti-Television at Its Finest." *TV Guide*, June 26, 2017, www.tvguide.com/news/twin-peaks-part-8-recap/.

Propp, Vladimir. 1968 (1928). *Morphology of the Folktale*, 2nd ed. Translated by Laurence Scott. Austin, TX: University of Texas Press.

Reeder, Glenn D., and David Trafimow. 2005. "Attributing Motives to Other People." In *Other Minds*, edited by Bertram F. Malle and Sara D. Hodges, 106–123. New York: Guilford Press.

Thain, Alanna. 2016. "One Way Out Between Two Worlds: The Dance Moves of *Twin Peaks*." *Senses of Cinema* 79. http://sensesofcinema.com/2016/twin-peaks/dance-in - twin-peaks/.

Thompson, Kristin. 2003. *Storytelling in Film and Television*. Cambridge, MA: Harvard University Press.

Williams, Linda. 1991. "Film Bodies: Gender, Genre, and Excess." *Film Quarterly* 44, no. 4: 2–13.

12 Parallelism and complex storytelling in film and TV

Malcolm Turvey

In the pilot of *Mad Men* (AMC 2007–2015), titled "Smoke Gets in Your Eyes" and first broadcast on July 19, 2007, Peggy Olson (Elisabeth Moss), who has just started work as Donald Draper's (Jon Hamm) secretary at the advertising agency in Manhattan where Don is creative director, makes a pass at him. It is 1960, and the agency, Sterling Cooper, is steeped in the sexism of the era, as the show somewhat heavy-handedly makes clear in its early episodes. Peggy has been informed by Joan Holloway (Christina Hendricks), the firm's office manager, that (female) secretaries are expected to look attractive and be sexually available to their (male) bosses, and Peggy offers herself to Don by clumsily putting her hand over his as he rests it on his desk, her face full of trepidation. However, he rebuffs her, asserting that he is her boss, not her boyfriend. Don has just scored a major victory over a younger rival, account man Peter Campbell (Vincent Cartheiser), in a meeting with Lucky Strike, one of Sterling Cooper's most important clients, and he is basking in the praise bestowed on him by the firm's staff. A hard-drinking, handsome womanizer with a mistress in Greenwich Village and, we later find out, a home with a beautiful wife and two children in the suburbs, Don is brilliant, successful, and full of confidence, and he seemingly has the world at his fingertips.

Five story-years later, in episode seven of season four, which originally aired on September 5, 2010, things have changed. Don's wife, Betty (January Jones), has divorced him because in addition to his infidelities, she has discovered that Donald Draper is not his real name, and he lied to her about his true identity throughout their relationship. She is, for the most part, happily remarried, while Don lives alone in a small, gloomy apartment in Greenwich Village, and his life has begun to spiral out of control due to his heavy drinking. Anna (Melinda Page Hamilton), his only close friend, is dying of cancer, and Don is now a partner in a fledgling advertising agency, Sterling Cooper Draper Pryce, that will soon lose Lucky Strike, its only big client, and come close to bankruptcy. Meanwhile, under Don's often-abusive tutelage, Peggy, Don's former secretary, has become one of the few female copywriters in the advertising business, and her star is rising as she proves herself to be as talented as Don. In the episode, Don and Peggy fall asleep on the couch in Don's office after a night of drinking in which they share personal information for the first

DOI: 10.4324/9781003188643-12

time, including that they both lost parents at a young age, and in the morning, Don awakes to a phone call informing him that his friend Anna has died. Devastated, he breaks down in tears before Peggy, and she tries to comfort him as he explains that Anna was "the only person in the world who really knew me." Even though he is embarrassed and sends Peggy away, this is the first time he has allowed himself to be emotionally vulnerable in front of her. When Peggy returns to check on him, he places his hand on hers, which is resting on his desk, just as she did to him in the series' pilot. However, this time the gesture is one of genuine affection and solidarity, and Peggy smiles in return. As she leaves, she asks him if he wants his door open or closed, and he says "open," as if to signify the new intimacy between them.

Toward the end of the following season, which takes place in 1967, the ground has shifted once more. After a short period of happiness with Megan (Jessica Paré), his new, young wife, Don's life is beginning to fall apart again. Megan, who worked with Don at his company and showed great promise as a copywriter, has left to pursue her dream of becoming a professional actress, and Don and Megan are starting to drift apart. Sterling Cooper Draper Pryce, having barely avoided bankruptcy, is finally flourishing, and in episode 11, titled "The Other Woman" and initially shown on May 27, 2012, the company lands its first big car account, Jaguar. However, amid the celebrations, Don discovers that they haven't won the account because of his stunning advertising campaign, which likened a Jaguar car to a beautiful, temperamental, unobtainable woman whom "at last … you can truly own." Rather, the account is theirs because Joan Holloway, the office manager, slept with Herb Rennet, a member of Jaguar's advertising selection committee, in a quid pro quo organized by the other partners. Disgusted and demoralized, Don retreats to his office to drink, inviting Peggy, whom he has increasingly bullied as his relationship to Megan has deteriorated, to join him. Peggy then tells him that she is leaving Sterling Cooper Draper Pryce to work for Don's competitor, Ted Chaough (Kevin Rahm). Don bitterly attempts to persuade her to stay, using both emotional manipulation and the promise of a higher salary, but she refuses. As she stands over him while he sits, they once again touch hands when Peggy reaches out for a handshake. But on this occasion Don clutches her hand desperately, kissing it in supplication until, crying, she pulls away and then leaves the building triumphantly. Don has now lost the four women to whom he was closest – Betty, Anna, Megan, and Peggy – and in the following season, after a neighbor with whom he has been having a passionate affair ends their relationship, he again starts drinking heavily and is suspended from his job.

Although only the most attentive viewer will have noticed, given that these three episodes were originally broadcast several years apart, the creators of *Mad Men* have marked the evolution of Don and Peggy's relationship – from one in which Don has near total power to dictate the terms of their professional and personal interaction to one in which he is far more professionally and emotionally dependent on Peggy than she is on him – through a series of comparable hand gestures that recur in Don's office. To put it more formally, by using similar body language, locations, and situations involving the same characters, they have created narrative events that *parallel* each other. Parallelism often occurs in films and television shows, and, I argue in this chapter, it is an important device for fashioning narrative complexity and richness, which can be a source of pleasure for viewers.[1] It comes in many shapes and sizes, some of which I will delineate before concluding with a brief discussion of its relation to artistic value. However, unlike in literary studies, where, thanks to the work of theorists such as Roman Jakobson, parallelism has long been analyzed, especially in the context of poetry, it has not been given much attention in film studies and even less in television studies. David Bordwell, Kristin Thompson, and Jeff Smith are among the few film scholars to have briefly defined it. "Parallels cue us to compare two or more distinct elements by highlighting some similarity," and they may involve "characters, settings, situations, times of day, or any other elements," Bordwell, Thompson and Smith claim (2017, 66, 73). Parallelism, in other words, does not only consist of elements that are alike or are repeated, as is the case with a motif such as a musical theme that is heard every time a particular character appears. Rather, a parallel prompts the viewer to compare and contrast two or more corresponding elements and to reflect on their similarities and differences. Moreover, parallels usually occur at narratively significant moments to underscore important milestones and themes. In the case of the hand gestures between Don and Peggy, the resemblances between them and the situations in which they occur encourage us to compare the emotions and power dynamics they manifest and thereby contemplate how the relationship between Don and Peggy has changed over time.

This example also shows why parallelism is a broader category than metaphor, which likewise involves comparing two (or more) elements. Although there is much debate about how precisely to define metaphor, contemporary cognitive film studies tends to draw on George Lakoff and Mark Johnson's famous formulation: "The essence of metaphor is understanding and experiencing one kind of thing in terms of another" (Lakoff and Johnson, 1980, 5; Fahlenbrach, 2015). When one type of thing – what Lakoff and Johnson call the target domain – is presented in terms of another – what they call the source domain – the discrepancy between them ("time is money"; "all the world's a stage") encourages us to transfer or "map" aspects of the source domain onto the target to determine in what ways they are related, thereby transforming our understanding of the target (Whittock 1990, 5). Dziga Vertov, in one of the most famous metaphors in film history, refers to the movie camera (the target) as an eye (the source) in his writings ("I am kino-eye, I am a mechanical eye. I, a machine, show you the world as only I can see it") and superimposes an eye onto a camera lens in *Man with a Movie Camera* (1929). The fact that a camera is not literally an eye prompts us to contemplate in what respects they might be comparable by mapping features of the eye onto the camera, thereby altering our conception of the latter. Although parallels may involve metaphors, they do not require that we think of one thing in terms of another or that our understanding of it is transformed as a result. The second time that Don and

Peggy touch hands, in episode seven of season four, is not a metaphor for the first time they do so in the series pilot. We are not compelled to find ways in which these two events relate to each other because of a discrepancy between them, as we are with the metaphors of camera as eye or world as stage. Rather, the parallel encourages us to compare and contrast the situations in which they touch hands. Moreover, our attention is drawn to the similarities *and differences* between these situations rather than the ways in which one thing can be seen as another, as in metaphor.

As Bordwell, Thompson, and Smith point out, by cuing us to relate two or more elements that we might not otherwise think to compare, parallelism makes works "more complex" and denser (2017, 74). Not only must we follow the work's narrative, but we must also consider how its elements can be connected beyond their place within the spatial, temporal, and causal patterns of the story. The quid pro quo arrangement that secures the Jaguar account in *Mad Men* is a good example. Don, having learned of the arrangement, visits Joan's apartment to tell her it's "not worth it" and that they shouldn't be "in business with people like that." The following day he makes his pitch to Jaguar's advertising committee believing, along with the viewer, that Joan hasn't slept with Herb Rennet. However, as he does so, we see flashbacks to Joan's assignation with Rennet while hearing Don's pitch in voice-over. Causally and spatially, we realize that Sterling Cooper Draper Pryce will likely win the Jaguar account because Joan has already visited Herb in his hotel to have sex with him. And temporally, we now understand that Don must have gone to Joan's apartment to dissuade her from sleeping with Herb *after* she had already done so. But the narration also encourages us to make another, more conceptual connection. As he makes the case that Jaguar cars are like beautiful, unobtainable women except that they can be owned, we see shots of Joan in Herb's room and realize that Joan is an example of just such a woman. Normally, she wouldn't give a man like Herb, who is a corpulent, lecherous, and vulgar philistine, the time of day. However, unlike the women described by Don, Joan is obtainable because she is prostituting herself and is, in a sense, being bought by Herb like a car. The commodification of femininity in advertising ("men want her and women want to be her" is a maxim constantly repeated by Don and the other male advertisers in the show) is thereby literalized. But this doesn't do justice to the complexity of the situation, as Joan is receiving a partnership and a 5% stake in Sterling Cooper Draper Pryce for sleeping with Herb. Unlike a beautiful car, which can only ever be owned, she has used her beauty to become a part owner of the company, thereby giving her some, albeit limited, power and money. Whatever one's ultimate judgment about the price Joan has had to pay for her newfound status, the parallel created by intercutting Joan's visit to Herb with Don's pitch prompts us to reflect on the weave of similarities and differences between Joan and a Jaguar car and the larger theme of the commodification of women, in addition to understanding the place of these elements within the narrative. If we rely on the ordinary definition of complexity as consisting of many intricately related parts, then parallelism makes narratives more complex by increasing the number of relations between their elements. It also places an additional cognitive burden on the viewer, who must think through the conceptual and other relations between the elements being compared, especially if they are both similar and different, as is the case with Joan and a Jaguar car.

It is perhaps because it is found in cinema that Jason Mittell doesn't address parallelism in his influential account of narrative complexity in television. Arguing against Kristin Thompson, who has claimed that the importation of art cinema conventions into television has given rise to an "art TV" (Thompson 2003), Mittell maintains that "television's narrative complexity is predicated on *specific* facets of storytelling that seem *uniquely* suited to the television series structure apart from film and literature" (2015, 18, my emphasis). For Mittell, the medium-specific conventions that comprise narrative complexity in TV are, first and foremost, a redefinition of the boundary between episodic and serial narration in which storylines confined to single episodes are intermixed to varying degrees with ones that cross multiple episodes; an "operational aesthetic" or "heightened degree of self-consciousness in storytelling mechanics" wherein TV creators foreground their experimentation with the form of storytelling in a manner evident to and enjoyed by viewers (2015, 53); and a more intensified engagement on the part of fans with shows in online and other forums. Drawing on David Bordwell's concept of a mode of narration (1985, 150), Mittell asserts that these three features constitute a new mode of storytelling on North American TV that has emerged since the 1990s due to economic, technological, and industrial factors. This mode can be distinguished from the conventional episodic and serial forms, such as police procedurals and soaps, that have dominated television since its inception, and it is exemplified by many of the shows that are associated with the new "Golden Age of TV," or "quality TV," such as *Mad Men* and *The Sopranos* (1999–2007).

Mittell's account certainly goes some way towards pinpointing important aspects of contemporary television. However, one might question whether it succeeds in isolating a medium-specific mode of televisual storytelling. Unlike the classical, art, and other modes of narration identified by Bordwell in cinema, each of which consists of a number of distinct, interlocking narrational conventions, Mittell's category of narrative complexity on TV is comprised of just two norms: the intermingling of episodic and serial narration, and narrational self-consciousness. (The third attribute of narrative complexity, intensified fan engagement, is not a narrational norm.) Moreover, only the conjunction of episodic and serial narration seems essential, since Mittell gives as examples of narrative complexity shows that do not display much narrational self-consciousness or do so – like most shows – only intermittently, such as *The Sopranos* and *Breaking Bad* (2008–2013). One might worry, therefore, that the category of narrative complexity is too broad and lacks discriminatory power. After all, many shows combine episodic with serial forms of storytelling and include moments of narrational self-awareness, including what are thought of as fairly routine sitcoms and dramas, such as *Friends* (1994–2004), *The Big*

Bang Theory (2007–2019), and *ER* (1994–2009). Are shows such as these to be included within the category of narratively complex TV? If so, one wonders what Mittell means by complexity and what the criteria are for identifying it, given that these shows are not usually thought of as complex. Indeed, Mittell does not devote much time to defining complexity or explaining how the features he pinpoints make shows complex, and it is hard to see how these features alone necessarily result in complexity in the ordinary sense in which I have defined it. A show such as *Lemony Snicket's A Series of Unfortunate Events* (2017–2019), which my nine-year-old and I are currently enjoying on Netflix, is one of the most narratively self-conscious TV shows I have ever seen. For example, it uses an onscreen narrator who talks to viewers, encouraging us to "look away" from the unfortunate events that befall the show's major protagonists, the Baudelaire children. And it intermixes episodic with serial narration, often ending episodes with cliffhangers (quite literally at the end of season two, when two of the Baudelaire children are about to plunge to their deaths from a cliff). But even though its irony, dark humor, and high degree of stylization make it unusual, *A Series of Unfortunate Events* is not narratively complicated, and my son follows it quite easily (not to mention his father). At the very least, it seems, we need to fill out Mittell's category by identifying other narrational conventions that make TV shows narratively complex. Meanwhile, rather than a distinct mode of narration, narrative complexity, like narrational self-consciousness, seems more like a quality that different kinds of TV shows can possess to varying degrees, including soap operas and other conventional forms of television.

More importantly, balancing episodic and serial narration (not to mention narrational self-consciousness) is hardly specific to TV and has a long history in literature, comics, cinema, and radio. Indeed, it is because it is so hard to isolate features specific to a medium that the doctrine of medium-specificity has been rejected by many, and Mittell does not explain what he means by medium-specificity or which version of the doctrine he subscribes to.[2] Even if some version of medium-specificity is defensible, as I suspect it is, given that episodic and serial storytelling are present in other media, it seems unlikely that the storytelling conventions used in television are specific to it even if they have been adapted to TV's peculiarities. Mittell writes: "In the past 15 years, television's storytelling possibilities and practices have undergone drastic shifts *specific to the medium*. What was one a risky innovative device, such as subjective narration or jumbled chronology, is now almost a cliché" (2015, 2, my emphasis). But this is to forget that "subjective narration" and "jumbled chronology" are hardly specific to television and have a long history in literature, cinema, and other narrative arts. Just as cinematic storytelling leans heavily on prior narrative forms from literature and theater, it is probable that televisual storytelling borrows its conventions from these media as well as cinema and radio while modifying them to suit TV's contingencies.

This, at least, is the case with parallelism, a narrational device or "principle" that was used in cinema long before it was imported into television but that can take a distinct form in TV due to the medium's predilection for seriality, as I will argue in the last part of this chapter. In cinema, parallelism sometimes occurs in classical narration, although it is usually momentary. The endings of classical films, for example, often briefly resemble their beginnings, prompting us to compare them and take stock of how much things have, and haven't, changed in the interim. Alfred Hitchcock's *Rear Window* (1954) provides a famous example. Following the opening credits, which are superimposed on a shot of a window with blinds rising, a circular pan moving from right to left reveals the apartments around the courtyard outside the window and comes to rest on the perspiring forehead of a sleeping man, Jeffries (James Stewart), the film's major protagonist. The film's penultimate shot is a similar right-to-left pan of the courtyard that shows us what has happened to the apartments' inhabitants, who have been an object of Jeffries's (and the viewer's) fascination throughout the film, before ending on Jeffries, who is again asleep but who is now accompanied by his girlfriend, Lisa (Grace Kelly). The film ends with the blind closing on Jeffries' window and the Paramount studio logo superimposed on it. Some of the courtyard's denizens are happier than at the beginning (Miss Lonelyhearts (Judith Evelyn), Miss Torso (Georgine Darcy)), while others are unhappier (the newlyweds), and one might wonder to which group Jeffries and Lisa belong. Either way, the visual similarities between the first and final two shots of the film encourage us to contrast the situations of the characters at the end relative to the beginning, a form of parallelism that can be called *situational* and which includes the example of Don and Peggy touching hands from *Mad Men*. In situational parallelism, it is the circumstances of the characters at different moments in the narrative that we are asked to consider in relation to each other. In classical narration, situational parallelism helps unify the narrative by focusing our attention on the trajectory of the characters. If occurring at the end, it can also bring about narrative closure (or undermine it) by foregrounding the extent to which the questions posed at the narrative's beginning have been answered and the narrative's major causal chains have been resolved.

As these examples attest, situational parallelism in moving image media is often cued by visual (and sometimes aural) similarities between the different situations depicted, much as in poetry, according to Jakobson, "equivalence in sound … inevitably involves semantic equivalence" (1987, 83). In Max Ophuls's *Letter from an Unknown Woman* (1948), which is set in Vienna in the early 20th century, Lisa Berndle (Joan Fontaine), a teenager living in an apartment building, falls in love with a neighbor, famous pianist Stefan Brand (Louis Jourdan), although they cross paths only once at the entrance to the building. When her mother remarries and she is forced to move to another town, Lisa runs away and returns to the apartment building, hoping to find Brand and "throw herself at his feet." But he is not there, and she waits in the dark at the top of the interior staircase for him. Finally, he returns early in the morning, but he is accompanied by a woman, and together they walk up the staircase and into his apartment. Lisa watches unseen from the floor above, and as Brand and his companion ascend the stairs, Ophuls films them with a distinctive high-angle 90-degree pan from left to right behind Lisa. Devastated, Lisa goes back to her mother, but a few years later, when she is estranged from her family and is working as a model back in Vienna, she waits for Brand each evening outside his apartment building until he finally notices her, although he does not remember her. After a night out, they go back to his building in the early morning and climb the staircase together to his apartment, just as she had seen him do with the other woman years earlier, and Ophuls films them with the same high-angle 90-degree pan from left to right. Lisa is ecstatic, believing that Brand is finally hers, and once inside, they make love. But the identical 90-degree pan warns the attentive viewer that for Brand, Lisa is a one-night stand just like the woman who accompanied him before, and after Brand fails to contact her when he returns from a two-week concert tour, Lisa gives birth to their child alone and does not see him again for many years. In this example, the repetition of a distinctive shot creates an ironic situational parallel. Lisa does not understand what the resemblance between the pans makes clear: that she is just one in a long line of women Brand has brought back to his apartment and subsequently forgotten.[3] Here, the visual similarities between the pans underscore the situational similarities between Lisa and her predecessors.

The parallels established by visual resemblances sometimes foreground situational *differences* rather than similarities. In episode six of season three of *The Sopranos*, titled "University," Ralph Cifaretto (Joe Pantoliano), one of Tony Soprano's (James Gandolfini) henchmen, brutally beats to death his (Ralph's) girlfriend, Tracee (Ariel Kiley), outside the Bada Bing, the strip club where Tony keeps an office. Tracee worked as a stripper in the club and had tried to make friends with Tony before her death, even baking some bread for him as thanks for giving her advice about her son. In one scene, Tracee approaches Tony who rebuffs her, and she walks away, the camera behind her. As she goes to open a door, there is a graphic match to a shot of Meadow (Jamie-Lynn Sigler), Tony's daughter, walking away from the camera as she opens the door to her dorm room at Columbia University. Thereafter, the episode consistently intercuts between Meadow's and Tracee's storylines, often using other visual likenesses between them. Meadow pulls her top off as she prepares to sleep with her boyfriend in his dorm room, and then Tracee, topless, again tries to befriend Tony at the strip club. Ralph forces Tracee to perform oral sex on a cop at the club. As she bends down, we cut to Meadow's roommate bent down crying as she recounts a traumatic experience to Meadow in their room. Meadow goes home and gets into her mother's bed to hug her. There follows a scene in which Tracee asks Tony about whether she should keep Ralph's unborn child, and we learn that her mother abused her as a child by holding her hand over a stove. At the end of the scene, a medium shot of Tracee looking down to her left as she contemplates Tony's advice is followed by a graphic match to a medium shot of Meadow, also looking down to her left, at her family's kitchen table while her mother makes her breakfast. These visual similarities seem designed to make us contemplate the differences between Tracee's and Meadow's circumstances. Meadow comes from a wealthy family, attends an Ivy League school, and is loved and protected by her parents, while Tracee is a pregnant stripper who was physically abused by her mother and is sexually exploited (and worse) by Ralph and the other men at the Bada Bing. After she is murdered by Ralph outside the Bing, a low-angle shot of her body shows a drain surrounded by trash in the foreground, suggesting that she has been discarded like garbage, and immediately we cut to Meadow studying happily with her boyfriend, Noah (Patrick Tully), in the library at Columbia, underscoring just how far apart their worlds are. However, Noah then proceeds to "throw her away" too by abruptly breaking up with Meadow, and as we shall see, a later episode revisits the parallel to suggest that Meadow's and Tracee's situations are more alike than they first appeared.

Not all parallels are cued by visual resemblances. In "Waldorf Stories," episode six of season four of *Mad Men*, Roger Sterling (John Slattery), a senior partner at Don Draper's advertising agency, forces Don to interview his (Roger's) wife's cousin, Danny Siegel (Danny Strong), for a copywriter position. Danny is woefully unqualified for the job and attends the interview with a portfolio containing only five original ads, each of which is a variation on the catchphrase "a cure for the common cold." Don laughs about Danny, whom he has no intention of hiring, as he and Roger start drinking in preparation for the CLIO awards ceremony for television advertising, which is taking place that night. Don is up for an award, which he wins before returning to the office for an advertising pitch to representatives from Life cereal. The client likes the ad but not the slogan. Drunk and overconfident from his win, Don proceeds to invent some alternative slogans on the spot including "Life, cure for the common cold," thereby inadvertently borrowing Danny's one original idea. The client loves it, and Don goes on a bender for the weekend before Peggy visits him to remind him that "cure for the common cold" belongs to Danny. The next week, Don tries to buy the catchphrase from Danny, who insists instead on being hired, which Don, although it pains him, is forced to do because he needs the slogan for Life cereal. Despite his lack of qualifications, Danny therefore gets the job because of his connection to Roger and Don's drunkenness.

Meanwhile, the situation with Danny reminds Roger of how Don got hired at Sterling Cooper, which is revealed in a series of flashbacks distributed throughout the episode. Don was a fur coat salesman Roger first met when he purchased a fur for his mistress, Joan Holloway, in the early 1950s. However, Don wanted to become an advertiser, and he slipped his advertising portfolio into the coat box, hoping Roger would look at it and hire him. Roger discards it with contempt, but Don then deliberately runs into Roger at the entrance to his building on the false pretext that he is there to see a client, and Don takes Roger drinking. A drunk Roger tells Don he won't hire him, but the next day Don shows up again at Roger's building, claiming that Roger had hired him the previous day. Because he had been drunk, Roger cannot remember what he really said, and he begrudgingly assents. Together they enter the elevator to Sterling Cooper as the Skeeter Davis song "Ladder of Success" plays. It turns out that Don, just like Danny, got his job not because he was qualified for it but because of forgetfulness due to intoxication and a connection to Roger. Indeed, unlike Danny, who is unaware of the true reasons for his employment, Don hustled his way into Roger's company by getting him drunk and then misleading him. Here, as in the other examples, we are prompted to compare and contrast what is happening to Don and Danny. But while visual resemblances between the present and the past cue Roger's flashbacks, there are no such similarities between the scenes in which Don and Danny are hired. We are supposed to grasp the parallel based on the correspondences between their storylines.

As this example suggests, it isn't just the situations that characters find themselves in that can be paralleled in films and TV shows. Rather, resemblances between storylines can also form the basis of what can be called *narrative* parallelism. Whereas situational parallelism focuses on the circumstances of characters at particular moments in a story, narrative parallelism concerns correspondences between events that occur over time within a story, although in practice, these two kinds of parallelism often overlap. Danny's situation is similar to the one Don was in – he wants to break into advertising, just like Don did, but is young and unqualified, as was Don. However, the parallelism extends beyond their circumstances to include homologous narrative events. Both use their connections to Roger to get a foot in the door at Sterling Cooper, and in both cases, the doorkeeper reluctantly lets them in due to his intoxication. Narrative parallelism can certainly be found in cinema, a classic example being Hitchcock's *Vertigo* (1958), in which the love affair between Scottie (James Stewart) and Madeleine (Kim Novak) that takes place in the first part of the film is repeated in the second following Madeleine's apparent death, this time involving Scottie and Judy (Kim Novak), the woman who pretended to be Madeleine. The viewer is supposed to compare and contrast the two love stories and notice similarities between them as well as the stories of Carlotta Valdes, the woman who was cast aside by her lover a century before and who possessed Madeleine, and Gavin Elster (Tom Helmore), who hired Scottie to follow Madeleine in order to conceal the murder of his wife. All these stories involve women who are controlled and then discarded by powerful men, and through the parallels between them, Hitchcock addresses one of his recurrent themes: the misogynistic, often destructive power of male sexuality and fantasy. However, while films certainly can create narrative parallels, television series and serials are particularly suited to them due to their multiple characters and storylines. These are a norm in TV, unlike in cinema, and narrative parallels between the so-called A, B, and even C plots in TV episodes are one way that televisual storytellers can connect storylines and create unity.

Before examining a form of parallelism that is distinctive to TV, it is important to mention two other varieties that can be found in both media. Unlike situational and narrative parallelisms, which involve comparing and contrasting the circumstances and storylines of characters, what can be termed *character* parallelism prompts us to consider the similarities and differences between characters themselves. In *Letter from an Unknown Woman*, Lisa is compared to other women with whom Brand has had affairs. But the comparison concerns the similar way Brand behaves towards them rather than anything about the women's characters, and in fact, we learn little about Lisa's predecessors. Similarly, the resemblance between Don and Danny only goes as far as the illegitimate manner in which they both gain employment at Sterling Cooper. Some narratives, however, ask us to consider the extent to which characters are alike because they possess similar traits, personalities, or other psychological features, often to the point that one character can be described as the "double" of another. Again, Hitchcock's films provide a *locus classicus* for this kind of parallelism. In *Shadow of a Doubt* (1943), Hitchcock employs visual resemblances as well as the same name to parallel the serial killer Uncle Charlie (Joseph Cotten) with his niece, young Charlie (Teresa Wright). When Uncle Charlie is first introduced at the beginning of the film, establishing shots of a run-down neighborhood are followed by several shots of a street, each closer to a boarding house on the street than the last. A canted shot of the boarding house's bedroom window precedes a shot that dollies towards a man, whom we soon discover is Uncle Charlie, lying on a bed inside, the shadows cast by the window curtains visible on the wall behind him. Five minutes of screen time later, a similar sequence of shots of young Charlie's neighborhood and street, each getting closer to Charlie's house and culminating in a canted show of her bedroom window, is followed by a forward dolly shot introducing Charlie lying on her bed in the same position as her uncle had lain on his, likewise with shadows from the window on the wall behind her. By way of the correspondences between these sequences of shots, the viewer is encouraged to contemplate the extent to which uncle and niece are alike despite their obvious differences. It should be noted that the similarities between these sequences extend beyond visual resemblances between the shots themselves to include the *arrangement* of the shots, much as syntactical parallelism in prose is predicated on the arrangement of words, as in "Nature gave women too much power, the law gives them too little."[4] In moving image media, editing combined with shot length and *mise-en-scène* can establish correspondences between the order, composition, and duration of sequences of shots at different moments in a work.

Character parallelism can involve comparisons between more than two characters and can structure an entire narrative, especially in art cinema, where, as Bordwell argues, "parallelisms come to the fore" due to the weakening of causality (1985, 207). Whereas in classical narrative there tends to be strong causal connections between events as characters pursue their goals, in art cinema characters are less goal-oriented and often "slide passively from one situation to another" as they struggle with psychological and existential issues (1985, 207). Hence, the causal relation between narrative events is weaker than in classical narrative, and art cinema narratives tend to be more episodic, aleatory, and elliptical than classical ones with events linked by parallels. In Ingmar Bergman's *Wild Strawberries* (1957), Professor Isak Borg (Victor Sjöström), an isolated, widowed scientist in his seventies, travels by car to Lund to be awarded an honorary degree, accompanied by his pregnant daughter-in-law Marianne (Ingrid Thulin), who admits she doesn't like her father-in-law much and that she is considering separating from Isak's son, Evald (Gunnar Björnstrand). During the journey, a series of chance meetings with strangers who parallel people in his life forces Isak to evaluate his past and confront his estrangement from his son. On the road, they meet a young woman, Sara (Bibi Andersson), hitchhiking with two young men, Anders (Folke Sundquist) and Viktor (Björn Bjelfvenstam), one of whom is a scientist, the other a poet. Sara reminds Isak of his sister-in-law, Sara, who in flashbacks is played by the same actress and whom Isak loved when they were young. However, she chose to marry his brother, Sigfrid (Per Sjöstrad), just as Sara the hitchhiker is trying to decide between Viktor and Anders. They also encounter a married couple, Sten (Gunnar Sjöberg) and Berit (Gunnel Broström), who argue aggressively and incessantly, and Isak acknowledges that his own marriage was just like theirs. Most significantly, Isak is paralleled with his son, Evald. Not only are both highly principled and righteous, but both see themselves as dead even though they are alive, and this is the source of their estrangement from others. While Isak is accepting his honorary degree, in voice-over he remarks on the "extraordinary logic" discernible in the "jumble of events" of the day's journey, and we understand him to be referring to the meaningful parallels between people in his life and the strangers he encountered on the road.

Finally, narratives can establish *conceptual* or *thematic* parallels instead of ones based on situations, storylines, and the traits of characters. We have already seen an example of this in the momentary comparison between Joan Holloway and a Jaguar car in *Mad Men*, although sometimes entire narratives can be predicated on such thematic parallels. A notorious example in the history of cinema is D.W. Griffith's *Intolerance* (1916), which intercuts four separate storylines from different periods in human history: the Babylonian story, which depicts the fall of Babylon in 539 BC; the Biblical story about Christ's crucifixion; the story of the St. Bartholomew's Day Massacre in 1572 in which Protestant Huguenots are killed by Catholics; and a story set in the present day about the ruthlessness of capitalists and moral puritans. Although their stories and characters differ, they are connected by the common theme of human intolerance, which, the film asserts, is responsible for the violent events that befall the characters. Watching it, viewers are supposed to grasp the thematic resemblance between the four stories, an interpretation prompted by the intercutting. For example, the sentencing of The Boy in the present-day story for a murder he did not commit is intercut with the crucifixion of Christ, suggesting that both are victims of the forces of intolerance of their eras.

The television show *The Wire* (2002–2008) does something similar in its juxtaposition of separate institutions and groups of characters in the present in the city of Baltimore. The first episode of season five, for instance, introduces a storyline about the metropolitan newspaper, *The Baltimore Sun*, undergoing cuts and forced layoffs due to its profit-seeking, out-of-town owners and a decline in advertising revenue, and one of its employees mutters, "Someday, I want to find out what it feels like to work on a real newspaper." Meanwhile, Baltimore's Mayor Carcetti (Aiden Gillen) cuts funding to the police due to the city's education deficit, forcing the Major Crimes Unit to shut down. Detective Jimmy McNulty (Dominic West), who has been a regular on the show and has successfully prosecuted high-level criminals as part of the Unit, must return to Homicide, which is far less satisfying due to the ineffectual nature of the work. He comments: "I wonder what it feels like to work in a real police department." This verbal repetition establishes a parallel between the newspaper and the police force as institutions in which individuals struggle to varying degrees to maintain professional standards in the face of drastic budget cuts, which, the show implies, are the result of the rapacious, neoliberal capitalism afflicting the United States in the early 21st century. One might think of this as a form of situational parallelism, given that the police and journalists are up against similar financial constraints. However, *The Wire* is widely viewed as a show that uses situational parallelisms to make a thematic point about the ways institutions that are controlled by economic interests constrain the actions of even their best-intentioned employees and in the process fail to properly serve Baltimore's inhabitants. Just as *Intolerance* employs its four separate storylines to suggest that the transhistorical force of human intolerance shapes the events it depicts, so *The Wire*, as series creator David Simon puts it, is

> a Greek tragedy in which the postmodern institutions are the Olympian forces. It's the police department, or the drug economy, or the political structures, or the school administration, or the macroeconomic forces that are throwing the lightning bolts and hitting people in the ass for no decent reason. … The show [is] about untethered capitalism run amok, about how power and money actually route themselves in a postmodern American city, and, ultimately, about why we as an urban people are no longer able to solve our problems or heal our wounds.
>
> (Hornby 2007)

Both *The Wire* and *Intolerance*, in other words, move beyond resemblances between the specific situations of their characters to make thematic claims about the similar forces structuring these situations.

The parallel between *The Baltimore Sun* and the police force continues in later episodes of season five. In order to attract funding that can be surreptitiously diverted to surveilling drug dealer Marlo Stanfield (Jamie Hector), McNulty begins making the deaths of homeless people look like homicides at the hands of a serial killer, and the mayor is forced to provide funding to capture the killer. At *The Baltimore Sun*, reporter Scott Templeton (Tom McCarthy) starts to fabricate stories about the homeless to advance his career. When he finds out about the supposed serial killer targeting homeless people, he fakes a phone call from the killer to his cell phone and thereby attracts national attention to his reporting. Both McNulty and Templeton, therefore, engage in deception, although for very different reasons, and the ramifications of their deceit for themselves, their respective institutions, and the city of Baltimore play out across the rest of the season. This exemplifies a distinctive form of parallelism that, while certainly not unique to television, is made possible by its norm of serial narration. A film typically consists of a single narrative viewed in one sitting lasting between 75 and 180 minutes, and parallels of the sort discussed in this chapter must be established within this temporal limit, which doesn't leave much time to develop them. By contrast, due to what Ted Nannicelli aptly calls television's "temporal prolongation," television shows can return in later episodes to parallels originated in earlier ones, expanding upon, nuancing, and complicating them to the point that they are enriched and even transformed (Nannicelli 2017, 65).

Take the example of the situational parallel between Tony's daughter Meadow and Tracee the stripper in *The Sopranos*. As we have seen, when this parallel is introduced in "University," episode six of season three, its point seems to be to highlight the differences between Meadow's and Tracee's circumstances in life, and after Tracee's death in episode six, the parallel isn't revisited in episode seven. However, in the following episode, titled "He Is Risen," Tony looks at Meadow as she approaches him with a plate of bread in their kitchen, and this triggers a short flashback, again linked by a graphic match, to Tracee walking towards him in the Bada Bing with the plate of bread she baked for him as thanks. Tony then tells Meadow how much he loves her, saying, "If anything were ever to happen to you …" before they are interrupted. It seems that Tony's memory of Tracee prompts him to express loving concern about his daughter, suggesting he sees a connection between them and thinks Meadow might be in danger, as was Tracee. This primes the viewer to wonder whether Meadow's situation is more like Tracee's than it initially seemed, and in fact, Meadow has just started to date Jackie Aprile, Jr. (Jason Cerbone), son of former mob boss Jackie Aprile, Sr. (Michael Rispoli), who died of cancer at the beginning of the series and was Tony's close friend. Jackie Jr. is making a big show of not following in his father's footsteps and attending college, but in truth, he is falling into a life of crime and is increasingly exploiting his family's ties to the mob for personal gain. Meadow is, therefore, potentially at risk as she becomes more involved with Jackie, and although he isn't initially concerned, Tony comes to see the danger as Jackie's true nature is gradually revealed. One of the themes of *The Sopranos* is the extent to which Tony can keep his family separate from his life of crime, and Meadow's involvement with Jackie threatens this separation. Despite her privilege, Meadow's life is not as divorced from Tony and his criminal associates as it might have seemed when she was initially contrasted with Tracee. This shows how a television serial can develop a parallel over time, a technique I call serial parallelism.

Season five of *Mad Men* uses serial parallelism to signal the growing gulf between Don and his wife Megan. The season begins with the couple happily married and working together at Sterling Cooper Draper Pryce, and in episode seven, Megan devises a brilliant advertising strategy that persuades Heinz Baked Beans, one of SCDP's most difficult clients, to remain with the company. Don finally seems to have found the all-encompassing, passionate relationship with a woman he has always yearned for, one that fuses work and domestic life, and the couple enjoy a brief moment of bliss. But Megan quickly realizes that advertising is not for her, and in the next episode she confesses to Don that she wants to leave SCDP to pursue her dream of an acting career. He agrees with equanimity, and on her last day at work, walks her to the elevator, seemingly supportive. But as the doors close, he appears to change his mind, and he pushes the call button in an attempt to follow her. The doors to another elevator open to reveal an empty elevator shaft, and Don peers down into it, clearly troubled, before retreating to his office to drink. That night, he returns home just as Megan is leaving to attend an acting class, and she gives him the Beatles' album *Revolver*, advising him to listen to a particular track, which turns out to be "Tomorrow Never Knows." The lyrics of the song have occasioned many conflicting interpretations, but the second verse says, "Lay down all thoughts, surrender to the void, It is shining, it is shining," which calls to mind the void of the elevator shaft that Don looked down into earlier in the day. The impression of an absence or void is intensified when Don abruptly switches off the record and silence ensues. In the remaining episodes of the season, Don finds Megan's pursuit of her acting career increasingly difficult to deal with, and they drift apart. In the final episode, Megan, who is desperate for an acting job after repeated rejections, persuades Don to use his influence to get her a part on a commercial for one of his clients. In the penultimate scene, Don and Megan are on the set of the commercial, and Megan, ecstatic that she has work, kisses Don and tells him that she loves him. But as the shoot begins, Don walks away into the darkness of the adjoining studio, leaving Megan behind in the light to shoot her commercial, and goes and drinks alone at a bar, where a woman tries to pick him up, asking, "Are you alone?" In this example, the creators of *Mad Men* use the emptiness of the elevator shaft to create a visual parallel for the abandonment Don feels when Megan leaves SCDP to pursue her own career. The fact that there is no elevator car when the elevator doors open literally separates them, as Don cannot travel down to the ground floor to reach Megan. But the emptiness of the elevator shaft also provides a figurative representation of the beginning of Megan's absence in Don's life, one that is echoed by the lyrics to the Beatles song that Don listens to that night. This visual parallel is then completed in the final episode of the season, when Don, in a breathtaking backward tracking shot, walks into the darkness of the studio, thereby surrendering to the void of the elevator shaft, and in the subsequent two seasons his marriage to Megan falls apart as he again begins having affairs and drinking heavily. What is distinctive about this example is the way the elevator shaft and the Beatles song introduce the looming rupture between Don and Megan in episode eight of season five, and that rupture is then completed by the walk into the darkness of the studio in episode 13.

Season five of *The Sopranos* offers another variant on this technique. Tony's wife, Carmela (Edie Falco), has separated from him due to his infidelities, and in episode one, a black bear wanders into their backyard while their son, AJ (Robert Iler), is taking out the trash. Carmela, who is on her own now that Tony has reluctantly left, scares the bear away and phones animal control, who come and inspect their property and tell Carmela that Tony's birdfeed probably attracted the bear. Carmela refuses to call Tony for help because she is trying to assert her independence, but the bear returns a few days later, and Tony drops by just as Carmela is phoning animal control again. Tony, worried about his family's safety now that he isn't living at the house, has one of his men sit outside in the garden each night with a gun in case the bear returns. However, this also enables him to keep a watchful eye on his wife and is just one of several ways he finds to stay involved in Carmela's life and impede her attempt to break free of him. As the season unfolds, he repeatedly shows up at the house unannounced to use the swimming pool and eat food, and he tightly controls the purse strings, forcing her to ask him for money. The incidents with the bear are soon forgotten, and in episode nine, Carmela decides to move ahead with divorcing Tony and calls an attorney. To her surprise, the lawyer tells her he must recuse himself, and when she asks why, we cut to a shot of the bear, which has returned to her backyard, unbeknownst to Carmela. The man then explains that Tony has already met him for a consultation, which is why he cannot take her case, and when Carmela mentions that Tony has done the same with other top divorce attorneys in the state, he implies that Tony has done so to make it difficult for her to find somebody to represent her in divorce proceedings. Devastated, she hangs up, and the bear wanders away without making its presence known. Things seem to be looking up for Carmela later in the episode when she finds a lawyer willing to represent her and investigate Tony's assets using a forensic accountant. However, the man then phones her to say that no forensic accountant wants to work on her case because of her husband's ties to the mob and that his own caseload is full, and she breaks down in tears. When she arrives home, Tony is once again outside in the pool.

The reappearance of the bear during the conversation with the first attorney might seem mysterious until we realize that it is a parallel for Tony. Like the bear, which is initially attracted by Tony's birdfeed, Tony refuses to go away, and is an unwanted and unpredictable presence in Carmela's life who lurks threateningly in her backyard. Moreover, just as the bear scavenges for food, so Tony often takes food from Carmela's kitchen. Carmella cannot be free of Tony because he has effectively trapped her in their marriage by contaminating her relationship to divorce attorneys and scaring them away with his reputation for violence and criminality. He is also dangerous like the bear, and in the subsequent episode, after he discovers she has drained the pool because of the expense of heating it, he appears to be on the verge of throwing her onto its concrete bottom. Carmela and Tony subsequently reconcile, and Tony moves back home. But at the end of the final episode of the season, the parallel between Tony and the bear is confirmed when, having escaped on foot from an FBI raid on the nearby house of fellow mob boss Johnny Sacrimoni (Vince Curatola), Tony lumbers through the woods in his black coat. Over a shot of his garden, we hear branches breaking, and a slow-motion close-up of some bushes shows an indeterminate black figure moving among them. It could be the bear, but it turns out to be Tony as he emerges from the bushes, climbs his fence, and is welcomed inside by Carmela. In this example of serial parallelism, rather than a parallel that is introduced and subsequently developed, an element of the narrative – the bear that appears in episode one – retroactively becomes part of a conceptual parallel with Tony that is established in later episodes. What makes this particularly interesting is that the bear initially seems to be a threat to Carmela against which Tony himself is concerned to protect her by stationing his men in her backyard. However, as the conceptual parallel between the bear and Tony dawns on us, we realize that Tony is as threatening to Carmela as the bear, thereby complicating our understanding of the bear's meaning. One might call this retroactive serial parallelism to distinguish it from the developing serial parallelism between Tracee and Meadow. Either way, it is once again made possible by the serial narration characteristic of television.

I do not pretend to have provided in this chapter a taxonomy of all possible types of parallelism in film and television, an impossible task given that creative moving image artists will always innovate new and varied forms of the device. Rather, I have aimed merely to delineate some of its most common manifestations in order to help lay the foundations for further study of this neglected yet widely used formal feature. I have suggested that parallelism is an important technique for creating complexity, at least in the ordinary language sense of consisting of many intricately related parts. Parallelism makes narratives richer by increasing the number of relations between their elements and prompting the viewer to think through these relations. Additionally, I have pointed to some of the distinctive forms that parallelism assumes in television due to the medium's widespread use of serial narration, although I don't believe these are by any means specific in the sense of being unique to TV, given that serial narration can be found in a variety of media and artforms. Nevertheless, what I have called serial parallelism is surely a significant source of aesthetic pleasure for viewers of many television shows. Not only does it help unify seasons by connecting episodes, but it rewards those who are paying close attention to shows and can therefore discern the often subtle ways later elements relate to (or "call back" to) earlier ones. It is only if one has noticed and thought about the appearances of the bear and its similarities to Tony in season five of *The Sopranos* that one will appreciate and understand the final scene of the season in which Tony stumbles through the bushes in his backyard, just as one must be struck by Don's unusual encounter with the elevator shaft in episode eight of season five of *Mad Men* in order to grasp the awful significance of his plunge into darkness in the season's final episode.

I have also claimed that serial parallelism in television shows is distinctive because the temporal prolongation made possible by the medium allows the elaboration and enrichment of parallels over time in serial narration. This is in contrast to the limited parallels that are typically found in movies due to the temporal constraints of single-narrative films. Of course, serial narration also occurs in cinema, and parallels can be developed from episode to episode in a film series. In the *Harry Potter* films, the character parallelism between Harry and Lord Voldemort, which is only hinted at in the earlier installments, is expanded in the later ones until we discover that part of Voldemort's soul actually resides in Harry, which explains their similarities and telepathic communication. Nevertheless, serial narration is much more of a norm in television than in cinema, which means that serial parallelism is more pervasive and has a somewhat different relation to artistic value in television shows than parallelism does in films. The topic of artistic value is an enormously complex one and cannot be addressed in any depth here. Suffice it to say that for many philosophers, artworks have value because they elicit certain kinds of experiences that are "intrinsically worthwhile," in the words of Jerrold Levinson:

> because one's cognitive faculties are notably exercised or enlarged; because one's eyes and ears are opened to certain spatial and temporal possibilities; because one is enabled to explore unusual realms of emotion; because one's consciousness is integrated to a degree out of the ordinary; because one is afforded a distinctive feeling of freedom or transcendence; because certain moral truths are made manifest to one in concrete dress; or because one is provided insight, in one way or another, into human nature.
>
> (Levinson 1996, 19)

Artistic value should not, of course, be confined to and equated with the worth of the experiences elicited by artworks. Levinson, for example, points out: "Part of an artwork's value might reside in its art-historical relations to other artworks, e.g., ones of anticipation, or originality, or influence, independent of the value of experiencing the work in the appropriate manner" (1996, 19). And David Davies argues that artworks also have "artistic value in virtue of being particular performances or 'doings'" in formulating his theory of art as performance (2004, 265). But as even Davies acknowledges, it is "indisputable" that the experiences artworks afford "are among the things for which we value works of art" (2004, 256). This is why, when we engage with artworks, we evaluate the means artists use to elicit these experiences. For example, recently, a fierce debate has occurred online and elsewhere about the much anticipated third episode of the eighth and final season of the TV serial *Game of Thrones* (HBO, 2011–2019), titled "The Long Night," which has just been broadcast for the first time (on April 28, 2019) in the United States. For some, the climactic battle between the armies of the living and the dead that is depicted in the episode was difficult to discern because of the low lighting, and this diminished their ability to experience the spectacle of the battle. For others, the low lighting was a good-making feature of the episode because it allowed them to experience some of the confusion that must be inherent in war. Part of the disagreement was over the goals of the show's creators. If one believes that the episode's aim was, or should have been, perceptual and narrative clarity in its depiction of the battle so that we could appreciate its spectacle, then one might find the episode's cinematography wanting. If one thinks the episode was aiming to impart a visceral experience of the battlefield, then one might conclude that it had succeeded. Whichever side of the debate one is on, the point is that it is an example of our attention to the means through which artists realize their goals and the importance we place on these means in shaping our experience of the artwork. We pay attention to and evaluate the artistry of artists' creative choices, especially when we perceive these choices to be enhancing or diminishing the perceptual, cognitive, emotive, and other experiences we value in engaging with their artworks.

Parallels, I have suggested in this chapter, can heighten our cognitive experience of films and television shows by increasing the number of relations between their parts and thereby creating complexity and richness. Situational, narrative, character, and thematic parallels can make audiovisual narratives more fascinating and intriguing because they give us more to think about, especially when they are unexpected and complicate our understanding of the characters, their actions, and their worlds. Thus, when engaging with these narratives, we may take note of and evaluate the parallels they draw and debate the merits of their execution. However, due to temporal prolongation and the norm of seriality, television shows are capable of enhancing our cognitive experience through parallelism further than most films because they have the time to develop parallels in new and surprising ways, as we have seen in the examples of Meadow and Tracee as well as Tony and the bear in *The Sopranos*. Hence, we might well place a higher value on serial parallelism in television shows than we typically do on parallelism in films because of its greater ability to augment and deepen our cognitive experience.

Notes

1 Todd Berliner argues that moderate forms of complexity are pleasurable for film viewers and cites empirical studies in support of this claim (2017, 15–22).
2 Within film studies, a well-known critic of medium-specificity is Noël Carroll. See, for example, Carroll (2008, chapter 2).
3 See Wilson (1986, chapter 6).
4 This example is given in Sopher (1982, 37).

References

Berliner, Todd. 2017. *Hollywood Aesthetic: Pleasure in American Cinema*. New York: Oxford University Press.

Bordwell, David, Kristin Thompson, and Jeff Smith. 2017. *Film Art: An Introduction*, 11th edition. New York: McGraw-Hill.

Bordwell, David. 1985. *Narration in the Fiction Film*. Madison: University of Wisconsin Press.

Carroll, Noël. 2008. *The Philosophy of Motion Pictures*. Malden, MA: Blackwell.

Davies, David. 2004. *Art as Performance*. Malden, MA: Blackwell.

Fahlenbrach, Kathrin, ed. 2015. *Embodied Metaphors in Film, Television, and Video Games: Cognitive Approaches*. New York: Routledge.

Hornby, Nick. 2007. "An Interview with David Simon." *The Believer* 46 (August 2007), https://believermag.com/an-interview-with-david-simon, accessed January 4, 2019.

Jakobson, Roman. 1987. *Language in Literature*, edited by Krystyna Pomorska and Stephen Rudy. Cambridge, MA: Belknap Press.

Lakoff, George, and Mark Johnson. 1980. *Metaphors We Live By*. Chicago, IL: University of Chicago Press.

Levinson, Jerrold. 1996. "Pleasure and the Value of Works of Art." In *The Pleasures of Aesthetics: Philosophical Essays*, edited by Levinson, 11–24. Ithaca, NY: Cornell University Press.

Mittell, Jason. 2015. *Complex TV: The Poetics of Contemporary Television Storytelling*. New York: New York University Press, 2015.

Nannicelli, Ted. 2017. *Appreciating the Art of Television: A Philosophical Perspective*. New York: Routledge, 2017.

Sopher, Haifa. 1982. "Parallelism in Modern English Prose." *English Studies* 63, no. 1: 37–48.

Thompson, Kristin. 2003. *Storytelling in Film and Television*. Cambridge, MA: Harvard University Press.

Whittock, Trevor. 1990. *Metaphor and Film*. Cambridge: Cambridge University Press.

Wilson, George M. 1986. *Narration in Light: Studies in Cinematic Point-of-View*. Baltimore, MD: Johns Hopkins University Press.

Part IV

Value

Aesthetic and beyond

13 Audiovisual atmospheres, moods, and metaphoric spaces

Aesthetically rich spaces in complex TV series

Kathrin Fahlenbrach

Introductory remarks

With the growing success of serial narratives on cable TV and on streaming platforms, new forms of televisual expressions and styles have emerged. Current research has been focused, rather, on narrative complexity (e.g., Mittell 2015) in TV series. But how does style contribute to the experience of complexity? As current research in the realm of cognitive media theories shows (e.g., Vaage 2016), most significant for the experience of complexity in TV series is that they confront viewers with multi-branched plots, unexpected courses of events, and ambivalent characters and morality. As a result, viewers are constantly challenged, over the long run of a series, to change their perspective, interpretative schemata, and appraisals of characters and events. Accordingly, complexity is considered as a narrative quality that challenges its viewers cognitively and emotionally. As this chapter will argue, narrative complexity is, furthermore, typically related to rich styles (e.g., in cinematography, sound design, production design, and editing) to enhance the viewer's experience of complexity.[1] More specifically, densely composed moods, atmospheres, and sensorially rich styles (e.g., Jacobs and Peacock 2013; Guffey 2014) might significantly feed into the viewer's experience of complexity in certain shows, offering dense compositions of sensorial, cognitive, and emotional cues.

Obviously, such shows do not only aim at entertaining and engaging viewers. Furthermore, they tend to evoke what media psychologists call "appreciation." Following Oliver and Bartsch (2010), this implies, on the one hand, a culturally grounded estimation of a moving image and its contents and styles. On the other hand, appreciation is based on emotional gratifications related to the positive emotional experience of 'deeper insights'. The cultural and aesthetic value of a show is appreciated not just cognitively but also emotionally. Appreciations emerge from challenging, sometimes even negative or frustrating, experiences of a fictional world. This often results in "an experiential state that is characterized by the perception of deeper meaning, the feeling of being moved, and the motivation to elaborate on thoughts and feelings inspired by the experience" (Bartsch 2010, 76). Accordingly, aesthetically rich experiences can feed into cognitive and emotional challenges

DOI: 10.4324/9781003188643-13

that the viewer undergoes over a serial narrative. This is often paralleled by 'deeper insights' and appreciation. These are anchored in narrative discourses and structures that challenge their viewers, e.g., by creating moral ambivalences.

This chapter will discuss the role of televisual spaces in creating intense and rich embodied experiences and understanding of narrative meanings that can, in some cases, contribute to narrative complexity. The spaces of rich and complex TV series, I will go on to argue, create distinct geographic topographies and meaningful topologies, which evolve over the long run of a series; also, they typically create an original spatial style, conveying specific global and local atmospheres and moods within a series' world.

The chapter will first outline some general dimensions of TV spaces that, put together, contribute to the spatial and aesthetic richness and, sometimes, complexity of a series. In a case study of *Bloodline*, it will be demonstrated how these dimensions interact on both the local and the global scales of a series.[2]

Aesthetic and experiential dimensions of televisual spaces in TV series

Jeremy Butler (2010) distinguishes some general functions of television style by following David Bordwell's functions of film style: *to denote*, *to express emotions*, *to symbolize*, *to decorate* or *intrinsically express* televisual style, to *persuade*, to *hail*, and to *signify liveness*. While he refers to the whole range of styles in different TV genres, the first four matter specifically in the case of complex TV series. As for the styles of their spaces and their experiential qualities, it seems rewarding to distinguish some general dimensions: (1) the *denotative* dimension of TV spaces; (2) the *emotional* dimension of TV spaces, including *affective moods and atmospheres*; (3) the *symbolic* dimension of TV spaces; and (4) the *expressive* dimension of TV spaces. In their interplay, these dimensions significantly contribute to viewers' cognitive, affective, and sensorial experience of complexity.

The *denotative* dimension can be mentioned here only briefly. Adding to the canonical definitions of Bordwell and Butler, I would just argue that this is the level of building a basic *topographical* structure by architecture, set design, and spatial motifs as well as by their spatio-temporal manifestation in editing and cinematography throughout a serial world. Just as in movies (cf. Bordwell and Thompson 1990), we can consider this the most elementary dimension of TV spaces, created in the interaction of creators, moving images, and viewers. From this interaction, stylistically and mentally based topographies emerge that provide the very ground for the emotional, symbolical, and expressive topologies that will be discussed in the following paragraphs.

Emotional topologies, moods, and atmospheres of serial TV spaces

Generally, TV spaces both reflect character emotions and aim at involving viewer affects and emotions in a certain way. As will be explored in the following, the emotional dimension is paralleled by affectively loaded atmospheres and moods as well as *emotional topologies*.

In entertaining moving images, emotions obviously play a key role for storytelling and styles. As G. Smith (2003) has argued, moving images typically create single short and intense emotional moments, evoked by a dramatic conflict or a burst of emotions between characters. The audiovisual space fully reflects the emotions in the *mise-en-scène*. In other words: Such scenes create an emotional topology that stages the cognitive, affective, and bodily qualities of the emotions performed in a movie. Also, in TV series, I would argue, intense and singular moments significantly contribute to a transcending emotional topology in a serial world. More specifically, emotional topologies dynamically evolve throughout the long run of a series in the interplay of (a) emotional events at specific places in a series, (b) the way in which style and storytelling refer to such emotional places, and (c) the mental and affective maps built by viewers around such places (Fahlenbrach 2016). Throughout the emerging emotional topologies, the affective appearance of the series' places often varies, reflecting the different emotional shades in the storyworld.

Obviously, emotional topologies are significantly shaped by affectively loaded atmospheres and moods. Moving images do not only aim at evoking intense emotions. Rather, they establish moods that embrace a longer episode, which might prepare viewers for intense emotions to follow (G. Smith 2003). As Sinnerbrink states, movies and other moving images create moods that are not necessarily tied to single characters and their emotions. Rather, affective states are established as "affective background or encompassing 'mood' against which our complex flow of emotional responsiveness becomes manifest: the background against which we are able to recognize, align and ally ourselves with particular characters within specific narrative scenarios" (2012, 152). Moods as "affective background" are explained also by psychology. Accordingly, moods do not need a specific cause (e.g., event or conflict) to emerge but are a constant part of our lives, related to vital bodily and affective states. Psychologist Stern (cf. 1999) shows that we continuously experience specific *vitality affects* that continuously accompany our existence (see also Koppe et al. 2008). These are related to vital processes like breathing, sleeping, or just "being" in any kind of bodily and mental activity (e.g., feeling calm or aroused). Vitality affects have a gestalt dimension (Koppe et al. 2008, 170) that might be experienced by the whole body (mimics, gestures, voice, movements, etc.), such as 'surging' 'fading away,' 'fleeting,' 'exploding,' or 'bursting' (e.g.. Stern 1999, 68). We experience these gestalts in a synesthetic, or more precisely, in a cross-modal way as coherent. This is because they always imply qualities that are felt by all senses, like *intensity*, *tempo/rhythm*, and *duration*.[3]

While moods can be expressed in moving images by the whole *mise-en-scène* of images, sounds, and music, we can distinguish atmospheres being anchored more specifically in the spatial appearance of an audiovisual scenery. According to the phenomenological approach of Böhme (2001), atmospheres are rooted in the way we are sensing a place synesthetically: The "total atmospheric impression" (Böhme 2001, 78) of a place is sensually initiated in our experience by its spatial dimensions, forms, colors, smells, sounds, etc. Spatial atmospheres and affective moods often closely intermingle – especially by being both rooted in the experience of vitality effects.

Movies and TV series create atmospheres and moods by shaping audiovisual spaces in cinematography, sound design, music, and acting, which are akin to the gestalts of vitality affects. The house of Joyce Byers in *Stranger Things* (Netflix, 2016ff), for instance, is presented for the first time in soft morning light that, together with the warm colors of the wooden furniture, creates a bright and friendly atmosphere based on harmonious gestalts. The camera moves in rather long shots, showing Jonathan making breakfast and Joyce searching for her keys. We are invited to appraise the spatial atmosphere of the place on a reflexive and affective level as 'pleasant' and 'harmonious.' Later in the series, when Joyce is desperately searching for her little son Will, the atmosphere of her house changes fundamentally: We mostly see it in the evening, while only single lights are shining in the dark rooms; the interior is getting increasingly messy and destroyed by Joyce's attempts to get into contact with Will, who is locked in the "dark side." Dark lighting and somber colors, together with the messiness of things in the rooms, establish opaque gestalts and create a disharmonious and chaotic atmosphere.

Based on gestalt perception, such affective appraisal is the result of experiencing the colors, lights, dimensions, and sounds of a specific place – all of which factors together create its atmosphere. While the atmosphere is rooted in the spatial qualities of a place and its experience, the mood is the result of bodily performances of characters and the affective tone of the *mise-en-scène*. The appraisal of a spatial atmosphere can fuse, but also contrast, with the affective mood of a situation. In *Stranger Things*, the harmonious atmosphere of the first sequence in Joyce's house contrasts with a nervous and increasingly tense mood. This is firstly evoked by Joyce's hectic search for the keys and then intensified by her rising panic after she discovers that little Will is missing. Already at the end of the first episode, the atmosphere of the place is changing in a way that is now congruent with the reigning mood. The sadness of Joyce and Jonathan is fully reflected by the spatial atmosphere: They are sitting together in the dark living room, with single lamps producing a warm light; they are talking and crying quietly; their rather reluctantly expressed sadness and tears correlate with the gentle sound of rain and single slow, long sounds of music. Atmosphere and mood intermingle here in somber and soft gestalts and by slow performances of the characters, the camera, and the sound. It is only when the telephone rings that we experience a drastic shift of both atmosphere and mood: The distorted voice and breathings coming from the phone receiver, Joyce's yelling, and finally, the flash traversing and cutting the telephone line mark a significant turn of events and an emotion marker that is followed by a considerable change of atmosphere and mood. From now on and until Will's return, the house is a place of fear and horror, which is displayed both in its spatial and atmospheric settings – as mentioned before – and in the moods performed by characters and *mise-en-scène*.

Obviously, affective moods and spatial atmospheres contribute significantly to the affective experience of an audiovisual space and the related storyworld. As Plantinga (2014) argues, they also affect viewers' moral appraisals and attitudes. According to Plantinga, moods often imply moral meanings and attitudes by triggering positive or negative feelings in viewers. They enable them to appraise the situation both emotionally and cognitively, including *moral appraisals*:

> If a film … triggers powerful and memorable moral intuitions, then a story can be effective in affirming and/or altering our moral intuitions about types of characters and situations. Mood plays an important role in the triggering of such intuitions, in part by providing an atmosphere within which such intuitions seem right and compelling.
>
> (Plantinga 2014, 155)

In other words, viewers might appreciate the "world view" and the moral attitude of a narrative, which is conveyed through its global moods. Sometimes, even cognitively and emotionally complex experiences are rendered by moods, e.g., when contrasted with the morality of its characters and their actions. An example would be the murders in the TV show *Dexter*, performed in a cheerful mood.

What Plantinga observes in film is obviously also true for fictional worlds in TV narration. This is especially the case in TV stories with a "psychological realism" that provides a "centripetal complexity," as Mittell (2015) calls it: Stories that unveil the psychological depth of a character and his biographical background step by step during the seasons and episodes. Prototypical examples would be Walter White in *Breaking Bad* (AMC 2008-2013) and Don Draper in *Mad Men* (AMC 2007-2015). As Mittell and other scholars observe, different moral and psychological shades of such characters are conveyed by densely composed visual styles – especially, I would add, by the visual and audiovisual style of key narrative places and their atmospheres, affectively loaded by the reigning moods.

As will be elaborated more specifically in the case study, movies and TV series can share a cinematic manner of shaping atmospheres and moods in a narrative way. They both create places with cognitively, sensorially, and affectively rich atmospheres and moods, which offer viewers evaluative cues for appraising the presented fictional world. Even more than movies, TV series can elaborate on their dramaturgical way of guiding viewers affectively and emotionally through a narrative by the interplay of local and global moods. This offers viewers the chance to experience different shades of affective tones and perspectives in a narrative.

Symbolic and metaphoric topologies of serial TV spaces

Spaces of movies and TV series regularly create a symbolic dimension that reflects more abstract conceptual meanings anchored in a narrative. Symbolic meanings in serial narratives transcend the local denotative and emotional meanings of a represented place. This can imply symbolic meanings related to the choice of spatial motifs, established in culture and/or media conventions. Furthermore, audiovisual spaces can generate quite specific symbolic meanings on the global scale of a fictional world. TV series particularly can elaborate different symbolic meanings of spaces in the long run. By the recurring use of spatial motifs and their aesthetic staging, their symbolic meanings can gradually evolve during the episodes. A well-known example is the inserts of an air crash in *Breaking Bad*, which repeatedly shows, ahead of several episodes, single short-cuts of the catastrophe near Walter's house. It is only over the run of the series that viewers can make sense of them and that they become a symbol for the fatal decline of Walter White. Obviously, even motifs with no evident symbolic character at the beginning might generate such transitional conceptual semantics via serial repetition and reframing.

Symbolic meanings of televisual spaces are often conveyed by audiovisual metaphors (e.g., Fahlenbrach 2016). Films and TV series regularly create metaphoric spaces that allow viewers to grasp and experience symbolic meanings in a reflexive and embodied way. Canonic examples would be the display of social hierarchies in a storyworld by creating hierarchies between high and low in set design and by filmmaking, or the metaphoric display of characters being 'emotionally overwhelmed' by showing them in heavy rain. It is by the choice of motifs, but also by the specific audiovisual composition of images, sounds, and movements, that TV series can make use of metaphoric displays to let viewers experience and understand quickly more complex meanings and emotions.

The cognitive and emotional impact of such metaphoric displays can be explained by drawing on cognitive metaphor theory (e.g., Johnson 1987). Accordingly, metaphors are mental tools that enable us to imagine in our minds both abstract and complex concepts, ideas, and relations as well as complex and invisible emotions in terms of embodied image schemata: As physical *forces* (e.g., 'emotion is a natural force'), spatial *paths* (e.g., 'life is a journey'), or *containers* (e.g., 'society is a building'). We permanently activate mental image schemata that genuinely rely on bodily experiences (Johnson 1987).

As studies in cinematic and audiovisual metaphors demonstrate (e.g., Forceville 2008; Fahlenbrach 2016; Coëgnarts and Kravanja 2014), metaphors are constantly created in moving images – movies, TV shows, or video games. Mental image schemata (e.g., container or path) are created in every audiovisual composition and by the very display of motifs of an audiovisual artifact. Filmmakers can intuitively or intentionally make use of our mental capacity of metaphoric thinking to guide our experiences. They metaphorically shape meanings so that viewers can experience them immediately, even without being aware of it. On the one hand, metaphors can be triggered in viewers that are anchored in our minds as mental schemata, such as 'good is up – bad is down,' 'power is big – weakness is small,' or 'good is bright' – 'evil is dark.' It is also through sound design and musical composition that such well-established embodied metaphoric associations are initiated quickly in viewers by the very topographic composition of spatial gestalts (up/down, etc.). On the other hand, every audiovisual piece creates original metaphors by its specific use of images, sounds, and movements, drawing on embodied gestalt perception, affective experience, and cognition of viewers. In *Twin Peaks*, for example, the forest as a recurrent leitmotiv is metaphorically shaped as an 'intelligent being' (Fahlenbrach 2016) and a key audiovisual metaphor that guides the viewer's experience of the narrative.

As will be exemplified in the following case study, we can observe in many complex TV series a salient metaphorical shaping of key action places that conceptually structure the appearances and embodied meanings of other elements in the fictional world. They give basic meanings a multi-sensorial gestalt throughout the whole narrative discourse. However, a significant difference is that metaphoric meanings of recurrently shown places might evolve only during a longer period, related to a more progressively emerging salience of the key narrative topics (Fahlenbrach 2016). Hence, with the broader establishment of narrative information and of atmospheres, the metaphoric meaning of a specific place might emerge only during the long-run series. This goes ahead with a reframing of gestalt qualities of such a place, which can also be experienced pre-consciously. In *Twin Peaks* (Frost and Lynch, USA 1990–1991), for instance, key locations such as the forest (as an 'intelligent being') or the little town surrounded by nature ('society is a natural place') evolve their metaphoric meanings progressively across the series (Fahlenbrach 2016). *Breaking Bad* develops a global metaphoric spatial structure by foregrounding in set design, cinematography, and editing Walter White's house as a 'family place' that is first threatened by an 'internal evil force,' then, after Walter moves out, an 'external evil force,' and after his return with the crawlspace as a key action space for hiding drug money, an 'evil force from below.' Each time, the concrete gestalt of the house functions in the filmmaking as a spatial source for providing metaphorically embodied pictures of a broader, abstract idea: 'The ambivalent evil.'

Hence, on the global scale of a series, complex metaphoric networks might emerge, interrelating conceptual and symbolic meanings of different key action spaces. Key action places then act as audiovisual metaphors that provide relevant narrative meanings with a cross-modal gestalt, allowing viewers a reflexive embodied experience of higher narrative or cultural meanings. Through their recurrent appearance in TV series, a global metaphoric network emerges that significantly shapes the symbolic topology of a serial world and its embodied and affective experience by viewers in the long run.

Expressive topologies of TV spaces

One of the most significant characteristics of complex TV series is certainly their exposed use of audiovisual styles, sometimes even autonomous forms of expression. With Mittell (2015), we can observe here a tendency towards 'spectacular moments' akin to the 'cinema of attractions.' Yet, expressive style is not necessarily a purely decorative surplus. As Vermeulen and Rustad (2013) have aptly argued, the specific visual style of a series' aesthetics can attain a quality of its own, also beyond storytelling and diegetic functionality. Hence, images, and certainly also sound, do not simply illustrate the narrative. Rather, audiovisual forms – such as flashbacks or flash-forwards, Match-Cuts, or specific compositional styles in cinematography – may develop autonomous ways of expression. In their analysis of *Mad Men*, for example, Vermeulen and Rustad (2013) gave the example of so-called "late cuts," considering that the editing of the series often puts forward the very audiovisual presence of televisual spaces, e.g., by showing places where relevant characters have already left, where no action is taking place yet or anymore, or by drawing attention to details of a situation that are somewhat irrelevant in narrative terms. Foregrounding such audiovisual elements can intensify the cognitive and affective involvement of viewers. Cognitive attention is intensified by letting viewers puzzle over their meanings. Sometimes, these autonomous forms notably expand the overarching atmospheres and moods of the series' spaces. This typically aims at intensified bodily and affective viewer experiences, combined with distinctive artifact emotions (Tan 1996). Even if evoked admiration and pleasure at expressive styles can momentarily distance the viewer from involvement in the diegetic world, it is apt to intensify the viewer's overall experience of the series by expanded appreciation.

The global expressive dimension of a series is essentially generated by the repetition and variation of such autonomous elements. Following Jacobs and Peacock (2013), I would argue that complex series often establish a self-referential system of stylistic forms and codes that the viewers learn to specifically interpret and appraise in a series' world. Hence, these forms can attain a key role within a series in both the affective experience and the cognitive understanding of a series' spaces. Furthermore, they significantly contribute to the viewer's experience of aesthetic richness and sometimes, of complexity. As I will demonstrate in the following case study, expressive forms contribute significantly to the symbolic and emotional display of spatio-temporal structures and action places in the long run of a series.

In the previous paragraphs, I claimed that the complexity of TV series depends not only on the cognitive and emotional challenges for the viewers related to the narrative, but also on their aesthetic richness, provided by style. More specifically, the creation of aesthetically dense televisual spaces offers viewers rich affective and mental cues that feed into their experience of narrative complexity. As I have argued, this happens on different levels of televisual spaces: By providing denotative information about spaces and by creating local and global atmospheres, moods, and emotional topologies as well as symbolic and metaphoric spaces. All these dimensions are closely interconnected and feed into each other. Furthermore, specific styles of televisual spaces express an original aesthetic character of a series to further enhance the viewer's appreciation. While televisual spaces share these different levels of aesthetic creation with other moving images, their serial structure creates a significant difference. As I will show in a more detailed fashion in the following case study, televisual spaces might profit in terms of aesthetic richness from their global and serial latitude, e.g., by repetition and recontextualization of spatial motifs, or by letting symbolic meanings of single places emerge only during the long run of the series.

Case study: Audiovisual spaces in *Bloodline* (Netflix/Sony Pictures/KZK Productions, 2015–2017)

For my case study, I chose a complex TV series that densely composes spatial atmospheres, moods, symbolic topologies, as well as expressive forms around the story of several tragic traumas in a family. *Bloodline* tells the story of the Rayburn family, who own a small hotel at the Florida Keys. The parents, Sally and Robert, live at the hotel, while John, a police officer, Meg, a lawyer, and Kevin, owner of a small marina, live in the surroundings with their partners and children. As we learn during the series, they all suffer from traumatic memories of losing their daughter and sister Sarah during a boat trip with their son and brother Danny when they were children. While most family members have, however, become able to handle this memory by the time the series starts, their psychological and social balance becomes more and more disrupted when Danny returns from a long absence. Even more so, his return and wish to stay initiates a row of further tragic events, increasingly expanding their original feelings of guilt caused by the death of Sarah – feelings that each of them has, for specific reasons, lurking in the past. From a highly respected family in the local community, we witness the involuntary moral decline and continuous fall into criminality of all family members.

As I will demonstrate, the settings and aesthetic staging of the series' spaces significantly contribute to the way viewers are mentally and emotionally involved in the traumatic memories and psychological conflicts of the characters. And in this case, the emotional topologies and moods do not relate just to single characters but to the whole family and their psychic dynamics. As we will see, this is prominently reflected in an expressive use of editing, producing a fragmentary and associative narrative discourse that jumps from one character to another, sometimes relating their memories.

Starting with the *denotative dimension*, we can observe the following key topographical characteristics: The series is situated in the Florida Keys, an island chain off the southern coast of Florida, close to Cuba. More specifically, the key places are located around the community of Islamorada. Its topography is regularly revealed by the camera, starting with the very first pictures of the show, by high-angle tracking shots that show us a long and narrow highway as the sole road leading to the island. These tracking shots also saliently put forward the geographical environment of Islamorada: The mangrove swamps on the island and the sea that surrounds it. Similarly, the second key site of the action is introduced during the first sequence and then regularly during the three episodes by high-angle tracking shots: The Rayburn house. These shots reveal that the hotel is located near the sea and is naturally enclosed by palms and brushes. Some other recurrent action places are Kevin's office at the marina, the bar at Islamorada, the house of Danny's friend Chelsea O'Bannon, and the house of police officer John Rayburn and his family, as well as Danny's abandoned apartment and restaurant in Miami. As we know from other series (e.g., *Twin Peaks*, cf. Fahlenbrach 2016), the geographical relations between these different locations are kept opaque. However, given the general topography of Islamorada, it is obvious to viewers that all places *there* are rather close. In contrast, Miami is revealed as a distant place that people reach by bus or car, but often they fail to reach it and are stuck on the island.

Symbolic and metaphoric topology in **Bloodline**

As the reconstruction of the denotative topographical structure might already indicate, it implies a symbolic dimension, and hence a conceptually based topology, closely related to the narrative. With its geographical isolation, and being surrounded by the sea, Islamorada provides a setting that allows the filmmakers to create the diegetic place of a rather closed community. More specifically, this regards the Rayburn family, whose members are shown several times as being trapped there. The very first sequence of the series shows Danny approaching Islamorada by bus. Struggling with doubts about this journey, he leaves the bus at a previous station, but finally ends up arriving at the Rayburn residence. During the seasons, we also learn from other family members, like Sally, Meg, and John, that they have been trying in vain, at moments of deep crisis, to leave the place. It is only after a considerable breakup of the family ties in the last season that most of them leave. As a key spatial motif, a basic metaphoric concept of the island is established throughout the episodes: 'Family is a place surrounded by a natural force.' Considering the fragility of the narrow island and the omnipresent power of the surrounding sea, put forward in cinematography, a more specific metaphoric concept is generated: 'Family is a house surrounded by an encroaching natural force.' The aforementioned tracking shots of the Rayburn house offer further stylistic support to these metaphoric concepts. Throughout the second and third seasons, the sea's water increasingly permeates the ground and the house of the Rayburns, and in the last episode, an expert even predicts that the house will be fully submerged within the next ten years. Sally Rayburn even comments: "The sea takes everything! My children, my home ...." Hence, at the global scale of the show, the initial metaphoric concept of the settings is further specified: 'Family is a place threatened by an encroaching, fluid force.'

The pervasively presented sea provides a symbolic spatial motif for the destructive forces that slowly but constantly destroy the unity of the family. Significantly, storytelling and filmmaking locate the most traumatic moments of the family at sea: Little Sarah is drowned on a boat trip; father Robert nearly dies of a heart attack on his canoe after a dispute with his son Danny on the beach; finally, Danny dies at the end of season 2 when he is drowned by his brother John during an escalating struggle – just to mention the most traumatic moments, which are repeatedly remembered throughout the series. Hence, the sea is symbolically and conceptually linked with family trauma. It creates metaphoric meanings like 'Family trauma is falling into a sea' – 'is losing body control in a fluid space.' This is already established during the trailer sequence, presenting a quasi-static shot from a huge beach, with the change of times of the day and weather being shown in fast forward – paralleled by the song lyrics and the refrain: "(…) and you'll drown before the water lets you in." As is often the case in trailers for complex TV series, viewers are cognitively and affectively primed here for the series' world with its specific conflicts, atmospheres, and moods (cf. Fahlenbrach and Flückiger 2014) – and its key metaphors. Furthermore, within the series, flashbacks to the traumas expose the very moment of falling into the sea, losing control over the body, which is mostly emphasized by slow motion. The moment they lost their sister is not only remembered but reimagined by Danny and John at moments of diving. As a convention in other moving images, too, water is used here as a metaphor (Urios-Apararisi 2016). It indicates vividly the power of emotions and traumata, which are constantly challenging the protagonists' inner control; more specifically, the sea as a huge and autonomous natural space is metaphorically performed to evidence the unforeseeable and sometimes destructive power of emotional dynamics in families, friendships, and other social bonds. As we will see in the following analysis, the symbolic and metaphoric shapes of series' spaces are also significant elements in their expressive and emotional topologies. More specific expressive, emotional, and affective metaphors are created, which feed into the metaphoric network around the key locations shown so far.

Expressive topologies: Edited spaces in Bloodline

Like other complex TV series, *Bloodline* creates expressive stylistic forms that develop over the long run self-referential meanings, most notably a specific system of flashbacks, flash-forwards, and epiphanies of past characters and objects that viewers learn to understand only over time. Here, styles of montage build edited spaces that expressively add to the symbolic and emotional topologies by addressing viewers' mind and imagination. During the first episodes, these integrated fragments of the edited spaces work, rather, as autonomous segments and let viewers puzzle about their meanings. The first flashback to the traumatic death of Sarah, for example, occurs in 1/I, during a night-time dive by Danny after his return. The editing combines his actual dive with another one during daytime, shown some minutes before, when he imagines seeing

Figure 13.1 *Bloodline* season 1, episode 1: Traumatic flashback memories.

and grasping a necklace from the bottom, and finally, the blurred and bluish pictures of a little girl running towards the camera. It is by repetition of the same and by inserting further flashbacks around this past event on the global scale of the series, also from different character memories, that we can continuously put together in our mind the different pieces and form a coherent picture of what happened back then. Thereby, the editing evokes in viewers a mental space around the memory of this and other traumatic events, which intermingles with the events happening in the diegetic present. Most significantly, though, these memories are not focused on one single character, as is conventionally often the case. Rather, the editing artfully creates a discourse of *collectively shared* memory of the *whole* family. This is often realized by inserting flashback memories of different characters that relate to each other on the global scale of the series. The traumatic death of Sarah, for example, is remembered several times by different family members. Hence, by combining these different flashback memories in the long run of the series, viewers might create in their mind a complex memory discourse of the family. But shared memory is also construed on the local level. In this case, the edited spaces combine one moment of the family past that is remembered by different characters at the same time, with their memories even completing each other. In one flashback

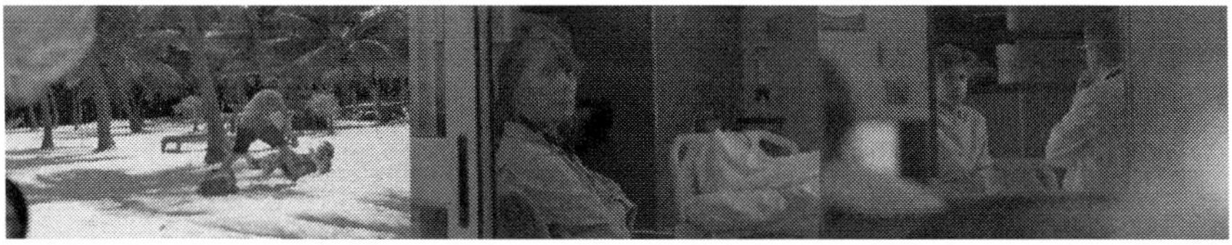

Figure 13.2 Shared memory in *Bloodline* season 1, episode 2.

Figure 13.3 Shared memory in *Bloodline* season 1, episode 2.

sequence, in 2/I, we see Kevin attacking Danny after their father's heart attack, guessing that this was Danny's fault. Images of John in the present, who witnesses their fight in the past, are cross-cut with pictures of Sally at the hospital visiting her husband in the present. Inserted in the flashback is an epiphany of Danny as a young boy at the hospital. This refers to another family trauma, as we learn later: Danny was seriously beaten by his father after Sarah's accident, a fact that has been covered up by the whole family in dealings with doctors and police – and a collective guilt that significantly pervades the family's destiny. The cross-cutting between John and Sally at different places, related by their epiphanies about Danny as a young and injured boy, and the flashback to the past hospital situation exposes a moment of shared memory between two family members.

Obviously, the editing involves viewers in the inter-dynamic psychological experiences within the family by confronting them with different memory perspectives. The editing space is built on a specific spatio-temporal order. It is not based on linear chronology but rather, on associative and affective dynamics of the family members' memories, and as we learn at the end of the first and of the third episode of season 3, partly by John's confessions to his police colleagues. By connecting different memories of the single characters within single sequences, the editing spaces establish a metaphoric expression: 'Family trauma is shared seeing.'

The metaphoric staging of memories by the editing also affects how viewers are confronted with the series' spaces. The Rayburn house, particularly, is repeatedly presented as the center of the family, often by showing it from above, inserted before a sequence of a family meeting. As a key spatial metaphor for the family ('family is a house'), it is furthermore exposed in the edited space as a place where past and present moments of guilt, trauma, and conflicts are culminating. As a result, the somewhat associative structure of the editing enables the viewers' mental image of the house to be more and more enriched by pictures performing these experiences of crisis and guilt feelings. Hence, the expressive style of the montage creates edited spaces that go beyond the symbolic or emotional representation of concrete locations in the storyworld. More so, it aims at letting viewers anticipate the memories and traumas of the characters in terms of mental spaces, characterized by psychologically based spatio-temporal structures. Finally, as an expressive style of the series, the editing spaces also significantly contribute to its aesthetic richness.

Emotional topologies, atmospheres, and moods in **Bloodline**

Obviously, emotional topologies of spaces in complex TV series are closely connected with the aspects outlined before and partly emerge from these. This is especially the case here for the building of an emotional topology around the psychologically charged memories of the characters. Still, some aspects must be considered that mark the emotional qualities of the spaces and the way they are displayed. As mentioned before, the spatial atmospheres may lay the ground for affective contours and moods. On the global scale, we may observe two distinct kinds of atmosphere around the Rayburn house. One is a bright atmosphere in daytime, showing us the family during happy meetings in the house and along the beach in front of it. Here, daytime, the sunny beach, and the blue sea are chosen as the setting for affectively positive, cheerful moods, related to the laughing and chatting of the characters as mood cues. However, these positive atmospheres and moods are rather singular and restricted to the first season. In contrast, the house is increasingly shown by night, and especially in dramatic scenes, in heavy rain. This dark spatial atmosphere lays the gestalt ground for global oppressive, and even catastrophic, moods, related to conflicts, crises, and new traumatic events in the diegetic present.

An extreme correlation of intense tension, darkness, rain, and somber mood is performed at the intercutting between the last episode of the second season and the first episode of season 3. Both episodes present one and the same night, in which another traumatic event happens, and John tries to flee Islamorada in despair, finally returning. The editing directly relates the two seasons by cross-cutting Kevin's murder and John's getaway on the highway by night, as well as Meg at home with her mother Sally, telling her the truth about John being his brother Danny's murderer. This montage across episodes creates a dense com-

Figure 13.4 *Bloodline* season 2, episode 10 and season 3, episode 1: Expressive edited space across episodes.

Figure 13.5 *Bloodline* season 2, episode 10 and season 3, episode 1: Expressive edited space across episodes.

position of mixed negative moods that are anchored both in the global mood of the series' world and the current situation of the characters and their physically expressed fear, panic, and sad resignation. By alternately cross-cutting the different places and characters of this night, the editing allows a comprehensive mood to emerge around these emotions, accentuating again the psychic dynamics between the family members – even if they are in different places.

For grounding these moods, the atmospheres around three places in particular are alternately presented in the editing: The house of Marco, who is murdered by Kevin; the highway with John, fleeing the island; and the Rayburn house with Meg and Sally. All these places are congruently related in atmosphere and mood by audiovisually created affective gestalts that imply cross-modal experiences of intensity and tempo: After Kevin's murder is presented as a strong marker of emotion, the tempo of everything that follows is decelerated: camera movements, music, and movements of action at the different places. Even the tempo of John's escape is subjectively lowered by showing him sitting motionless in his car, staring ahead. As a result, an overarching cross-modal gestalt of 'slowing down' is created by images and sounds. In contrast to the dramatic events and emotional stress performed by the actors before, this deceleration intensifies the tension that is related to both the global development of the series and the local events (Kevin's murder and Meg's confession). In other words, viewers' suspenseful expectation of how these simultaneous dramatic events might escalate and play out is intensified by the deceleration of their display. Most significantly, the suspenseful expectation is blocked by the sharp cut in a shot of John in his car, which abruptly ends the second season and acts as a suspenseful cliffhanger. In 1/III, the series continues the display of these interrupted events. The tension is now further conveyed by music and sound: Single sounds, such as a constant pumping noise associating inner sounds such as heartbeat and breathing, as well as a rising high-frequency sound significantly put forward the overarching gestalt of strong affective tension; the loud noises of crickets and other animals bodily indicate the constant presence of nature and wilderness. Finally, the sequence is accompanied by a solemn choral music score that connotes a religious acceptance of fate and creates a mood of sad resignation.

The tempo of the sequence is then slightly accelerated when Kevin flees Marco's house and runs through the woods towards the Rayburn residency. Additionally, throughout several cuts, we see a crocodile slowly rising from water, walking ashore, and heading towards the highway. The editing closely alternates shots of the crocodile and of John in the car as two constantly forwardly propulsive forces that in the end will collide when the animal reaches the highway and is run over by his car. The cross-modal tempo and intensity are further increased towards the end of the sequence: In an augmented frequency of cuts, the editing alternates more rapidly between the different places and their protagonists, even including a new one: A house guest of Sally, who is looking for her dog. While we see the dog following Kevin's footprints in several inserts, we hear his owner calling him with growing impatience. These inserts do not only contrast with the culminating drama around the family members by their banality. They also feed into the growing intensity of tension and catastrophic feelings by further decelerating the display of the dramatic events and 'interrupting' the narrative flow.

Hence, the composition of the editing, including moments of disruption, significantly serves to heighten the intensity of the atmospheres and moods. This is most evident when Sally realizes that her son John has killed his brother.

It is Meg who forces her to accept this truth ("Mom, did you hear what I said?"). The camera shows Sally, looking out of the window, being visually enclosed by the window frame, accompanied by an arousing, high-frequency sound when she finally whispers "Yea – he didn't mean to do it." While we are still looking at her, we hear a cell phone ringing; the editing switches to John looking at the display of his cell phone, but he refuses to answer; then, the little dog, barking at a high frequency, is included as well as his owner calling him; this is followed by a very short insert of the crocodile moving slowly ashore. Hence, Sally's ongoing realization of her family's guilt is interrupted by shots of John's cell phone, the crocodile, and the dog with his increasingly angry owner. The affective cross-modal gestalt of a constantly up-swelling tension is built up in this montage and finally erupts in the crash of John and the crocodile, the only moment in this montage across episodes when two actors meet in one and the same insert.

Atmospheres and moods are congruently created in this sequence and generate metaphoric shapes of the spaces that offer viewers an aesthetically rich experience of the family's drama. This concerns, for example, the inserts showing the crocodile. As a 'wild animal' emerging from the water, it is another metaphoric motif for the power of negative emotions of guilt and fear that constantly erupt within the family. Also, by its very gestalt and appearance as a dark, cold, and dangerous animal, it significantly contributes to the sequence's overall fraught mood. Across the montage, its slow movements affectively and metaphorically correlate in the audiovisual composition with the gradual culmination of the catastrophic moods. On a more general scale, the expressive style of the whole montage creates a metaphoric dimension that transcends the above-mentioned metaphoric network: The collective family guilt is conveyed by its editing as a 'shared affective space,' permanently connecting the different places of the characters by the cuts, by a tense overarching soundscape, and by the overall dark atmosphere. In this, cinematography and sound editing shape a slowly, but constantly, rising intensity of tension and a cross-modal up-swelling gestalt, combined with somber moods, related to anxiety and sadness. Construing a closely interlinked edited space, the filmmaking further accentuates within it two significant image schemata: *Paths* of escape (John in the car, Kevin's run) and interior spaces as closed *containers* where dramatic events are happening (Kevin's murder, Meg's confession). Both John and Kevin are blocked in their escape (by the crocodile and by the dog). Regarding the close connection of the places as one shared affective space, both the characters moving on paths and those in the house are equally staged as being stuck at one place. Accordingly, affective gestalts, spatial atmospheres, and moods in this montage across episodes merge to an overarching embodied audiovisual metaphor: 'Collective family guilt is a continuously up-swelling gestalt of tension in a shared space.'

It is through metaphoric performances of the filmmaking that the moral appraisal of the inclined moods might be experienced in a reflexive way. Hence, it is certainly true that this piece also offers by its comprehensive mood what Plantinga calls the *worldview* of a narrative: Generally, the series deals with prototypical psychological, in part psychotic, dynamics in families. It shows how family roles evolve by implied expectations, prejudices, and deeply anchored needs of all family members. As an artwork, the series adds to such a psychological analysis Biblical themes, such as the stories of Cain and Abel, of the prodigal son, and of the apocalyptic deluge that is to destroy the family house. The aesthetically created global moods of the series significantly contribute to letting viewers experience and appreciate such 'deeper insights' and collective knowledge by their very senses and affects.

Conclusion

As the case study should demonstrate, complex TV spaces result from a multifaceted interplay of denotative, symbolic, emotional, and expressive dimensions. More specifically, it is in the blending of topographic features, symbolic and metaphoric topologies, affective atmospheres and moods, as well as specific aesthetic styles of televisual expression that serial spaces can be experienced and appreciated by viewers as aesthetically rich and complex.

In film and media studies, it is always tricky to deal with such complexities, especially if rather 'fuzzy' phenomena such as moods, affects, and bodily associations are included. At the same time, those phenomena especially matter for the aesthetic experience of TV series, as they do for movies. Drawing on psychology and cognitive metaphor theory, different gestalt-based aspects of audiovisual aesthetics and reception have been discussed that might help to seize these difficult-to-grasp dimensions of TV aesthetics. It has been suggested that atmospheres prepare the spatial ground of moods and are themselves shaped in the gestalt of affective gestalts, akin to vitality affects, which accompany us in our bodily and affective being. Atmospheres are created in the filmmaking, which conveys cross-modal gestalts of affective qualities, related to intensities, tempo, rhythm, or duration – qualities that viewers can experience with all their senses. Consequently, atmospheric gestalts in an audiovisual piece can trigger multisensory associations that often transcend ears and eyes. While embodied and affective associations of a series' atmospheres might already cause rich sensorial experiences, they might further shape the ground of moods, emotions, and more abstract meanings in a storyworld. Atmospheres and moods on the local and global scale are saturated by metaphoric meanings, by building metaphoric networks around key action places that are repeatedly displayed in a serial storyworld. Accordingly, it is by metaphors that moods can convey more narrative meanings and worldviews – while their very aesthetic and atmospheric gestalt mostly remains below conscious notice. At the same time, it is this almost hidden saturation of aesthetic forms, symbolic meanings, and emotional and affective experiences across a series' spaces of which viewers only gradually become aware in the long run of a series, and it is this that allows them to appreciate its complexity.

Notes

1 I am grateful to Héctor J. Pérez for his suggestion of differentiating richness and complexity. He presented a first draft of his approach at the SCSMI conference 2018, Bozeman.
2 This chapter elaborates arguments presented in Fahlenbrach 2018.
3 Cross-modal gestalts are mentally processed by integrating information across different senses and thus form the fundament of coherent multisensory perceptions; cf. Marks 1989; Stern 1999.

References

Bartsch, Anne. 2010. "Embodied Emotion Metaphors in Moving Images". In *Embodied Metaphors in Film, Television, and Video Games: Cognitive Approaches*, edited by Kathrin Fahlenbrach. London/New York: Routledge.

Böhme, Gernot. 2001. *Aisthetik. Vorlesungen über Ästhetik als Allgemeine Wahrnehmungslehre.* München: Fink.

Bordwell, David, and Kristin Thompson. 1990. *Film Art. An Introduction.* New York: McGraw Hill.

Bruun-Vaage, Margrethe. 2016. *The Antihero in American Television.* New York/London: Routledge.

Butler, Jeremy. 2010. *Televisual Style.* New York/London: Routledge.

Caldwell, John T. 1995. *Televisuality. Style, Crisis, and Authority in American Television.* New Brunswick: Rutgers.

Coëgnarts, Maarten, and Peter Kravanja, eds. 2014. "Metaphor, Bodily Meaning, and Cinema." Special issue of *Image [&] Narrative. Metaphor, Bodily Meaning, and Cinema* 15, no. 1.

Fahlenbrach, Kathrin, and Barbara Flückiger. 2014. "Immersive Entryways into Televisual Worlds. Affective and Aesthetic Functions of Title Sequences in Quality Series." *Projections. Journal for Movies and Mind* 8, no. 1: 84–103.

Fahlenbrach, Kathrin. 2016. "Audiovisual Metaphors as Embodied Narratives in Moving Images." In *Embodied Metaphors in Film, Television, and Video Games. Cognitive Approaches*, edited by Kathrin Fahlenbrach, 33–50. London/New York: Routledge.

Fahlenbrach, Kathrin. 2018. Audiovisuelle Atmosphären, Stimmungen und metaphorische Räume in komplexen Fernsehserien. *montage/AV* 27, no. 2: 45–60.

Forceville, Charles. 2008. "Metaphor in Pictures and Multimodal Representations." In *Cambridge Handbook of Metaphor and Thought*, edited by Ray Gibbs, 462–482. Cambridge: Cambridge University Press.

Guffey, Ensely F. 2014. "Buying the House. Places in *Breaking Bad*." In *Breaking Bad, Critical Contexts of the Contexts, Politics, Style, and Reception of the Television Series*, edited by David P. Pierson. Lanham, MD: Lexington Books.

Jacobs, Jason, and Steven Peacock, ed. 2013. *Television Aesthetics and Style.* New York: Bloomsbury.

Johnson, Mark. 1987. *The Body in the Mind: The Bodily Basis of Meaning, Imagination, and Reason.* Chicago, IL: Chicago UP.

Koppe, Simo, Susanne Harder, and Mette Vaever. 2008. "Vitality Affects." *International Forum of Psychoanalysis* 17: 169–179.

Marks, L. E. 1989. "On Cross-Modal Similarity: The Perceptual Structure of Pitch, Loudness, and Brightness." *Journal of Experimental Psychology: Human Perception and Performance* 15: 586–602.

Mittell, Jason. 2015. *Complex TV. The Poetics of Contemporary Television Storytelling*. New York: New York UP.

Oliver, Mary Beth, and Anne Bartsch. 2010. "Appreciation as Audience Response: Exploring Entertainment Gratifications Beyond Hedonism." *Human Communication Research* 36: 53–81.

Plantinga, Carl. 2014. "Mood and Ethics in Narrative Film." In *Cognitive Media Theory*, edited by Ted Nannicelli and Paul Taberham, 141–157. New York/London: Routledge.

Sinnerbrink, Robert. 2012. "Stimmung: Exploring the Aesthetics of Mood." *Screen* 52, no. 2: 148–163.

Smith, Greg M. 2003. *Film Structure and the Emotion System*. Cambridge: Cambridge UP.

Stern, Daniel N. 1999. "Vitality Contours: The Temporal Contour of Feelings as a Basic Unit for Constructing the Infant's Social Experience." In *Early Social Cognition: Understanding Others in the First Months of Life*, edited by Philippe Rochat, 67–80. London: Lawrence Erlbaum.

Tan, Ed S. 1996. *Emotion and the Structure of Narrative Film. Film as an Emotion Machine*. Mahwah NJ.: Erlbaum.

Urios-Aparisi, Eduardo. 2016. "Stormy Weather: An Intercultural Approach to the Water-Metaphor in Cinema." In *Embodied Metaphors in Film, Television, and Video Games: Cognitive Approaches*, edited by Kathrin Fahlenbrach, 67–81. London/New York: Routledge.

Vermeulen, Timotheus, and Rustad, Gruy C. 2013. "Watching Television with Jacques Rancière: US 'Quality Television', *Mad Men* and the 'Late Cut.'" *Screen* 54: 341–354.

14 Repetition, familiarity, and aesthetic pleasure

Formulaic generic television series

Iris Vidmar Jovanović

The longevity of some of the longest-running genre fiction television series suggests that these shows inspire and reward continual viewers' interest over an extensive period of time. Now in its 23rd season, *Law and Order: Special Victims Unit* (NBC 1999–) is still a roaring success and attracting millions of viewers with each new episode, as do numerous similar crime fiction series. *Criminal Minds* (CBS) has been around since 2005; *NCIS: Naval Criminal Investigative Service* (CBS) was originally released in 2003 and is still piling up episodes; and *Bones* (Fox) ran for 12 years, as did *NYPD Blue* (NBC). Hospital dramas routinely hold attention for over a decade, as evidenced by *ER* (NBC 1994–2009), and some courtroom dramas, such as *The Practice* (ABC1997–2004) and *L.A. Law* (NBC 1986–1994), compiled hundreds of episodes before their termination. My aim in this chapter is to explore what sustains such *long-term interest*, given that viewers are usually well familiar with genre-characteristic storylines, repeatedly found *in series pertaining to the same genre*, and with the series-specific manner of implementing such stories, repeatedly instantiated *in episodes pertaining to the same series*.

To answer this question, I look at some of the currently dominant theories on the appeal of mass art and television programs.[1] In particular, Noël Carroll's work on junk fiction (1994) and mass art (1998, 2013) goes a long way towards explaining why we like familiar generic stories, but, I'll argue, not far enough to explain the prolonged appeal of the two-tiered familiarity of generic television series. The long-term appeal of such series raises a particular puzzle given the extremely high level of repetitious, formulaic structures repeatedly implemented in their episodes. As stand-alone units that tell individual stories, episodes pertaining to a series exhibit salient homogeneity with respect to subject and theme, plot development, ensemble of recurrent characters and their interactions, narrative structures, dramatic situations and their resolutions, and the overall aesthetic design – notwithstanding, of course, a surprise here or there.[2] Having seen but a few episodes, one can get a rough idea of how others will play out, as it is easy to identify the underlying formulaic patterns around which structural, narrative, thematic, and aesthetic details are developed and with minor modifications, repeatedly reprised from one episode to the next. In light of such two-tiered familiarity – familiarity with the genre-characteristic

DOI: 10.4324/9781003188643-14

stories and familiarity with the series-specific details of developing such stories episodically – the paradox of junk fiction has a double force in the context of generic television series. However, rather than asking about viewers' rationality in watching such stories, as Carroll does, I ask: Why do viewers remain interested in a series that tells roughly the same stories in the same manner over an extended period of time?

Presupposing that formulaic generic series' continual appeal invites more philosophical attention than received so far, I set out to explore factors that might constitute it. I take them to be inherently connected to the *fictional world* of particular series: To the details of what the spectators experience and to the kinds of cognitive and emotional engagements that these worlds invite. The solution I offer recognizes the combined attraction of appealing characters struggling in circumstances that keep attracting viewers' attention in light of the particular kind of intellectual interest and emotional bonds they develop with the characters. I proceed as follows. In the first part, I analyze some of the solutions to the paradox of junk fiction in order to show why they cannot accommodate the case of generic series. In the second part, I develop my account.

The paradox of generic television series

Genre fiction television programs, such as crime, hospital, and legal series, are nowadays one of the most widely consumed forms of mass art. On Noël Carroll's (1985, 1998) view, the wide appeal of mass art relates primarily to its easy accessibility – no significant cognitive effort is needed to grasp such art. To secure such easy access, mass art relies on structures that are widely familiar to consumers, one of which is genre.[3] As numerous scholars working on genre have pointed out, viewers have empirically based working knowledge of specific norms that regulate the development of generic stories. Such "stereotyped knowledge reservoirs of the imaginary" (Schweinitz 2011, 57–58) consist of the relevant schemas used to organize the content and development of stories by series-makers and viewers alike. The audiences know prior to watching a crime fiction story that its content is going to reverberate around good guys chasing bad guys. Whether the good guys are hardboiled detectives tormented by the horrors they see on a daily basis, forensic experts of the highest moral and epistemic virtues, or experts in behavioral psychology makes little difference to viewers' capacity to understand what is going on. As Raphaëlle Moine explains, "The pleasure of a genre does not derive from prolonged suspense, but rather from the reaffirmation of conventions that the viewer knows and recognizes" (2008, 102). In a similar vein, on Thomas Roberts's (1990) account, when we read generic stories, we are in fact observing how a particular story relates to, and differs from, other stories of the same genre. When we read generic fiction, he argues, we "read in a system," and the satisfaction is derived from the system more than from the stories. Carroll (1994) disagrees. We read for the stories, not for the genre, he argues, but this raises the paradox: Given the extremely limited and highly familiar repertoire of story-types available in formulaic genre fiction, why do we keep attending to them? On Carroll's (1994, 1998) view, familiarity with the stories enhances our pleasure because it enables us to exercise certain interpretative activities, such as filling in presuppositions and making moral and emotional judgments with respect to the events described. Such "transactional values" we get from these stories neutralize their familiarity, as we take recourse to what we know about the general structure of such stories in order to predict how the one we are attending to will develop. Familiarity with the stories makes it possible for the viewers to participate in the guessing game of "who did it" while also exercising moral judgments over the details of why someone did it. There is nothing irrational in attending to generic stories we already know, Carroll concludes, as long as we use that knowledge to reinforce our interpretive skills.

Despite their differences, Carroll's and Roberts's accounts are complementary and give us a resourceful framework within which to search for an explanation of our continued interest in generic television series. The mere fact that so many series of the same genre catch spectators' attention supports the idea that viewers are interested in the genre itself, as an interest in seeing how a particular series develops generic norms is a powerful motivation for viewers to attend to a series in the first place. The grand success of the *CSI* franchise had a lot to do with, at the time, unfamiliar techniques in the forensic sciences that the series brought into view. Various cross-generic mergings, such as *Law and Order*'s integration of police procedural and courtroom drama, make for an interesting and inviting combination, keeping viewers alert to the narrative, thematic, and aesthetic possibilities of both genres. Introducing novelties with respect to generic characters, as *Castle* does by incorporating a fiction writer into a homicide investigation team, is a good strategy for diversifying the stereotyped characters' interaction, as are modifications with respect to homogeneous pairs of regularly appearing characters – *Elementary*'s female Watson (Lucy Liu) allowed the series to introduce a romantic note and sexual tension to what might have been yet another "detective and side-kick" pair. "Watching in the system" explains attending to individual series, as viewers stay attentive to see how the next episode in line will instantiate the formulaic patterns characteristic of the series itself. Such watching, I maintain, is indicative of viewers' exercising their interpretive skills and moral assessments along the lines suggested by Carroll. With series like *Poirot* or *The Mentalist*, viewers follow the main detectives in order to identify the culprit, with particular care towards clues they get from the pool of potential suspects. Series that are more open towards social and psychological realism, such as the *Law and Order* franchise, offer plenty of opportunities to exercise moral and emotional judgments, as viewers are constantly invited to take sides with respect to the moral puzzles depicted by the show.

The role of familiarity in maintaining aesthetic pleasure that underlies Carroll's and Roberts's accounts has been supported by recent research in cognitive aesthetics (Hogan 2016; Berliner 2017). As an audience, we like to see something new in what we are otherwise familiar with. Such a balance fits best with our need to be cognitively challenged but not to the point where too much effort is needed to track the novelties introduced into what we already know and can easily absorb. This "familiarity balances novelty thesis" explains why we feel comfortable when watching an episode of a show we know well or a show whose generic affiliation is familiar to us: Particularities of the episode are new and thus motivate us to stay focused and follow the action, which we can easily do since we are familiar with the series' overall design, plot lines, and recurring characters.

However, with respect to generic series' longevity, both Carroll's and Roberts's accounts face the same problem: Isn't there a point when too much familiarity is just – well, too much? Having seen several episodes of a series, we know how it reaffirms the conventions, how it develops stereotypes, and how it awards our genre-preferences. Shouldn't we assume that with the accumulation of episodes, the aesthetics of the show, the sharpness of its stories, the suspense of its dramatic situations, the aesthetics of its design, and the appeal of its characters will wear off? Going into an episode, we know that Horatio (David Caruso) will outsmart the baddies and that House (Hugh Laurie) will have an epiphany just in time to save the patient. Even if we enjoy the action sequences regularly depicted in a series, sooner or later, their "wow" effect diminishes – how often, after all, can we be swept off our feet by Sherlock's skills of deduction, amused by Monk's pathologies, or horrified by *Criminal Minds*' deviant psychopaths? Having seen 200 episodes of *CSI*, little do we marvel at the state-of-the-art forensic technology in the remaining 135 episodes, and hardly are we fascinated by flashy colors and sporty cars if we regularly feast on *Miami Vice*. The longevity of a show neutralizes its capacity to entertain when formulaic patterns are episodically implemented. In the course of the seven years that it took the *Mentalist*'s Patrick Jane (Simon Baker) to catch Red John and marry his boss (Robin Tunney), his unorthodox methods of investigation became predictable, and his witty remarks lost their sharpness. Long-time exposure to a series might tone down the pleasures of transactional value, as the regular reaffirmation of certain clues, like old family portraits in *Poirot*, diminishes the appeal of the interpretive activities for viewers.

Similar worries plague Roberts' account. An interest in *how* a series develops generic patterns is satisfied by seeing several of its episodes – usually, the pilot suffices to instruct and educate the audience on what the series brings into view and how it differs from the next series in the same generic line. Once viewers recognized that the role traditionally awarded to detectives was delegated to forensic experts in *CSI*, it was crime business as usual – not much was left to decipher afterwards, as Grissom (William Petersen) did roughly the same as Sipowitz (Dennis Franz). More than an interest in the system is needed to account for the long-term commitment to the series, even if the relevant system is the series, not the genre. It is unlikely that the audience will stick to the show in the long run if they are only interested in episodic modifications – particularly because such modifications are not regularly inserted into episodes, as series are by definition generated by multiplying the same kinds of structures. Were a series to introduce significant modifications on a regular basis, it would not count as formulaic in the sense which I am concerned with here.

Carroll and Roberts, it seems, can account for viewers' non-discriminatory interest in formulaic generic series on offer but have difficulties explaining their longevity. Building on the grounds they provide, I turn to explaining the phenomenon of longevity, taking further into consideration another aspect of spectators' engagements with mass art that does not feature in the two accounts: The fact that viewers often have their preferred series, even among those that are part of the same franchise, such as *Law and Order*, or are generated into existence as spin-offs. Series pertaining to the *CSI* franchise are saliently similar with respect to *how* they reaffirm the generic norms, and *Law and Order* and *Law and Order: Special Victims Unit* offer saliently similar opportunities for implementing one's interpretive skills, moral judgments, and emotional appraisal. However, a fervent spectator of the latter would not rest satisfied with the former, and neither would a *CSI: Miami* fan give it up for the original *CSI*. A different explanation is needed to account for the spectators' continual interest in their preferred formulaic series, one that takes into consideration the plausibility of Carroll's and Roberts' solutions but can also accommodate the highly formulaic episodic form of these series, their longevity, and the fact that spectators have preferences. Let us, then, turn to providing such an explanation.

Sustaining long-term interest in formulaic generic television series

Our discussion so far has shown that pointing to the pleasures of familiarity does not explain the paradox of junk fiction, if the junk fiction in question comprises generic series: The homogeneity of episodes threatens to suffocate such pleasures by continually providing saliently similar kinds of stimuli to the audience. Part of the explanation as to why viewers attend to a particular series relates to factors that are external to the series itself, such as a series' genre, producers, network, scheduling time on TV, advertisement and fandom surrounding it, etc. Such factors have more to do with the series *as an artifact* than with its *particular fictional world* (Plantinga 2009; Maes 2017). The difference is blurry – arguably, many of the features of the artifact determine many of the features of the fictional world generated by the artifact – but it does explain a distinction between audiences' *motivation* to initially attend to a series and their *long-term interest* in it. Factors related to the series as artifact cannot explain such interest for roughly the same reasons why Roberts's take on junk fiction does not work: None of these factors suffices, jointly or separately, to ensure viewers' repeated return to episodes from one season to the next. What we need, then, is an explanation of why the series becomes a source of repeated pleasure for the viewers – factors, in other words, that explain why we, as Hans Maes (2017) would put it, love it!

The first such factor relates to the actors. Actors' performances are a particularly rich source of aesthetic pleasure, and it is plausible to claim that the aesthetic and artistic appeal of some series (think of *Poirot* or *Columbo*) and serials (*Breaking Bad* and the *Sopranos*) is greatly advanced by actors' performances. Star actors are powerful bait for the audience – Halle Berry, Kevin Spacey, and Jennifer Lopez most likely triggered some to attend to the science fiction (*Extant*), political (*House of Cards*), and detective (*Shades of Blue*) dramas they starred in, respectively, independently of audience's genre-preferences. The "star" status of TV actors might not be as influential as that of film actors, but it is not as negligible a factor as is usually the case with soap opera actors, exceptions aside (see Butler 1995). Other factors potentially inviting the audience come to mind, such as actors' reprising generic roles in different series as different characters. David Caruso's and Kim Delaney's performances in *NYPD Blue* made them popular with the audience; no wonder that spectators were curious to see them transform from traditional cops into forensic experts when they joined forces in *CSI: Miami*. Genre-determined slots, stereotyped as they are, offer limited space for an actor to exhibit his or her skills, making it all the more inviting to see their performances and evaluate them on those bases – think about the interest surrounding the performance of Ted Danson, famous for his roles in comedies, upon entering the world of crime drama. The fact that more often than not, a character disappears from the series when an actor quits the show speaks in favor of the actor's (rather than the character's) centrality to the series' appeal.

However, we should not put all the emphasis on the actors. While I am certainly not denying actors' enormous contribution to the appeal of a series and a particular character, the question here isn't whether we gain satisfaction from an actor's performance but whether such satisfaction might account for the sustained interest in a series in the long run, and this I find questionable. On the one hand, there is a phenomenological difference in caring for the actor as opposed to caring for the character: we are worried for Benson's, not Hargitay's, wellbeing when she is assaulted – though we may admire Hargitay's portrayal of Benson – and we admire Hargitay, not Benson, for setting up the Joyful Heart Foundation.[4] Moreover, actors come and go, but series remain – David Caruso leaving *NYPD Blue* or Chris Meloni leaving *L&O: SVU* shows that series can survive the loss of their stars, while Berry's incapacity to salvage *Extant* indicates that sometimes, not even stars can be sufficiently inviting. Examples, of course, work in the other direction, as so many fans of *The X-Files* who still mourn David Duchovny's exit know all too well. The relevant difference might have to do with the overall character distribution in relation to the series' focus. Series that feature numerous characters in formulaic generic roles – doctors, lawyers, detectives – are arguably less affected by the loss of the particular actor/character duo, particularly if such changes are scattered throughout several seasons. It took 15 seasons for *CSI* to lose its audience, although most of the original cast was long gone by then. On the other hand, character-based series face harder challenges when they lose the actor and have to go on without the character. The novelty and the appeal of *The X-Files* was not only in fueling crime genre stories with extra-terrestrial villains but also with invigorating the detective pair's chemistry by having them repeatedly clash over one's belief in the supernatural and the other's faith in science. With Duchovny's exit, both of these plotlines were compromised. The attempt to invigorate the series by turning Scully (Gillian Anderson) into a believer and putting her in Mulder's position with respect to Doggett's (Robert Patrick) skepticism did not work for viewers who had seen it before with the original plotline. For a series whose main appeal revolved around the dialectics of a particular couple and the mutual chemistry of particular actors, the absence of both a character and an actor was too much to handle.

Our discussion so far testifies to the strength of the alluring power of what Murray Smith (1995, 2011a) calls "the twofoldedness of character."[5] In watching a fictional character, Smith claims, we are aware not only of "virtual persons," whom we respond to as if they were actual people but also of their "configurational aspect" – the fact that characters are embodied by performers and that they serve a particular role within the artifact that is a fictional world. With respect to generic television series, let me add, such awareness is additionally fueled by what we know about the stereotypical generic character slots definitive of a particular genre. Convinced by Carroll's (2013) take on star personae, I am inclined to add yet another aspect of character-foldedness: Characters resonate with the audience in light of the actors embodying them, but sometimes, it is the character who lives on in the audience's mind – how many, after all, see David Suchet, as opposed to Poirot, in *The Bank Job*? On the whole, however, more than the recognition of the relevance of an actor is needed to explain my concern here. Part of viewers' interest in a series – recall Roberts – is an interest in seeing how it portrays yet another detective or yet another doctor. However, "recognizing" a character, as Smith puts it, and enjoying its two-, three-, or more-foldedness, I argue, is still not enough to sustain viewers' long-term commitment in the absence of additional inviting factors. *In the long run*, viewers primarily attend to the series for the satisfaction it provides when one engages with the fictional worlds it generates, *repeatedly* and *continually*, from one episode to the next. What gives us pleasure is watching a particular character in a particular set of intellectually stimulating circumstances derived from the fictional world: Pitching these together, so that neither can be modified without the loss of aesthetic appeal, is crucial in keeping viewers committed to the series in the long run.

Engaging, entertaining, and thought-provoking fictional worlds

There are different ways in which fictional worlds can be engaging. For all the fun we have in watching House bending the rules when it comes to patients' rights, the professional code of conduct, and pretty much everything in between, the series problematizes medical and bioethical concerns and shows moral conundrums underlying our health service. Although the approach it takes to these themes is devoid of any theoretical background that surrounds such issues in more formal contexts, its ease in depicting the topics makes the series all the more accessible, by Carroll's criteria, to an untrained audience. As an extra bonus, viewers get to understand what is at stake in various social practices. The appeal of an intellectually stimulating fictional world is quite evident in the case of crime fiction and courtroom dramas. *The Practice* repeatedly gave viewers a chance to look into the legal system and to probe its underlying rationale, challenging along the way the permeable distinction between ethical and legal, guilty and innocent. The themes of victims' rights as opposed to the perpetrators', or the state's authority in the face of personal freedoms, were episodically contextualized and thus developed into concrete cases rather than abstract principles, as did numerous issues ranging from euthanasia to self-defense.

Fascination with the crime genre and the fact that it has so often and so continuously served as a mirror into the real world, a source of beliefs regarding the operation of the criminal justice system and an instrument for probing its foundations, hint at the possibility that viewers continuously attend to it because it responds to the uncertainties and moral conundrums that viewers encounter in their daily experience. Notably, this isn't always the case with genre series; character-based series such as *Columbo* hardly ever engage in any substantial way with social concerns, and the appeal they exhibit is best explained by the unique mixture of intriguing, inviting characters and particularly pleasurable ways of developing genre-determined formulas. Rather than inviting reflection on challenging themes, these series provide entertainment, where the central focus of interest for the viewers is the main character and his particular way of being in the world. However, some of the most popular contemporary series are open to embracing social realism, and their popularity is related to tackling issues that are relevant for the viewers, who, in turn, feel challenged to reflectively engage with these issues. Series are thus continuing a trend set by soap operas, which often served as a platform for highlighting social issues not publicly debated in other ways (Hayward 1992; Katzman 1972; LaPota and LaPota 1973). In light of 9/11, the war on terrorism, and ethical issues triggered by it, an explanation that insists on the embeddedness of TV series in the real world explains the sustained interest in series systematically tackling terrorism, surveillance, torture, and human rights, such as *24* (Fox, 2001–2010 – though *24* is not episodically formulaic, unlike my main examples, it does work by seasonally implementing the same formula, similarly to *Prison Break* or *Dexter*) or *NCIS* (CBS 2003–). An even more compelling case is *L&O: SVU*, famous and repeatedly praised for providing a public platform for discussion on sexual crimes in the widest sense of the word. While the series' thematic concerns are constant – crimes of a sexual nature – the particular instances of such crimes, the circumstances in which these happen, and their various aftermaths are extremely heterogeneous. Consequently, every episodic case, while formulaic in depicting certain kinds of crimes and detectives' methods in solving them, is original in portraying the much wider context of particular crimes. In addition, the series relentlessly scrutinizes social institutions, from police procedures and the legal system, medical practices and the educational system to the United States' external and internal politics, giving viewers an insight into the operation of these practices and more importantly, a chance to actively engage (via fandom, internet sites, or small talk) in issues raised by certain thematic concerns driving individual episodes. At least some of these issues permeate either the personal or the social experience of viewers, and watching a show enables them to engage with these concerns in diverse contexts and from varying perspectives.

A prominent way in which series cash out the relevance of thematic concerns is by making them personal to the inhabitants of the fictional world, namely, the characters. As many have suggested, characters are the key aspect of viewers' engagement with works of narrative art. My take on this claim, in the context of television series' longevity, is to suggest that the factor most responsible for keeping viewers committed to a series has to do with the recurrent characters within a series and the emotional reaction they inspire in viewers. Unlike some philosophers, I am not committed to the claim that emotional experience is the most rewarding aspect of our engagements with narrative, mostly because I think reflective engagements with thematic concerns make up a substantial part of it. However, my claim here is that fictional characters invite emotional bonding, which plays a crucial role in sustaining viewers' engagement with a series. On the whole, the way characters relate to the thematic concerns makes up the richness and depth of our sense of satisfaction provided by series.

Fictional characters as human beings

A long-term interest in a series is sustained when viewers take *internal perspective* on its characters, i.e., start to consider them as real human beings rather than as textual presentations, narrative construction, a product of filmmakers and actors' performances (Thomasson 2003; Lamarque 2010). This process is much more complex than the notions of sympathy and empathy – the two most popular views on character-engagements currently on offer – suggest. It is crucial in this process to assess characters in light of their ethical, psychological, emotional, and other real-world character traits not determined by genre. It is an interest in humans, in their personal stories, that explains why the highly formulaic nature of generic series is not an obstacle to viewers' sustained engagement. As long as a series keeps addressing the audience's interests along these lines, the continual return of the audience is secured.

Various explanations are on offer as to why we are intrigued by others, including fictional others. From simulation theory and theory of mind (see Currie 1995, 2016), to theories that emphasize our empathic responses (Plantinga 1999; Vaage 2010; Smith 2011b),[6] evolutionary theories (Davies 2012) and theories that more specifically explicate circumstances in which individuals develop an interest in particular characters (Robinson 2005), to first-hand experience of (dis)liking certain characters, plenty of evidence suggests that we care for the characters as much as, if not more than, for what happens next in the story. And given the formulaic nature of TV series, the "what happens next" variations are limited to those outcomes that the genre allows, notwithstanding occasional departures from the stereotypical stories. Consequently, it is the caring relationships we develop towards the characters, mixed with curiosity with respect to what happens to them, that keep us motivated to return to the series, in the long run, after the novelty of the series fades.

To properly explain how my account differs from other theories on character-engagements on offer, let me elaborate on the two accounts most similar to mine and show why they are insufficient in the face of series' longevity and viewers' preferences. Noël Carroll (2013) argued that emotional responses we develop to the characters are "the ties that bind" us to works of mass art. In order to secure such ties, mass art presents characters that are either likable or dislikable, mostly due to their moral valence: They deserve our love and sympathy because they are morally praiseworthy or our contempt in light of their rotten nature. On the first go, this seems right. Who would, after all, dislike Grissom's (or Hotchner's (Thomas Gibson) or Rush's (Kathryn Morris)) selfless dedication to finding the culprit at the expense of their safety and wellbeing, and who would deny that Benson is still one of our favorite detectives in light of her unyielding fight against sexual deviants? Even when characters deviate from the path of moral supremacy, as they occasionally do – think of Sipowitz's alcoholism and homophobia – we still love them because in the end, they *are* the good guys.

However, Carroll's solution might be too general in the context of television series – his examples are all from films. Because genres are determined by characteristic story-types and by repeatedly appearing types of characters, the overall character distribution does not vary significantly from one series to the next one of the same genre. Poirot, Derek Morgan, Scotty Valens, Olivia Benson, and Temperance Brennan occupy the same genre-determined slot and perform the same function within the fictional world of a crime fiction story – that of a detective (see Jenner 2016; Lamarque 2010; Malmgren 2010) – and are thus a priori inviting of viewers' sympathy. Based only on Carroll's criterion of moral valence, they are all likable. Empirically, however, viewers have preferences with respect to characters, both interserially and intraserially, which suggests that the ties that bind us are more complex than like versus dislike. There are morally praiseworthy detectives who annoy us, even though they are doing what all the good guys are doing: Fighting crime. Moreover, most of the regular characters in quality television series are far more psychologically complex than Carroll's distinction – morally praiseworthy versus morally blameworthy – leaves room for. For all the similarities in moral and epistemic virtues of Grissom, Taylor (Gary Sinise), and Caine (David Caruso), the three characters are worlds apart, as are Amaro and Valens, even though both are embodied by Danny Pino. A defining aspect of quality television is the characters' development and complexity, and our interest in such characters is motivated by our desire to understand them and our curiosity about what happens to them. This isn't to say that characters don't invite the pro-attitude of sympathetic care – certainly, as Carroll argues, such an interest accommodates a wide variety of responses we have for them. However, our interest in them is characterized not only by our sympathy (even empathy) for them but, as I will show, by our overall interest in their life-story and their personality.

Another prominent account of viewers' long-term commitment is the one developed by Robert Blanchet and Margrethe Bruun Vaage (2012). Reiterating cognitive sciences' view on the role of familiarity in enjoyment, they "suggest that it is pleasurable to engage with characters in television series partly because, *after a season or two*, we *have become so used to them and know them so well*" (2012, 24; my emphasis). This is certainly right, but what worries me about this suggestion is that it doesn't answer the question of why we would stick with a series "for a season or two" if we didn't find something appealing in it *prior to* the time needed for "becoming used to characters and loving them." The caring relations that they speak of – the metaphor of friendship they use – only develop after a prolonged exposure (a season or two, as they suggest). Certainly, at that point, familiarity plays an important role in our moral evolution of characters (as Vaage (2014) argues, convincingly, in other work), but – to reiterate my point – it is not clear what motivates viewers to stay committed to a series for that long. Furthermore, the familiarity by itself hardly suffices to keep viewers' interest if they do not have deeper reasons to attend to the series – I am well familiar with my neighbor's out-of-tune singing but would much rather skip it than attend to her singing concert, just as the familiarity of annoying jingle commercials does not inspire me to play them on repeat. Blanchet and Vaage also do not take into consideration the fact that viewers have preferences among characters they are equally familiar with. Numerous series featuring numerous characters are regularly on TV, providing equal opportunities for viewers to become "used to them," but viewers make choices regarding the shows they attend to *regularly and care for profoundly*. Moreover, viewers have preferences with respect to the characters within a series. Although the set of recurrent characters is, exceptions aside, permanent throughout a season, even from one season to the next, viewers have their preferred characters independently of how familiar with the cast they are overall.

The emotional bonds we develop with the characters that populate our generic fictional worlds cannot be explicated via sympathy for or familiarity with them, as these two approaches do not consider the complexity of such characters and viewers' preferences. On my suggestion, considering such characters as real people can explain these bonds. The question before us now is this: How does an interest in a character-as-person existing in a particular fictional world counterbalance the underlying tediousness of formulaic generic series?

Solving the paradox: Characters, longevity, and preferences

I suggested earlier that it is by virtue of compressing psychologically complex characters and the intellectually stimulating circumstances in which they find themselves that viewers keep *returning* to a series. An interest in character-as-human-being is motivated by the details of a character's personal story, his or her "significant life events" (O'Meara 2015) that jointly and successively add up to who the character is, what is happening to him, and how he reacts to these events. From one episode to the next, characters develop their personal stories, thus transcending their genre-specific functions and formulaic patterns of interaction definitive of a genre. Lily Rush and Olivia Benson occupy the same genre-specific slot, perform the same function within their fictional worlds, and are even similar with respect to a character-type – both are lone female detectives tormented by conflicts with their loveless alcoholic mothers, struggling to establish themselves as equals to their male partners, firmly committed to their jobs, and unwilling to compromise their moral code. However, differences accumulate as the series progress, as each outgrows the genre-determined slot and becomes a psychologized individual. While we know what a detective will do given the conventions of a genre, we are curious to see how a particular character – Benson or Rush or any other of our favorites – will do it, given the particularities of her personal story. To the extent that we are interested in what happens to people, we will be interested in what happens to the characters in the fictional world – though only while they contribute to mimetic lines of the series. Once Stabler (Chris Meloni) retired, he became irrelevant for the series' episodic cases, though he remained a powerful presence for Benson's personal story.

Different narrative techniques enable personal stories to develop. Series often organize their content so that initial episodes of the first season bring to the fore series-specific formulaic patterns, introduce the recurrent characters, and provide a framework for their future interactions – for example, the pilot episode of *CSI: Crime Scene Investigation* introduces the viewers to motives repeatedly depicted in subsequent episodes, such as Warwick's (Gary Dourdan) gambling issues. As the series progresses, more space is given to characters' individuation and personalization – a process whereby each becomes a rounded individual rather than an executioner of a genre-specific, stereotyped character-slot. Depending on how central to the plot a certain character is, more or less space is given to her individuation, and more details from her personal story become relevant for plot lines. Some episodes unite a particular moral, social, or political concern with characters' individual situations, as when *L&O: SVU* channels homophobic and hate crimes through the character of Fin's (Ice-T) son. Occasionally, the two aspects are merged, as when Hotchner searches for the man who killed his wife or when House's team members become his patients.

Characters' individual storylines are not constrained within episodes but extend from one to another, accumulatively adding bits to the arc story of a character, thus creating ongoing stories that transcend individual episodes and seasons and postpone narrative closure, as is typical of series. Given that characters' storylines extend throughout seasons, they are, in principle, as open-ended as the series itself. To keep track of what happens to the characters, viewers need to pay attention to events that relate to them, following characters' reactions to these events and the aftermaths of these events for the characters and for the series' subsequent storylines – in other words, they have to attend to a sequence of episodes. The search for Mr. Scratch (Bodhi Elfman) drew the action of most episodes in seasons 11 to 13 of *Criminal Minds*, affecting the individual stories of all the characters to the point where the boundary between episodic cases and personal stories was occasionally annihilated. Many formulaic shows are series-like, in that they keep reprising series-specific formulaic ways of implementing generic norms, and serials-like in characters' storylines, thus resembling the plots typical of soap operas: Searching for love, finding it, messing it up, being at the mercy of external forces, and the like. A difference, however, from the character stories in series as opposed to soap operas is that they remain connected to the series' genre-specific subject, occasionally personalizing the stories – as when detectives end up fighting criminals who are after them or their families – but never entirely defamiliarizing series' formulaic patterns. In other words, many of their personal events are merged with who they are as generic characters, and even when the spotlight is turned on a character rather than on the mimetic focus of the series, the action sequences remain formulaic – Hotchner relies on behavioral analysis to find Foyet (C. Thomas Howell), and House employs his usual mastery in diagnosing Thirteen (Olivia Wilde). In other words, the serial aspect of generic series does not annihilate the paradox, because independently of the details of characters' personal stories, the solutions to their dramatic situations are provided by what is unique to the series in question: Thirteen can only be saved by House's diagnostics, while Foyet is ultimately tracked down due to Hotchner's excellence in behavioral analysis. From the narrative perspective, series are not as character-based as serials, as they necessarily remain primarily an instrument of executing genre-characteristic story-types. Only exceptionally is the focus of an entire episode exclusively on a character's story. Throughout the season, each episode presents a new problem, and solving that particular problem takes most of the running time. Personal stories of characters develop over entire seasons, but from one episode to the next, such stories remain secondary to the main storyline. Awareness of these two aspects – series' generic stories and characters' personal stories – influences viewers' emotional reactions to characters and their narrative and character desires (Currie 1999). We empathize with Jane's pain over the death of his family and want him to get his revenge, all the while knowing that if this happens, the series will come to its end.

In addition to securing viewers' return to the next episode, an interest in a character (or characters) can be a powerful mechanism that keeps viewers alert to thematic issues they might be unaware of, independently of the stimuli provided by the series. It is also a platform for addressing social and other concerns, as when repeated references to mental disorder in relation to Stabler help raise awareness of mental health issues. In the course of attending to a series, viewers are not only interested in (as Smith puts it) "recognizing and aligning" with characters but start forming "allegiances" with them, loving some and disliking others. Such bonding emotions are not developed indiscriminately; spectators "pick and choose," consciously or not, whom they prefer. How exactly this happens is not easy to explain, but I think Jenefer Robinson (2005) has a point in insisting on recognizing the similarities between our own concerns and those of the characters we feel attached to. Patrick Colm Hogan (2016) shows how one's aesthetic preferences are determined by one's memories and formative experiences in addition to publicly available standards of beauty and stimuli that one is repeatedly exposed to. Such an account explains why different people fall for different characters, fictional and otherwise, particularly if we assume that a character's appeal embraces that character's traits in addition to his looks. Arguably, our own experiences and affective memories have a role in aligning us with certain characters and distancing us from certain others, as does the extent to which we share characters' moral code and value system. These are the nuances that set apart different stereotyped characters who are all, in Carroll's sense, morally deserving of our sympathy, and explain why we care for some but not for others. If the overall character distribution does not seem appealing to a viewer, she might not develop an interest in a series, independently of her genre-preferences. Naturally, it takes more than a pilot to align with a character – familiarity is, doubtlessly, a relevant factor – but that is still a long way from sticking to the series for a "season or two," particularly given the numerous series on offer. If the characters are not sufficiently engaging, viewers might give up on a series even if it falls into their preferred genre. The fact that *Criminal Minds: Suspect Behavior* did not manage to live up to the standards set by *Criminal Minds* has to do with the fact that the character ensemble of the original series captivated viewers' attention in a more profound way. Not only are their personal stories more inviting and better embedded within the series' overall thematic concerns, but their interactions are structurally more intertwined – look no further than the attachments that the character of Garcia shares with other team members in *Criminal Minds*. Lacking such attachments, her character, though not her genre-determined role, seems out of place in the spin-off.

Conclusion

My concern in this chapter was the long-lasting appeal of generic television series. I argued that they are imbued with double familiarity – familiarity with genre-characteristic storylines and with the series-specific manner of implementing such stories episodically – and thus give rise to a variation of the junk fiction paradox. Building upon the grounds provided by Roberts and Carroll, I developed an account of how the particular fictional world of a series, and in particular its characters, sustain and maintain viewers' interest and return to the series.

I argued that formulaic nature is not an obstacle to aesthetic pleasure because it is diluted by the details of the fictional world created by a series and by characters' storylines *not entirely* determined by the genre. Such storylines relate to characters acting not solely as genre-slot executioners but as fully rounded, individuated, personalized people with their own psychological, ethical, political, sexual, and other traits. Emphasizing the impact of an interest in characters-as-human-beings in a particular fictional world explains the interest in accumulation of episodes, i.e., a series' longevity: once characters grow out of their genre-specific roles, their stories are potentially open-ended, allowing the series to grow. In addition, I argued that an interest in particular characters explains why viewers have a preference for a particular series against others of the same genre.

My account is not meant to explain generic preferences and is not intended as a "one fits all solution." I take the factors I emphasize as relevant for inspiring aesthetic pleasure and sustaining viewers' interest as the most effective, though not unique, for this job. However, their implementation and mutual reinforcement always remain liable to numerous circumstantial factors – as always in life and show business, sometimes they work and sometimes they do not.[7]

Notes

1 Carroll (1994, 1985, 2013); Nannicelli (2016).
2 For an account of series – serials distinction, see Kazloff (1992); Mittell (2006); Andrzejewski and Salwa (2018); Nannicelli (2010).
3 Carroll (2013). For a theory of genre, see Bavarshi (2000); Currie (2004); Mittell (2015); Knight (1997); Schweinitz (2011); Moine (2008).
4 http://www.joyfulheartfoundation.org/tags/mariska-hargitay
5 See also Johannes (2010); Perez (2015).
6 I share Carroll's (2011) worries regarding empathy, which is partly a reason why I am, in this chapter, more concerned with elaboration on the notion of internal perspectives on characters as human beings. We can certainly empathize with such beings, but as evident from my take on sympathy, we can exhaust our engagement with fictional characters by putting it all on empathy.
7 I am grateful to Hector Perez and Ted Nannicelli for their helpful comments on the earlier draft of this paper.

References

Andrzejewski, Adam, and Mateusz Salwa. 2018. *Law and TV Series*. Leiden: Brill.

Berliner, Todd. 2017. *Hollywood Aesthetic: Pleasure in American Cinema*. Oxford: Oxford University Press.

Blanchet, Robert, and Margrethe Bruun Vaage. 2012. "Don, Peggy, and Other Fictional Friends? Engaging with Characters in Television Series." *Projections* 6, no. 2: 18–41.

Butler, Jeremy G. 1995. "'I am Not a Doctor, But I Play One on TV.' Characters, Actors and Acting in Television Soap Opera." In *To Be Continued: Soap Operas Around the World*, edited by Robert Allen Robert, 145–163. London: Routledge.

Carl, Malmgren. 2010. "The Pursuit of Crime: Characters in Crime Fiction." In *A Companion to Crime Fiction*, edited by Rzepka Charles and Lee Horsley. Wiley Blackwel.

Carroll, Noël. 1985. "The Power of Movies." *Daedalus* 114, no. 4: 79–103.

Carroll, Noël. 1994. "The Paradox of Junk Fiction." *Philosophy and Literature* 18, no. 2: 225–241.

Carroll, Noël. 1998. *A Philosophy of Mass Art*. Oxford: Oxford University Press.

Carroll, Noël. 2011. "On Some Affective Relations between Audiences and the Characters in Popular Fictions." In *Empathy: Philosophical and Psychological Perspectives*, edited by Amy Coplan and Peter Goldie, 162–184. Oxford: Oxford University Press.

Carroll, Noël. 2013. *Minerva's Night Out: Philosophy, Pop Culture and Moving Pictures*. Malden, MA: Wiley-Blackwell.

Currie, Gregory. 1995. *Image and Mind: Film, Philosophy, and Cognitive Science*. Cambridge: Cambridge University Press.

Currie, Gregory. 1999. "Narrative Desire." In *Passionate Views: Film, Cognition, and Emotion*, edited by Carl Plantinga and Greg M. Smith, 183–199. Baltimore: The Johns Hopkins University Press.

Currie, Gregory. 2016. "Literature and 'Theory of Mind.'" In *The Routledge Companion to Philosophy of Literature*, edited by Noël Carroll and John Gibson, 419–429. New York: Routledge.

Davies, Stephen. 2012. *The Artful Species: Aesthetics, Art and Evolution*. Oxford: Oxford University Press.

Hayward, Jennifer. 1992. "'Day after Tomorrow': Audience Interaction and Soap Opera Production." *Cultural Critique* 23: 83–109.

Hogan, Patrick Colm. 2016. *Beauty and Sublimity: A Cognitive Aesthetics of Literature and the Arts*. Cambridge: Cambridge University Press.

James, Mittell. 2015. *Complex TV and the Poetics of Contemporary Television Storytelling*. New York: New York Press.

Jenner, Mareike. 2016. *American TV Detective Dramas: Serial Investigations*. Basingstoke: Palgrave Macmillan.

Katzman, Natan. 1972. "Television Soap Operas: What's Been Going on Anyway?" *The Public Opinion Quarterly* 36, no. 2: 200–212.

Kozloff, Sarah. 1992. "Narrative Theory and Television." In *Channels of Discourse, Reassembled*, edited by Robert C. Allen, 67–98. Chapel Hill: University of North Carolina Press.

Lamarque, Peter. 2010. "How to Create Fictional Character." In his *Work and Object*, 188–207. Oxford: Oxford University Press.

LaPota, Margerite, and Bruce LaPota. 1973. "The Soap Opera: Literature to Be Seen and Not Read." *The English Journal* 62, no. 4: 556–567

Maes, Hans. 2017. "Truly, Madly, Deeply." *The Philosophers' Magazine*: 53–57.

Mittell, Jason. 2006. "Narrative Complexity in Contemporary American Television." *The Velvet Light Trap* 58: 29–40.

Moine, Raphaëlle. 2008. *Cinema Genre*. Oxford: Blackwell.

O'Meara, Radha. 2015. "Changing the Way We Think about Character Change in Episodic Television Series." *Journal of Screenwriting* 6, no. 2: 189 – 201.

Plantinga, Carl. 1999. "The Scene of Empathy and the Human Face on Film." In *Passionate Views: Film, Cognition, and Emotion*, edited by Carl Plantinga and Greg M. Smith, 239–255. Baltimore: The Johns Hopkins University Press.

Plantinga, Carl. 2009. *Moving Viewers, American Film and the Spectators Experience*. Berkeley, CA: University of California Press.

Roberts, Thomas. 1990. *An Aesthetics of Junk Fiction*. Athens, GA: University of Georgia Press.

Robinson, Jenefer. 2005. *Deeper than Reason*. Oxford: Oxford University Press.
Schweinitz, Jörg. 2011. *Film and Stereotype: A Challenge for Cinema and Theory*. New York: Columbia University Press.
Smith, Murray. 1995. *Engaging Characters. Fiction, Emotion, and the Cinema*. Oxford: Oxford University Press.
Smith, Murray. 2011a. "On the Twofoldness of Character." *New Literary History* 42, no. 2: 277–294.
Smith, Murray. 2011b. "Empathy, Expansionism, and the Extended Mind." In *Empathy: Philosophical and Psychological Perspectives*, edited by Amy Coplan and Peter Goldie, 99–117. Oxford: Oxford University Press.
Ted, Nannicelli. 2010. "It's All Connected: Televisual Narrative Complexity". In *The Wire: Urban Decay and American Television*, edited by Tiffany Potter and C.W. Marshall. New York: Continuum.
Thomasson, Amie. 2003. "Fictional Characters and Literary Practice." *British Journal of Aesthetics* 43, no. 2: 138–157.
Vaage, Margrethe Bruun. 2010. "Fiction Film and the Varieties of Empathic Engagement." *Midwest Studies in Philosophy* 34: 158–179.
Vaage, Margrethe Bruun. 2014. "Blinded by Familiarity: Partiality, Morality, and Engagement with Television Series." In *Cognitive Media Theory*, edited by Ted Nannicelli and Paul Taberham, 268–284. New York: Routledge.

15 Ethics and bad protagonists in serial television drama

Carl Plantinga

By now, the phenomenon of the bad protagonist in long-form serial dramas is well known. Shows like *Breaking Bad* (2008–2013), *Dexter* (2006–2013), *The Sopranos* (1999–2007), *Game of Thrones* (2011–present), and *House of Cards* (2013–present) have become very popular and figure in numerous discussions of television ethics. In *Breaking Bad*, mild-mannered, terminally ill chemistry teacher Walter White (Bryan Cranston) gradually transforms into a homicidal drug dealer. In *Dexter*, forensic technician Morgan (Michael C. Hall) leads a secret double life as a vigilante serial killer. *The Sopranos* features Tony Soprano (James Gandolfini), a loyal family man and also a violent mobster. Until Netflix fired Kevin Spacey in 2017 after charges of sexual misconduct were leveled against him, *House of Cards* starred the actor as Frank Underwood, a political opportunist who, together with his wife Claire Underwood (Robin Wright), lies, extorts, and even murders to attain and maintain political power.

My assumption here is that the kinds of stories we circulate contribute to what I call the "cultural ecology" of a time and place. If we assume that stories on screens have the potential to contribute to or detract from this cultural ecology, to make it healthier and more vibrant, or conversely, unhealthy and dysfunctional, what should we say about these shows with ethically flawed main characters? Should they be condemned? Celebrated? Grudgingly accepted? Feared? Loved? Do screen stories with bad protagonists present any special ethical considerations?

These shows, and several others like them, are part of a trend in television towards what many critics see as more complex, quality television drama.[1] I suspect that many contemporary critics and viewers would dismiss ethical concerns as priggish or naïve. These shows are clearly designed to elicit complex responses towards the bad protagonists – mixtures of repulsion, disgust, allegiance, and fascination. Certainly, audiences are not meant to have uncomplicated allegiances to or identification with these antiheroes. Viewers are not meant to approve of their behavior and certainly not to emulate it. One could argue that the shows create mixed responses that generate complex ethical thinking, and that such thinking is beneficial to viewers and to the cultural ecology for that reason. Certainly, this is a plausible argument to make.

DOI: 10.4324/9781003188643-15

The purpose of this chapter, however, is to complicate and question that argument. My suggestion will be that the phenomenon of bad protagonists may be plausibly taken to confuse us ethically, perhaps drawing on problematic masculinist perspectives and even misogyny. My purpose is not to define a new genre such as the bad-protagonist-serial-drama. Rather, it is to describe the kinds of spectatorial processes that some serial dramas with bad protagonists may elicit in viewers. Thus, my argument will be that ethical worries about recent serial dramas with bad protagonists have some merit and seem to warrant further discussion.

Bad fans and good fans

One reason why we might fear the influence of shows with antihero protagonists is that they seem to encourage what television critic Emily Nussbaum calls "bad fans." Bad fans are the fans who fail to have the prescribed responses to the characters in a serial. These are the fans, for example, who rooted for Walter White as he blazed a trail of crime across New Mexico, manufacturing and selling meth, deceiving his family and putting them at risk, poisoning a child, and killing his rivals. Actress Anna Gunn, who played Walt's wife Skyler White on *Breaking Bad*, noted that many of these "bad fans" reacted strongly against her during the show's first season, when she resents Walt's lying and tries to figure out what her husband is up to. Then she tries to stop him. She wrote an op ed piece in the *New York Times* in which she notes that her character, "to judge from the popularity of Web sites and Facebook pages devoted to hating her, has become a flash point for many people's feelings about strong, nonsubmissive, ill-treated women."[2]

The point here is not to argue about whether or not Skyler should be liked; it is, rather, to note the extreme level of hateful discourse that some fans generated in relation to her character. It is also to note the level of allegiance carried by some fans for Walter White despite his despicable behavior. Nussbaum first identified the phenomenon of bad fans in a series of articles in *The New Yorker*, initially in relation to *Breaking Bad*. During the show's fourth season, it is strongly implied that Walt poisons Brock, the six-year-old son of partner Jesse's girlfriend, to get Jesse's allegiance back. Nussbaum writes:

> Once the truth came out, and Brock recovered, I read posts insisting that Walt was so discerning, so careful with the dosage, that Brock could never have died. The audience has been trained by cable television to react this way: to hate the nagging wives, the dumb civilians, who might sour the fun of masculine adventure. *Breaking Bad* increases that cognitive dissonance, turning some viewers into not merely fans but enablers.[3]

These are the bad fans, the viewers who, as Nussbaum flat out says, are "watching wrong."[4]

The bad fan phenomenon did not begin with *Breaking Bad*, of course. In regard to television, Nussbaum points to the famous situation comedy *All in the Family* (1971–1979) as signaling the rise of the bad fan. *All in the Family* did something groundbreaking in American television; it dealt with racism, homophobia, and sexism head-on by featuring a bigoted protagonist. Showrunner Norman Lear intended audiences to respond to Archie Bunker's reprehensible views with laughter and disdain, thereby making the show a critique of bigotry through satire. Lear had hoped that audiences would embrace Archie but reject his beliefs, and many did. A subset of viewers, however, took Archie's bigotry at face value and accepted it; this subset failed to see the show as a satire but rather, celebrated and embraced Archie's perspectives.[5]

The bad fans Nussbaum writes about are typically male, but they need not be. In her essay on the female bad fan, Nussbaum notes that fans of the morally ambiguous *The Good Wife* (2009–2016) sometimes mistook it for a "You go girl!" fantasy and became "outraged and confused" when protagonist Alicia Florick (Julianna Margulies) performed morally questionable acts. Other fans of *The Mindy Project* (2012–2017) seemingly hold unproblematic, adoring allegiance for protagonist Mindi Lahiri (Mindy Kaling) despite showrunner Kaling's intention to represent some of her character's actions and intentions as ethically suspect.[6] Kaling insists that despite the reactions of some fans, she never meant the character to be a spunky role model like Mary Tyler Moore.

Although Nussbaum toys with the idea that the elicitation of bad fan responses may be somehow triggered by the shows' designs, she mostly treats the phenomenon of bad fandom as something that some fans just get wrong. They don't respond to the shows as they ought; they fail to understand the show's intentions. This leaves the question of how an ethical critic might respond to shows with bad protagonists and to bad fans, and it is here that Nussbaum simply punts (to use a football metaphor). Of course, no one wants to become that prissy schoolmarm who tut-tuts her way through life, telling other people how they ought to behave. Thus, Nussbaum bristles at the suggestion that she is a "moral" critic. She makes fun of Newton Minows's famous reference to commercial television as a "vast wasteland," saying that his language sounds "prissy and laughable" from a modern perspective. She even suggests that few people take seriously the possibility that television "turns people into monsters," but that today we reserve such fears for the internet.[7]

For Nussbaum, artistic originality is the chief ethical good, a good so valuable that it outweighs (and perhaps banishes) other ethical concerns. As Nussbaum notes, she would like to "imagine an ethical quality embedded in real originality."[8] She writes that when praised by an "ethicist" during a visit to a university, she told the commenter that she wanted originality, "even if it was ugly, and that I'd rather watch a show that unsettled me than something that was merely 'good.'" To value originality, artistic exploration, boundary-crossing, etc. is, of course, understandable. One of the important functions of the arts is to challenge us, to shock us, to defamiliarize. To make this the chief or *only* ethical value of a work of television, however, is less plausible. Nussbaum seems to argue that artistic originality can make up for many of a show's potential ethical lapses. Is she contending that *any* ethical problem is trumped by artistic originality?

Constructing bad fans?

Nussbaum makes a distinction between bad fans and good fans. But what if shows with bad protagonists *work* to make bad fans? What if these shows build bad fandom into the very fabric of their construction? To answer these questions, we need to consider what kind of ethical experience these stories offer and how spectators interact with and respond to such stories. What sorts of psychological relationships do spectators have with bad protagonists?

The best consideration of the moral psychology of shows with bad protagonists comes from Norwegian scholar Margrethe Bruun Vaage, whose book *The Antihero in American Television* is the most thorough examination of the spectatorship of antihero shows.[9] Vaage's argument about how people view these shows, and the psychological strategies the shows employ, is radical, even if her calm prose and balanced manner disguise that fact. She believes that when viewers engage with fictions they typically bracket the rational, deliberative aspects of moral evaluation and instead, rely on quick, largely automatic moral intuitions. She calls this "fictional relief" or in other words, relief from "real-world" moral evaluation. When fictions deliberately engage a re-activation of the deliberate, rational route of moral evaluation, Vaage calls this a "reality check." The vast majority of Vaage's theory, however, emphasizes the *irrational* element of the psychology of viewing. In the case of long-form television serials with bad protagonists, time after time, Vaage argues that the shows engage largely irrational, low-level psychological processes to get viewers to like, identify with, and have allegiance to the antihero protagonists. Although Vaage does not claim this explicitly, her theory implies that the shows create ethical confusion and moral dumbfounding.

Media psychologist Dolf Zillman calls "affective disposition theory" the idea that viewers evaluate characters on a moral basis and then enjoy narratives that reward good and punish evil.[10] We like the protagonist because she or he does good things and exhibits good character. We dislike the antagonist because she or he does bad things and exhibits bad character. We take pleasure in seeing the protagonist succeed and the antagonist punished, and we greatly enjoy stories in which this occurs. While the outlines of this theory are in many cases correct, Vaage argues that the moral psychology of stories is often much more complicated and ambiguous. She cites the arguments of psychologist Arthur Rainey and various associates that dispositions towards characters can be formed without moral judgment.[11] She also cites my claim, made in relation to the film *Legends of the Fall* (1994) and the protagonist Tristan (Brad Pitt), that viewers can be encouraged by textual strategies to confuse nonmoral and moral judgments of characters and perhaps, to mistake one for the other.[12] In other words, viewers can be manipulated, even confused, by various textual strategies.

Sympathizing with murderers

One would think that it would be difficult to get viewers to have allegiance to, or at least to like, protagonists who are morally evil – who kill, beat, extort, maim, lie, deal drugs, etc. But it turns out not to be so difficult, as the popularity of and critical acclaim won by shows with bad protagonists attest. Yet to facilitate our liking or allegiance with bad protagonists, the shows must have to do some psychological work. What sorts of strategies are employed to win the viewer's liking for or allegiance to the bad protagonist?

The first strategy would be to develop a *strong initial sympathy* for the protagonist. Consider how this occurs in *The Sopranos*. Tony Soprano (James Gandolfini), the protagonist of *The Sopranos*, crime boss and patriarch, is a violent man. Over the course of its six seasons, Tony is involved in too many "whackings" to count, either directly or indirectly. The man is clearly a murderer. Yet, *The Sopranos* and similar shows with bad protagonists encourage a kind of identification with or allegiance to their featured baddies. It needs to be pointed out that even while we are sympathetic with Tony, we nonetheless understand that his behavior is often reprehensible. Our sympathies are mixed at best. Yet, those sympathies still exist. How are they elicited?

A central way that *The Sopranos* establishes sympathy for Tony is by showing him to be a devoted family man. If stories can have a persuasive impact on viewers, one means of persuasion is to elicit emotions that embody the attitudes the storytellers intend to persuade viewers to take. Noël Carroll has argued, for example, that the film *Philadelphia* (1991), in a context in which disgust for gays and HIV/AIDS victims was common, transfers its gay protagonist Andrew Beckett (Tom Hanks) from the potentially reviled category of gay man to the universally revered category of family man. It does this by consistently showing Andrew with his loving family, who support him through a nasty lawsuit and eventually, as he dies from his disease. We see that Andy's family love him, and that he loves them. Carroll argues that moral change in this case can occur because the spectator is encouraged to "file" Andy Beckett under the category "beloved family man." By the end of *Philadelphia*, the film has not done its work if the viewer does not feel deep sympathy for Andrew Beckett and his family.

If this strategy works to change viewer attitudes towards gay men suffering from HIV/AIDS, perhaps it can also work to establish sympathy, however mixed, for gangsters and murderers like Tony Soprano. Tony is not the ideal patriarch by any means; he cheats on his wife and has a temper. But the series' first three episodes work hard to establish Tony as a devoted family man who cares about his wife and children, and especially for his ungrateful mother. As Tony admits to his therapist, Dr. Melfi (Lorraine Bracco), he desperately fears losing his family. We see Tony at family picnics, attending his daughter's volleyball game, playing video games with his son, and interceding in family squabbles. Tony cares for his sour mother, who returns his favors with scorn and derision. He lavishes her with gifts such as flowers or her favorite macaroons. He brings over a CD player and CDs of her favorite music. He cries while cleaning out her house after she is moved into a retirement community. He argues against Dr. Melfi when she suggests that he is harboring rage towards his mother. He is a momma's boy. Vaage notes that the moral system at play in *The Sopranos* is quite simple: Loyalty to one's group. In *The Sopranos*, she writes, the loyalty of the antihero to his family "contributes to making the antihero appear to the spectator as morally preferable to any character who violates this norm" (40). By conventional standards, Tony is a very bad man indeed. But he loves his family, so viewers are cued to like him.

The initial episodes of *Breaking Bad* are another good example of this strategy. Walter White, who later becomes a savage manufacturer and dealer of drugs, is initially motivated to engage in illegal behavior by a diagnosis of terminal cancer, by his inability to care for his family financially, and by various humiliations he suffers as a high school chemistry teacher and later, as a car wash attendant. That all of this is established in the early episodes speaks to the importance of establishing sympathy for a character who will later commit evil acts. In this case, we are cued to like Walter White not because he is a family man so much as because he is a victim – of cancer, of the lack of affordable health care, of the indifferent high school students he tries to teach, and of a bad break early in his career that led to his missing out on the great wealth accumulated by former associates.

The second strategy is *familiarity and tribalism*. Social scientists note that tribal affiliation is notorious for clouding moral judgment, as we are far more likely to judge outsiders harshly and in-group members with excessive leniency.[13] Vaage claims that as we become familiar with bad protagonists, we begin to see them as something like a member of our tribe. Not only that, but viewers tend to prefer *familiar* characters, whatever their moral failings. An objective moral judge, one who could be depended on to determine the ethical parameters of a situation in a rational way, would not in theory be influenced by familiarity or by tribal considerations but rather, by the nature of an incident or action solely in relation to moral or ethical standards. Viewers of shows with bad protagonists are incapable of maintaining such objectivity. Once viewers side with a character, Vaage claims, they become stubborn sympathizers. Vaage notes that after *The Sopranos*, it has

> become standard for antihero series to copy this structure of sympathy; first enhancing sympathy with a morally bad antihero through various narrative means, and then deliberately putting the spectator's sympathy to the test, thus demonstrating time and again how much it takes for that bond to snap once it has been consolidated.
>
> (56)

Vaage describes this as an intuitive response that undermines a fully rational evaluation of the character because it is rooted in partiality; this partiality is born of the human tendency to tribalism and to prefer the familiar.

Vaage notes that the antiheros in series like *The Sopranos* often murder people, but they do not rape. Why? This is the third strategy, what I would call *rape an unforgivable transgression* strategy. For Vaage, rape serves in fictional narrative as the unforgivable sin. Whether a character commits rape or not distinguishes the bad but redeemable from the unredeemable. In the realm of fiction, at least, murder, extortion, cruelty, bribery, and theft are all forgivable. Rape is not. If you doubt this claim, imagine Dexter in the show *Dexter* as a rapist rather than a serial killer. Would audiences still have been able to sympathize with Dexter?[14] As Vaage notes, in antihero stories, "when rape occurs, the main sympathetic characters are not the perpetrators" (127). Some characters in antihero narratives do rape; Vaage calls these characters "contrast characters," their central function being to cause viewers to take the antihero as morally preferable.

Television scholar Jason Mittell has suggested that in order for shows like *The Wire* (2002–2008) to develop sympathies for many of its characters, it had to leave rape off the show's agenda, at least for the most part.[15] Life on the streets among dealers and thugs might be expected to involve a certain amount of rape. Yet during its run, as Vaage notes, *The Wire* suggests only two unambiguous instances of rape. In one instance, Wee-Bey (Hassan Johnson) apparently rapes a barely conscious woman at a party; I say "apparently" because although he later admits to having "fucked her silly," the suggestion that he raped her is based on her statement to Wee-Bey as he carries her to the bedroom that she doesn't feel well. Later, she is found to be dead (apparently of a drug overdose). While Wee-Bey seems cold-blooded and remorseless (126), D'Angelo (Lawrence Gilliard, Jr.) discovers the young woman's dead body and is obviously mortified by what has happened. This is one of the ways that *The Wire* differentiates between the good and bad gang member – by their committing of rape and their perspective on the dignity of women.

Murray Smith first raised the issue of "apparently perverse allegiances," as he called the viewer's siding with or liking bad protagonists.[16] Smith's explanation was a more general version of Vaage's claim; we root for the bad protagonist because he or she is surrounded by even worse characters, thus making the bad protagonist look good by comparison. Vaage's claims here are more specific in that she is pointing out one strategy for making the bad protagonist morally preferable. Vaage also points out that rape is often used as the justification for the viewer's wholesale approval of vigilante revenge. Why is rape singled out as unforgivable? Vaage says that viewers find rape to be not only morally disgusting but physically disgusting, and it is thus singled out for a special kind of intense disapproval. Rape elicits sheer bodily disgust that ramps up and amplifies the moral disgust it generates. The antihero is a very bad man; but he does not rape, and so, we can sympathize with him.

The fourth strategy for maintaining sympathy for bad protagonists is *suspense*. How can suspense play into sympathy for a devil? Alfred Hitchcock demonstrated decades ago that a suspenseful scene can cause viewers to root for an evil character. In *Strangers on a Train* (1951), for example, the antagonist

Bruno (Robert Walker) reaches down a sewer drain for his dropped lighter; he needs the lighter to exonerate himself from a murder. In *Frenzy* (1972), the sex-murderer Rusk (Barry Foster) struggles to extract his monogrammed tie-pin from the grasp of a victim with rigor mortis. In each case, the forward-momentum of suspense, and the viewer's fear that an agent will not achieve a desired goal, may cause the viewer to root for the antagonist. Hitchcock prided himself on his ability to cause viewers to align themselves with the goals of evil characters, or in other words, to desire results in the narrative that are morally questionable.

Vaage argues that the strong emotion of suspense is often amoral and is used to foster sympathetic responses to antiheroes even as they engage in unethical behavior. Daniel Barratt calls this tendency "goal contagion";[17] viewers have a kind of completion compulsion, wanting the character to finish a task or reach a goal, even if the task or goal is clearly wrong. In *Dexter*, Dexter may engage in an elaborate and dangerous plan to ensnare and then kill a victim. In *Breaking Bad*, Walter White might be eluding the detection of his DEA brother-in-law, hiding a large amount of illicit cash, or planning the murder of a rival. In each case, suspense causes us to desire narrative outcomes that are immoral. Since both suspense and empathy, Vaage claims, are low-level psychological processes, they can operate independently of considered moral judgment. As Vaage writes, "one of the strategies recent American television series use to ensure engagement with their morally bad main characters is moral inversion of suspense" (77):

> The suspenseful sequences are so enjoyable that they make the spectator circumvent moral evaluation of what Walter and Jesse are doing. They offer the spectator instant gratification. As we gave seen, suspense can make the spectator engage in a character's perspective on its own, and humor and chases further facilitate the pleasurable and thrilling feeling of suspense.
>
> (80)

The four strategies I have discussed so far are applied to all or most audiences; the fifth strategy – the strategy of *misogyny* – is most effective for some male viewers. Most antiheroes are male; Vaage notes that it is still perceived as less acceptable "to portray non-conformist, difficult, and transgressive female characters on screen" (151). She notes that despite their oft-celebrated innovations, the representation of women is conventional, with female roles divided between "morally good" mothers or daughters, on the one hand, or fallen women (strippers, prostitutes, lovers), on the other. Vaage notes that in *Breaking Bad*, the domestic sphere is typically depicted as stifling and boring. As Vaage writes, suspenseful scenes of action and excitement are contrasted with Walt's life in the domestic setting (80). These sequences are extended in duration to suggest unease, feature an unmoving camera, a feature soundtrack without underscoring and consisting of awkward breaks in conversation during which we hear only the ticking of a clock. As Vaage notes, in his home, Walter is portrayed as disillusioned and entrapped, diffident and disempowered (80–81). These sequences serve not only to contrast with and emphasize the pleasures of the suspense sequences but also to elicit negative perspectives on Skyler, Walter's long-suffering wife. Skyler is rendered unlikeable in part because she is "not as carefully presented and constructed as is Walter" (162). As noted earlier, some viewers took a strong dislike to Skyler, but their reasoning is often opaque. Vaage notes that their explanations for their dislike often sound confused or "dumbfounded." One commenter on Reddit entitled his post "I hate Skyler White":

> so [*sic*] i just started watching Breaking Bad (never got the chance to see it) im half way into season 4, and i absolutely cannot stand Skyler oh my gosh. Ive come to the point where i just skip ahead when shes on the screen im not even joking. Shes spoiling the show for me. Im not even sexist or anything, i dont hate any other women on the show nor do i hate the women from walking dead or daredevil but Sorry to say that this SKyler character enrages me, she literally is ruining breaking bad for me. Theres so many reasons i hate her.[18]

Tellingly, the poster is unable to give a single reason for hating her. This might well be expected in a case of moral dumbfounding, where one's intuitions are powerful but their genesis opaque, lying somewhere beneath the level of consciousness. The post did trigger a contagion, however, leading dozens of others to weigh in with their shared hatred of Skyler White. Vaage concludes that in *Breaking Bad*, "the antihero's wife is a drag," functioning as a "prolonged, lingering reality check" who offers "little attraction amidst the enjoyable transgressions her husband offers" (169).

Ethics and the bad protagonist

In conclusion, then, we have reasons to be worried about the ethical implications of long-form serial dramas with bad protagonists. One worry might be what Emily Nussbaum dubbed the bad fan. Bad fans "go rogue," so to speak, ignoring moral commonplaces and complexities to respond to the series' masculinized fantasies that celebrate sheer power, transgression, and freedom from conventional ethical constraint. Walter White's drug manufacture and dealing is excused because he was disrespected and he needs the money. Tony Soprano's violence is excused because he needs to protect his family.

Yet if there is a problem in this regard, it is not merely that of bad fans. The problem is that the series build such responses into their very fabric, into their design. As we have seen, it is not by accident that spectators are able to like and perhaps sympathize (to some extent) with Walter White, Tony Soprano, and Dexter; it is by intention. We have seen that the shows employ various strategies to create and maintain sympathy for their protagonists. They elicit strong initial sympathy for the protagonists and then make use of intuitive, sometimes irrational human tendencies towards moral judgment. The bad protagonist is loyal to his family; he is given lots of screen time and thus is familiar to the viewer; though he murders and extorts, he does not rape, one strategy of depicting him as morally superior to other criminal characters; his crimes are represented as suspenseful and exciting; and his domestic life – a place where he can be "good" – is so dull by comparison.

One could defend these series by contrasting them with simplistic melodramas that depict good and evil in dualistic and moralistic terms. Surely, these long-form serial dramas with bad protagonists offer a sophisticated viewing experience that is superior to television programs like any of the *Star Trek* series, crime dramas, or soaps that present good and evil as easy to identify and in which good is rewarded and evil punished. Is not moral complexity preferable to the sentimental moralism of Disney or soaps? Surely, the long-form serial dramas with bad protagonists are more realistic and offer a viewing experience that can lead to ethical reflection, sophistication, and sensitivity.

That could be the case, of course. But notice that Vaage identifies all of the strategies that the shows use to elicit sympathy for bad protagonists as *irrational.* For viewers to excuse the protagonist's wrongdoing because it is depicted as suspenseful or exciting, because he is familiar to us, or because he loves his family, is hardly the sort of experience that leads to ethical sophistication. To sympathize with a murderer because he doesn't rape is not constitutive of critical thinking. Do shows like *The Sopranos* and *Breaking Bad* lead to ethical reflection and questioning during or after viewing? Or do they confuse viewers ethically by dumbfounding them, by playing on instinctual intuitions that in reality are flaws in our ethical thinking?

Of that great Hollywood genre of the past, the Western, it is often said that it explores the boundaries between wilderness and civilization, with the Western hero straddling that boundary. The Westerner, almost always a man, nominally supports the values inherent in civilization but also enjoys the freedoms of the wilderness. The Westerner is typically untied by the bonds of domesticity, rejecting the home and family for the freedom to move about as he pleases through the dangerous and beautiful expanses of the untamed frontier. The classic Westerner is also a man of violence, although he uses violence only reluctantly, sparingly, and always in the context of a fair fight.

Shows like *The Sopranos* and *Breaking Bad* are a different sort of masculine fantasy, albeit with clear ties to the Western. The Western hero will ultimately use violence against those who threaten civilization or those he loves. The bad protagonist will use violence against anyone who threatens his business interests, his gang, or those he loves. The difference is that the bad protagonist's business interests and his gang are both opposed to civilization and not representative of it.

These antiheroes have one foot in domesticity and one foot in organized crime. It is often their ties to domesticity that make them human, but it is their activities in organized crime that make them exciting, that energize and fascinate audiences. That Tony Soprano loves his mother is not a sufficient reason to watch *The Sopranos*; that he both loves his mother and strangles people with his bare hands creates a friction that makes *The Sopranos* and shows like it so fascinating.

Nothing in what I have written implies a wholesale ethical rejection of serial dramas with bad protagonists. The shows may feature ethical goods that are significant and that weigh against potential worries. My aim in this chapter, however, is to argue that such worries are justified. Let the conversation continue.

Notes

1 For a more comprehensive list of these shows and a discussion of their critical reception, see Margrethe Bruun Vaage, *The Antihero in American Television* (New York and London: Routledge, 2016), xi–xii.
2 Anna Gunn, "I Have a Character Issue," *The New York Times,* August 23, 2013. www.nytimes.com/2013/08/24/opinion/i-have-a-character-issue.html
3 Emily Nussbaum, "Child's Play," *The New Yorker,* August 27, 2012. www.newyorker.com/magazine/2012/08/27/childs-play-5. Accessed January 31, 2018.
4 Emily Nussbaum, "That Mind-Numbing Phone Call on Last Night's *Breaking Bad,*" *The New Yorker,* September 16, 2013. www.newyorker.com/culture/culture-desk/that-mind-bending-phone-call-on-last-nights-breaking-bad
5 Emily Nussbaum, "The Great Divide: Norman Lear, Archie Bunker, and the Rise of the Bad Fan," April 7, 2014. www.newyorker.com/magazine/2014/04/07/the-great-divide-emily-nussbaum
6 Emily Nussbaum, "The Female Bad Fan," *The New Yorker,* October 17, 2014. www.newyorker.com/culture/cultural-comment/female-bad-fan
7 Nussbaum, "The Great Divide."
8 Nussbaum, "The Great Divide."
9 Margrethe Bruun Vaage, *The Antihero in American Television* (New York: Routledge, 2016), 12. Further references to this book will be made parenthetically within the text.
10 See Vaage, pp. 7–9. Also see Dolf Zillman, "Basal Morality in Drama Appreciation," in Ib Bondebjerg, ed., *Moving Images, Culture, and the Mind* (Luton: University of Luton Press, 2000), pp. 53–63.
11 A.A. Rainey, "Expanding Disposition Theory: Reconsidering Character Liking, Moral Evaluations, and Enjoyment." *Communication Theory*, 2004, 14 (4), 348–369.
12 Carl Plantinga, "'I Followed the Rules, and They All Loved You More': Moral Judgment and Attitudes Toward Fictional Characters in Film." *Midwest Studies in Philosophy*, 2010, 34 (1), 34–51. This material has been revised and reworked in Carl Plantinga, *Screen Stories: Emotion and the Ethics of Engagement* (New York: Oxford University Press, 2018), 191–210.
13 For an overview, see Joshua Greene, *Moral Tribes: Emotion, Reason, and the Gap Between Us and Them* (New York: The Penguin Press, 2013), 28–65.
14 This example was originally given by Jason Mittell, as quoted in Vaage, 122. For a full account of the representation of rape on television, see Lisa M. Cuklanz, *Rape on Prime Time: Television, Masculinity, and Sexual Violence* (Philadelphia: University of Philadelphia Press, 2000).
15 Drake Bennet, "This Will Be on the Midterm. You Feel Me? Why So Many Colleges are Teaching *The Wire,*" *Slate*, 2010, www.slate.com/id/2245788/. Accessed February 28, 2018.
16 Murray Smith, "Gangsters, Cannibals, Aesthetes, or Apparently Perverse Allegiances," in Carl Plantinga and Greg M. Smith, eds., *Passionate Views: Film, Cognition, and Emotion* (Baltimore: Johns Hopkins University Press, 1999), 217–238.

17 Daniel Barratt, "Tracing the Routes to Empathy: Association, Simulation, or Appraisal?" *Film Studies: An International Review*, 8 (1) 2006, 39–52.

18 Reddit, www.reddit.com/r/breakingbad/comments/4eorzk/i_hate_skyler_white/. Accessed February 28, 2018.

References

Bennett, Drake. 2010. "This Will Be on the Midterm. You Feel Me? Why So Many Colleges are Teaching The Wire." *Slate*, http://www.slate.com/id/2245788/. Accessed 28 February 2018.

Cuklanz, Lisa M. 2000. *Rape on Prime Time: Television, Masculinity, and Sexual Violence*. Philadelphia, PA: University of Philadelphia Press.

Greene, Joshua. 2013. *Moral Tribes: Emotion, Reason, and the Gap Between Us and Them*. New York: Penguin Press.

Gunn, Anna. 2013. "I Have a Character Issue." *New York Times*. August 23, 2013. Accessed February 9, 2018. http://www.nytimes.com/2013/08/24/opinion/i-have-a-character-issue.html

Nussbaum, Emily. 2012. "Child's Play." *The New Yorker*. August 27, 2012. Accessed 31 January 2018. https://www.newyorker.com/magazine/2012/08/27/childs-play-5

Nussbaum, Emily. 2013. "That Mind-Numbing Phone Call on Last Night's *Breaking Bad*." *The New Yorker*. September 16, 2013. Accessed 31 January 2018. https://www.newyorker.com/culture/culture-desk/that-mind-bending-phone-call-on-last-nights-breaking-bad

Nussbaum, Emily. 2014. "The Great Divide: Norman Lear, Archie Bunker, and the Rise of the Bad Fan." *The New Yorker*. April 7, 2014. Accessed 31 January 2018. https://www.newyorker.com/magazine/2014/04/07/the-great-divide-emily-nussbaum

Nussbaum, Emily. 2014. "The Female Bad Fan." *The New Yorker*. October 17, 2014. Accessed 31 January 2017. https://www.newyorker.com/culture/cultural-comment/female-bad-fan

Plantinga, Carl. 2018. *Screen Stories: Emotion and the Ethics of Engagement*. New York: Oxford University Press.

Plantinga, Carl. 2010. "'I Followed the Rules, and They All Loved You More': Moral Judgment and Attitudes Toward Fictional Characters in Film." *Midwest Studies in Philosophy* 34, no. 1: 34–51.

Rainey, A.A. 2004. "Expanding Disposition Theory: Reconsidering Character Liking, Moral Evaluations, and Enjoyment." *Communication Theory* 14, no. 4, 348–369.

Smith, Murray. 1999. "Gangsters, Cannibals, Aesthetes, or Apparently Perverse Allegiances." In *Passionate Views: Film, Cognition, and Emotion*, edited by Carl Plantinga and Greg M. Smith, 217–238. Baltimore: Johns Hopkins University Press.

Vaage, Margrethe Bruun. 2016. *The Antihero in American Television*. NewYork: Routledge.

Zillman, Dolf. 2000. "Basal Morality in Drama Appreciation." In *Moving Images, Culture, and the Mind*, edited by Ib Bondebjerg, 53–63. Luton: University of Luton Press.

16 A sense of moment

Appreciating television serials from aesthetic and cognitive perspectives

Sarah Cardwell

This book's existence and its breadth of contributions attest that television aestheticians and cognitivists share an important endeavor.[1] Both groups are driven to explore the compelling emotional, cognitive, and aesthetic appeals of contemporary television serials. In other words, whether we take up a broadly aesthetic perspective or a cognitive approach towards TV, we are engaged in an ongoing act of appreciative engagement. We share a mutual fascination with the televisual works that captivate us and an urge to address our sense of their potential significance or moment.

Our apparent commonalities, however, lead us not only in diverse directions but often also into disagreements and mistrust, as noted in the Editors' Introduction. I write as someone committed to television aesthetics, who embraces the arrival of new perspectives and recognizes the usefulness of much cognitive work, but who nonetheless will admit to some uneasiness about the presumptions underlying cognitive science and trepidation regarding its deployment within TV studies. This chapter is a preliminary foray into the two approaches side by side. But rather than comparing and contrasting, I aim to uncover something a little more nuanced and elusive: the distinctive sensibility of each perspective and the implicit values which inform it.

The chapter proceeds by identifying some of the commonest notes of concord and discord between aesthetic and cognitive television scholars, uncovering differences of purpose, scope, and values, in order to better appreciate the points of urgent distinction that separate the approaches and to illuminate the hazards of speaking at cross purposes.

So that I might grasp more positively the specific strengths and merits of each perspective, I briefly consider how a specific moment of television might seize the attention of its practitioners. I have chosen two moments drawn from recent U.S. television series – *The Closer* (Fox 2005–2012) and *Desperate Housewives* (ABC 2004–2012) – that I argue are most sensitively and persuasively appreciated via cognitive and aesthetic perspectives, respectively.

My exploration of these two examples leads me, finally, to revisit this book's core focus – the television serial – via a consideration of "moment." The "sense of moment" in this chapter's title consciously denotes two meanings of the word. The first is more commonplace: a moment is a short time, an

DOI: 10.4324/9781003188643-16

instant. The second refers to importance, weight, significance. What is the "moment" of a particular fragment within a long-running serial? How do cognitive and aesthetic approaches weigh this moment? As we shall see, cognitivists and aestheticians take up subtly dissimilar stances in relation to seriality and moment(s), and in each approach, the two meanings of "moment" are differently interconnected. Attending to these distinctions helps us uncover something of the sensibility of each perspective. And in keeping with the values and sensibility of a television aesthetician, I ultimately aver that it is television programs themselves, or the unique particularities of selected moments within them, that will guide us – if we let them – to choose the most appropriate appreciative approach in each case.

Common ground, common cause, and common interests

Television aestheticians and cognitivists already share common ground. Both believe experiences of television to be valuable in their own right, offering us narrative absorption, emotional engagement and aesthetic pleasure. Both are fascinated by our engagement with television works and are driven to reflect upon that engagement. To the reader located outside television studies, these may sound obvious foci, but television studies' long-standing distrust of aesthetics and philosophy of art has meant that television aestheticians have had to argue for decades in favor of paying close attention to the details of specific programs in a spirit of critical and evaluative appreciation.

This common ground leads to common cause. Aesthetic and cognitive television scholars' primary focus on the material of television (programs or works), rather than on television as a social, cultural, or ideological construct, constitutes a challenge to a number of established theoretical and critical notions precious to the wider field of TV studies. Furthermore, at a conceptual level, in different ways and to different ends, cognitivists and aestheticians concur on certain fundamental ideas concerning the television work, its creators, and its viewers. Both groups are willing to accept, broadly, the ontological integrity of television works. Both acknowledge and engage with the creative process and the individuals (or agencies) involved in it. Both work from a presumption of the possibility of intersubjective agreement, whether shared perceptions, reactions or experiences when viewing, or shared interpretative or evaluative responses. Both assume that references to details of specific programs constitute viable support for their theses.

These ideas are far from universally accepted by the wider TV studies community. Television aestheticians, rooted within that community, are keenly aware of the contentiousness of these precepts, and of their approach, within that wider field.[2] The first forays by cognitivists into television studies are likely to elicit similarly wary responses for reasons explored later. In that sense, there is potential solidarity among those who are keen to break new and contentious ground. Recent cognitive scholarship on television implicitly but effectively supplements and complements existing work by television aestheticians, strengthening the case for conceptual revision within TV studies. Together, both groups can continue to engage constructively with critics and skeptics within television studies, whose uneasy concerns about even the words "cognitive" and "aesthetic" continue to demand from their proponents careful, reflective, and ideally, persuasive and inspiring defenses. In this, at least, aestheticians and cognitivists might be allies.

Aestheticians' and cognitivists' common cause has been curiously overlooked, or at least unacknowledged, until now, but is worth highlighting in the present context, since it reveals terrain on which we might fruitfully meet and potential grounds for rapprochement. There are already examples of overt overlap and collaboration: areas of common interest. Nikos Metallinos's early work (1996) on television aesthetics explicitly connected aesthetic with perceptual and cognitive elements. Today, some television aestheticians are excited by how the methods and material of analytic (philosophical) aesthetics might enhance their work – a stance shared by many cognitivists. Consider, for instance, the work of Ted Nannicelli, which constantly crosses the boundaries between cognitive and aesthetic perspectives. His incisive exploration of the practice of appreciating television, his elucidation of the ontology of the televisual work, and his defense of interpretative and evaluative criticism go to the nub of what we do when we appreciate TV aesthetically (Nannicelli 2017). Nannicelli draws heavily upon the literature and methods of analytic aesthetics. His approach is echoed in my work within television aesthetics, originating more recognizably in television studies but nonetheless adopting enthusiastically a perspective inspired by analytic aesthetics, incorporating material from that field, such as on aesthetic experience (Cardwell 2013), and drawing upon its characteristic manner of argumentation and meta-critical reflection. Philosophical aesthetics in the Anglo-American, analytic tradition provides fertile ground for cross-germination between cognitivists and television aestheticians.

Other strands of writing in television aesthetics proffer latent, promising connections with cognitive work. For instance, some scholars have argued for the importance of aesthetic education, recognizing that via our scholarship, via our attention to works of TV art, we remain open to learning and developing, to deepening both our aesthetic sense and our understanding of the human condition and our society (see, for instance, Nelson 1997). Such work might be helpfully complemented and supported by cognitive material which shares similar preoccupations.

It is clear, then, that aestheticians and cognitivists share several areas of common ground, common cause, and common interests. But, as some readers will doubtless have noted, the preceding depiction of "television aesthetics" is rather misleading.[3] In truth, conceptual, philosophical, and meta-critical literature constitutes only a small fraction of work in the field. By far the most dominant strand, and the most frequently practiced, is appreciative, close stylistic analysis; accordingly, this conception of television aesthetics is the rightful focus in this chapter. True, this "'television aesthetics" chimes less readily with cognitive approaches – but there is an important crossover we might use as a starting point: both aestheticians and cognitivists depend upon a model of *attentiveness*, which also distinguishes their work from literature in TV studies that more often prioritizes dispersed attention to multimedia sources.

Both cognitivists and aestheticians closely attend. Both believe that attentiveness has some kind of value.[4] But as we shall see, the nature of that attention (and its relationship to appreciation, interpretation, and evaluation) differs. Moreover, the two groups have divergent remits and purposes, which arise from their particular, distinct experiences of attending and which are supported by what one might consider the values of their scholarly fields. The upshot is that cognitivists and aestheticians, while appearing to engage closely in appreciation of the same program, are frequently talking quite literally at cross purposes.

Thus, scholars of television aesthetics are likely to clash – sometimes heatedly – with cognitivists despite our mutual interest in accounting for the appeal of TV works and our engagement with them. Conversations at cross purposes are uncomfortable. In this case, they provoke uneasiness, even skepticism, on the part of TV aestheticians towards accounts of works offered by cognitivists, as regular attendees of academic conferences and seminars will likely attest. In turn, cognitivists may feel surprised or frustrated by the rancor directed towards them by television aestheticians (and by television scholars more broadly). Once we acknowledge our differences of remit and purpose, and if we accept that each approach is equally appropriate and valid in given circumstances, some heat is removed from the dissension between us.

Terms of engagement: attending, appreciating, explaining

Consider, as a brief indicative example, the different tenors of attention paid to the acclaimed U.S. serial *Breaking Bad* (AMC 2008–2013) by scholars engaging from broadly aesthetic or cognitive perspectives, respectively.

Elliott Logan introduces his book on the serial with a commitment: "This book appreciates the artistry of *Breaking Bad*" (Logan 2016a, 1). His extensive engagement with the serial focuses on how its "expressiveness and meaning" arise from its specific "narrative and stylistic palette" (Logan 2016a, 2, 1); as this implies, his writing moves persistently between detailed stylistic analysis and scrutiny of the program's complex characterization and wider themes. Logan engages confidently in evaluative critique, writing of the program's unique achievements. His vocabulary and register, alongside his stated remit and intentions, situate this account of *Breaking Bad* firmly within television aesthetics.

"Television aesthetics" is sometimes characterized as "close textual analysis". Certainly, the latter is a crucial and defining element. But it must be acknowledged that many traditions in TV studies use close textual analysis to support their theses and investigations. Logan's approach to *Breaking Bad* exemplifies those additional factors which specifically delineate an aesthetic approach. His writing pays particular attention to the work's stylistic choices and artistic qualities, as well as its narrative and thematic concerns, and it does not shy away from evaluation. Moreover, rather than using close textual analysis to explore pre-determined questions and concerns, or to direct the reader's attention out and away from the program towards wider social or cultural concerns, as might be more common in television studies,[5] Logan chooses "an appreciative, focused and sustained engagement with the programme under scrutiny, in order to offer a critical appreciation of the achievements of the programme as an artwork – a potential source of joy, illumination and value" (Cardwell 2017, 12).

Logan adopts what one might call an "aesthetic attitude." I have argued elsewhere that television aesthetics rests broadly upon a notion of aesthetic attitude or frame of mind (Cardwell 2013).[6] We conceive of the work (the TV program under scrutiny) as a potential source of aesthetic pleasure or – to use a more familiar term – aesthetic experience.[7] Of course, aesthetic experience is only one of many legitimate and varied kinds of viewing experiences, and a viewer may appropriately take up other kinds of attitudes towards a work. I would aver that each program itself guides us towards the most appropriate and rewarding vantage point from which to view, experience, and evaluate it. The nature of aesthetic experience/attitude is rarely explicitly addressed or conceptualized by television aestheticians, who tend to prefer close textual analysis over conceptual and philosophical investigations. Nonetheless, a pre-theoretical notion of aesthetic experience or attitude underpins and enables these ongoing acts of appreciation, interpretation, and evaluation.

Writing from broadly cognitive and analytic perspectives, Margrethe Bruun Vaage's and Ted Nannicelli's responses to *Breaking Bad* also address the program's textual details and stylistic choices, but more fleetingly. Instead, despite their very different projects (Vaage's account of antiheroes in U.S. television; Nannicelli's philosophy of the art of television), both writers find themselves drawn to two key areas: the program's overarching structure of suspense and its function in arresting viewers' attention, and the moral and ethical questions prompted by its narrative and characters (Vaage 2015 *passim*; Nannicelli 2016 *passim*).

Vaage's and Nannicelli's concerns arise instinctively and directly from attentiveness to *Breaking Bad* itself, its stylistic particularities and thematic preoccupations, and the artistic choices made by its creators. Interestingly, we can see that the impetus behind these cognitive and analytic accounts actually aligns with the spirit of television aesthetics, moving from "a close analysis of thematic, formal and stylistic qualities ... to explore some of the questions that arise from peculiarities of a single work" (Cardwell 2005). "Part-time cognitivist" David Bordwell (2010) advocates a similar trajectory, arguing that film scholars should begin by attending to distinctive "smaller-scale problems" within a particular work (10–11) and then move outwards towards pertinent, broader matters. Bordwell insists that "we still want generalizations" (10), which might perhaps prove a step too far for many television aestheticians – but this is a disagreement over degree and emphasis more than fundamental methodology. The aim of television aesthetics has been stated thus: "to capture something of the individuality and distinctiveness of the program, evaluate its achievements and also address the more conceptual questions that the program raises" (Cardwell 2005, 180).[8] While aestheticians tend to concern themselves primarily with the first two parts, cognitivists emphasize – and expand upon – the last element, broadening their remit to consider viewers' responses to the program.

Many television scholars are concerned with audiences' experiences and responses within a real-world context, of course. But, as in the case of Vaage and Nannicelli, cognitivism uniquely conceives of the viewer as human (social) animal, drawing on literature from evolutionary psychology and cognitive science, ethics, and moral philosophy to explain viewers' engagement. Cognitivist accounts explore "the general mental operations of viewers and the individual media works that cue them" (Nannicelli 2018) (the order of emphasis here is indicative). They attempt to reflect upon the likely ways a person might respond to a work, evincing evidence not only from within the work itself but also from cognitive science and psychology, to moot explanations linked to the broader human experience in evolutionary, psychological, and socio-cultural terms. The cognitive explanation shares with the aesthetic account close reference to details of the work, but engagement with the work is typically couched in terms of likely shared responses.

It is understandable that cognitive scholars are more often drawn to especially ambivalent, morally complex, or troublesome programs containing unsavory or dubious characters (such as in the case of *Breaking Bad*). These are the kinds of works that invite viewers to interrogate further, reflect, and seek explanations. Cognitive accounts acknowledge that such works pose problems for, or at least raise knotty questions about, the nature of our engagement and explicitly challenge viewers' established perspectives. Cognitivists presume that our pleasure in these works must be explained, and they roll up their sleeves to do so.

Both groups enter the work attentively, sensitive to its particularities, but once inside, they take very different routes. In short, aestheticians and cognitivists undertake their analyses under different terms of engagement, motivated by distinct impulses.

Why do we write? Aesthetic and other experiences, and the individual

Cognitive scholars appear typically more excited by the questions raised in or by a work than by the act of appreciative critique itself. Underlying a cognitive account is an urge to clarify, to understand, to contextualize. Cognitivists prioritize analysis and explanation, proffering reasonable and, it is hoped, persuasive evidence for the responses of viewers to the work in question. Their analyses direct the reader outwards, towards a recognition of the human, social animal to whom the program speaks. One might say that the movement is centrifugal.

As we have seen, television aestheticians, in contrast, undertake an appreciative act from the starting point of assuming some kind of aesthetic attitude or experience. Their close analyses, rooted as they are in the details of the particular program, are offered in a spirit of elucidation rather than explanation. The unique qualities of the specific work take center stage. Furthermore, aestheticians often attempt manifestly to approximate in their writing their own aesthetic experience, as provoked by the work under scrutiny. There is an inherent element of individual self-awareness within the writer's response. An aesthetic account is often evocative, expressively encapsulating something of the particular writer's felt experience of the work. This can be seen especially in instances of expressive criticism, which proffer distinctly individual, even idiosyncratic, appreciative accounts of specific programs, exhibiting a sincere commitment to render something of the writer's experience. The reader is entreated to share in that experience and is directed to return, repeatedly, insistently, to the program itself. The impulse of such writing is centripetal.

Clearly, different weight is given, in these two approaches, to two key elements: aesthetic experience and the individual (work and viewer). For cognitivists, aesthetic experience is only one type of viewing experience. If appreciation and concomitantly, aesthetic experience underlie television aesthetics, cognitive studies takes as its remit a wide range of viewing experiences, considering many types of engagement, from analysis of the "startle effect" when watching a program in the horror genre to the correspondence between long-term serial viewing and real-life friendship. Cognitivists might be interested in aesthetic experiences, but they also focus on many other aspects and kinds of viewing experiences. Their explanations do not necessarily address the form of engagement that most interests TV aestheticians, that is, aesthetic engagement.

The broadly centrifugal movement of the cognitivist television scholar frustrates the kind of insistent value the aesthetician would place upon the achievements of the particular program and his or her individual appreciation of them. Consequently, to the TV aesthetician, the cognitivist's account can feel impersonal, diffuse, or even lacking in respect for the individual specificity of the work, its creators, and/or one person's particular experience of it.

It should be noted that cognitive approaches need not downplay the importance of creative individuals' work. In fact, a cognitivist might argue that since many television artworks are consciously designed in the hope of soliciting particular physiological and psychological responses from viewers, it is entirely reasonable to investigate concurrently both those responses and the ways in which the artworks achieve – or attempt to achieve – them. The aesthetician can surely empathize with this rationale, which recognizes the fundamental importance of creative intentions, choices, and achievements. A larger stumbling block is the particular nature of cognitivists' explanations: drawing as they do on cognitive science, they can be suspected of undermining individuals' diversity by postulating reductive "norms" for human responses, from which television scholars of all stripes historically and instinctively rebound.

Of course, one might contend that (television) aestheticians hold to their own normative conceits: specifically, it is contended that "normative force [is] ... a feature of evaluative discourse" (Nannicelli 2017, 185). In his incisive exploration of this topic, Nannicelli observes that aesthetic accounts of TV programs appear to rest upon an expectation that different viewers are able to reach intersubjective agreement about the works in question – that they can share responses, experiences, and judgments despite their individual subjectivities – and that they do so by means of unexamined but powerful norms of judgment (Nannicelli 2017, 185–193).

Television aestheticians are not unaware of the "problem" of norms within aesthetic criticism, especially since it is mobilized by a number of their peers within television studies as part of an ideological critique of the very project of TV aesthetics.[9] Quite possibly, their awareness has contributed to the development of a distinctive sensibility, a mode of critique with a pronounced emphasis on the individual and the singular. As I noted earlier, much close critical analysis in TV aesthetics is either "demonstrative" or expressive. Noël Carroll summarizes the aim of the former as "ideally, the promotion of a certain kind of experience – what is generally called an aesthetic experience – in the audience" (Carroll 2001, 42). In other words, those engaged in demonstrative criticism hope that by drawing attention to the details that they believe have contributed to their experience of the work under scrutiny, they might induce the reader to revisit the work, look more closely, and appreciate it more fully; perhaps he or she might even share, in subsequent viewings, something of the writer's experience.

Expressive criticism embraces even more readily its subjective, individual nature.[10] Each instance of criticism in this vein might be understood as being silently prefaced by the words "My experience of this work is ..." or "I see in this work ..." (though it is true that sometimes a reader less familiar with this mode might not grasp the unspoken preface, which is where misunderstandings can arise). This form of aesthetic engagement does not presume one's own experience to be universal, or naturally or instinctively common to all, but potentially accessible, given appropriate circumstances, to a number of others. There is the distinct possibility and hope of broad intersubjective agreement, but the response of this individual, in this moment, is necessarily his or her own. Such an aesthetic account generally avoids claims about how other people either will or should respond to a work, taking up instead a stance that prioritizes the work and the individual's experience of it.

Nannicelli has examined some of the conceptual and methodological flaws in these attempts to sidestep the role of norms within aesthetic criticism. Clearly, aestheticians have good reasons to reflect more deeply upon the presence, nature, and function of norms within their practice. For our purposes here, however, we need not assess the relative coherence of TV aestheticians' stance on the subject; instead, we need only appreciate what it reveals about the particular sensibility of their approach. The elevated role of the individual within much writing in TV aesthetics betrays an awareness of the potential pitfall of norms and a desire not to allow them to presume, define, or contain one's own, or others', experience of a particular artwork. Generally speaking, TV aestheticians try to avoid assumptions and assertions about "natural" or universal human responses or experiences. Cognitivists have a greater liability with which to contend in this regard, given their connection with the natural and neurological sciences and what that means, or implies, for their explanations of television and us, its viewers.

The scientific register: cognitivism in the context of TV studies

Cognitive studies of television are still nascent, but television aesthetics is on a comparatively firmer and more intimate footing within TV studies, with more scholars longer established in the wider field. Although television aestheticians may often find themselves at odds with some of their peers, they nevertheless share with them a number of fundamental commitments, including particular regard for diversity and plurality in terms of works, viewers, and viewing experiences.[11] As described earlier, television scholars mostly eschew assertions about "universal" experiences and responses. It can sometimes seem that cognitivism does not share these important commitments, especially given its connections with cognitive science.

While cognitivists' concerns with moral and ethical questions, and social implications, correspond readily to television scholars' existing interests, the role of science and its adoption within TV studies is a sticking point. Scientific, psychophysiological accounts of engagement with television drama might employ familiar key terms, thereby implying common interests with TV scholars, but they often redefine these terms in ways that have little resonance with those who write and teach about television every day. In a recent example, an article promises to reveal '"how to evaluate the emotional experiences [of viewers of] television drama" (Heiselberg and Bjørne 2018, 884). The project redefines "evaluation" and "emotion," salient topics for television aestheticians, in laboratory terms of stimuli and responses, measured via skin conductance tests and self-reports. Individual viewers become human (laboratory) subjects. It is nigh impossible to forge convincing connections between this kind of research and current scholarship within the field of television studies. The fields remain completely isolated from one another.

Scientific psychologist Alexis Makin astutely warns of "the gap between aesthetic science and aesthetic experience," counselling that "the future of scientific aesthetics depends on how successfully we can transcend reductive, quasi-psychophysical approaches" (Makin 2017, 184). Notably, much recent cognitive work on TV attempts to strike a productive balance with existing television scholarship, abjuring a resolutely scientific register and following in the footsteps of cognitive film studies by adopting the language of analytic aesthetics, which enables broad congruence on key terms such as emotion, evaluation, and aesthetic experience.[12]

Nonetheless, it is understandable, at this relatively early stage, that TV scholars might feel trepidatious about cognitivism's scientific roots. As cognitivists Marcus Pearce et al. caution:

> It is important to acknowledge a genuine tension here between an approach often taken in the humanities in which a given artefact is studied in detail, relating it to the particular historical circumstances in which it was created and experienced, and that of the sciences, where the tendency is to pose and corroborate general predictive models of a given phenomenon.
>
> (2016, 271)

Television aestheticians in particular might feel detached from, or even reject as superfluous and reductive, cognitivist accounts which seem to demote the singular, the individual, and the particular in favor of the many, the average, and the norm. Indeed, in the case of aesthetic experience, several cognitivists have explicitly acknowledged aestheticians' fear that cognitive accounts risk "los[ing] the quintessential essence of those experiences: their unique, privileged, and individual quality" (Pearce et al. 2016, 271).

Notions of individuality and reflexivity, specificity and particularity have long underlain television aesthetics and remain central to aestheticians' close analyses. That is, they retain great pre-theoretical importance, even if they have enjoyed only sporadic conceptual investigation or philosophical attention. They constitute part of the sensibility of television aesthetics, if not part of its explicit ethos.

The particular: serials, episodes, fragments, and moments

Television aestheticians and cognitivists are equally fascinated by the dramatic potential of long-running serial form, especially its manifestation in "quality US drama." Jason Jacobs and Steven Peacock, in their edited collection on television aesthetics and style, celebrate "the expansive structure of television fictions" (2013: 6–7); Logan explores "the associations between quality television and serial form" (2016b, 160); and Robin Nelson (1997) and Jason Mittell (2015) have commended contemporary "quality" TV serials' complex narrative and character development. Both Nannicelli's philosophical account of the art of television and Vaage's exploration of the antihero in U.S. television dramas, aforementioned, dwell admiringly on long-run serials.

The tendency of cognitive work to develop centrifugally, and its wont to focus on the wider picture, corresponds neatly with its preferred focus on long-run serials, deflecting attention away from smaller divisions such as episodes, fragments, and moments. In the spirit of expansive explanation outlined earlier, cognitivists are well placed to address viewers' involvement with these sustained dramas, tackling why we keep watching, investing so much time and mental energy in these characters and this storyline. A centrifugal cognitive approach enables the scholar to move sure-footedly from one specific moment in a program, outwards to the broad arc of a serial, and beyond, exploring our engagement over a long period.

In comparison, television aestheticians have often exhibited greater concern with moments. Close analyses frequently foreground singular, selected moments rather than broader commentary. Similarly, in more conceptual work, some scholars have found the idea of a moment an inspiring starting point (see, for example, Nelson 2016) – interestingly chiming with writers in philosophical aesthetics who recognize that even fleeting moments can provoke profound aesthetic experiences, in the same way that, as Diané Collinson observes, we "notice the world in small bits" (1992, 168). A television aesthetician wishes to account for why he or she is engaged by a specific instance of television, to capture something about his or her engagement – to explain, even evoke it in appreciative terms. Given this value placed upon the particular, the moment, and the local, it is unsurprising that some scholars have observed an enduring tension within the aesthetic account between the moment and the whole, captured provocatively in Jacobs's writing on televisual fragments (2001). In what way can one best do justice to, and fully appreciate, a long-running serial without losing attentiveness to the singular moment?

Perhaps aestheticians' ongoing unease around the relationship of the moment to its wider context is one further reason for their caution regarding the explanations of cognitivists, who happily shift from the small particularities of one moment to explore long-running narrative arcs, the development of character(s) over time, or indeed, matters beyond the work's formal boundaries, such as broader questions about audience responses, engagement, and judgments. But our differences of emphasis are not detrimental. Indeed, I would entreat that we maintain them and that aestheticians continue to give due weight, in their evaluative close analyses, to the particular moment in itself and on its own terms.

I have written elsewhere of some of the risks of over-valuing seriality and serial form, specifically in terms of the interpretation and evaluation of television performances (Cardwell 2019). In celebrating the achievements of long-running serials, we must be careful not to institute expectations of value proportionate to a program's perceived level of seriality. It is certainly one kind of achievement to develop a narrative and characters over a very long period of time, and it requires considerable skill on the part of the actors to offer engaging, credible, and persuasive performances within that context. Yet, this does not mean that performances within the context of episodic series, which rely less upon notions of change and development and more upon confirmation and repetition, are less valuable or impressive. Indeed, the challenges of creating successful, sustained performances within classic, often generic, episodic series are considerable. Performance is merely one facet – one example. Television is fundamentally episodic before it is serial. We must take care not to overlook the smaller building blocks, such as episodes, fragments, and moments, in our desire to grapple with the more obvious complexities of contemporary long-run serials.[13]

Close analyses within television aesthetics are broadly centripetal, always gravitating (back) inwards towards the particulars of the program under scrutiny, rejoicing in this writer's intimate connection with this moment in this work. This approach exhibits a sense of vital immediacy. Any moment may elicit such a response. it need not be problematic, unusual, or unconventional; it need not inspire curiosity, discomfort, or awkward questions; it need not contribute to a broader theoretical account; it need not even be pivotal or transformative within the work. "It can be intense or gentle, sustained or fleeting, immediate or cumulative, or combinations of any of these" (Collinson 1992, 117). The moment needs only to touch this viewer, provoking an aesthetic attitude, experience, or response, demanding closer and more sustained attention for its own sake.

An aesthetic perspective is more obviously fitting when responding to an ephemeral moment of television, especially given the often fleeting nature of a moment of intense aesthetic experience. And yet, certain moments, as we shall see, encourage us, once we have entered, to take up a cognitive path.

Moments of significance (examples from *The Closer* and *Desperate Housewives*)[14]

Let us take, briefly, two moments from within two different serial contexts. *Desperate Housewives*, which ran for eight seasons, was notable for its pacey proliferation of plots and storylines of varying length and import (some light-hearted and episodic, some of greater magnitude, stretching across several seasons). *The Closer* was an episodic, generic cop series, but it contained various serial elements, the weightiest of which reached its pinnacle as the program concluded, in its seventh season.[15]

In the concluding season of *The Closer*, protagonist Chief Brenda Leigh Johnson (Kyra Sedgwick), responsible for "closing" cases by eliciting confessions from guilty parties, falls under scrutiny for her role in cases in which her behavior or decisions were in some way contentious or morally dubious. The implications are serious: Brenda faces losing her job, and criminal charges. Initially, Brenda and members of her team are sued by the family of a teenage murder suspect who was beaten to death by a gang after he was released by the police. In episode ten, "Fresh Pursuit," this case is dismissed. As the team celebrates, Brenda is called into a meeting room by civil litigator Peter Goldman (Curtis Armstrong), where, drawing files from a large cardboard box on the table in front of him, he confronts her with the evidence he has assembled against her for his new lawsuit: six cases, which together "add up to a past practice and pattern of denying suspects their constitutional privilege to a fair trial." Goldman vows: 'It's my intention, Chief Johnson, to put an end to you – and all your works." His attack is brutal and unrelenting, and delivered with repellent relish. Brenda is battered by his allegations.

At first, it is understandable if we root for Brenda, around whose charismatic and impressive character the previous seven series have revolved. Our

Figure 16.1 Goldman and his box of files, *The Closer* (TNT 2005–12).

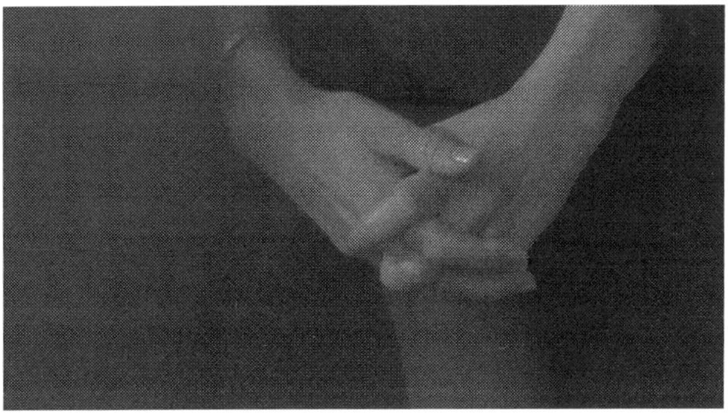

Figure 16.2 Brenda's trembling hands, *The Closer* (TNT 2004–12).

allegiance to her is likely increased by the disposition of her nemesis, who is tenacious and sharp but also ruthless, underhand and weaselly in manner. Goldman is a difficult character to like and appears driven by egotism as much as a sense of justice. This scene foregrounds the two individuals; the familiar, dingy office surroundings are unobtrusive, and only Goldman's portentous box of files draws any attention. The camera moves, through a series of cuts, progressively closer to each character's face, except for one moment in which it cuts to a shot of Brenda's clasped, trembling hands.

Outwardly, Brenda retains her poise and composure, standing neatly erect, saying little – and in the occasional long shot, she remains apparently unflustered. But every close-up discloses the tiny tremors of her head, the stifled quivering of her lips. These details of performance convey Brenda's profound distress, which is likely to elicit sympathy in regular viewers. But the evident intensity of Brenda's disorientation mirrors something more troubling: our own discombobulation, as we are shaken from our previous allegiance and, perhaps, complacency. All along, we have observed the unconventional methods by which Brenda excels in provoking confessions from killers: "She cajoles, she yells, she soothes. She bluffs about plea deals and lies about evidence. She's a walking weekly reminder to always shut up and call a lawyer" (Smith 2012). But now we are asked to take a broader overview. We are reminded, if we need such a reminder, that Brenda has, in the past, made decisions that crossed a line. Worse, we are compelled to confront the likelihood that, far from a series of discrete incidences, there is a *pattern* here of morally suspect behavior, one that was previously, stubbornly, overlooked. Any previous tolerance of Brenda's quirks is now troubled by new levels of discomfort and uncertainty. Moral ambiguity denies viewers a cozy ending as the final season draws to its close. As reviewer Sara Smith (2012) observed at the time, "Brenda's hands shook in fear as she listened, realizing she came off on paper like a dirty cop who deserved to be taken down. And maybe she is. *The Closer* isn't finished asking that question." Nor are its viewers.

Goldman's assault pulls together moments from across the series that were otherwise separate and distinct, due in great part to the episodic form. His undeniably persuasive case rests upon connectedness. It demands that we travel outwards, centrifugally, from here. In this moment, *The Closer* evokes seriality. The meeting between Brenda and Goldman is not a climax but a culmination, a revelation of an accretion of individual instances, which, we are now asked to consider, form a serial thread previously unobtrusive and unacknowledged – and that thread troubles the very integrity of the program's protagonist.

This disruption has potential ramifications beyond the program. It constitutes a bold provocation, asking us to examine ourselves and the judgments we have made up to this point. Have we, given our affection for Brenda, our eagerness to engage with her over seven seasons, turned a blind eye to and even endorsed immoral behavior? Did we make allowances we should not have made? Is this something we do in real life? Could we have found ourselves in Brenda's situation? As we confront these disturbing questions, as we consider our routine judgment of character and the ways in which familiarity and intimacy distort our moral evaluations, we are responding instinctively, with a greater or lesser degree of formality, as cognitivists. A consciously cognitive approach, considering appropriate literature on character, morality, and so on, would enhance our appreciation and understanding of *The Closer*'s achievements.

Consider, in contrast, an apparently climactic scene from the penultimate episode of the long-running serial *Desperate Housewives*, in which Lynette and Tom Scavo (Felicity Huffman and Doug Savant), who have been separated for some time, reunite. As with *The Closer*, the scene inhabits a familiar context: Wisteria Lane, at night. The more obviously important action is happening elsewhere: a celebration party for Bree (Marcia Cross), who has been dramatically acquitted of murder after a long-running and seemingly hopeless battle. Elsewhere, Tom has been visiting his neighbor Roy (Orson Bean), who is tending to his terminally ill wife, Karen (Kathryn Joosten). In a moving scene, Roy has told Tom of his recent conversation with Karen, in which they shared memories and previously unexpressed truths, both small (Karen's pot roast recipe) and momentous (Roy told Karen that "she was the love of my life"). Roy's timely advice to Tom – "It's so important to say these things when you can, because when it's over, it's over" – prompts Tom's expression of love to Lynette in this scene.

Where the preceding scenes at Bree's house and at Roy's place were emotionally vivid (joyful and relieved in the first case, moving and poignant in the latter), the setting for this reunion is quiet, grey, understated. As Tom and Lynette, who stand at some distance from one another, framed separately, begin to speak, they are subdued, each believing that all hope of reuniting with the other has gone. We have heard so many conversations between these two. They have been back and forth, on and off. We, too, perhaps, are tired. It seems improbable that they might reach across the space that separates them.

And yet, there is one moment, one gesture, that beseeches us – if we let it – to draw closer. Tom tries to explain to Lynette that he has had a change of perspective:

> Look – at the end, when I left, our problems looked (he extends his arms to his sides) this big (and drops them, putting his hands in his pockets). So I went away. But now I realize they only seemed that way because we were so close up against them. And … and they were blocking me from seeing how much (he slows) I love you. Which is …

In place of words, Tom raises his arms from his sides, tracing a huge circle in the air until he pauses, arms outstretched to heaven. A cut to a close-up from just behind him shows Tom's right arm shaking, straining with the effort to reach out and up as far as he can, as if he is unable quite to convey the size and scale of his feelings, to encompass them in his embrace. In a beat, Tom's uncharacteristically grand and effortful gesture encapsulates the urgency of this moment: his last chance to lay it all on the line and let Lynette know how he really feels.

Tom does not hope for a reunion; he incorrectly believes Lynette has moved on and is in a relationship with another man. He wishes her well: "I hope you'll be happy. Because you, Lynette" (he presses his right hand to his chest, over his heart), "you'll always be the love of my life."

Tom's boldness provokes Lynette to correct his misapprehension and confirm that the man she is actually in love with is "You." (She drops the bag of ice she is carrying and walks towards him). "You." (She presses her hands together, touching her fingertips to her lips, then opens her palms as if to sing out) "You." As they meet, finally sharing the frame: "You." They kiss, lingeringly, and the camera begins slowly to encircle them, winding around and up, swirling and rising ultimately to the rooftops and the sky above.

Figure 16.3 Tom gestures, *Desperate Housewives* (ABC 2004–12).

Figure 16.4 Tom's arm shaking, *Desperate Housewives* (ABC 2004–12).

I would contend that this scene reverses the direction of that in *The Closer*. This moment is not a culmination; it does not ask us to look outwards and seek connections. Instead, the scene is offered to us as an exceptional, joyful hiatus. Its isolation from the dramatic action elsewhere, its quiet, everyday locale, its understated pretext, the muted tiredness of the actors – these elements create a sense of action suspended, set aside from its lively serial context. Finely judged performances that incorporate conspicuously theatrical gestures, and careful choices of framing and focus, catch and draw our attention repeatedly inwards. The moment has centripetal force.

This moment beseeches us to set aside cynicism, just for a moment, and embrace it on its own terms. As the camera soars in the scene's closing moments, we might reflect upon the exceptional dramatic weight placed upon the maneuvers of this quite ordinary, messy, middle-aged relationship: the trembling of Tom's arm and his uncharacteristically expressive declaration of eternal love, the use of expansive theatrical gestures denoting passion and honesty, Lynette's gentle but assured assertion – "You. You. You" and finally "You" – and the swirling, swooping camera are suggestive of epic romance and immortal love. But above all, the power of this scene rests in its particularities: this gesture, these words, this man, this woman, here and now.

Moments and movements: feeling a way in

In each of these examples, particular moments of style and performance prompted me to look more closely. Both programs presented fleeting moments of defamiliarization, breaking to some extent with their established formal choices and patterns. But then, they drew me in different directions.

The Closer, an episodic series, in a pivotal moment of finale, gestured decisively towards seriality, revealing a previously unperceived, underlying theme, which provoked a reconsideration of its beloved protagonist and further reflection upon ethical, moral, and psycho-sociological matters. A broadly cognitive approach respects the program here by allowing consideration of the wider concerns to inform our appreciation of this moment; it recognizes that "cognitive value is often a significant component of artistic value" (Nannicelli 2017, 196).

The moment from *Desperate Housewives* moves in an opposite direction. We appreciate it most if we embrace it. The scene unburdens itself of its responsibilities to the wider serial and revels in its particularity. In that sense, it constitutes an episodic moment in the context of a complex, expansive, and long-running serial. This is not uncharacteristic of *Desperate Housewives*, which despite its serial form, not only incorporates single scenes (often comedic) that do not contribute to sustained narrative strands but also famously "forgets" or sets aside characters who have played previously key roles in certain storylines; this is particularly true in relation to pets and children (two dogs, a cat, Gaby's biological daughter, and Lynette's grandchild all disappear or are forgotten by the time the series ends). While the serial sustains complex plots across seasons, still, much of the joy within the program can be found in a series of moments, in episodic spirit: the thrill of the here and now. Television aesthetics offers a sensitive route into the appreciation of scenes such as these.

Both scenes are in some sense climactic or culminatory, but they differ in weight, in their elevation of thought or of feeling, and in the extent to which they are self-contained or gesture beyond – towards other scenes and seasons, the wider social world, and the viewer's sense of his or her relationship with that world. A sense of this informed my instinct for which approach was most fitting in each case in order to appreciate fully each moment's significance and achievements.

Of course, there are many other modes of engagement with each program that would be equally appropriate. *The Closer* is stylistically interesting throughout and would certainly benefit from close stylistic analysis in an aesthetic vein. *Desperate Housewives* could be helpfully examined via cognitive perspectives. But these particular moments suggested one approach before the other. *The Closer* inspired questions, reflections, reconsideration; before these responses, it felt unfinished and unresolved. *Desperate Housewives* inspired me to watch again, to re-embrace and unpack the moment. It felt complete in itself. These differences capture something of the sensibility of cognitive and aesthetic approaches, respectively.

Cognitivism and aesthetics: working alongside each other

Like Lynette and Tom in *Desperate Housewives*, perhaps, cognitivists and aestheticians can find a way to reach out and connect across the gap. It is important to be realistic, to recognize the different projects and remits of the two approaches, and to acknowledge when we are speaking at cross purposes. Given that the boundaries between cognitivism and aestheticism are not set in stone, it makes sense to attend to the particular sensibilities of each writer's contribution and assess it on its own terms. Is the person offering appreciative evaluation or explanation? Is the broad movement of their analysis centripetal or centrifugal? What kinds of claims are being made? What values are implicit?

Television aesthetics rests upon a commitment to a notion of aesthetic experience that informs its values, principles, and methods. Television aestheticians might fruitfully recognize that when cognitivists attempt to account for our engagement with a program, they are not necessarily or exclusively interested in aesthetic engagement or appreciation. They are addressing different questions. In turn, cognitivists might further address the legitimate concerns of television scholars about the perceived normalizing and universalizing tendencies of cognitive science.

It would also be beneficial to thrash out in more detail the ways in which we can constructively disagree. In television aesthetics, several scholars have explicitly addressed the question of disagreement in interpretative and evaluative practice (see, for example, Mittell 2015; Nannicelli 2016), and there is supporting literature in film studies and philosophical aesthetics. Some interpretative disagreements might be ironed out through returning to the program under scrutiny to explore its details further. Many evaluative disagreements will persist, given individual subjectivity. Yet, it is generally agreed that while two people might not share the same conclusions, each response harbors its own integrity. This is even truer in the case of demonstrative or expressive criticism. We might remain unpersuaded by a writer's account: able to perceive and agree upon the stylistic details to which they draw our attention, but ultimately, individually unmoved by the work, despite the other person's attempts to disclose it to us. In such a case, we do not share the other person's experience or conclusions – we disagree – but nonetheless, his or her evaluative judgement is sincerely held: it is true for them (as is ours for ourselves).

As we have seen, cognitivism, relatively speaking, downplays the individual and particular. This makes the matter of disagreement more fraught. When we disagree with an aesthetic account, we disagree with another individual. When we disagree with a cognitive account, often couched in terms of average human responses within a given social context, we are being asked to accept that our response is atypical of the group. This is an uncomfortable, if not implausible, position. Cognitive scholars may tire of addressing this allegation, but its endurance merely indicates its importance within the humanities context; it is not going to go away. Cognitivists could explain further how someone might legitimately and constructively disagree with their conclusions.

It would be a mistake to underestimate the differences in our aims, methods, and premises. But as was noted at the beginning, we share a sustained concern with what is there in the work and a desire to appreciate it fully. We share interests in key matters, including emotions, mood, characterization, morality, ethics, and more. We might better address all of these side by side.

Reflections

For cognitivists or aestheticians, critical engagement with the work of the other can prove of immense value. Our disagreements are actually an opportunity: they compel scholars on both sides to reflect upon and expose our respective underlying commitments and the fundamental purposes, scope, and values upon which our work is based, but which may not have received enough explicit attention.

In this spirit, this chapter constitutes a personal attempt to uncover something of the sensibility and underlying values of cognitive and aesthetic approaches. It is a necessarily somewhat rudimentary, impressionistic, and self-reflective pursuit. Even the decision to include brief consideration of two moments from specific programs was, I now reflect, expressive of the sensibility of television aesthetics. These were two moments that gave me pause and urged me to revisit them. In *The Closer*, I met with something unsettling, which led me outwards to question, reconsider, and animatedly debate with fellow viewers its implications. *Desperate Housewives* led me inwards to embrace, scrutinize, and appreciate. The first inspired an attitude of curiosity; the second an attitude of wonder. For me, these differing experiences encapsulate something of the essences of cognitive and aesthetic perspectives, respectively.

The work itself often leads, or draws, us towards an appropriate perspective or approach. But of course, it is also true that our own sensibilities, our preferences and passions, play their part. In undertaking the explorations contained herein, I realized that certain moments of television entreat me to take up a cognitive-inspired perspective, and that I might heed that call more often.

Yet, I was also reminded of my instinctive predisposition towards an aesthetic stance. I did not expect to discover in each of the programs I selected an intriguing playfulness with the balance between seriality and episodic moment. As I elucidated this, I became more keenly aware of the value of "the moment" to my own aesthetic pleasure; I uncovered something of myself. While both cognitive and aesthetic approaches persuasively address seriality and moment (in the sense of weight or significance), for me, an aesthetic perspective accords more intuitively with the joyful engagement I experience, and wish to share, when absorbed by a striking, singular moment of television.

Notes

1 There is no straightforward delineation of cognitive and aesthetic approaches, especially because, as observed later, several scholars work across both. This chapter offers a partial exploration of the sensibilities and values that might help distinguish the two perspectives.

2 Criticism of the very project of television aesthetics has become less frequent but persists from some quarters in TV studies. See, for instance, Matt Hills (2001).

3 For a balanced introductory overview of television aesthetics, see Cardwell (2006).

4 I gloss over a larger question here, regarding the source of "value" and where it resides: in the artwork, in the experience afforded by it, or in some combination of the two. This is a long-debated issue in philosophical aesthetics. Correspondingly, disagreements on this matter are likely both between and among cognitivists and aestheticians – though one might broadly expect aestheticians to prioritize the work as a source of value and cognitivists the experience of the person attending to it.

5 See, for comparison, David Pierson (2014) on *Breaking Bad*.

6 It should be noted that "aesthetic attitude" is a contentious topic within philosophical aesthetics, reflecting both the complexity of the concept and its potential value to the field. Responding to earlier accounts, George Dickie proffered an influential rebuttal of the "myth" of the aesthetic attitude (1964), which many aestheticians found persuasive. Nevertheless, the notion persists and inspires ongoing scholarship. For a balanced historical overview, see David Fenner (1996).

More saliently in the current context, the work (teaching and writing) of many television aestheticians tacitly presumes the existence of such an attitude as a constituent and defining feature. Whether aesthetic attitude is ultimately sound as a philosophical concept or not, it is nevertheless important to the contemporary venture of television aesthetics, as it distinguishes its specific approach, principles, and sensibility within the broader context of TV studies.

7 I am conscious here of eliding aesthetic attitude and aesthetic experience – two much-debated terms. I undertake a more detailed exploration of aesthetic attitude and experience in Cardwell (2013). The observations offered in this chapter are not dependent upon the reader accepting one term over the other or concurring with any particular formulation of either. The key point is one of sensibility: that the practice of television aestheticians implicitly presupposes the reality and value of aesthetic experience and/or attitude, and that these are understood as a certain kind of attention or attentiveness. Bence Nanay's recent account of aesthetic experience persuasively develops the idea that it is best understood in terms of particular modes of attention (Nanay 2016).

8 The word "conceptual" here respects a revision (from "theoretical") offered in Cardwell (2006, 73).

9 In television studies, the kind of conceptual investigation Nannicelli undertakes is still rare, and socio-political concerns still hold sway. Unsurprisingly, in this context, then, the

"problem" of implicit normativity in aesthetic criticism is typically refigured in ideological terms. Television aestheticians have been accused of ascribing to out-of-date norms of value, which, via the evaluative criticism of particular TV works, esteem certain qualities and experiences over others, and consequently perpetuate elitist and exclusionary cultural and social hierarchies. (See, for instance, Hills (2001), who alleges that the very existence of television aesthetics as it stands constitutes a "pre-structuralist danger," or more recently, Michael Z. Newman and Elena Levine (2012).)

Beleaguered TV aestheticians who accept the dependence of their practice upon normative values might look to philosophical aesthetics for support: Paul Crowther, for instance, offers a provocative and detailed defense of normativity against these ideological objections, arguing that normative meanings can exhibit "universal orientation" rather than "marginal Western idioms" (2007, 15). In addition, television aestheticians can continue to address concerns about canon-building and critical conservatism by challenging current hierarchies of value with regard to artistic and aesthetic qualities – for instance, by celebrating simplicity in the face of current enthusiasm for complexity, or episodic form as opposed to long-form serial structure (as I do, briefly, later in this chapter). Both routes accept a role for norms within aesthetic criticism but challenge hasty presumptions that these are inherently reactionary or unchangeable.

Also helpful is Nannicelli's account of "instrumental" evaluation, in which a work is judged on the basis of criteria determined by its specific context and purposes rather than evaluative norms (2017, 194–204); Nannicelli's argument echoes Jacobs (2001) and Christine Geraghty (2003), who recommend evaluating programs in relation to their genre/category. I would aver that many instances of evaluative criticism in TV aesthetics already implicitly, if not explicitly, adopt this approach.

10 Indeed, in this tradition, the writing process might in itself constitute part of the aesthetician's experience of the work and thereby, a further source of pleasure.

11 Television aesthetics might place stronger emphasis upon the singular, creative individual, while other television studies might prioritize a diversity of individuals within a social context, but in each case, individual voices and subjectivities pre-exist their coalescence into larger groups or communities.

12 Recent work within cognitive film studies sustains this positive approach. Murray Smith's recent book (2017), for example, in pursuit of his focus on film, emotion, and cognition, argues powerfully for closer and more collaborative and productive conversations between science- and humanities-based scholars.

13 It may also be the case that there are different, nesting works that need to be appreciated both distinctly and collectively, depending on one's particular critical aims. I thank Ted Nannicelli for this valuable observation.

14 These two serials have been previously overlooked by aestheticians and perhaps offer a nice counterpoint to the male-dominated examples more often examined.

15 *The Closer* was followed by a spin-off, *Major Crimes* (2012–2018), without protagonist Brenda Leigh Johnson but including most of her original team.

References

Bordwell, David. 2010. "The Part-time Cognitivist: A View from Film Studies." *Projections* 4, no. 2: 1–18.

Cardwell, Sarah. 2019 (In press). "In Small Packages: Particularities of Performance in Episodic Series." In *Performance in Television*, edited by James Walters and Lucy Donaldson. Basingstoke: Palgrave Macmillan.

Cardwell, Sarah. 2017. "Season to Taste: Television Cookery Programmes, Aesthetics and Seasonality." *Journal of Popular Television* 5, no. 1: 11–29.

Cardwell, Sarah. 2013. "Television Aesthetics: Stylistic Analysis and Beyond." In *Television Aesthetics and Style*, edited by Jason Jacobs and Steven Peacock, 23–44. London: Bloomsbury.

Cardwell, Sarah. 2006. "Television Aesthetics." *Critical Studies in Television* 1, no. 1 (Spring): 72–80.

Cardwell, Sarah. 2005. "'Television Aesthetics' and Close Analysis: Style and Mood in *Perfect Strangers* (Stephen Poliakoff, 2001)." In *Style and Meaning*, edited by Doug Pye and John Gibbs, 179–194. Manchester: Manchester University Press.

Carroll, Noël. 2001. *Beyond Aesthetics: Philosophical Essays*. Cambridge: Cambridge University Press.

Collinson, Diané. 1992. "Aesthetic Experience." In *Philosophical Aesthetics: An Introduction*, edited by Oswald Hanfling, 111–178. Oxford: Open University Press/Blackwell Publishers.

Crowther, Paul. 2007. *Defining Art, Creating the Canon: Artistic Value in an Era of Doubt*. Oxford: Oxford University Press.

Dickie, George. 1964. "The Myth of the Aesthetic Attitude." *American Philosophical Quarterly* 1: 56–65.

Fenner, David. 1996. *The Aesthetic Attitude*. Atlantic Highlands, New Jersey: Humanities Press.

Geraghty, Christine. 2003. "Aesthetics and Quality in Television Drama." *International Journal of Cultural Studies* 6, no. 1: 25–45.

Heiselberg, Lene, and Thomas Bjørner. 2018. "How to Evaluate Emotional Experiences in Television Drama Series: Improving Viewer Evaluations Using A Combination of Psychophysiological Measurements and Self-reports." *Behaviour and Information Technology* 37, no. 9: 884–893.

Hills, Matt. 2001. "Television Aesthetics: A Pre-structuralist Danger?" *Journal of British Cinema and Television* 8, no. 1: 99–117.

Jacobs, Jason, and Steven Peacock. 2013. *Television Aesthetics and Style*. London: Bloomsbury.

Jacobs, Jason. 2001. "Issues of Judgement and Value in Television Studies." *International Journal of Cultural Studies* 4, no. 4: 435–437.

Logan, Elliott. 2016a. *Breaking Bad and Dignity: Unity and Fragmentation in the Television Serial Drama*. Basingstoke: Palgrave Macmillan.

Logan, Elliott. 2016b. Summer 2016. ""Quality Television" as a Critical Obstacle." *Screen* 57, no. 2 (Summer): 114–162.

Makin, Alexis D.J. 2017. "The Gap Between Aesthetic Science and Aesthetic Experience." *Journal of Consciousness Studies* 24, no. 1–2: 184–213.

Metallinos, Nikos. 1996. *Television Aesthetics: Perceptual, Cognitive and Compositional Bases*. Mahwah, NJ: Lawrence Erlbaum Associates.

Mittell, Jason. 2015. *Complex TV: The Poetics of Contemporary Television Storytelling*. New York & London: NYU Press.

Nanay, Bence. 2016. *Aesthetics as Philosophy of Perception*. Oxford: OUP.

Nannicelli, Ted. 2018. "Cognitivism." In *The Craft of Criticism: Critical Media Studies in Practice*, edited by Michael Kackman and Mary Celeste Kearney, 157–168. New York: Routledge.

Nannicelli, Ted. 2017. *Appreciating the Art of Television: A Philosophical Perspective*. New York & London: Routledge.

Nelson, Robin. 2016. "The Emergence of 'Affect' in Contemporary TV Fictions." In *Emotions in Contemporary TV Series*, edited by Alberto N. Garcia, 26–51. Basingstoke: Palgrave Macmillan.

Nelson, Robin. 1997. *TV Drama in Transition: Forms, Values and Cultural Change*. Basingstoke: Macmillan.

Newman, Michael Z., and Elena Levine. 2012. *Legitimating Television: Media Convergence and Cultural Status*. New York & Oxon: Routledge.

Pearce, Marcus T., et al. 2016. "Neuroaesthetics: The Cognitive Neuroscience of Aesthetic Experience." *Perspectives on Psychological Science* 11, no. 2: 265–279.

Pierson, David P., ed. 2014. *Breaking Bad: Critical Essays on the Contexts, Politics, Style, and Reception of the Television Series*. Lanham, MD: Lexington Books.

Smith, Murray. 2017. *Film, Art and the Third Culture: A Naturalised Aesthetics of Film*. Oxford: Oxford University Press.

Smith, Sara. 2012. "TV Review: Moral Complexity Deepens Drama on *The Closer*." *The Kansas City Star*. https://www.kansascity.com/entertainment/article304974.html. Accessed 15 January 2019.

Vaage, Margrethe Bruun. 2015. *The Antihero in American Television*. New York & London: Routledge.

Index

Note: References in *italic* refers figures and references following "n" refer endnotes.

Made in the USA
Las Vegas, NV
28 October 2024

8f888ce3-3cea-4424-871f-66072b61dd3cR01